John Locke's Two Essays Concerning Civil Government

re:Organizing America

Edited by Thomas Adamo

A Woodbine Cottage Publication

A Woodbine Cottage Publication
PO Box 211
Lakehurst, NJ 08733-0211
awcpublications@aol.com

Edited by Thomas Adamo
Copyright 2011

*Cover photography "Lower Falls 3" provided courtesy of Tommy Graef.
View his extensive collection of natural photography and art at
www.tomstwin.com.*

ISBN: 1-4538-1859-6

EAN-13: 978-1-4538-1859-6

John Locke's Two Essays

Concerning Civil Government

re:Organizing America

Table of Contents

PREFACE

Reader, you have here the beginning and end of a discourse concerning government; what fate has otherwise disposed of the papers that should have filled up the middle, and were more than all the rest, it is not worthwhile to tell you. These, which remain, I hope are sufficient to establish the throne of our great restorer, our present King William; to make good his title, in the consent of the people, which being the only one of all lawful governments, he has more fully and clearly, than any prince in Christendom; and to justify to the world the people of England, whose love of their just and natural rights, with their resolution to preserve them, saved the nation when it was on the very brink of slavery and ruin. If these papers have that evidence, I flatter myself is to be found in them, there will be no great miss of those which are lost, and my reader may be satisfied without them: for I imagine, I shall have neither the time, nor inclination to repeat my pains, and fill up the wanting part of my answer, by tracing Sir Robert again, through all the windings and obscurities, which are to be met with in the several branches of his wonderful system. The king, and body of the nation, have since so thoroughly confuted his Hypothesis, that I suppose nobody hereafter will have either the confidence to appear against our common safety, and be again an advocate for slavery; or the weakness to be deceived with contradictions dressed up in a popular style, and well-turned periods: for if anyone will be at the pains, himself, in those parts, which are here untouched, to strip Sir Robert's discourses of the flourish of doubtful expressions, and endeavor to reduce his words to direct, positive, intelligible propositions, and then compare them one with another, he will quickly be satisfied, there was never so much glib nonsense put together in well-sounding English. If he think it not worthwhile to examine his works all through, let him make an experiment in that part, where he treats of usurpation; and let him try, whether he can, with all his skill, make Sir Robert intelligible, and consistent with himself, or common sense. I should not speak so plainly of a gentleman, long since past answering, had not the pulpit, of late years, publicly owned his doctrine, and made it the current divinity of the times. It is necessary those men who, taking on them to be teachers, have so dangerously misled others, should be openly showed of what authority this their Patriarch is, whom they have so blindly followed, that so they may either retract what upon so ill grounds they have vented, and cannot be maintained; or else justify those principles which they preached up for gospel; though they had no better an author than an English courtier: for I should not have writ against Sir Robert, or taken the pains to show his mistakes, inconsistencies, and want of (what he so much boasts of, and pretends wholly to build on) Scripture-proofs, were there not men among us, who, by crying up his books, and espousing his doctrine, save me from the reproach of writing against a dead adversary. They have been so zealous in this point, that, if I have done him any wrong, I cannot hope they should spare me. I wish, where they have done the truth and the public wrong, they would be as ready to redress it, and allow its just weight to this reflection, that is that there cannot be done a greater mischief to prince and people, than the propagating of wrong notions concerning government; that so at last all times might not have reason to complain of the Drum Ecclesiastic. If anyone, concerned really for truth, undertakes the confutation of my Hypothesis, I promise him either to recant my mistake, upon fair conviction; or to answer his difficulties. But he must remember two things.

First, that quibbling here and there, at some expression, or little incident of my discourse, is not an answer to my book.

Secondly, That I shall not take railing for arguments, nor think either of these worth my notice, though I shall always look on myself as bound to give satisfaction to anyone, who shall appear to be conscientiously scrupulous in the point, and shall show any just grounds for his scruples.

I have nothing more, but to advertise the reader, that "Observations" stands for *Observations on Hobbs, Milton, etc.* and that a bare quotation of pages always means pages of his *Patriarcha, Edition 1680.*

OF GOVERNMENT

BOOK I

CHAPTER I.

Section 1. Slavery is so vile and miserable an estate of man, and so directly opposite to the generous temper and courage of our nation; that it is hardly to be conceived, that an Englishman, much less a gentleman, should plead for it. And truly I should have taken Sir Robert Filmer's Patriarcha, as any other treatise, which would persuade all men, that they are slaves, and ought to be so, for such another exercise of wit, as was his who writ the encomium of Nero; rather than for a serious discourse meant in earnest, had not the gravity of the title and epistle, the picture in the front of the book, and the applause that followed it, required me to believe, that the author and publisher were both in earnest. I therefore took it into my hands with all the expectation, and read it through with all the attention due to a treatise that made such a noise at its coming abroad, and cannot but confess myself mightily surprised, that in a book, which was to provide chains for all mankind, I should find nothing but a rope of sand, useful perhaps to such, whose skill and business it is to raise a dust, and would blind the people, the better to mislead them; but in truth not of any force to draw those into bondage, who have their eyes open, and so much sense about them, as to consider, that chains are but an ill wearing, how much care soever has been taken to file and polish them.

Section 2. If anyone think I take too much liberty in speaking so freely of a man, who is the great champion of absolute power, and the idol of those who worship it; I beseech him to make this small allowance for once, to one, who, even after the reading of Sir Robert's book, cannot but think himself, as the laws allow him, a freeman: and I know no fault it is to do so, unless anyone better skilled in the fate of it, than I, should have it revealed to him, that this treatise, which has lain dormant so long, was, when it appeared in the world, to carry, by strength of its arguments, all liberty out of it; and that from thenceforth our author's short model was to be the pattern in the mount, and the perfect standard of politics for the future. His system lies in a little compass; it is no more but this, that all government is absolute monarchy; and the ground he builds on, is this, that no man is born free.

Section 3. In this last age a generation of men has sprung up among us, that would flatter princes with an opinion, that they have a divine right to absolute power, let the laws by which they are constituted, and are to govern, and the conditions under which they enter upon their authority, be what they will, and their engagements to observe them never so well ratified by solemn oaths and promises. To make way for this doctrine, they have denied mankind a right to natural freedom; whereby they have not only, as much as in them lies, exposed all subjects to the utmost misery of tyranny and oppression, but have also unsettled the titles, and shaken the thrones of princes: (for they too, by these men's system, except only one, are all born slaves, and by divine right are subjects to Adam's right heir;) as if they had designed to make war upon all government, and subvert the very foundations of human society, to serve their present turn.

Section 4. However we must believe them upon their own bare words, when they tell us, we are all born slaves, and we must continue so, there is no remedy for it; life and thralldom we entered into together, and can never be quit of the one, till we part with the other. Scripture or reason I am sure do not anywhere say so, notwithstanding the noise of divine right, as if divine authority has subjected us to the unlimited will of another. An admirable state of mankind, and that which they have not had wit enough to find out until this latter age. For, however Sir Robert Filmer seems to condemn the novelty of the contrary opinion, Patr. p. 3, yet I believe it will be hard for him to find any other age, or country of the world, but this, which has asserted monarchy to be *jure divino*. And he confesses, Patr. p. 4. that Heyward, Blackwood, Barclay, and others, that have bravely vindicated the right of kings in most points, never thought of this, but with one consent admitted the natural liberty and equality of mankind.

Section 5. By whom this doctrine came at first to be broached, and brought in fashion among us, and what sad effects it gave rise to, I leave to historians to relate, or to the memory of those, who were contemporaries with Sibthorp and Manwering, to recollect. My business at present is only to consider what Sir Robert Filmer, who is allowed to have carried this argument farthest, and is supposed to have brought it to perfection, has said in it; for from him everyone, who would be as fashionable as French was at court, has learned, and runs away with this short system of politics, that is Men are not born free, and therefore could never have the liberty to choose either governors, or forms of government. Princes have their power absolute, and by divine right; for slaves could never have a right to compact or consent. Adam was an absolute monarch, and so are all princes ever since.

CHAPTER II.

Of Paternal and Regal Power.

Section 6. Sir Robert Filmer's great position is that men are not naturally free. This is the foundation on which his absolute monarchy stands, and from which it erects itself to an height, that its power is above every power, *caput inter nubila*, so high above all earthly and human things, that thought can scarce reach it; that promises and oaths, which tie the infinite Deity, cannot confine it. But if this foundation fails, all his fabric falls with it, and governments must be left again to the old way of being made by contrivance, and the consent of men (Ἀνϑϛωπίνη Χτίσιϛ) making use of their reason to unite together into society. To prove this grand position of his, he tells us, p. 12. Men are born in subjection to their parents, and therefore cannot be free. And this authority of parents, he calls royal authority, p. 12, 14. Fatherly authority, right of fatherhood, p. 12, 20. One would have thought he would, in the beginning of such a work as this, on which was to depend the authority of princes, and the obedience of subjects, have told us expressly, what that fatherly authority is, have defined it, though not limited it, because in some other treatises of his he tells us, it is unlimited, and unlimitable; he should at least have given us such an account of it, that we might have had an entire notion of this fatherhood, or fatherly authority, whenever it came in our way in his writings: this I expected to have found in the first chapter of his Patriarcha. But instead thereof, having, 1. *en passant*, made his obeisance to the *arcana imperii*, p. 5. 2. made his compliment to the rights and liberties of this, or any other nation, p. 6. which he is going presently to null and destroy; and, 3. made his leg to those learned men, who did not see so far into the matter as himself, p. 7. he comes to fall on Bellarmine, p. 8. and, by a victory over him, establishes his fatherly authority beyond any question. Bellarmine being routed by his own confession, p. 11. the day is clear got, and there is no more need of any forces: for having done that, I observe not that he states the question, or rallies up any arguments to make good his opinion, but rather tells us the story, as he thinks fit, of this strange kind of domineering phantom, called the fatherhood, which whoever could catch, presently got empire, and unlimited absolute power. He assures us how this fatherhood began in Adam, continued its course, and kept the world in order all the time of the patriarchs until the flood, got out of the ark with Noah and his sons, made and supported all the kings of the earth until the captivity of the Israelites in Egypt, and then the poor fatherhood was under hatches, until God, by giving the Israelites kings, re-established the ancient and prime right of the lineal succession in paternal government. This is his business from p. 12. to 19. And then obviating an objection, and clearing a difficulty or two with one half reasons, p. 23. to confirm the natural right of regal power, he ends the first chapter. I hope it is no injury to call an half quotation an half reason; for God says, Honor your father and mother; but our author contents himself with half, leaves out your mother quite, as little serviceable to his purpose. But of that more in another place.

Section 7. I do not think our author so little skilled in the way of writing discourses of this nature, nor so careless of the point in hand, that he by over-sight commits the fault, that he himself, in his Anarchy of a mixed Monarchy, p. 239. objects to Mr. Hunton in these words: Where first I charge the author that he has not given us any definition or description of monarchy in general; for by the rules of method he should have first defined. And by the like rule of method Sir Robert should have told us, what his fatherhood or fatherly authority is, before he had told us, in whom it was to be found, and talked so much of it. But perhaps Sir Robert found, that this fatherly authority, this power of fathers, and of kings, for he makes them both the same, p. 24. would make a very odd and frightful figure, and very disagreeing with what either children imagine of their parents, or subjects of their kings, if he should have given us the whole draught together in that gigantic form, he had painted it in his own fancy; and therefore, like a wary physician, when he would have his patient swallow some harsh or corrosive liquor, he mingles it with a large quantity of that which may dilute it; that the scattered parts may go down with less feeling, and cause less aversion.

Section 8. Let us then endeavor to find what account he gives us of this fatherly authority, as it lies scattered in the several pieces of his writings. And first, as it was vested in Adam, he says, not only Adam, but the succeeding patriarchs, had, by right of fatherhood, royal authority over their children, p. 12. This lordship which Adam by command had over the whole world, and by right descending from him the patriarchs did enjoy, was as large and ample as the absolute dominion of any monarch, which has been since the creation, p. 13. Dominion of life and death, making war, and concluding peace, p. 13. Adam and the patriarchs had absolute power of life and death, p. 35. Kings, in the right of parents, succeed to the exercise of supreme jurisdiction, p. 19. As kingly power is by the law of God, so it has no inferior law to limit it; Adam was lord of all, p. 40. The father of a family governs by no other law, than by his own will, p. 78. The superiority of princes is above laws, p. 79. The unlimited jurisdiction of kings is so amply described by Samuel, p. 80. Kings are above the laws, p. 93. And to this purpose see a great deal more which our author delivers in Bodin's words: It is certain, that all laws, privileges, and grants of princes, have no force, but during their life; if they be not ratified by the express consent, or by sufferance of the prince following, especially privileges, Observations, p. 279. The reason why laws have been also made by kings, was this; when kings were either busied with wars, or distracted with public cares, so that every private man could not have access to their persons, to learn their wills and pleasure, then were laws of necessity invented, that so every particular subject might find his prince's pleasure deciphered unto him in the tables of his laws, p. 92. In a monarchy, the king must by necessity be above the laws, p. 100. A perfect kingdom is that, wherein the king rules all things according to his own will, p. 100. Neither common nor statute laws are, or can be, any diminution of that general power, which kings have over their people by right of fatherhood, p. 115. Adam was the father, king, and lord over his family; a son, a subject, and a servant or slave, were one and the same thing at first. The father had power to dispose or sell his children or servants; whence we find, that the first reckoning up of goods in Scripture, the man-servant and the maid-servant, are numbered among the possessions and substance of the owner, as other goods were, Observations, Pref. God also has given to the father a right or liberty, to give his power over his children to any other; whence we find the sale and gift of children to have much been in use in the beginning of the world, when men had their servants for a possession and an inheritance, as well as other goods; whereupon we find the power of castrating and making eunuchs much in use in old times, Observations, p. 155. Law is nothing else but the will of him that has the power of the supreme father, Observations, p. 223. It was God's ordinance that the supremacy should be unlimited in Adam, and as large as all the acts of his will; and as in him so in all others that have supreme power, Observations, p. 245.

Section 9. I have been loath to trouble my reader with these several quotations in our author's own words, that in them might be seen his own description of his fatherly authority, as it lies scattered up and down in his writings, which he supposes was first vested in Adam, and by right belongs to all princes ever since. This fatherly authority then, or right of fatherhood, in our author's sense, is a divine unalterable right of sovereignty, whereby a father or a prince has an absolute, arbitrary, unlimited, and unlimitable power over the lives, liberties, and estates of his children and subjects; so that he may take or alienate their estates, sell, castrate, or use their persons as he pleases, they being all his slaves, and he lord or proprietor of everything, and his unbounded will their law.

Section 10. Our author having placed such a mighty power in Adam, and upon that supposition sounded all government, and all power of princes, it is reasonable to expect, that he should have proved this with arguments clear and evident, suitable to the weightiness of the cause; that since men had nothing else left them, they might in slavery have such undeniable proofs of its necessity, that their consciences might be convinced, and oblige them to submit peaceably to that absolute dominion, which their governors had a right to exercise over them. Without this, what good could our author do, or pretend to do, by erecting such an unlimited power, but flatter the natural vanity and ambition of men, too apt of itself to grow and increase with the possession of any power? and by persuading those, who, by the consent of their fellowmen, are advanced to great, but limited, degrees of it, that by that part which is given them, they have a right to all, that was not so; and therefore may do what they please, because they have authority to do more than others, and so tempt them to do what is neither for their own, nor the good of those under their care; whereby great mischiefs cannot but follow.

Section 11. The sovereignty of Adam, being that on which, as a sure basis, our author builds his mighty absolute monarchy, I expected, that in his Patriarcha, this his main supposition would have been proved, and established with all that evidence of arguments, that such a fundamental tenet required; and that this, on which the great stress of the business depends, would have been made out with reasons sufficient to justify the confidence with which it was assumed. But in all that treatise, I could find very little tending that way; the thing is there so taken for granted, without proof, that I could scarce believe myself, when, upon attentive reading that treatise, I found there so mighty a structure raised upon the bare supposition of this foundation: for it is scarce credible, that in a discourse, where he pretends to confute the erroneous principle of man's natural freedom, he should do it by a bare supposition of Adam's authority, without offering any proof for that authority. Indeed he confidently says that Adam had royal authority, p. 12, and 13. Absolute lordship and dominion of life and death, p. 13. A universal monarchy, p. 33. Absolute power of life and death, p. 35. He is very frequent in such assertions; but, what is strange, in all his whole Patriarcha I find not one pretence of a reason to establish this his great foundation of government; not anything that looks like an argument, but these words: To confirm this natural right of regal power, we find in the Decalogue, that the law which enjoins obedience to kings, is delivered in the terms, Honor your father, as if all power were originally in the father. And why may I not add as well, that in the Decalogue, the law that enjoins obedience to queens is delivered in the terms of Honor your mother, as if all power were originally in the mother? The argument, as Sir Robert puts it, will hold as well for one as the other: but of this, more in its due place.

Section 12. All that I take notice of here, is, that this is all our author says in this first, or any of the following chapters, to prove the absolute power of Adam, which is his great principle: and yet, as if he had there settled it upon sure demonstration, he begins his second chapter with these words, By conferring these proofs and reasons, drawn from the authority of the Scripture. Where those proofs and reasons for Adam's sovereignty are, bating that of Honor your father, above mentioned, I confess, I cannot find; unless what he says, p. 11. In these words we have an evident confession, that is of Bellarmine, that creation made man prince of his posterity, must be taken for proofs and reasons drawn from Scripture, or for any sort of proof at all: though from thence by a new way of inference, in the words immediately following, he concludes, the royal authority of Adam sufficiently settled in him.

Section 13. If he has in that chapter, or anywhere in the whole treatise, given any other proofs of Adam's royal authority, other than by often repeating it, which, among some men, goes for argument, I desire anyone to show me the place and page, that I may be convinced of my mistake, and acknowledge my oversight. If no such arguments are to be found, I beseech those men, who have so much cried up this book, to consider, whether they do not give the world cause to suspect, that it is not the force of reason and argument, that makes them for absolute monarchy, but some other by interest, and therefore are resolved to applaud any author, that writes in favor of this doctrine, whether he support it with reason or no. But I hope they do not expect, that rational and indifferent men should be brought over to their opinion, because this their great doctor of it, in a discourse made on purpose, to set up the absolute monarchical power of Adam, in opposition to the natural freedom of mankind, has said so little to prove it, from whence it is rather naturally to be concluded, that there is little to be said.

Section 14. But that I might omit no care to inform myself in our author's full sense, I consulted his Observations on Aristotle, Hobbes, etc. to see whether in disputing with others he made use of any arguments for this his darling tenet of Adam's sovereignty; since in his treatise of the Natural Power of Kings, he has been so sparing of them. In his Observations on Mr. Hobbes's Leviathan, I think he has put, in short, all those arguments for it together, which in his writings I find him anywhere to make use of: his words are these: If God created only Adam, and of a piece of him made the woman, and if by generation from them two, as parts of them, all mankind be propagated: if also God gave to Adam not only the dominion over the woman and the children that should issue from them, but also over all the earth to subdue it, and over all the creatures on it, so that as long as Adam lived, no man could claim or enjoy anything but by donation, assignation or permission from him, I wonder, etc. Observations, 165. Here we have the sum of all his arguments, for Adam's sovereignty and against natural freedom, which I find up and down in his other treatises: and they are these following; God's creation of Adam, the dominion he gave him over Eve, and the dominion he had as father over his children: all which I shall particularly consider.

CHAPTER III.

Of Adam's Title to Sovereignty by Creation.

Section 15. Sir Robert, in his preface to his Observations on Aristotle's politics, tells us, a natural freedom of mankind cannot be supposed without the denial of the creation of Adam: but how Adam's being created, which was nothing but his receiving a being immediately from omnipotence and the hand of God, gave Adam a sovereignty over anything, I cannot see, nor consequently understand, how a supposition of natural freedom is a denial of Adam's creation, and would be glad anybody else (since our author did not vouchsafe us the favor) would make it out for him: for I find no difficulty to suppose the freedom of mankind, though I have always believed the creation of Adam. He was created, or began to exist, by God's immediate power, without the intervention of parents or the pre-existence of any of the same species to beget him, when it pleased God he should; and so did the lion, the king of beasts, before him, by the same creating power of God: and if bare existence by that power, and in that way, will give dominion, without any more ado, our author, by this argument, will make the lion have as good a title to it, as he, and certainly the anteater. No! For Adam had his title by the appointment of God, says our author in another place. Then bare creation gave him not dominion, and one might have supposed mankind free without the denying the creation of Adam, since it was God's appointment made him monarch.

Section 16. But let us see, how he puts his creation and this appointment together. By the appointment of God, says Sir Robert, as soon as Adam was created, he was monarch of the world, though he had no subjects; for though there could not be actual government until there were subjects, yet by the right of nature it was due to Adam to be governor of his posterity: though not in action, yet at least in habit, Adam was a king from his creation. I wish he had told us here, what he meant by God's appointment: for whatsoever providence orders, or the law of nature directs, or positive revelation declares, may be said to be by God's appointment: but I suppose it cannot be meant here in the first sense, i.e. by providence; because that would be to say no more, but that as soon as Adam was created he was *de facto* monarch, because by right of nature it was due to Adam, to be governor of his posterity. But he could not *de facto* be by providence constituted the governor of the world, at a time when there was actually no government, no subjects to be governed, which our author here confesses. Monarch of the world is also differently used by our author; for sometimes he means by it a proprietor of all the world exclusive of the rest of mankind, and thus he does in the same page of his preface before cited: Adam, says he, being commanded to multiply and people the earth, and to subdue it, and having dominion given him over all creatures, was thereby the monarch of the whole world; none of his posterity had any right to possess anything but by his grant or permission, or by succession from him. 2. Let us understand then by monarch proprietor of the world, and by appointment God's actual donation, and revealed positive grant made to Adam, i. Gen. 28. as we see Sir Robert himself does in this parallel place, and then his argument will stand thus, by the positive grant of God: as soon as Adam was created, he was proprietor of the world, because by the right of nature it was due to Adam to be governor of his posterity. In which way of arguing there are two manifest falsehoods. First, it is false, that God made that grant to Adam, as soon as he was created, since, though it stands in the text immediately after his creation, yet it is plain it could not be spoken to Adam, till after Eve was made and brought to him: and how then could he be monarch by appointment as soon as created, especially since he calls, if I mistake not, that which God says to Eve, iii. Gen. 16, the original grant of government, which not being till after the fall, when Adam was somewhat, at least in time, and very much distant in condition, from his creation, I cannot see, how our author can say in this sense, that by God's appointment, as soon as Adam was created, he was monarch of the world. Secondly, were it true that God's actual donation appointed Adam monarch of the world as soon as he was created, yet the reason here given for it would not prove it; but it would always be a false inference, that God, by a positive donation, appointed Adam monarch of the world, because by right of nature it was due to Adam to be governor of his posterity: for having given him the right of government by nature, there was no need of a positive donation; at least it will never be a proof of such a donation.

Section 17. On the other side the matter will not be much mended if we understand by God's appointment the law of nature, (though it be a pretty harsh expression for it in this place) and by monarch of the world, sovereign ruler of mankind: for then the sentence under consideration must run thus: By the law of nature, as soon as Adam was created he was governor of mankind, for by right of nature it was due to Adam to be governor of his posterity; which amounts to this, he was governor by right of nature, because he was governor by right of nature: but supposing we should grant, that a man is by nature governor of his children, Adam could not hereby be monarch as soon as created: for this right of nature being founded in his being their father, how Adam could have a natural right to be governor, before he was a father, when by being a father only he had that right, is, methinks, hard to conceive, unless he will have him to be a father before he was a father, and to have a title before he had it.

Section 18. To this foreseen objection, our author answers very logically, he was governor in habit, and not in act: a very pretty way of being a governor without government, a father without children, and a king without subjects. And thus Sir Robert was an author before he writ his book; not in action it is true, but in habit; for when he had once published it, it was due to him by the right of nature, to be an author, as much as it was to Adam to be governor of his children, when he had begot them: and if to be such a monarch of the world, an absolute monarch in habit, but not in action, will serve the turn, I should not much envy it to any of Sir Robert's friends, that he thought fit graciously to bestow it upon, though even this of act and habit, if it signified anything but our author's skill in distinctions, be not to his purpose in this place. For the question is not here about Adam's actual exercise of government, but actually having a title to be governor. Government, says our author, was due to Adam by the right of nature: what is this right of nature? A right fathers have over their children by begetting them; generatione *jus acquiritur parentibus in liberos*, says our author out of Grotius, Observations, 223. The right then follows the begetting as arising from it; so that, according to this way of reasoning or distinguishing of our author, Adam, as soon as he was created, had a title only in habit, and not in act, which in plain English is, he had actually no title at all.

Section 19. To speak less learnedly, and more intelligibly, one may say of Adam, he was in a possibility of being governor, since it was possible he might beget children, and thereby acquire that right of nature, be it what it will, to govern them, that accrues from thence: but what connection has this with Adam's creation, to make him say, that as soon as he was created, he was monarch of the world? for it may be as well said of Noah, that as soon as he was born, he was monarch of the world, since he was in possibility (which in our author's sense is enough to make a monarch, a monarch in habit,) to outlive all mankind, but his own posterity. What such necessary connection there is between Adam's creation and his right to government, so that a natural freedom of mankind cannot be supposed without the denial of the creation of Adam, I confess for my part I do not see; nor how those words, by the appointment, etc. Observations, 254. however explained, can be put together, to make any tolerable sense, at least to establish this position, with which they end, that is Adam was a king from his creation; a king, says our author, not in act, but in habit, i.e. actually no king at all.

Section 20. I fear I have tried my reader's patience, by dwelling longer on this passage, than the weightiness of any argument in it seems to require: but I have unavoidably been engaged in it by our author's way of writing, who, huddling several suppositions together, and that in doubtful and general terms, makes such a medley and confusion, that it is impossible to show his mistakes, without examining the several senses wherein his words may be taken, and without seeing how, in any of these various meanings, they will consist together, and have any truth in them: for in this present passage before us, how can anyone argue against this position of his, that Adam was a king from his creation, unless one examine, whether the words, from his creation, be to be taken, as they may, for the time of the commencement of his government, as the foregoing words import, as soon as he was created he was monarch; or, for the cause of it, as he says, p. 11. creation made man prince of his posterity? How farther can one judge of the truth of his being thus king, until one has examined whether king be to be taken, as the words in the beginning of this passage would persuade, on supposition of his private dominion, which was, by God's positive grant, monarch of the world by appointment; or king on supposition of his fatherly power over his off-spring, which was by nature, due by the right of nature; whether, I say, king be to be taken in both, or one only of these two senses, or in neither of them, but only this, that creation made him prince, in a way different from both the other? For though this assertion, that Adam was king from his creation, be true in no sense, yet it stands here as an evident conclusion drawn from the preceding words, though in truth it be but a bare assertion joined to other assertions of the same kind, which confidently put together in words of undetermined and dubious meaning, look like a sort of arguing, when there is indeed neither proof nor connection: a way very familiar with our author: of which having given the reader a taste here, I shall, as much as the argument will permit me, avoid touching on hereafter; and should not have done it here, were it not to let the world see, how incoherence in matter, and suppositions without proofs put handsomely together in good words and a plausible stile, are apt to pass for strong reason and good sense, till they come to be looked into with attention.

CHAPTER IV.

Of Adam's Title to Sovereignty by Donation, Gen. i. 28.

Section 21. Having at last got through the foregoing passage, where we have been so long detained, not by the force of arguments and opposition, but the intricacy of the words, and the doubtfulness of the meaning; let us go on to his next argument, for Adam's sovereignty. Our author tells us in the words of Mr. Selden, that Adam by donation from God, Gen. i. 28. was made the general lord of all things, not without such a private dominion to himself, as without his grant did exclude his children. This determination of Mr. Selden, says our author, inconsonant to the history of the Bible, and natural reason, Observations, 210. And in his Preface to his Observations on Aristotle, he says thus, the first government in the world was monarchical in the father of all flesh, Adam being commanded to multiply and people the earth, and to subdue it, and having dominion given him over all creatures, was thereby the monarch of the whole world: none of his posterity had any right to possess anything, but by his grant or permission, or by succession from him: The earth, said the Psalmist, has he given to the children of men, which show the title comes from fatherhood.

Section 22. Before I examine this argument, and the text on which it is founded, it is necessary to desire the reader to observe, that our author, according to his usual method, begins in one sense, and concludes in another; he begins here with Adam's propriety, or private dominion, by donation; and his conclusion is, which show the title comes from fatherhood.

Section 23. But let us see the argument. The words of the text are these; and God blessed them, and God said unto them, be fruitful and multiply, and replenish the earth and subdue it, and have dominion over the fish of the sea, and over the fowl of the air, and over every living thing that moves upon the earth, i. Gen. 28. from whence our author concludes, that Adam, having here dominion given him over all creatures, was thereby the monarch of the whole world: whereby must be meant, that either this grant of God gave Adam property, or as our author calls it, private dominion over the earth, and all inferior or irrational creatures, and so consequently that he was thereby monarch; or secondly, that it gave him rule and dominion over all earthly creatures whatsoever, and thereby over his children; and so he was monarch: for, as Mr. Selden has properly worded it, Adam was made general lord of all things, one may very clearly understand him, that he means nothing to be granted to Adam here but property, and therefore he says not one word of Adam's monarchy. But our author says, Adam was hereby monarch of the world, which, properly speaking, signifies sovereign ruler of all the men in the world; and so Adam, by this grant, must be constituted such a ruler. If our author means otherwise, he might with much clearness have said, that Adam was hereby proprietor of the whole world. But he begs your pardon in that point: clear distinct speaking not serving everywhere to his purpose, you must not expect it in him, as in Mr. Selden, or other such writers.

Section 24. In opposition therefore to our author's doctrine, that Adam was monarch of the whole world, founded on this place, I shall show,

1. That by this grant, i. Gen. 28. God gave no immediate power to Adam over men, over his children, over those of his own species; and so he was not made ruler, or monarch, by this charter.

2. That by this grant God gave him not private dominion over the inferior creatures, but right in common with all mankind; so neither was he monarch, upon the account of the property here given him.

Section 25. 1. That this donation, i. Gen. 28. gave Adam no power over men, will appear if we consider the words of it: for since all positive grants convey no more than the express words they are made in will carry, let us see which of them here will comprehend mankind, or Adam's posterity; and those, I imagine, if any, must be these, every living thing that moves: the words in Hebrew are, היה השמרה i.e. Bestiam Reptantem, of which words the Scripture itself is the best interpreter: God having created the fishes and fowls the 5th day, the beginning of the 6th, he creates the irrational inhabitants of the dry land, which, v. 24. are described in these words, let the earth bring forth the living creature after his kind; cattle and creeping things, and beasts of the earth, after his kind, and, v. 2. and God made the beasts of the earth after his kind, and cattle after their kind, and everything that creeps on the earth after his kind: here, in the creation of the brute inhabitants of the earth, he first speaks of them all under one general name, of living creatures, and then afterwards divides them into three ranks, 1. Cattle, or such creatures as were or might be tame, and so be the private possession of particular men; 2. היח which, ver. 24, and 25. in our Bible, is translated beasts, and by the Septuagint θηϛία, wild beasts, and is the same word, that here in our text, ver. 28. where we have this great charter to Adam, is translated living thing, and is also the same word used, Gen. ix. 2. where this grant is renewed to Noah, and there likewise translated beast. 3. The third rank was the creeping animals, which ver. 24, and 25. are comprised under the word, השמרח, the same that is used here, ver. 28. and is translated moving, but in the former verses creeping, and by the Septuagint in all these places, ἑϱπετά, or reptiles; from whence it appears, that the words which we translate here in God's donation, ver.28. living creatures moving are the same, which in the history of the creation, ver. 24, 25. signify two ranks of terrestrial creatures, that is wild beasts and reptiles, and are so understood by the Septuagint.

Section 26. When God had made the irrational animals of the world, divided into three kinds, from the places of their habitation, that is fishes of the sea, fowls of the air, and living creatures of the earth, and these again into cattle, wild beasts, and reptiles, he considers of making man, and the dominion he should have over the terrestrial world, ver. 26. and then he reckons up the inhabitants of these three kingdoms, but in the terrestrial leaves out the second rank חיה or wild beasts: but here, ver. 28. where he actually exercises this design, and gives him this dominion, the text mentions the fishes of the sea, and fowls of the air, and the terrestrial creatures in the words that signify the wild beasts and reptiles, though translated living thing that moves, leaving out cattle. In both which places, though the word that signifies wild beasts be omitted in one, and that which signifies cattle in the other, yet, since God certainly executed in one place, what he declares he designed in the other, we cannot but understand the same in both places, and have here only an account, how the terrestrial irrational animals, which were already created and reckoned up at their creation, in three distinct ranks of cattle, wild beasts, and reptiles, were here, ver. 28. actually put under the dominion of man, as they were designed, ver. 26. nor do these words contain in them the least appearance of anything that can be wrested to signify God's giving to one man dominion over another, to Adam over his posterity.

Section 27. And this further appears from Gen. ix. 2. where God renewing this charter to Noah and his sons, he gives them dominion over the fowls of the air, and the fishes of the sea, and the terrestrial creatures, expressed by חיה and שמרר wild beasts and reptiles, the same words that in the text before us, i. Gen. 28. are translated every moving thing, that moves on the earth, which by no means can comprehend man, the grant being made to Noah and his sons, all the men then living, and not to one part of men over another: which is yet more evident from the very next words, ver. 3. where God gives every שמר every moving thing, the very words used ch. i. 28. to them for food. By all which it is plain that God's donation to Adam, ch. i. 28. and his designation, ver. 26. and his grant again to Noah and his sons, refer to and contain in them neither more nor less than the works of the creation the 5th day, and the beginning of the 6th, as they are set down from the 20th to 26th ver. inclusively of the 1st ch. and so comprehend all the species of irrational animals of the terraqueous globe, though all the words, whereby they are expressed in the history of their creation, are nowhere used in any of the following grants, but some of them omitted in one, and some in another. From whence I think it is past all doubt, that man cannot be comprehended in this grant, nor any dominion over those of his own species be conveyed to Adam. All the terrestrial irrational creatures are enumerated at their creation, ver. 25. under the names beasts of the earth, cattle and creeping things; but man, being not then created, was not contained under any of those names; and therefore, whether we understand the Hebrew words right or no, they cannot be supposed to comprehend man, in the very same history, and the very next verses following, especially since that Hebrew word שמר which, if any in this donation to Adam, ch. i. 28. must comprehend man, is so plainly used in contradistinction to him, as Gen. vi. 20. vii. 14, 21, 23. Gen. viii. 17, 19. And if God made all mankind slaves to Adam and his heirs by giving Adam dominion over every living thing that moves on the earth, ch. i. 28. as our author would have it, methinks Sir Robert should have carried his monarchical power one step higher, and satisfied the world, that princes might eat their subjects too, since God gave as full power to Noah and his heirs, ch. ix. 2. to eat every living thing that moves, as he did to Adam to have dominion over them, the Hebrew words in both places being the same.

Section 28. David, who might be supposed to understand the donation of God in this text, and the right of kings too, as well as our author in his comment on this place, as the learned and judicious Ainsworth calls it, in the 8th Psalm, finds here no such charter of monarchical power, his words are, You have made him, i.e. man, the Son of man, a little lower than the angels; you maddest him to have dominion over the works of your hands; you have put all things under his feet, all sheep and oxen, and the beasts of the field, and the fowls of the air, and fish of the sea, and whatsoever passeth through the paths of the sea. In which words, if anyone can find out, that there is meant any monarchical power of one man over another, but only the dominion of the whole species of mankind, over the inferior species of creatures, he may, for aught I know, deserve to be one of Sir Robert's monarchs in habit, for the rareness of the discovery. And by this time, I hope it is evident, that he that gave dominion over every living thing that moves on the earth gave Adam no monarchical power over those of his own species, which will yet appear more fully in the next thing I am to show.

Section 29. 2. Whatever God gave by the words of this grant, i. Gen. 28. it was not to Adam in particular, exclusive of all other men: whatever dominion he had thereby, it was not a private dominion, but a dominion in common with the rest of mankind. That this donation was not made in particular to Adam, appears evidently from the words of the text, it being made to more than one; for it was spoken in the plural number, God blessed them, and said unto them, Have dominion. God says unto Adam and Eve, Have dominion; thereby, says our author, Adam was monarch of the world: but the grant being to them, i.e. spoke to Eve also, as many interpreters think with reason, that these words were not spoken till Adam had his wife, must not she thereby be lady, as well as he lord of the world? If it be said, that Eve was subjected to Adam, it seems she was not so subjected to him, as to hinder her dominion over the creatures, or property in them: for shall we say that God ever made a joint grant to two, and one only was to have the benefit of it?

Section 30. But perhaps it will be said, Eve was not made until afterward: grant it so, what advantage will our author get by it? The text will be only the more directly against him, and show that God, in this donation, gave the world to mankind in common, and not to Adam in particular. The word them in the text must include the species of man, for it is certain them can by no means signify Adam alone. In the 26th verse, where God declares his intention to give this dominion, it is plain he meant, that he would make a species of creatures, that should have dominion over the other species of this terrestrial globe: the words are, And God said, Let us make man in our image, after our likeness, and let them have dominion over the fish, etc. They then were to have dominion. Who? even those who were to have the image of God, the individuals of that species of man, that he was going to make; for that them should signify Adam singly, exclusive of the rest that should be in the world with him, is against both Scripture and all reason: and it cannot possibly be made sense, if man in the former part of the verse do not signify the same with them in the latter; only man there, as is usual, is taken for the species, and them the individuals of that species: and we have a reason in the very text. God makes him in his own image, after his own likeness; makes him an intellectual creature, and so capable of dominion: for wherein soever else the image of God consisted, the intellectual nature was certainly a part of it, and belonged to the whole species, and enabled them to have dominion over the inferior creatures; and therefore David says in the 8th Psalm above cited, You have made him little lower than the angels, you have made him to have dominion. It is not of Adam king David speaks here, for verse 4. it is plain; it is of man, and the son of man, of the species of mankind.

Section 31. And that this grant spoken to Adam was made to him, and the whole species of man, is clear from our author's own proof out of the Psalmist. The earth, said the Psalmist, has he given to the children of men; which shows the title comes from fatherhood. These are Sir Robert's words in the preface before cited, and a strange inference it is he makes; God has given the earth to the children of men, *ergo* the title comes from fatherhood. It is pity the propriety of the Hebrew tongue had not used fathers of men, instead of children of men, to express mankind: then indeed our author might have had the countenance of the sound of the words, to have placed the title in the fatherhood. But to conclude, that the fatherhood had the right to the earth, because God gave it to the children of men, is a way of arguing peculiar to our author: and a man must have a great mind to go contrary to the sound as well as sense of the words, before he could light on it. But the sense is yet harder, and more remote from our author's purpose: for as it stands in his preface, it is to prove Adam's being monarch, and his reasoning is thus, God gave the earth to the children of men, ergo Adam was monarch of the world. I defy any man to make a more pleasant conclusion than this, which cannot be excused from the most obvious absurdity, till it can be shown, that by children of men, he who had no father, Adam alone is signified; but whatever our author does, the Scripture speaks not nonsense.

Section 32. To maintain this property and private dominion of Adam, our author labors in the following page to destroy the community granted to Noah and his sons, in that parallel place, ix. Gen. 1, 2, 3. and he endeavors to do it two ways.

1. Sir Robert would persuade us against the express words of the Scripture that what was here granted to Noah, was not granted to his sons in common with him. His words are, As for the general community between Noah and his sons, which Mr. Selden will have to be granted to them, ix. Gen. 2. the text does not warrant it. What warrant our author would have, when the plain express words of Scripture, not capable of another meaning, will not satisfy him, who pretends to build wholly on Scripture, is not easy to imagine. The text says, God blessed Noah and his sons, and said unto them, i.e. as our author would have it, unto him: for, faith he, although the sons are there mentioned with Noah in the blessing, yet it may best be understood, with a subordination or benediction in succession, Observations, 211. That indeed is best, for our author to be understood, which best serves to his purpose; but that truly may best be understood by anybody else, which best agrees with the plain construction of the words, and arises from the obvious meaning of the place; and then with subordination and in succession, will not be best understood, in a grant of God, where he himself put them not, nor mentions any such limitation. But yet, our author has reasons, why it may best be understood so. The blessing, says he in the following words, might truly be fulfilled, if the sons, either under or after their father, enjoyed a private dominion, Observations, 211. which is to say, that a grant, whose express words give a joint title in present (for the text says, into your hands they are delivered) may best be understood with a subordination or in succession; because it is possible, that in subordination, or in succession, it may be enjoyed. Which is all one as to say, that a grant of anything in present possession may best be understood of reversion; because it is possible one may live to enjoy it in reversion. If the grant be indeed to a father and to his sons after him, who is so kind as to let his children enjoy it presently in common with him, one may truly say, as to the event one will be as good as the other; but it can never be true, that what the express words grant in possession, and in common, may best be understood, to be in reversion. The sum of all his reasoning amounts to this: God did not give to the sons of Noah the world in common with their father, because it was possible they might enjoy it under, or after him. A very good sort of argument against an express text of Scripture: but God must not be believed, though he speaks it himself, when he says he does anything, which will not consist with Sir Robert's hypothesis.

Section 33. For it is plain, however he would exclude them, that part of this benediction, as he would have it in succession, must needs be meant to the sons, and not to Noah himself at all: Be fruitful, and multiply, and replenish the earth, says God, in this blessing. This part of the benediction, as appears by the sequel, concerned not Noah himself at all; for we read not of any children he had after the flood; and in the following chapter, where his posterity is reckoned up, there is no mention of any; and so this benediction in succession was not to take place until 350 years after: and to save our author's imaginary monarchy, the peopling of the world must be deferred 350 years; for this part of the benediction cannot be understood with subordination, unless our author will say, that they must ask leave of their father Noah to lie with their wives. But in this one point our author is constant to himself in all his discourses, he takes great care there should be monarchs in the world, but very little that there should be people; and indeed his way of government is not the way to people the world: for how much absolute monarchy helps to fulfill this great and primary blessing of God Almighty, Be fruitful, and multiply, and replenish the earth, which contains in it the improvement too of arts and sciences, and the conveniences of life, may be seen in those large and rich countries which are happy under the Turkish government, where are not now to be found one third, nay in many, if not most parts of them one thirtieth, perhaps I might say not one hundredth of the people, that were formerly, as will easily appear to anyone, who will compare the accounts we have of it at this time, with ancient history. But this by the by.

Section 34. The other parts of this benediction, or grant, are so expressed, that they must needs be understood to belong equally to them all; as much to Noah's sons as to Noah himself, and not to his sons with subordination, or in succession. The fear of you, and the dread of you, says God, shall be upon every beast, etc. Will anybody but our author say, that the creatures feared and stood in awe of Noah only, and not of his sons without his leave, or until after his death? And the following words, into your hands they are delivered, are they to be understood as our author says, if your father please, or they shall be delivered into your hands hereafter? If this be to argue from Scripture, I know not what may not be proved by it; and I can scarce see how much this differs from that fiction and fantasy, or how much a surer foundation it will prove, than the opinions of philosophers and poets, which our author so much condemns in his preface.

Section 35. But our author goes on to prove, that it may best be understood with a subordination, or a benediction in succession; for, says he, it is not probable that the private dominion which God gave to Adam, and by his donation, assignation, or cession to his children, was abrogated, and a community of all things instituted between Noah and his sons——Noah was left the sole heir of the world; why should it be thought that God would disinherit him of his birthright, and make him of all men in the world the only tenant in common with his children? Observations, 211.

Section 36. The prejudices of our own ill-grounded opinions, however by us called probable, cannot authorize us to understand Scripture contrary to the direct and plain meaning of the words. I grant, it is not probable, that Adam's private dominion was here abrogated: because it is more than improbable, (for it will never be proved) that ever Adam had any such private dominion: and since parallel places of Scripture are most probable to make us know how they may be best understood, there needs but the comparing this blessing here to Noah and his sons after the flood, with that to Adam after the creation, i. Gen. 28. to assure anyone that God gave Adam no such private dominion. It is probable, I confess, that Noah should have the same title, the same property and dominion after the flood, that Adam had before it: but since private dominion cannot consist with the blessing and grant God gave to him and his sons in common, it is a sufficient reason to conclude, that Adam had none, especially since in the donation made to him, there are no words that express it, or do in the least favor it; and then let my reader judge whether it may best be understood, when in the one place there is not one word for it, not to say what has been above proved, that the text itself proves the contrary; and in the other, the words and sense are directly against it.

Section 37. But our author says, Noah was the sole heir of the world; why should it be thought that God would disinherit him of his birthright? Heir, indeed, in England, signifies the eldest son, who is by the law of England to have all his father's land; but where God ever appointed any such heir of the world, our author would have done well to have showed us; and how God disinherited him of his birthright, or what harm was done him if God gave his sons a right to make use of a part of the earth for the support of themselves and families, when the whole was not only more than Noah himself, but infinitely more than they all could make use of, and the possessions of one could not at all prejudice, or, as to any use, straighten that of the other.

Section 38. Our author probably foreseeing he might not be very successful in persuading people out of their senses, and, say what he could, men would be apt to believe the plain words of Scripture, and think, as they saw, that the grant was spoken to Noah and his sons jointly; he endeavors to insinuate, as if this grant to Noah conveyed no property, no dominion; because, subduing the earth and dominion over the creatures are therein omitted, nor the earth once named. And therefore, says he, there is a considerable difference between these two texts; the first blessing gave Adam a dominion over the earth and all creatures; the latter allows Noah liberty to use the living creatures for food: here is no alteration or diminishing of his title to a property of all things, but an enlargement only of his commons, Observations, 211. So that in our author's sense, all that was said here to Noah and his sons, gave them no dominion, no property, but only enlarged the commons; their commons, I should say, since God says, to you are they given, though our author says his; for as for Noah's sons, they, it seems, by Sir Robert's appointment, during their father's life-time, were to keep fasting days.

Section 39. Anyone but our author would be mightily suspected to be blinded with prejudice, that in all this blessing to Noah and his sons, could see nothing but only an enlargement of commons: for as to dominion, which our author thinks omitted, the fear of you, and the dread of you, says God, shall be upon every beast, which I suppose expresses the dominion, or superiority was designed man over the living creatures, as fully as may be; for in that fear and dread seems chiefly to consist what was given to Adam over the inferior animals; who, as absolute a monarch as he was, could not make bold with a lark or rabbit to satisfy his hunger, and had the herbs but in common with the beasts, as is plain from i Gen. 2, 9, and 30. In the next place, it is manifest that in this blessing to Noah and his sons; property is not only given in clear words, but in a larger extent than it was to Adam. Into your hands they are given, says God to Noah and his sons; which words, if they give not property, nay, property in possession, it will be hard to find words that can; since there is not a way to express a man's being possessed of anything more natural, nor more certain, than to say, it is delivered into his hands. And ver. 3. to show, that they had then given them the utmost property man is capable of, which is to have a right to destroy anything by using it; Every moving thing that lives, said God, shall be meat for you; which was not allowed to Adam in his charter. This our author calls, a liberty of using them for food, and only an enlargement of commons, but no alteration of property, Observations, 211. What other property man can have in the creatures, but the liberty of using them, is hard to be understood: so that if the first blessing, as our author says, gave Adam dominion over the creatures, and the blessing to Noah and his sons, gave them such a liberty to use them, as Adam had not; it must needs give them something that Adam with all his sovereignty wanted, something that one would be apt to take for a greater property; for certainly he has no absolute dominion over even the brutal part of the creatures; and the property he has in them is very narrow and scanty, who cannot make that use of them, which is permitted to another. Should anyone who is absolute lord of a country, have bidden our author subdue the earth, and given him dominion over the creatures in it, but not have permitted him to have taken a kid or a lamb out of the flock, to satisfy his hunger, I guess, he would scarce have thought himself lord or proprietor of that land, or the cattle on it; but would have found the difference between having dominion, which a shepherd may have, and having full property as an owner. So that, had it been his own case, Sir Robert, I believe, would have thought here was an alteration, nay, an enlarging of property; and that Noah and his children had by this grant, not only property given them, but such a property given them in the creatures, as Adam had not: For however, in respect of one another, men may be allowed to have propriety in their distinct portions of the creatures; yet in respect of God the maker of heaven and earth, who is sole lord and proprietor of the whole world, man's propriety in the creatures is nothing but that liberty to use them, which God has permitted; and so man's property may be altered and enlarged, as we see it was here, after the flood, when other uses of them are allowed, which before were not. From all which I suppose it is clear, that neither Adam, nor Noah, had any private dominion, any property in the creatures, exclusive of his posterity, as they should successively grow up into need of them, and come to be able to make use of them.

Section 40. Thus we have examined our author's argument for Adam's monarchy, founded on the blessing pronounced, i. Gen. 28. Wherein I think it is impossible for any sober reader, to find any other but the setting of mankind above the other kinds of creatures, in this habitable earth of ours. It is nothing but the giving to man, the whole species of man, as the chief inhabitant, who is the image of his Maker, the dominion over the other creatures. This lies so obvious in the plain words, that anyone, but our author, would have thought it necessary to have shown, how these words, that seemed to say the quite contrary, gave Adam monarchical absolute power over other men, or the sole property in all the creatures; and methinks in a business of this moment, and that whereon he builds all that follows, he should have done something more than barely cite words, which apparently make against him; for I confess, I cannot see anything in them, tending to Adam's monarchy, or private dominion, but quite the contrary. And I the less deplore the dullness of my apprehension herein, since I find the apostle seems to have as little notion of any such private dominion of Adam as I, when he says, God gives us all things richly to enjoy, which he could not do, if it were all given away already, to Monarch Adam, and the monarchs his heirs and successors. To conclude, this text is so far from proving Adam sole proprietor, that, on the contrary, it is a confirmation of the original community of all things among the sons of men, which appearing from this donation of God, as well as other places of Scripture, the sovereignty of Adam, built upon his private dominion, must fall, not having any foundation to support it.

Section 41. But yet, if after all, anyone will have it so, that by this donation of God, Adam was made sole proprietor of the whole earth, what will this be to his sovereignty? And how will it appear, that propriety in land gives a man power over the life of another? Or how will the possession even of the whole earth, give anyone a sovereign arbitrary authority over the persons of men? The most specious thing to be said, is, that he that is proprietor of the whole world, may deny all the rest of mankind food, and so at his pleasure starve them, if they will not acknowledge his sovereignty, and obey his will. If this were true, it would be a good argument to prove, that there never was any such property, that God never gave any such private dominion; since it is more reasonable to think, that God, who bid mankind increase and multiply, should rather himself give them all a right to make use of the food and raiment, and other conveniences of life, the materials whereof he had so plentifully provided for them; than to make them depend upon the will of a man for their subsistence, who should have power to destroy them all when he pleased, and who, being no better than other men, was in succession likelier, by want and the dependence of a scanty fortune, to tie them to hard service, than by liberal allowance of the conveniences of life to promote the great design of God, increase and multiply: he that doubts this, let him look into the absolute monarchies of the world, and see what becomes of the conveniences of life, and the multitudes of people.

Section 42. But we know God has not left one man so to the mercy of another, that he may starve him if he please: God the Lord and Father of all has given no one of his children such a property in his peculiar portion of the things of this world, but that he has given his needy brother a right to the surplus of his goods; so that it cannot justly be denied him, when his pressing wants call for it: and therefore no man could ever have a just power over the life of another by right of property in land or possessions; since it would always be a sin, in any man of estate, to let his brother perish for want of affording him relief out of his plenty. As justice gives every man a title to the product of his honest industry, and the fair acquisitions of his ancestors descended to him; so charity gives every man a title to so much out of another's plenty, as will keep him from extreme want, where he has no means to subsist otherwise: and a man can no more justly make use of another's necessity, to force him to become his vassal, by with-holding that relief, God requires him to afford to the wants of his brother, than he that has more strength can seize upon a weaker, master him to his obedience, and with a dagger at his throat offer him death or slavery.

Section 43. Should anyone make so perverse an use of God's blessings poured on him with a liberal hand; should anyone be cruel and uncharitable to that extremity, yet all this would not prove that propriety in land, even in this case, gave any authority over the persons of men, but only that compact might; since the authority of the rich proprietor, and the subjection of the needy beggar, began not from the possession of the Lord, but the consent of the poor man, who preferred being his subject to starving. And the man he thus submits to, can pretend to no more power over him, than he has consented to, upon compact. Upon this ground a man's having his stores filled in a time of scarcity, having money in his pocket, being in a vessel at sea, being able to swim, etc. may as well be the foundation of rule and dominion, as being possessor of all the land in the world; any of these being sufficient to enable me to save a man's life, who would perish if such assistance were denied him; and anything, by this rule, that may be an occasion of working upon another's necessity, to save his life, or anything dear to him, at the rate of his freedom, may be made a foundation of sovereignty, as well as property. From all which it is clear, that though God should have given Adam private dominion, yet that private dominion could give him no sovereignty; but we have already sufficiently proved that God gave him no private dominion.

CHAPTER V.

Of Adam's Title to Sovereignty by the Subjection of Eve.

Section 44. The next place of Scripture we find our author builds his monarchy of Adam on, is iii. Gen. 26. And your desire shall be to your husband, and he shall rule over you. Here we have (says he) the original grant of government, from whence he concludes, in the following part of the page, Observations, 244. That the supreme power is settled in the fatherhood, and limited to one kind of government, that is, to monarchy. For let his premises be what they will, this is always the conclusion; let rule, in any text, be but once named, and presently absolute monarchy is by divine right established. If anyone will but carefully read our author's own reasoning from these words, Observations, 244. and consider, among other things, the line and posterity of Adam, as he there brings them in, he will find some difficulty to make sense of what he says; but we will allow this at present to his peculiar way of writing, and consider the force of the text in hand. The words are the curse of God upon the woman, for having been the first in the disobedience; and if we will consider the occasion of what God says here to our first parents, that he was denouncing judgment, and declaring his wrath against them both, for their disobedience, we cannot suppose that this was the time, wherein God was granting Adam prerogatives and privileges, investing him with dignity and authority, elevating him to dominion and monarchy: for though, as a helper in the temptation, Eve was laid below him, and so he had accidentally a superiority over her, for her greater punishment; yet he too had his share in the fall, as well as the sin, and was laid lower, as may be seen in the following verses; and it would be hard to imagine, that God, in the same breath, should make him universal monarch over all mankind, and a day-laborer for his life; turn him out of paradise to till the ground, ver. 23. and at the same time advance him to a throne, and all the privileges and ease of absolute power.

Section 45. This was not a time, when Adam could expect any favors, any grant of privileges, from his offended Maker. If this be the original grant of government, as our author tells us, and Adam was now made monarch, whatever Sir Robert would have him, it is plain, God made him but a very poor monarch, such a one, as our author himself would have counted it no great privilege to be. God sets him to work for his living, and seems rather to give him a spade into his hand, to subdue the earth, than a scepter to rule over its inhabitants. In the sweat of your face you shall eat your bread, says God to him, ver. 19. This was unavoidable, may it perhaps be answered, because he was yet without subjects, and had nobody to work for him; but afterwards, living as he did above 900 years, he might have people enough, whom he might command, to work for him; no, says God, not only while you are without other help, save your wife, but as long as you live, shall you live by your labor, In the sweat of your face, shall you eat your bread, till you return unto the ground, for out of it were you taken, for dust you are, and unto dust shall you return, v. 19. It will perhaps be answered again in favor of our author, that these words are not spoken personally to Adam, but in him, as their representative, to all mankind, this being a curse upon mankind, because of the fall.

Section 46. God, I believe, speaks differently from men, because he speaks with more truth, more certainty: but when he vouchsafes to speak to men, I do not think he speaks differently from them, in crossing the rules of language in use among them: this would not be to condescend to their capacities, when he humbles himself to speak to them, but to lose his design in speaking what, thus spoken, they could not understand. And yet thus must we think of God, if the interpretations of Scripture, necessary to maintain our author's doctrine, must be received for good: for by the ordinary rules of language, it will be very hard to understand what God says, if what he speaks here, in the singular number, to Adam, must be understood to be spoken to all mankind, and what he says in the plural number, i. Gen. 26, and 28. must be understood of Adam alone, exclusive of all others, and what he says to Noah and his sons jointly, must be understood to be meant to Noah alone, Gen. ix.

Section 47. Father it is to be noted, that these words here of iii. Gen. 16. which our author calls the original grant of government, were not spoken to Adam, neither indeed was there any grant in them made to Adam, but a punishment laid upon Eve: and if we will take them as they were directed in particular to her, or in her, as their representative, to all other women, they will at most concern the female sex only, and import no more, but that subjection they should ordinarily be in to their husbands: but there is here no more law to oblige a woman to such a subjection, if the circumstances either of her condition, or contract with her husband, should exempt her from it, than there is, that she should bring forth her children in sorrow and pain, if there could be found a remedy for it, which is also a part of the same curse upon her: for the whole verse runs thus, Unto the woman he said, I will greatly multiply your sorrow and your conception; in sorrow you shall bring forth children, and your desire shall be to your husband, and he shall rule over you. It would, I think, have been a hard matter for anybody, but our author, to have found out a grant of monarchical government to Adam in these words, which were neither spoke to, nor of him: neither will anyone, I suppose, by these words, think the weaker sex, as by a law, so subjected to the curse contained in them, that it is their duty not to endeavor to avoid it. And will anyone say that Eve, or any other woman, sinned, if she were brought to bed without those multiplied pains God threatens her here with? Or that either of our queens, Mary or Elizabeth, had they married any of their subjects, had been by this text put into a political subjection to him? or that he thereby should have had monarchical rule over her? God, in this text, gives not, that I see, any authority to Adam over Eve, or to men over their wives, but only foretells what should be the woman's lot, how by his providence he would order it so, that she should be subject to her husband, as we see that generally the laws of mankind and customs of nations have ordered it so; and there is, I grant, a foundation in nature for it.

Section 48. Thus when God says of Jacob and Esau, that the elder should serve the younger, xxv. Gen. 23. nobody supposes that God hereby made Jacob Esau's sovereign, but foretold what should de facto come to pass. But if these words here spoke to Eve must needs be understood as a law to bind her and all other women to subjection, it can be no other subjection than what every wife owes her husband; and then if this be the original grant of government and the foundation of monarchical power, there will be as many monarchs as there are husbands: if therefore these words give any power to Adam, it can be only a conjugal power, not political; the power that every husband has to order the things of private concernment in his family, as proprietor of the goods and land there, and to have his will take place before that of his wife in all things of their common concernment; but not a political power of life and death over her, much less over anybody else.

Section 49. This I am sure: if our author will have this text to be a grant, the original grant of government, political government, he ought to have proved it by some better arguments than by barely saying, that your desire shall be unto your husband, was a law whereby Eve, and all that should come of her, were subjected to the absolute monarchical power of Adam and his heirs. Your desire shall be to your husband, is too doubtful an expression, of whose signification interpreters are not agreed, to build so confidently on, and in a matter of such moment, and so great and general concernment: but our author, according to his way of writing, having once named the text, concludes presently without any more ado, that the meaning is as he would have it. Let the words rule and subject be but found in the text or margent, and it immediately signifies the duty of a subject to his prince; the relation is changed, and though God says husband, Sir Robert will have it king; Adam has presently absolute monarchical power over Eve, and not only over Eve, but all that should come of her, though the Scripture says not a word of it, nor our author a word to prove it. But Adam must for all that be an absolute monarch, and so down to the end of the chapter. And here I leave my reader to consider, whether my bare saying, without offering any reasons to evince it, that this text gave not Adam that absolute monarchical power, our author supposes, be not as sufficient to destroy that power, as his bare assertion is to establish it, since the text mentions neither prince nor people, speaks nothing of absolute or monarchical power, but the subjection of Eve to Adam, a wife to her husband. And he that would trace our author so all through, would make a short and sufficient answer to the greatest part of the grounds he proceeds on, and abundantly confute them by barely denying; it being a sufficient answer to assertions without proof, to deny them without giving a reason. And therefore should I have said nothing but barely denied, that by this text the supreme power was settled and founded by God himself, in the fatherhood, limited to monarchy, and that to Adam's person and heirs, all which our author notably concludes from these words, as may be seen in the same page, Observations, 244. it had been a sufficient answer: should I have desired any sober man only to have read the text, and considered to whom, and on what occasion it was spoken, he would no doubt have wondered how our author found out monarchical absolute power in it, had he not had an exceeding good faculty to find it himself, where he could not show it others. And thus we have examined the two places of Scripture, all that I remember our author brings to prove Adam's sovereignty, that supremacy, which he says, it was God's ordinance should be unlimited in Adam, and as large as all the acts of his will, Observations, 254. that is i. Gen. 28. and iii. Gen. 16. one whereof signifies only the subjection of the inferior ranks of creatures to mankind, and the other the subjection that is due from a wife to her husband, both far enough from that which subjects owe the governors of political societies.

CHAPTER VI.

Of Adam's Title to Sovereignty by Fatherhood.

Section 50. There is one thing more, and then I think I have given you all that our author brings for proof of Adam's sovereignty, and that is a supposition of a natural right of dominion over his children, by being their father: and this title of fatherhood he is so pleased with, that you will find it brought in almost in every page; particularly he says, not only Adam, but the succeeding patriarchs had by right of fatherhood royal authority over their children, p. 12. And in the same page, this subjection of children being the fountain of all regal authority, etc. This being, as one would think by his frequent mentioning it, the main basis of all his frame, we may well expect clear and evident reason for it, since he lays it down as a position necessary to his purpose, that every man that is born is so far from being free, that by his very birth he becomes a subject of him that begets him, Observations, 156. so that Adam being the only man created, and all ever since being begotten, nobody has been born free. If we ask how Adam comes by this power over his children, he tells us here it is by begetting them: and so again, Observations, 223. this natural dominion of Adam, says he, may be proved out of Grotius himself, who teaches, that generatione jus acquiritur parentibus in liberos. And indeed the act of begetting being that which makes a man a father, his right of a father over his children can naturally arise from nothing else.

Section 51. Grotius tells us not here how far this *jus in liberos*, this power of parents over their children extends; but our author, always very clear in the point, assures us, it is supreme power, and like that of absolute monarchs over their slaves, absolute power of life and death. He that should demand of him, how, or for what reason it is, that begetting a child gives the father such an absolute power over him, will find him answer nothing: we are to take his word for this, as well as several other things; and by that the laws of nature and the constitutions of government must stand or fall. Had he been an absolute monarch, this way of talking might have suited well enough; *proratione voluntas* might have been of force in his mouth; but in the way of proof or argument is very unbecoming, and will little advantage his plea for absolute monarchy. Sir Robert has too much lessened a subject's authority to leave himself the hopes of establishing anything by his bare saying it; one slave's opinion without proof is not of weight enough to dispose of the liberty and fortunes of all mankind. If all men are not, as I think they are, naturally equal, I am sure all slaves are; and then I may without presumption oppose my single opinion to his; and be confident that my saying, that begetting of children makes them not slaves to their fathers, as certainly sets all mankind free, as his affirming the contrary makes them all slaves. But that this position, which is the foundation of all their doctrine, who would have monarchy to be jure divino, may have all fair play, let us hear what reasons others give for it, since our author offers none.

Section 52. The argument, I have heard others make use of, to prove that fathers, by begetting them, come by an absolute power over their children, is this; that fathers have a power over the lives of their children, because they give them life and being, which is the only proof it is capable of: since there can be no reason, why naturally one man should have any claim or pretence of right over that in another, which was never his, which he bestowed not, but was received from the bounty of another. 1. I answer, that everyone who gives another anything, has not always thereby a right to take it away again. But 2. They who say the father gives life to his children, are so dazzled with the thoughts of monarchy, that they do not, as they ought, remember God, who is the author and giver of life: it is in him alone we live, move, and have our being. How can he be thought to give life to another that knows not wherein his own life consists? Philosophers are at a loss about it after their most diligent enquiries; and anatomists, after their whole lives and studies spent in dissections, and diligent examining the bodies of men, confess their ignorance in the structure and use of many parts of man's body, and in that operation wherein life consists in the whole. And does the rude plough-man, or the more ignorant voluptuary, frame or fashion such an admirable engine as this is, and then put life and sense into it? Can any man say he formed the parts that are necessary to the life of his child? Or can he suppose himself to give the life, and yet not know what subject is fit to receive it, or what actions or organs are necessary for its reception or preservation?

Section 53. To give life to that which has yet no being, is to frame and make a living creature, fashion the parts, and mould and suit them to their uses, and having proportioned and fitted them together, to put into them a living soul. He that could do this, might indeed have some pretence to destroy his own workmanship. But is there anyone so bold that dares thus far arrogate to himself the incomprehensible works of the almighty? Who alone did at first, and continues still to make a living soul, he alone can breathe in the breath of life. If anyone thinks himself an artist at this, let him number up the parts of his child's body which he has made, tell me their uses and operations, and when the living and rational soul began to inhabit this curious structure, when sense began, and how this engine, which he has framed, thinks and reasons: if he made it, let him, when it is out of order, mend it, at least tell wherein the defects lie. Shall he that made the eye not see? says the Psalmist, Psalm xciv. 9. See these men's vanities! The structure of that one part is sufficient to convince us of an all-wise contriver, and he has so visible a claim to us as his workmanship, that one of the ordinary appellations of God in Scripture is, God our Maker, and the Lord our Maker. And therefore though our author, for the magnifying his fatherhood, be pleased to say, Observations, 159. That even the power which God himself exercises over mankind is by right of fatherhood, yet this fatherhood is such an one as utterly excludes all pretence of title in earthly parents; for he is king, because he is indeed maker of us all, which no parents can pretend to be of their children.

Section 54. But had men skill and power to make their children, it is not so slight a piece of workmanship, that it can be imagined, they could make them without designing it. What father of a thousand, when he begets a child, thinks farther than the satisfying his present appetite? God in his infinite wisdom has put strong desires of copulation into the constitution of men, thereby to continue the race of mankind, which he does most commonly without the intention, and often against the consent and will of the begetter. And indeed those who desire and design children, are but the occasions of their being, and when they design and wish to beget them, do little more towards their making, than Deucalion and his wife in the fable did towards the making of mankind, by throwing pebbles over their heads.

Section 55. But grant that the parents made their children, gave them life and being, and that hence there followed an absolute power. This would give the father but a joint dominion with the mother over them: for nobody can deny but that the woman has an equal share, if not the greater, as nourishing the child a long time in her own body out of her own substance: there it is fashioned, and from her it receives the materials and principles of its constitution: and it is so hard to imagine the rational soul should presently inhabit the yet unformed embryo, as soon as the father has done his part in the act of generation, that if it must be supposed to derive anything from the parents, it must certainly owe most to the mother. But be that as it will, the mother cannot be denied an equal share in begetting of the child, and so the absolute authority of the father will not arise from hence. Our author indeed is of another mind; for he says, We know that God at the creation gave the sovereignty to the man over the woman, as being the nobler and principal agent in generation, Observations, 172. I remember not this in my Bible; and when the place is brought where God at the creation gave the sovereignty to man over the woman, and that for this reason, because he is the nobler and principal agent in generation, it will be time enough to consider, and answer it. But it is no new thing for our author to tell us his own fancies for certain and divine truths, though there be often a great deal of difference between his and divine revelations; for God in the Scripture says, his father and his mother that begot him.

Section 56. They who allege the practice of mankind, for exposing or selling their children, as a proof of their power over them, are with Sir Robert happy arguers; and cannot but recommend their opinion, by founding it on the most shameful action, and most unnatural murder, human nature is capable of. The dens of lions and nurseries of wolves know no such cruelty as this: these savage inhabitants of the desert obey God and nature in being tender and careful of their off-spring: they will hunt, watch, fight, and almost starve for the preservation of their young; never part with them; never forsake them, till they are able to shift for themselves. And is it the privilege of man alone to act more contrary to nature than the wild and most untamed part of the creation? does God forbid us under the severest penalty, that of death, to take away the life of any man, a stranger, and upon provocation? and does he permit us to destroy those, he has given us the charge and care of; and by the dictates of nature and reason, as well as his revealed command, requires us to preserve? He has in all the parts of the creation taken a peculiar care to propagate and continue the several species of creatures, and makes the individuals act so strongly to this end, that they sometimes neglect their own private good for it, and seem to forget that general rule, which nature teaches all things, of self-preservation; and the preservation of their young, as the strongest principle in them, over-rules the constitution of their particular natures. Thus we see, when their young stand in need of it, the timorous become valiant, the fierce and savage kind, and the ravenous tender and liberal.

Section 57. But if the example of what has been done, be the rule of what ought to be, history would have furnished our author with instances of this absolute fatherly power in its height and perfection, and he might have showed us in Peru, people that begot children on purpose to fatten and eat them. The story is so remarkable, that I cannot but set it down in the author's words. "In some provinces, says he, they were so liquorish after man's flesh, that they would not have the patience to stay till the breath was out of the body, but would suck the blood as it ran from the wounds of the dying man; they had public shambles of man's flesh, and their madness herein was to that degree, that they spared not their own children, which they had begot on strangers taken in war: for they made their captives their mistresses, and choicely nourished the children they had by them, till about thirteen years old they butchered and eat them; and they served the mothers after the same fashion, when they grew past child bearing, and ceased to bring them any more roasters," Garcilasso de la Vega hist. des Incas de Peru, l. i. c. 12.

Section 58. Thus far can the busy mind of man carry him to a brutality below the level of beasts, when he quits his reason, which places him almost equal to angels? Nor can it be otherwise in a creature, whose thoughts are more than the sands, and wider than the ocean, where fancy and passion must needs run him into strange courses, if reason, which is his only star and compass, be not that he steers by. The imagination is always restless, and suggests variety of thoughts, and the will, reason being laid aside, is ready for every extravagant project; and in this state, he that goes farthest out of the way, is thought fittest to lead, and is sure of most followers: and when fashion has once established what folly or craft began, custom makes it sacred, and it will be thought impudence, or madness, to contradict or question it. He that will impartially survey the nations of the world, will find so much of their religions, governments and manners, brought in and continued among them by these means, that he will have but little reverence for the practices which are in use and credit among men; and will have reason to think, that the woods and forests, where the irrational untaught inhabitants keep right by following nature, are fitter to give us rules, than cities and palaces, where those that call themselves civil and rational, go out of their way, by the authority of example. If precedents are sufficient to establish a rule in this case, our author might have found in holy writ children sacrificed by their parents, and this among the people of God themselves: the Psalmist tells us, Psalm. cvi. 38. They shed innocent blood, even the blood of their sons and of their daughters, whom they sacrificed unto the idols of Canaan. But God judged not of this by our author's rule, nor allowed of the authority of practice against his righteous law; but as it follows there, the land was polluted with blood; therefore was the wrath of the Lord kindled against his people, insomuch that he abhorred his own inheritance. The killing of their children, though it was fashionable, was charged on them as innocent blood, and so had in the account of God the guilt of murder, as the offering of them to idols had the guilt of idolatry.

Section 59. Be it then, as Sir Robert says, that anciently it was usual for men to sell and castrate their children, Observations, 155. Let it be, that they exposed them; add to it, if you please, for this is still greater power, that they begat them for their tables, to fat and eat them: if this proves a right to do so, we may, by the same argument, justify adultery, incest and sodomy, for there are examples of these too, both ancient and modern; sins, which I suppose have their principal aggravation from this, that they cross the main intention of nature, which wills the increase of mankind, and the continuation of the species in the highest perfection, and the distinction of families, with the security of the marriage bed, as necessary thereunto.

Section 60. In confirmation of this natural authority of the father, our author brings a lame proof from the positive command of God in Scripture: his words are, To confirm the natural right of regal power, we find in the Decalogue, that the law which enjoins obedience to kings, is delivered in the terms, Honor your father, p. 23. Whereas many confess, that government only in the abstract, is the ordinance of God, they are not able to prove any such ordinance in the Scripture, but only in the fatherly power; and therefore we find the commandment, that enjoins obedience to superiors, given in the terms, Honor your father; so that not only the power and right of government, but the form of the power governing, and the person having the power, are all the ordinances of God. The first father had not only simply power, but power monarchical, as he was father immediately from God, Observations, 254. To the same purpose, the same law is cited by our author in several other places, and just after the same fashion; that is, and mother, as apocryphal words, are always left out; a great argument of our author's ingenuity, and the goodness of his cause, which required in its defender zeal to a degree of warmth, able to warp the sacred rule of the word of God, to make it comply with his present occasion; a way of proceeding not unusual to those, who embrace not truths because reason and revelation offer them, but espouse tenets and parties for ends different from truth, and then resolve at any rate to defend them; and so do with the words and sense of authors, they would fit to their purpose, just as Procrustes did with his guests, lop or stretch them, as may best fit them to the size of their notions: and they always prove like those so served, deformed, lame, and useless.

Section 61. For had our author set down this command without garbling, as God gave it, and joined mother to father, every reader would have seen, that it had made directly against him; and that it was so far from establishing the monarchical power of the father, that it set up the mother equal with him, and enjoined nothing but what was due in common, to both father and mother: for that is the constant tenor of the Scripture, Honor your father and your mother, Exod. xx. He that smites his father or mother shall surely be put to death, xxi. 15. He that curses his father or mother shall surely be put to death, ver. 17. Repeated Lev. xx. 9. and by our Savior, Matthew. xv. 4. You shall fear every man his mother and his father, Lev. xix. 3. If a man have a rebellious son, which will not obey the voice of his father, or the voice of his mother; then shall his father and his mother lay hold on him, and say, This our son is stubborn and rebellious, he will not obey our voice, Deut. xxi. 18, 19, 20, 21. Cursed be he that sets light by his father or his mother, xxviii. 16. My son, hear the instructions of your father, and forsake not the law of your mother, are the words of Solomon, a king who was not ignorant of what belonged to him as a father or a king; and yet he joins father and mother together, in all the instructions he gives children quite through his book of Proverbs. Woe unto him that says unto his father, What did you beget or to the woman, What have you brought forth? Isa. xi. ver. 10. In you have they set light by father or mother, Ezek. xxviii. 2. And it shall come to pass, that when any shall yet prophesy, then his father and his mother that begat him, shall say unto him, You shall not live, and his father and his mother that begat him, shall thrust him through when he prophesied, Zech. xiii. 3. Here not the father only, but the father and mother jointly, had power in this case of life and death. Thus ran the law of the Old Testament and in the New they are likewise joined, in the obedience of their children, Eph. vi. 1. The rule is, Children, obey your parents; and I do not remember, that I anywhere read, Children, obey your father, and no more: the Scripture joins mother too in that homage, which is due from children; and had there been any text, where the honor or obedience of children had been directed to the father alone, it is not likely that our author, who pretends to build all upon Scripture, would have omitted it: nay, the Scripture makes the authority of father and mother, in respect of those they have begot, so equal, that in some places it neglects even the priority of order, which is thought due to the father, and the mother is put first, as Lev. xix. 3. from which so constantly joining father and mother together, as is found quite through the Scripture, we may conclude that the honor they have a title to from their children, is one common right belonging so equally to them both, that neither can claim it wholly, neither can be excluded.

Section 62. One would wonder then how our author infers from the 5th commandment that all power was originally in the father; how he finds monarchical power of government settled and fixed by the commandment, Honor your father and your mother. If all the honor due by the commandment, be it what it will, be the only right of the father, because he, as our author says, has the sovereignty over the woman, as being the nobler and principle agent in generation, why did God afterwards all along join the mother with him, to share in his honor? can the father, by this sovereignty of his, discharge the child from paying this honor to his mother? The Scripture gave no such license to the Jews, and yet there were often breaches wide enough between husband and wife, even to divorce and separation: and, I think, nobody will say a child may with-hold honor from his mother, or, as the Scripture terms it, set light by her, though his father should command him to do so; no more than the mother could dispense with him for neglecting to honor his father: whereby it is plain, that this command of God gives the father no sovereignty, no supremacy.

Section 63. I agree with our author that the title to this honor is vested in the parents by nature, and is a right which accrues to them by their having begotten their children, and God by many positive declarations has confirmed it to them: I also allow our author's rule, that in grants and gifts, that have their original from God and nature, as the power of the father, (let me add and mother, for whom God has joined together, let no man put asunder) no inferior power of men can limit, nor make any law of prescription against them, Observations, 158. so that the mother having, by this law of God, a right to honor from her children, which is not subject to the will of her husband, we see this absolute monarchical power of the father can neither be founded on it, nor consist with it; and he has a power very far from monarchical, very far from that absoluteness our author contends for, when another has over his subjects the same power he has, and by the same title: and therefore he cannot forbear saying himself that he cannot see how any man's children can be free from subjection to their parents, p. 12. which, in common speech, I think, signifies mother as well as father, or if parents here signifies only father, it is the first time I ever yet knew it to do so, and by such an use of words one may say anything.

Section 64. By our author's doctrine, the father having absolute jurisdiction over his children, has also the same over their issue; and the consequence is good, were it true, that the father had such a power: and yet I ask our author whether the grandfather, by his sovereignty, could discharge the grandchild from paying to his father the honor due to him by the 5th commandment. If the grandfather has, by right of fatherhood, sole sovereign power in him, and that obedience which is due to the supreme magistrate, be commanded in these words, Honor your father, it is certain the grandfather might dispense with the grandson's honoring his father, which since it is evident in common sense he cannot, it follows from hence, that Honor your father and mother, cannot mean an absolute subjection to a sovereign power, but something else. The right therefore which parents have by nature, and which is confirmed to them by the 5th commandment, cannot be that political dominion, which our author would derive from it: for that being in every civil society supreme somewhere, can discharge any subject from any political obedience to anyone of his fellow subjects. But what law of the magistrate can give a child liberty, not to honor his father and mother? It is an eternal law, annexed purely to the relation of parents and children, and so contains nothing of the magistrate's power in it, nor is subjected to it.

Section 65. Our author says, God has given to a father a right or liberty to give his power over his children to any other, Observations, 155. I doubt whether he can wholly give the right of honor that is due from them: but be that as it will, this I am sure, he cannot alien, and retain the same power. If therefore the magistrate's sovereignty be, as our author would have it, nothing but the authority of a supreme father, p. 23. it is unavoidable, that if the magistrate has all this paternal right, as he must have if fatherhood be the fountain of all authority; then the subjects, though fathers, can have no power over their children, no right to honor from them: for it cannot be all in another's hands, and a part remain with the parents. So that, according to our author's own doctrine, Honor your father and mother cannot possibly be understood of political subjection and obedience; since the laws both in the Old and New Testament, that commanded children to honor and obey their parents, were given to such, whose fathers were under civil government, and fellow subjects with them in political societies; and to have bid them honor and obey their parents, in our author's sense, had been to bid them be subjects to those who had no title to it; the right to obedience from subjects, being all vested in another; and instead of teaching obedience, this had been to foment sedition, by setting up powers that were not. If therefore this command, Honor your father and mother, concern political dominion, it directly overthrows our author's monarchy; since it being to be paid by every child to his father, even in society, every father must necessarily have political dominion, and there will be as many sovereigns as there are fathers: besides that the mother too has her title, which destroys the sovereignty of one supreme monarch. But if Honor your father and mother mean something distinct from political power, as necessarily it must, it is besides our author's business, and serves nothing to his purpose.

Section 66. The law that enjoins obedience to kings is delivered, says our author, in the terms, Honor your father, as if all power were originally in the father, Observations, 254: and that law is also delivered, say I, in the terms, Honor your mother, as if all power were originally in the mother. I appeal whether the argument is not as good on one side as the other, father and mother being joined all along in the Old and New Testament wherever honor or obedience is enjoined children. Again our author tells us, Observations, 254. that this command, Honor your father, gives the right to govern, and makes the form of government monarchical. To which I answer, that if by Honor your father be meant obedience to the political power of the magistrate, it concerns not any duty we owe to our natural fathers, who are subjects; because they, by our author's doctrine, are divested of all that power, it being placed wholly in the prince, and so being equally subjects and slaves with their children, can have no right, by that title, to any such honor or obedience, as contains in it political subjection: if Honor your father and mother signifies the duty we owe our natural parents, as by our Savior's interpretation, Matthew. xv. 4. and all the other mentioned places, it is plain it does, then it cannot concern political obedience, but a duty that is owing to persons, who have no title to sovereignty, nor any political authority as magistrates over subjects. For the person of a private father, and a title to obedience, due to the supreme magistrate, are things inconsistent; and therefore this command, which must necessarily comprehend the persons of our natural fathers, must mean a duty we owe them distinct from our obedience to the magistrate, and from which the most absolute power of princes cannot absolve us. What this duty is, we shall in its due place examine.

Section 67. And thus we have at last got through all, that in our author looks like an argument for that absolute unlimited sovereignty described, sect. 8. which he supposes in Adam; so that mankind ever since have been all born slaves, without any title to freedom. But if creation, which gave nothing but a being, made not Adam prince of his posterity: if Adam, Gen. i. 28. was not constituted lord of mankind, nor had a private dominion given him exclusive of his children, but only a right and power over the earth, and inferior creatures in common with the children of men; if also Gen. iii. 16. God gave not any political power to Adam over his wife and children, but only subjected Eve to Adam, as a punishment, or foretold the subjection of the weaker sex, in the ordering the common concernments of their families, but gave not thereby to Adam, as to the husband, power of life and death, which necessarily belongs to the magistrate: if fathers by begetting their children acquire no such power over them; and if the command, Honor your father and mother, give it not, but only enjoins a duty owing to parents equally, whether subjects or not, and to the mother as well as the father; if all this be so, as I think, by what has been said, is very evident; then man has a natural freedom, notwithstanding all our author confidently says to the contrary; since all that share in the same common nature, faculties and powers, are in nature equal, and ought to partake in the same common rights and privileges, till the manifest appointment of God, who is Lord over all, blessed forever, can be produced to show any particular person's supremacy; or a man's own consent subjects him to a superior. This is so plain, that our author confesses, that Sir John Hayward, Blackwood and Barclay, the great vindicators of the right of kings, could not deny it, but admits with one consent the natural liberty and equality of mankind, for a truth unquestionable. And our author has been so far from producing anything, that may make good his great position, that Adam was absolute monarch, and so men are not naturally free, that even his own proofs make against him; so that to use his own way of arguing, the first erroneous principle failing, the whole fabric of this vast engine of absolute power and tyranny drops down of itself, and there needs no more to be said in answer to all that he builds upon so false and frail a foundation.

Section 68. But to save others the pains, were there any need, he is not sparing himself to show, by his own contradictions, the weakness of his own doctrine. Adam's absolute and sole dominion is that, which he is everywhere full of, and all along builds on, and yet he tells us, p. 12. that as Adam was lord of his children, so his children under him had a command and power over their own children. The unlimited and undivided sovereignty of Adam's fatherhood, by our author's computation, stood but a little while, only during the first generation, but as soon as he had grand-children, Sir Robert could give but a very ill account of it. Adam, as father of his children, faith he, has an absolute, unlimited royal power over them, and by virtue thereof over those that they begot, and so to all generations; and yet his children, that is Cain and Seth, have a paternal power over their children at the same time; so that they are at the same time absolute lords, and yet vassals and slaves; Adam has all the authority, as grand-father of the people, and they have a part of it as fathers of a part of them: he is absolute over them and their posterity, by having begotten them, and yet they are absolute over their children by the same title. No, says our author, Adam's children under him had power over their own children, but still with subordination to the first parent. A good distinction that sounds well and it is pity it signifies nothing, nor can be reconciled with our author's words. I readily grant, that supposing Adam's absolute power over his posterity, any of his children might have from him a delegated, and so a subordinate power over a part, or all the rest: but that cannot be the power our author speaks of here; it is not a power by grant and commission, but the natural paternal power he supposes a father to have over his children. For 1. he says As Adam was lord of his children, so his children under him had a power over their own children: they were then lords over their own children after the same manner, and by the same title, that Adam was, i.e. by right of generation, by right of fatherhood. 2. It is plain he means the natural power of fathers, because he limits it to be only over their own children; a delegated power has no such limitation, as only over their own children, it might be over others, as well as their own children. 3. If it were a delegated power, it must appear in Scripture; but there is no ground in Scripture to affirm, that Adam's children had any other power over theirs, than what they naturally had as fathers.

Section 69. But that he means here paternal power, and no other, is past doubt, from the inference he makes in these words immediately following, I see not then how the children of Adam, or of any man else, can be free from subjection to their parents. Whereby it appears that the power on one side, and the subjection on the other, our author here speaks of, is that natural power and subjection between parents and children: for that which every man's children owed, could be no other; and that our author always affirms to be absolute and unlimited. This natural power of parents over their children, Adam had over his posterity, says our author; and this power of parents over their children, his children had over theirs in his life-time, says our author also; so that Adam, by a natural right of father, had an absolute unlimited power over all his posterity, and at the same time his children had by the same right absolute unlimited power over theirs. Here then are two absolute unlimited powers existing together, which I would have anybody reconcile one to another, or to common sense. For the salvo he has put in of subordination, makes it more absurd: to have one absolute, unlimited, nay unlimitable power in subordination to another, is so manifest a contradiction, that nothing can be more. Adam is absolute prince with the unlimited authority of fatherhood over all his posterity; all his posterity are then absolutely his subjects; and, as our author says, his slaves, children, and grand-children, are equally in this state of subjection and slavery; and yet, says our author, the children of Adam have paternal, i.e. absolute unlimited power over their own children: Which in plain English is, they are slaves and absolute princes at the same time, and in the same government; and one part of the subjects have an absolute unlimited power over the other by the natural right of parentage.

Section 70. If anyone will suppose, in favor of our author, that he here meant, that parents, who are in subjection themselves to the absolute authority of their father, have yet some power over their children; I confess he is something nearer the truth: but he will not at all hereby help our author: for he nowhere speaking of the paternal power, but as an absolute unlimited authority, cannot be supposed to understand anything else here, unless he himself had limited it, and showed how far it reached. And that he means paternal authority in that large extent, is plain from the immediate following words; This subjection of children being, says he, the foundation of all regal authority, p. 12. the subjection then that in the former line, he says, every man is in to his parents, and consequently what Adam's grand-children were in to their parents, was that which was the fountain of all regal authority, i.e. according to our author, absolute unlimitable authority. And thus Adam's children had regal authority over their children, while they themselves were subjects to their father, and fellow-subjects with their children. But let him mean as he pleases, it is plain he allows Adam's children to have paternal power, p. 12. as also all other fathers to have paternal power over their children, Observations, 156. From whence one of these two things will necessarily follow, that either Adam's children, even in his life-time, had, and so all other fathers have, as he phrases it, p. 12. by right of fatherhood, royal authority over their children, or else, that Adam, by right of fatherhood, had not royal authority. For it cannot be but that paternal power does, or does not, give royal authority to them that have it: if it does not, then Adam could not be sovereign by this title, nor anybody else; and then there is an end of all our author's politics at once: if it does give royal authority, then everyone that has paternal power has royal authority; and then, by our author's Patriarchal government, there will be as many kings as there are fathers.

Section 71. And thus what a monarchy he has set up, let him and his disciples consider. Princes certainly will have great reason to thank him for these new politics, which set up as many absolute kings in every country as there are fathers of children. And yet who can blame our author for it, it lying unavoidably in the way of one discoursing upon our author's principles? For having placed an absolute power in fathers by right of begetting, he could not easily resolve how much of this power belonged to a son over the children he had begotten; and so it fell out to be a very hard matter to give all the power, as he does, to Adam, and yet allow a part in his life-time to his children, when they were parents, and which he knew not well how to deny them. This makes him so doubtful in his expressions and so uncertain where to place this absolute natural power, which he calls fatherhood. Sometimes Adam alone has it all, as p. 13. Observations, 244, 245. & Preface:

- Sometimes parents have it, which word scarce signifies the father alone, p. 12, 19.

- Sometimes children during their father's life-time, as p. 12.

- Sometimes fathers of families, as p. 78, and 79.

- Sometimes fathers indefinitely, Observations, 155.

- Sometimes the heir to Adam, Observations, 253.

- Sometimes the posterity of Adam, 244, 246.

- Sometimes prime fathers, all sons or grand-children of Noah, Observations, 244.

- Sometimes the eldest parents, p. 12.

- Sometimes all kings, p. 19.

- Sometimes all that have supreme power, Observations, 245.

- Sometimes heirs to those first progenitors, who were at first the natural parents of the whole people, p. 19.

- Sometimes an elective king, p. 23.

- Sometimes those, whether a few or a multitude, that govern the commonwealth, p. 23.

- Sometimes he that can catch it, a usurper, p. 23. Observations, 155.

Section 72. Thus this new nothing, that is to carry with it all power, authority, and government; this fatherhood, which is to design the person, and establish the throne of monarchs, whom the people are to obey, may, according to Sir Robert, come into any hands, anyhow, and so by his politics give to democracy royal authority, and make an usurper a lawful prince. And if it will do all these fine feats, much good do our author and all his followers with their omnipotent fatherhood, which can serve for nothing but to unsettle and destroy all the lawful governments in the world, and to establish in their room disorder, tyranny, and usurpation.

CHAPTER VII.

Of Fatherhood and Property considered together as Fountains of Sovereignty.

Section 73. In the foregoing chapters we have seen what Adam's monarchy was, in our author's opinion, and upon what titles he founded it. The foundations which he lays the chief stress on, as those from which he thinks he may best derive monarchical power to future princes, are two, that is Fatherhood and property: and therefore the way he proposes to remove the absurdities and inconveniencies of the doctrine of natural freedom, is, to maintain the natural and private dominion of Adam, Observations, 222. Conformable hereunto, he tells us, the grounds and principles of government necessarily depend upon the original of property, Observations, 108. The subjection of children to their parents is the fountain of all regal authority, p. 12. And all power on earth is either derived or usurped from the fatherly power, there being no other original to be found of any power whatsoever, Observations, 158. I will not stand here to examine how it can be said without a contradiction, that the first grounds and principles of government necessarily depend upon the original of property, and yet, that there is no other original of any power whatsoever, but that of the father: it being hard to understand how there can be no other original but fatherhood, and yet that the grounds and principles of government depend upon the original of property;

property and fatherhood being as far different as lord of a manor and father of children. Nor do I see how they will either of them agree with what our author says, Observations, 244. of God's sentence against Eve, Gen. iii. 16. That it is the original grant of government: so that if that were the original, government had not its original, by our author's own confession, either from property or fatherhood; and this text, which he brings as a proof of Adam's power over Eve, necessarily contradicts what he says of the fatherhood, that it is the sole fountain of all power: for if Adam had any such regal power over Eve, as our author contends for, it must be by some other title than that of begetting.

Section 74. But I leave him to reconcile these contradictions, as well as many others, which may plentifully be found in him by anyone, who will but read him with a little attention; and shall come now to consider, how these two originals of government, Adam's natural and private dominion, will consist, and serve to make out and establish the titles of succeeding monarchs, who, as our author obliges them, must all derive their power from these fountains. Let us then suppose Adam made, by God's donation, lord and sole proprietor of the whole earth, in as large and ample a manner as Sir Robert could wish; let us suppose him also, by right of fatherhood, absolute ruler over his children with an unlimited supremacy; I ask then, upon Adam's death what becomes of both his natural and private dominion? and I doubt not it will be answered, that they descended to his next heir, as our author tells us in several places. But this way, it is plain, cannot possibly convey both his natural and private dominion to the same person: for should we allow, that all the property, all the estate of the father, ought to descend to the eldest son, (which will need some proof to establish it) and so he has by that title all the private dominion of the father, yet the father's natural dominion, the paternal power cannot descend to him by inheritance: for it being a right that accrues to a man only by begetting, no man can have this natural dominion over anyone he does not beget; unless it can be supposed, that a man can have a right to anything, without doing that upon which that right is solely founded: for if a father by begetting, and no other title, has natural dominion over his children, he that does not beget them cannot have this natural dominion over them; and therefore be it true or false, that our author says, Observations, 156. That every man that is born, by his very birth becomes a subject to him that begets him, this necessarily follows, that is That a man by his birth cannot become a subject to his brother, who did not beget him; unless it can be supposed that a man by the very same title can come to be under the natural and absolute dominion of two different men at once; or it be sense to say, that a man by birth is under the natural dominion of his father, only because he begat him, and a man by birth also is under the natural dominion of his eldest brother, though he did not beget him.

Section 75. If then the private dominion of Adam, i.e. his property in the creatures, descended at his death all entirely to his eldest son, his heir; (for, if it did not, there is presently an end of all Sir Robert's monarchy) and his natural dominion, the dominion a father has over his children by begetting them, belonged immediately, upon Adam's decease, equally to all his sons who had children, by the same title their father had it, the sovereignty founded upon property, and the sovereignty founded upon fatherhood, come to be divided; since Cain, as heir, had that of property alone; Seth, and the other sons, that of fatherhood equally with him. This is the best can be made of our author's doctrine, and of the two titles of sovereignty he sets up in Adam: one of them will either signify nothing; or, if they both must stand, they can serve only to confound the rights of princes, and disorder government in his posterity: for by building upon two titles to dominion, which cannot descend together, and which he allows may be separated, (for he yields that Adam's children had their distinct territories by right of private dominion, Observations, 210.p.40.) he makes it perpetually a doubt upon his principles where the sovereignty is, or to whom we owe our obedience, since fatherhood and property are distinct titles, and began presently upon Adam's death to be in distinct persons. And which then was to give way to the other?

Section 76. Let us take the account of it, as he himself gives it us. He tells us out of Grotius, that Adam's children by donation, assignation, or some kind of cession before he was dead, had their distinct territories by right of private dominion; Abel had his flocks and pastures for them: Cain had his fields for corn, and the land of Nod, where he built a city, Observations, 210. Here it is obvious to demand, which of these two after Adam's death was sovereign? Cain, says our author, p. 19. By what title? As heir; for heirs to progenitors, who were natural parents of their people, are not only lords of their own children, but also of their brethren, says our author, p. 19. What was Cain heir to? Not the entire possessions, not all that which Adam had private dominion in; for our author allows that Abel, by a title derived from his father, had his distinct territory for pasture by right of private dominion. What then Abel had by private dominion, was exempt from Cain's dominion: for he could not have private dominion over that which was under the private dominion of another; and therefore his sovereignty over his brother is gone with this private dominion, and so there are presently two sovereigns, and his imaginary title of fatherhood is out of doors, and Cain is no prince over his brother: or else, if Cain retain his sovereignty over Abel, notwithstanding his private dominion, it will follow, that the first grounds and principles of government have nothing to do with property, whatever our author says to the contrary. It is true, Abel did not outlive his father Adam; but that makes nothing to the argument, which will hold good against Sir Robert in Abel's issue, or in Seth, or any of the posterity of Adam, not descended from Cain.

Section 77. He runs into the same inconvenience with the three sons of Noah, who, as he says, p. 13. had the whole world divided among them by their father. I ask then, in which of the three shall we find the establishment of regal power after Noah's death? If in all three, as our author there seems to say; then it will follow, that regal power is founded in property of land, and follows private dominion, and not in paternal power, or natural dominion; and so there is an end of paternal power as the fountain of regal authority, and the so-much-magnified fatherhood quite vanishes. If the regal power descended to Shem as eldest, and heir to his father, then Noah's division of the world by lot to his sons, or his ten years sailing about the Mediterranean to appoint each son his part, which our author tells of, p. 15. was labor lost; his division of the world to them, was too ill, or to no purpose: for his grant to Cham and Japheth was little worth, if Shem, notwithstanding this grant, as soon as Noah was dead, was to be lord over them. Or, if this grant of private dominion to them, over their assigned territories, were good, here were set up two distinct sorts of power, not subordinate one to the other, with all those inconveniences which he musters up against the power of the people, Observations, 158. which I shall set down in his own words, only changing property for people. All power on earth is either derived or usurped from the fatherly power, there being no other original to be found of any power whatsoever: for if there should be granted two sorts of power, without any subordination of one to the other, they would be in perpetual strife which should be supreme, for two supreme's cannot agree: if the fatherly power be supreme, then the power grounded on private dominion must be subordinate, and depend on it; and if the power grounded on property be supreme, then the fatherly power must submit to it, and cannot be exercised without the license of the proprietors, which must quite destroy the frame and course of nature. This is his own arguing against two distinct independent powers, which I have set down in his own words, only putting power rising from property, for power of the people; and when he has answered what he himself has urged here against two distinct powers, we shall be better able to see how, with any tolerable sense, he can derive all regal authority from the natural and private dominion of Adam, from fatherhood and property together, which are distinct titles, that do not always meet in the same person; and it is plain, by his own confession, presently separated as soon both as Adam's and Noah's death made way for succession: though our author frequently in his writings jumbles them together, and omits not to make use of either, where he thinks it will sound best to his purpose. But the absurdities of this will more fully appear in the next chapter, where we shall examine the ways of conveyance of the sovereignty of Adam, to princes that were to reign after him.

CHAPTER VIII.

Of the Conveyance of Adam's sovereign Monarchical Power.

Section 78. Sir Robert, having not been very happy in any proof he brings for the sovereignty of Adam, is not much more fortunate in conveying it to future princes, who, if his politics be true, must all derive their titles from that first monarch. The ways he has assigned, as they lie scattered up and down in his writings, I will set down in his own words: in his preface he tells us, That Adam being monarch of the whole world, none of his posterity had any right to possess anything, but by his grant or permission, or by succession from him. Here he makes two ways of conveyance of anything Adam stood possessed of; and those are grants or succession. Again he says, All kings either are, or are to be reputed, the next heirs to those first progenitors, who were at first the natural parents of the whole people, p. 19. There cannot be any multitude of men whatsoever, but that in it, considered by itself, there is one man among them, that in nature has a right to be the king of all the rest, as being the next heir to Adam, Observations, 253. Here in these places inheritance is the only way he allows of conveying monarchical power to princes. In other places he tells us, Observations, 155. All power on earth is either derived or usurped from the fatherly power, Observations, 158. All kings that now are, or ever were, are or were either fathers of their people, or heirs of such fathers, or usurpers of the right of such fathers, Observations, 253. And here he makes inheritance or usurpation the only ways whereby kings come by this original power: but yet he tells us, This fatherly empire, as it was of itself hereditary, so it was alienable by patent, and sizable by a usurper, Observations, 190. So then here inheritance, grant, or usurpation, will convey it. And last of all, which is most admirable, he tells us, p. 100. It skills not which way kings come by their power, whether by election, donation, succession, or by any other means; for it is still the manner of the government by supreme power, that makes them properly kings, and not the means of obtaining their crowns. Which I think is a full answer to all his whole hypothesis and discourse about Adam's royal authority, as the fountain from which all princes were to derive theirs: and he might have spared the trouble of speaking so much as he does, up and down, of heirs and inheritance, if to make anyone properly a king, needs no more but governing by supreme power, and it matters not by what means he came by it.

Section 79. By this notable way, our author may make Oliver as properly king, as anyone else he could think of: and had he had the happiness to live under Massanello's government, he could not by his own rule have forborne to have done homage to him, with O king live forever, since the manner of his government by supreme power, made him properly king, who was but the day before properly a fisherman. And if Don Quixote had taught his squire to govern with supreme authority, our author no doubt could have made a most loyal subject in Sancho Pancha's island; and he must needs have deserved some preferment in such governments, since I think he is the first politician, who, pretending to settle government upon its true basis, and to establish the thrones of lawful princes, ever told the world, That he was properly a king, whose manner of government was by supreme power, by what means soever he obtained it; which in plain English is to say, that regal and supreme power is properly and truly his, who can by any means seize upon it; and if this be to be properly a king, I wonder how he came to think of, or where he will find, an usurper.

Section 80. This is so strange a doctrine, that the surprise of it has made me pass by, without their due reflection, the contradictions he runs into, by making sometimes inheritance alone, sometimes only grant or inheritance, sometimes only inheritance or usurpation, sometimes all these three, and at last election, or any other means, added to them, the ways whereby Adam's royal authority, that is, his right to supreme rule, could be conveyed down to future kings and governors, so as to give them a title to the obedience and subjection of the people. But these contradictions lie so open, that the very reading of our author's own words will discover them to any ordinary understanding; and though what I have quoted out of him (with abundance more of the same strain and coherence, which might be found in him) might well excuse me from any father trouble in this argument, yet having proposed to myself, to examine the main parts of his doctrine, I shall a little more particularly consider how inheritance, grant, usurpation or election, can any way make out government in the world upon his principles; or derive to anyone a right of empire, from this regal authority of Adam, had it been never so well proved, that he had been absolute monarch, and lord of the whole world.

CHAPTER IX.

Of Monarchy, by Inheritance from Adam.

Section 81. Though it be never so plain, that there ought to be government in the world, nay, should all men be of our author's mind, that divine appointment had ordained it to be monarchical; yet, since men cannot obey anything, that cannot command; and ideas of government in the fancy, though never so perfect, though never so right, cannot give laws, nor prescribe rules to the actions of men; it would be of no behoove for the settling of order, and establishment of government in its exercise and use among men, unless there were a way also taught how to know the person, to whom it belonged to have this power, and exercise this dominion over others. It is in vain then to talk of subjection and obedience without telling us whom we are to obey: for if I were never so fully persuaded that there ought to be magistracy and rule in the world; yet I am never the less at liberty still, until it appears who is the person that has right to my obedience; since, if there be no marks to know him by, and distinguish him that has right to rule from other men, it may be myself, as well as any other. And therefore, though submission to government be everyone's duty, yet since that signifies nothing but submitting to the direction and laws of such men as have authority to command, it is not enough to make a man a subject, to convince him that there is regal power in the world; but there must be ways of designing, and knowing the person to whom this regal power of right belongs: and a man can never be obliged in conscience to submit to any power, unless he can be satisfied who is the person who has a right to exercise that power over him. If this were not so, there would be no distinction between pirates and lawful princes; he that has force is without any more ado to be obeyed, and crowns and scepters would become the inheritance only of violence and rapine. Men too might as often and as innocently change their governors, as they do their physicians, if the person cannot be known who has a right to direct me, and whose prescriptions I am bound to follow. To settle therefore men's consciences, under an obligation to obedience, it is necessary that they know not only, that there is a power somewhere in the world, but the person who by right is vested with this power over them.

Section 82. How successful our author has been in his attempts, to set up a monarchical absolute power in Adam, the reader may judge by what has been already said; but were that absolute monarchy as clear as our author would desire it, as I presume it is the contrary, yet it could be of no use to the government of mankind now in the world, unless he also make out these two things.

First, That this power of Adam was not to end with him, but was upon his decease conveyed entire to some other person, and so on to posterity.

Secondly, That the princes and rulers now on earth are possessed of this power of Adam, by a right way of conveyance derived to them.

Section 83. If the first of these fail, the power of Adam, were it never so great, never so certain, will signify nothing to the present government and societies in the world; but we must seek out some other original of power for the government of polities than this of Adam, or else there will be none at all in the world. If the latter fail, it will destroy the authority of the present governors, and absolve the people from subjection to them, since they, having no better a claim than others to that power, which is alone the fountain of all authority, can have no title to rule over them.

Section 84. Our author, having fancied an absolute sovereignty in Adam, mentions several ways of its conveyance to princes, that were to be his successors; but that which he chiefly insists on, is that of inheritance, which occurs so often in his several discourses; and I having in the foregoing chapter quoted several of these passages, I shall not need here again to repeat them. This sovereignty he erects, as has been said, upon a double foundation, that is that of property, and that of fatherhood. One was the right he was supposed to have in all creatures, a right to possess the earth with the beasts, and other inferior ranks of things in it, for his private use, exclusive of all other men. The other was the right he was supposed to have, to rule and govern men, all the rest of mankind.

Section 85. In both these rights, there being supposed an exclusion of all other men, it must be upon some reason peculiar to Adam, that they must both be founded. That of his property our author supposes to arise from God's immediate donation, Gen. i. 28. and that of fatherhood from the act of begetting: now in all inheritance, if the heir succeeds not to the reason upon which his father's right was founded, he cannot succeed to the right which followed from it. For example, Adam had a right of property in the creatures upon the donation and grant of God almighty, who was lord and proprietor of them all: let this be so as our author tells us, yet upon his death his heir can have no title to them, no such right of property in them, unless the same reason, that is God's donation, vested a right in the heir too: for if Adam could have had no property in, nor use of the creatures, without this positive donation from God, and this donation were only personally to Adam, his heir could have no right by it; but upon his death it must revert to God, the lord and owner again; for positive grants give no title father than the express words convey it, and by which only it is held. And thus, if as our author himself contends, that donation, Gen. i. 28. were made only to Adam personally, his heir could not succeed to his property in the creatures; and if it were a donation to any but Adam, let it be shown, that it was to his heir in our author's sense, i.e. to one of his children, exclusive of all the rest.

Section 86. But not to follow our author too far out of the way, the plain of the case is this. God having made man, and planted in him, as in all other animals, a strong desire of self-preservation; and furnished the world with things fit for food and raiment, and other necessaries of life, subservient to his design, that man should live and abide for some time upon the face of the earth, and not that so curious and wonderful a piece of workmanship, by his own negligence, or want of necessaries, should perish again, presently after a few moments continuance; God, I say, having made man and the world thus, spoke to him, (that is) directed him by his senses and reason, as he did the inferior animals by their sense and instinct, which were serviceable for his subsistence, and given him as the means of his preservation. And therefore I doubt not, but before these words were pronounced, i. Gen. 28, 29. (if they must be understood literally to have been spoken) and without any such verbal donation, man had a right to an use of the creatures, by the will and grant of God: for the desire, strong desire of preserving his life and being, having been planted in him as a principle of action by God himself, reason, which was the voice of God in him, could not but teach him and assure him, that pursuing that natural inclination he had to preserve his being, he followed the will of his maker, and therefore had a right to make use of those creatures, which by his reason or senses he could discover would be serviceable thereunto. And thus man's property in the creatures was founded upon the right he had to make use of those things that were necessary or useful to his being.

Section 87. This being the reason and foundation of Adam's property, gave the same title, on the same ground, to all his children, not only after his death, but in his life-time: so that here was no privilege of his heir above his other children, which could exclude them from an equal right to the use of the inferior creatures, for the comfortable preservation of their beings, which is all the property man has in them; and so Adam's sovereignty built on property, or, as our author calls it, private dominion, comes to nothing. Every man had a right to the creatures, by the same title Adam had, that is by the right everyone had to take care of, and provide for their subsistence: and thus men had a right in common, Adam's children in common with him. But if anyone had began, and made himself a property in any particular thing, (which how he, or anyone else, could do, shall be shown in another place) that thing, that possession, if he disposed not otherwise of it by his positive grant, descended naturally to his children, and they had a right to succeed to it, and possess it.

Section 88. It might reasonably be asked here, how come children by this right of possessing, before any other, the properties of their parents upon their decease? For it being personally the parents, when they die, without actually transferring their right to another, why does it not return again to the common stock of mankind? It will perhaps be answered, that common consent has disposed of it to their children. Common practice, we see indeed, does so dispose of it; but we cannot say, that it is the common consent of mankind; for that has never been asked, nor actually given; and if common tacit consent has established it, it would make but a positive, and not a natural right of children to inherit the goods of their parents: but where the practice is universal, it is reasonable to think the cause is natural. The grounds then I think to be this. The first and strongest desire God planted in men, and wrought into the very principles of their nature, being that of self-preservation, that is the foundation of a right to the creatures for the particular support and use of each individual person himself. But, next to this, God planted in men a strong desire also of propagating their kind, and continuing themselves in their posterity; and this gives children a title to share in the property of their parents, and a right to inherit their possessions. Men are not proprietors of what they have, merely for themselves; their children have a title to part of it, and have their kind of right joined with their parents, in the possession which comes to be wholly theirs, when death, having put an end to their parents use of it, has taken them from their possessions; and this we call inheritance: men being by a like obligation bound to preserve what they have begotten, as to preserve themselves, their issue come to have a right in the goods they are possessed of. That children have such a right is plain from the laws of God; and that men are convinced that children have such a right is evident from the law of the land; both which laws require parents to provide for their children.

Section 89. For children being by the course of nature, born weak, and unable to provide for themselves, they have by the appointment of God himself, who has thus ordered the course of nature, a right to be nourished and maintained by their parents; nay, a right not only to a bare subsistence, but to the conveniences and comforts of life, as far as the conditions of their parents can afford it. Hence it comes, that when their parents leave the world, and so the care due to their children ceases, the effects of it are to extend as far as possibly they can, and the provisions they have made in their life-time, are understood to be intended, as nature requires they should, for their children, whom, after themselves, they are bound to provide for: though the dying parents, by express words, declare nothing about them, nature appoints the descent of their property to their children, who thus come to have a title, and natural right of inheritance to their fathers goods, which the rest of mankind cannot pretend to.

Section 90. Were it not for this right of being nourished and maintained by their parents, which God and nature has given to children, and obliged parents to as a duty, it would be reasonable, that the father should inherit the estate of his son, and be preferred in the inheritance before his grandchild: for to the grandfather there is due a long score of care and expenses laid out upon the breeding and education of his son, which one would think in justice ought to be paid. But that having been done in obedience to the same law, whereby he received nourishment and education from his own parents; this score of education, received from a man's father, is paid by taking care, and providing for his own children; is paid, I say, as much as is required of payment by alteration of property, unless present necessity of the parents require a return of goods for their necessary support and subsistence: for we are not now speaking of that reverence, acknowledgment, respect and honor, that is always due from children to their parents; but of possessions and commodities of life valuable by money. But though it be incumbent on parents to bring up and provide for their children, yet this debt to their children does not quite cancel the score due to their parents; but only is made by nature preferable to it: for the debt a man owes his father takes place, and gives the father a right to inherit the son's goods, where, for want of issue, the right of children does not exclude that title. And therefore a man having a right to be maintained by his children, where he needs it; and to enjoy also the comforts of life from them, when the necessary provision due to them and their children will afford it; if his son die without issue, the father has a right in nature to possess his goods, and inherit his estate, (whatever the municipal laws of some countries may absurdly direct otherwise;) and so again his children and their issue from him; or, for want of such, his father and his issue. But where no such are to be found, i.e. no kindred, there we see the possessions of a private man revert to the community, and so in politic societies come into the hands of the public magistrate; but in the state of nature become again perfectly common, nobody having a right to inherit them: nor can anyone have a property in them, otherwise than in other things common by nature; of which I shall speak in its due place.

Section 91. I have been the larger, in showing upon what ground children have a right to succeed to the possession of their fathers properties, not only because by it, it will appear, that if Adam had a property (a titular, insignificant, useless property; for it could be no better, for he was bound to nourish and maintain his children and posterity out of it) in the whole earth and its product, yet all his children coming to have, by the law of nature, and right of inheritance, a joint title, and right of property in it after his death, it could convey no right of sovereignty to anyone of his posterity over the rest: since everyone having a right of inheritance to his portion, they might enjoy their inheritance, or any part of it in common, or share it, or some parts of it, by division, as it best liked them. But no one could pretend to the whole inheritance, or any sovereignty supposed to accompany it; since a right of inheritance gave everyone of the rest, as well as anyone, a title to share in the goods of his father. Not only upon this account, I say, have I been so particular in examining the reason of children's inheriting the property of their fathers, but also because it will give us father light in the inheritance of rule and power, which in countries where their particular municipal laws give the whole possession of land entirely to the first-born, and descent of power has gone so to men by this custom, some have been apt to be deceived into an opinion, that there was a natural or divine right of primogeniture, to both estate and power; and that the inheritance of both rule over men, and property in things, sprang from the same original, and were to descend by the same rules.

Section 92. Property, whose original is from the right a man has to use any of the inferior creatures, for the subsistence and comfort of his life, is for the benefit and sole advantage of the proprietor, so that he may even destroy the thing, that he has property in by his use of it, where need requires: but government being for the preservation of every man's right and property, by preserving him from the violence or injury of others, is for the good of the governed: for the magistrate's sword being for a terror to evil doers, and by that terror to enforce men to observe the positive laws of the society, made conformable to the laws of nature, for the public good, i.e. the good of every particular member of that society, as far as by common rules it can be provided for; the sword is not given the magistrate for his own good alone.

Section 93. Children therefore, as has been showed, by the dependence they have on their parents for subsistence, have a right of inheritance to their fathers property, as that which belongs to them for their proper good and behoove, and therefore are fitly termed goods, wherein the first-born has not a sole or peculiar right by any law of God and nature, the younger children having an equal title with him, founded on that right they all have to maintenance, support, and comfort from their parents, and on nothing else. But government being for the benefit of the governed, and not the sole advantage of the governors, (but only for theirs with the rest, as they make a part of that politic body, each of whose parts and members are taken care of, and directed in its peculiar functions for the good of the whole, by the laws of society) cannot be inherited by the same title, that children have to the goods of their father. The right a son has to be maintained and provided with the necessaries and conveniences of life out of his father's stock, gives him a right to succeed to his father's property for his own good; but this can give him no right to succeed also to the rule, which his father had over other men. All that a child has right to claim from his father is nourishment and education, and the things nature furnishes for the support of life: but he has no right to demand rule or dominion from him: he can subsist and receive from him the portion of good things, and advantages of education naturally due to him, without empire and dominion. That (if his father has any) was vested in him, for the good and behoove of others: and therefore the son cannot claim or inherit it by a title, which is founded wholly on his own private good and advantage.

Section 94. We must know how the first ruler, from whom anyone claims, came by his authority, upon what ground anyone has empire, what his title is to it, before we can know who has a right to succeed him in it, and inherit it from him: if the agreement and consent of men first gave a scepter into anyone's hand, or put a crown on his head, that also must direct its descent and conveyance; for the same authority, that made the first a lawful ruler, must make the second too, and so give right of succession: in this case inheritance, or primogeniture, can in its self have no right, no pretence to it, any father than that consent, which established the form of the government, has so settled the succession. And thus we see, the succession of crowns, in several countries, places it on different heads, and he comes by right of succession to be a prince in one place, who would be a subject in another.

Section 95. If God, by his positive grant and revealed declaration, first gave rule and dominion to any man, he that will claim by that title, must have the same positive grant of God for his succession: for if that has not directed the course of its descent and conveyance down to others, nobody can succeed to this title of the first ruler. Children have no right of inheritance to this; and primogeniture can lay no claim to it, unless God, the author of this constitution, has so ordained it. Thus we see, the pretensions of Saul's family, who received his crown from the immediate appointment of God, ended with his reign; and David, by the same title that Saul reigned, that is God's appointment, succeeded in his throne, to the exclusion of Jonathan, and all pretensions of paternal inheritance: and if Solomon had a right to succeed his father, it must be by some other title, than that of primogeniture. A cadet, or sister's son, must have the preference in succession, if he has the same title the first lawful prince had: and in dominion that has its foundation only in the positive appointment of God himself, Benjamin, the youngest, must have the inheritance of the crown, if God so direct, as well as one of that tribe had the first possession.

Section 96. If paternal right, the act of begetting, give a man rule and dominion, inheritance or primogeniture can give no title: for he that cannot succeed to his father's title, which was begetting, cannot succeed to that power over his brethren, which his father had by paternal right over them. But of this I shall have occasion to say more in another place. This is plain in the mean time, that any government, whether supposed to be at first founded in paternal right, consent of the people, or the positive appointment of God himself, which can supersede either of the other, and so begin a new government upon a new foundation; I say, any government began upon either of these, can by right of succession come to those only, who have the title of him they succeed to: power founded on contract can descend only to him, who has right by that contract: power founded on begetting, he only can have that begets; and power founded on the positive grant or donation of God, he only can have by right of succession, to whom that grant directs it.

Section 97. From what I have said, I think this is clear, that a right to the use of the creatures, being founded originally in the right a man has to subsist and enjoy the conveniences of life; and the natural right children have to inherit the goods of their parents, being founded in the right they have to the same subsistence and commodities of life, out of the stock of their parents, who are therefore taught by natural love and tenderness to provide for them, as a part of themselves; and all this being only for the good of the proprietor, or heir; it can be no reason for children's inheriting of rule and dominion, which has another original and a different end. Nor can primogeniture have any pretence to a right of solely inheriting either property or power, as we shall, in its due place, see more fully. It is enough to have showed here, that Adam's property, or private dominion, could not convey any sovereignty or rule to his heir, who not having a right to inherit all his father's possessions, could not thereby come to have any sovereignty over his brethren: and therefore, if any sovereignty on account of his property had been vested in Adam, which in truth there was not, yet it would have died with him.

Section 98. As Adam's sovereignty, if, by virtue of being proprietor of the world, he had any authority over men, could not have been inherited by any of his children over the rest, because they had the same title to divide the inheritance, and everyone had a right to a portion of his father's possessions; so neither could Adam's sovereignty by right of fatherhood, if any such he had, descend to anyone of his children: for it being, in our author's account, a right acquired by begetting to rule over those he had begotten, it was not a power possible to be inherited, because the right being consequent to, and built on, an act perfectly personal, made that power so too, and impossible to be inherited: for paternal power, being a natural right rising only from the relation of father and son, is as impossible to be inherited as the relation itself; and a man may pretend as well to inherit the conjugal power the husband, whose heir he is, had over his wife, as he can to inherit the paternal power of a father over his children: for the power of the husband being founded on contract, and the power of the father on begetting, he may as well inherit the power obtained by the conjugal contract, which was only personal, as he may the power obtained by begetting, which could reach no farther than the person of the begetter, unless begetting can be a title to power in him that does not beget.

Section 99. Which makes it a reasonable question to ask, whether Adam, dying before Eve, his heir, (suppose Cain or Seth) should have by right of inheriting Adam's fatherhood, sovereign power over Eve his mother: for Adam's fatherhood being nothing but a right he had to govern his children, because he begot them, he that inherits Adam's fatherhood, inherits nothing, even in our author's sense, but the right Adam had to govern his children, because he begot them: so that the monarchy of the heir would not have taken in Eve; or if it did, it being nothing but the fatherhood of Adam descended by inheritance, the heir must have right to govern Eve, because Adam begot her; for fatherhood is nothing else.

Section 100. Perhaps it will be said with our author, that a man can alien his power over his child; and what may be transferred by compact, may be possessed by inheritance. I answer, a father cannot alien the power he has over his child: he may perhaps to some degrees forfeit it, but cannot transfer it; and if any other man acquires it, it is not by the father's grant, but by some act of his own. For example, a father, unnaturally careless of his child, sells or gives him to another man; and he again exposes him; a third man finding him, breeds up, cherishes, and provides for him as his own: I think in this case, nobody will doubt, but that the greatest part of filial duty and subjection was here owing, and to be paid to this foster-father; and if anything could be demanded from the child, by either of the other, it could be only due to his natural father, who perhaps might have forfeited his right to much of that duty comprehended in the command, Honor your parents, but could transfer none of it to another. He that purchased, and neglected the child, got by his purchase and grant of the father, no title to duty or honor from the child; but only he acquired it, who by his own authority, performing the office and care of a father, to the forlorn and perishing infant, made himself, by paternal care, a title to proportional degrees of paternal power. This will be more easily admitted upon consideration of the nature of paternal power, for which I refer my reader to the second book.

Section 101. To return to the argument in hand; this is evident, that paternal power arising only from begetting, for in that our author places it alone, can neither be transferred nor inherited: and he that does not beget, can no more have paternal power, which arises from thence, than he can have a right to anything, who performs not the condition, to which only it is annexed. If one should ask, by what law has a father power over his children? it will be answered, no doubt, by the law of nature, which gives such a power over them, to him that begets them. If one should ask likewise, by what law does our author's heir come by a right to inherit? I think it would be answered, by the law of nature too: for I find not that our author brings one word of Scripture to prove the right of such an heir he speaks of. Why then the law of nature gives fathers paternal power over their children, because they did beget them; and the same law of nature gives the same paternal power to the heir over his brethren, who did not beget them: whence it follows, that either the father has not his paternal power by begetting, or else that the heir has it not at all; for it is hard to understand how the law of nature, which is the law of reason, can give the paternal power to the father over his children, for the only reason of begetting; and to the first-born over his brethren without this only reason, i.e. for no reason at all: and if the eldest, by the law of nature, can inherit this paternal power, without the only reason that gives a title to it, so may the youngest as well as he, and a stranger as well as either; for where there is no reason for anyone, as there is not, but for him that begets, all have an equal title. I am sure our author offers no reason; and when anybody does, we shall see whether it will hold or no.

Section 102. In the mean time it is as good sense to say, that by the law of nature a man has right to inherit the property of another, because he is of kin to him, and is known to be of his blood; and therefore, by the same law of nature, an utter stranger to his blood has right to inherit his estate; as to say that, by the law of nature, he that begets them has paternal power over his children, and therefore, by the law of nature, the heir that begets them not, has this paternal power over them; or supposing the law of the land gave absolute power over their children, to such only who nursed them, and fed their children themselves, could anybody pretend, that this law gave anyone, who did no such thing, absolute power over those, who were not his children?

Section 103. When therefore it can be showed, that conjugal power can belong to him that is not an husband, it will also I believe be proved, that our author's paternal power, acquired by begetting, may be inherited by a son; and that a brother, as heir to his father's power, may have paternal power over his brethren, and by the same rule conjugal power too: but till then, I think we may rest satisfied, that the paternal power of Adam, this sovereign authority of fatherhood, were there any such, could not descend to, nor be inherited by, his next heir. Fatherly power, I easily grant our author, if it will do him any good, can never be lost, because it will be as long in the world as there are fathers: but none of them will have Adam's paternal power, or derive theirs from him; but everyone will have his own, by the same title Adam had his, that is by begetting, but not by inheritance, or succession, no more than husbands have their conjugal power by inheritance from Adam. And thus we see, as Adam had no such property, no such paternal power, as gave him sovereign jurisdiction over mankind; so likewise his sovereignty built upon either of these titles, if he had any such, could not have descended to his heir, but must have ended with him. Adam therefore, as has been proved, being neither monarch, nor his imaginary monarchy hereditable, the power which is now in the world, is not that which was Adam's, since all that Adam could have upon our author's grounds, either of property or fatherhood, necessarily died with him, and could not be conveyed to posterity by inheritance. In the next place we will consider, whether Adam had any such heir, to inherit his power, as our author talks of.

CHAPTER X.

Of the Heir to Adam's Monarchical Power.

Section 104. Our author tells us, Observations, 253. That it is a truth undeniable, that there cannot be any multitude of men whatsoever, either great or small, though gathered together from the several corners and remotest regions of the world, but that in the same multitude, considered by its self, there is one man among them, that in nature has a right to be king of all the rest, as being the next heir to Adam, and all the other subjects to him: every man by nature is a king or a subject. And again, p. 20. If Adam himself were still living, and now ready to die, it is certain that there is one man, and but one in the world, who is next heir. Let this multitude of men be, if our author pleases, all the princes upon the earth, there will then be, by our author's rule, one among them, that in nature has a right to be king of all the rest, as being the right heir to Adam; an excellent way to establish the thrones of princes, and settle the obedience of their subjects, by setting up an hundred, or perhaps a thousand titles (if there be so many princes in the world) against any king now reigning, each as good, upon our author's grounds, as his who wears the crown. If this right of heir carries any weight with it, if it be the ordinance of God, as our author seems to tell us, Observations, 244. must not all be subject to it, from the highest to the lowest? Can those who wear the name of princes, without having the right of being heirs to Adam, demand obedience from their subjects by this title, and not be bound to pay it by the same law? Either governments in the world are not to be claimed, and held by this title of Adam's heir; and then the starting of it is to no purpose, the being or not being Adam's heir signifies nothing as to the title of dominion: or if it really be, as our author says, the true title to government and sovereignty, the first thing to be done, is to find out this true heir of Adam, seat him in his throne, and then all the kings and princes of the world ought to come and resign up their crowns and scepters to him, as things that belong no more to them, than to any of their subjects.

Section 105. For either this right in nature, of Adam's heir, to be king over all the race of men, (for all together they make one multitude) is a right not necessary to the making of a lawful king, and so there may be lawful kings without it, and then kings titles and power depend not on it; or else all the kings in the world but one are not lawful kings, and so have no right to obedience: either this title of heir to Adam is that whereby kings hold their crowns, and have a right to subjection from their subjects, and then one only can have it, and the rest being subjects can require no obedience from other men, who are but their fellow subjects; or else it is not the title whereby kings rule, and have a right to obedience from their subjects, and then kings are kings without it, and this dream of the natural sovereignty of Adam's heir is of no use to obedience and government: for if kings have a right to dominion, and the obedience of their subjects, who are not, nor can possibly be, heirs to Adam, what use is there of such a title, when we are obliged to obey without it? If kings, who are not heirs to Adam, have no right to sovereignty, we are all free, till our author, or anybody for him, will show us Adam's right heir. If there be but one heir of Adam, there can be but one lawful king in the world, and nobody in conscience can be obliged to obedience till it be resolved who that is; for it may be anyone, who is not known to be of a younger house, and all others have equal titles. If there be more than one heir of Adam, everyone is his heir, and so everyone has regal power: for if two sons can be heirs together, then all the sons are equally heirs, and so all are heirs, being all sons, or sons of sons of Adam. Between these two the right of heir cannot stand; for by it either but one only man, or all men are kings. Take which you please, it dissolves the bonds of government and obedience; since, if all men are heirs, they can owe obedience to nobody; if only one, nobody can be obliged to pay obedience to him, till he be known, and his title made out.

CHAPTER XI.

Who Heir?

Section 106. The great question which in all ages has disturbed mankind, and brought on them the greatest part of those mischiefs which have ruined cities, depopulated countries, and disordered the peace of the world, has been, not whether there be power in the world, nor whence it came, but who should have it. The settling of this point being of no smaller moment than the security of princes, and the peace and welfare of their estates and kingdoms, a reformer of politics, one would think, should lay this sure, and be very clear in it: for if this remain disputable, all the rest will be to very little purpose; and the skill used in dressing up power with all the splendor and temptation absoluteness can add to it, without showing who has a right to have it, will serve only to give a greater edge to man's natural ambition, which of its self is but too keen. What can this do but set men on the more eagerly to scramble, and so lay a sure and lasting foundation of endless contention and disorder, instead of that peace and tranquility, which is the business of government, and the end of human society?

Section 107. This designation of the person our author is more than ordinary obliged to take care of, because he, affirming that the assignment of civil power is by divine institution, has made the conveyance as well as the power itself sacred: so that no consideration, no act or are of man, can divert it from that person, to whom, by this divine right, it is assigned; no necessity or contrivance can substitute another person in his room: for if the assignment of civil power be by divine institution, and Adam's heir be he to whom it is thus assigned, as in the foregoing chapter our author tells us, it would be as much sacrilege for anyone to be king, who was not Adam's heir, as it would have been among the Jews, for anyone to have been priest, who had not been of Aaron's posterity: for not only the priesthood in general being by divine institution, but the assignment of it to the sole line and posterity of Aaron, made it impossible to be enjoyed or exercised by anyone, but those persons who were the off-spring of Aaron: whose succession therefore was carefully observed, and by that the persons who had a right to the priesthood certainly known.

Section 108. Let us see then what care our author has taken, to make us know who is this heir, who by divine institution has a right to be king over all men. The first account of him we meet with is, p. 12. in these words: This subjection of children, being the fountain of all regal authority, by the ordination of God himself; it follows, that civil power, not only in general, is by divine institution, but even the assignment of it, specifically to the eldest parents. Matters of such consequence as this is, should be in plain words, as little liable, as might be, to doubt or equivocation; and I think, if language be capable of expressing anything distinctly and clearly, that of kindred, and the several degrees of nearness of blood, is one. It were therefore to be wished, that our author had used a little more intelligible expressions here, that we might have better known, who it is, to whom the assignment of civil power is made by divine institution; or at least would have told us what he meant by eldest parents: for I believe, if land had been assigned or granted to him, and the eldest parents of his family, he would have thought it had needed an interpreter; and it would scarce have been known to whom next it belonged.

Section 109. In propriety of speech, (and certainly propriety of speech is necessary in a discourse of this nature) eldest parents signifies either the eldest men and women that have had children, or those who have longest had issue; and then our author's assertion will be, that those fathers and mothers, who have been longest in the world, or longest fruitful, have by divine institution a right to civil power. If there be any absurdity in this, our author must answer for it: and if his meaning be different from my explication, he is to be blamed, that he would not speak it plainly. This I am sure, parents cannot signify male heirs, nor eldest parents an infant child: who yet may sometimes be the true heir, if there can be but one. And we are hereby still as much at a loss, who civil power belongs to, notwithstanding this assignment by divine institution, as if there had been no such assignment at all, or our author had said nothing of it. This of eldest parents leaving us more in the dark, who by divine institution has a right to civil power, than those who never heard anything at all of heir, or descent, of which our author is so full. And though the chief matter of his writing is to teach obedience to those, who have a right to it, which he tells us is conveyed by descent, yet who those are, to whom this right by descent belongs, he leaves, like the philosophers stone in politics, out of the reach of anyone to discover from his writings.

Section 110. This obscurity cannot be imputed to want of language in so great a master of style as Sir Robert is, when he is resolved with himself what he would say: and therefore, I fear, finding how hard it would be to settle rules of descent by divine institution, and how little it would be to his purpose, or conduce to the clearing and establishing the titles of princes, if such rules of descent were settled, he chose rather to content himself with doubtful and general terms, which might make no ill found in men's ears, who were willing to be pleased with them, rather than offer any clear rules of descent of this fatherhood of Adam, by which men's consciences might be satisfied to whom it descended, and know the persons who had a right to regal power, and with it to their obedience.

Section 111. How else is it possible, that laying so much stress, as he does, upon descent, and Adam's heir, next heir, true heir, he should never tell us what heir means, nor the way to know who the next or true heir is? This, I do not remember, he does anywhere expressly handle; but, where it comes in his way, very warily and doubtfully touches; though it be so necessary, that without it all discourses of government and obedience upon his principles would be to no purpose, and fatherly power, never so well made out, will be of no use to anybody. Hence he tells us, Observations, 244. That not only the constitution of power in general, but the limitation of it to one kind, (i.e.) monarchy, and the determination of it to the individual person and line of Adam, are all three ordinances of God; neither Eve nor her children could either limit

Adam's power, or join others with him; and what was given unto Adam was given in his person to his posterity. Here again our author informs us, that the divine ordinance has limited the descent of Adam's monarchical power. To whom? To Adam's line and posterity, says our author. A notable limitation, a limitation to all mankind: for if our author can find anyone among mankind, that is not of the line and posterity of Adam, he may perhaps tell him, who this next heir of Adam is: but for us, I despair how this limitation of Adam's empire to his line and posterity will help us to find out one heir. This limitation indeed of our author will save those the labor, who would look for him among the race of brutes, if any such there were; but will very little contribute to the discovery of one next heir among men, though it make a short and easy determination of the question about the descent of Adam's regal power, by telling us, that the line and posterity of Adam is to have it, that is, in plain English, anyone may have it, since there is no person living that has not the title of being of the line and posterity of Adam; and while it keeps there, it keeps within our author's limitation by God's ordinance. Indeed, p. 19. he tells us, that such heirs are not only lords of their own children, but of their brethren; whereby, and by the words following, which we shall consider anon, he seems to insinuate, that the eldest son is heir; but he nowhere, that I know, says it in direct words, but by the instances of Cain and Jacob, that there follow, we may allow this to be so far his opinion concerning heirs, that where there are divers children, the eldest son has the right to be heir. That primogeniture cannot give any title to paternal power, we have already showed. That a father may have a natural right to some kind of power over his children, is easily granted; but that an elder brother has so over his brethren, remains to be proved: God or nature has not anywhere, that I know, placed such jurisdiction in the first-born; nor can reason find any such natural superiority among brethren. The law of Moses gave a double portion of the goods and possessions to the eldest; but we find not anywhere that naturally, or by God's institution, superiority or dominion belonged to him, and the instances there brought by our author are but slender proofs of a right to civil power and dominion in the first-born, and do rather show the contrary.

Section 112. His words are in the foresighted place: And therefore we find God told Cain of his brother Abel; his desire shall be subject unto you, and you shall rule over him. To which I answer,

1. These words of God to Cain are by many interpreters, with great reason, understood in a quite different sense than what our author uses them in.

2. Whatever was meant by them, it could not be, that Cain, as elder, had a natural dominion over Abel; for the words are conditional, If you do well; and so personal to Cain: and whatever was signified by them, did depend on his carriage, and not follow his birthright; and therefore could by no means be an establishment of dominion in the first-born in general: for before this Abel had his distinct territories by right of private dominion, as our author himself confesses, Observations, 210. which he could not have had to the prejudice of the heirs title, if by divine institution, Cain as heir were to inherit all his father's dominion.

3. If this were intended by God as the charter of primogeniture, and the grant of dominion to elder brothers in general as such, by right of inheritance, we might expect it should have included all his brethren: for we may well suppose, Adam, from whom the world was to be peopled, had by this time, that these were grown up to be men, more sons than these two: whereas Abel himself is not so much as named; and the words in the original can scarce, with any good construction, be applied to him.

4. It is too much to build a doctrine of so mighty consequence upon so doubtful and obscure a place of Scripture, which may be well, nay better, understood in a quite different sense, and so can be but an ill proof, being as doubtful as the thing to be proved by it; especially when there is nothing else in Scripture or reason to be found, that favors or supports it.

Section 113. It follows, p. 19. Accordingly when Jacob bought his brother's birthright, Isaac blessed him thus; Be lord over your brethren, and let the sons of your mother bow before you. Another instance, I take it, brought by our author to evince dominion due to birthright, and an admirable one it is: for it must be no ordinary way of reasoning in a man, that is pleading for the natural power of kings, and against all compact, to bring for proof of it, an example, where his own account of it founds all the right upon compact, and settles empire in the younger brother, unless buying and selling be no compact; for he tells us, when Jacob bought his brother's birthright. But passing by that, let us consider the history itself, with what use our author makes of it, and we shall find these following mistakes about it.

1. That our author reports this, as if Isaac had given Jacob this blessing, immediately upon his purchasing the birthright; for he says, when Jacob bought, Isaac blessed him; which is plainly otherwise in the Scripture: for it appears, there was a distance of time between, and if we will take the story in the order it lies, it must be no small distance; all Isaac's sojourning in Gerar, and transactions with Abimelech, Gen. xxvi. coming between; Rebecca being then beautiful, and consequently young; but Isaac, when he blessed Jacob, was old and decrepit: and Esau also complains of Jacob, Gen. xxvii. 36. that two times he had supplanted him; He took away my birthright, says he, and behold now he has taken away my blessing; words, that I think signify distance of time and difference of action.

2. Another mistake of our author's is, that he supposes Isaac gave Jacob the blessing, and bid him be lord over his brethren, because he had the birthright; for our author brings this example to prove, that he that has the birthright, has thereby a right to be lord over his brethren. But it is also manifest by the text, that Isaac had no consideration of Jacob's having bought the birthright; for when he blessed him, he considered him not as Jacob, but took him for Esau. Nor did Esau understand any such connection between birthright and the blessing; for he says, He has supplanted me these two times, he took away my birthright, and behold now he has taken away my blessing: whereas had the blessing, which was to be lord over his brethren, belonged to the birthright, Esau could not have complained of this second, as a cheat, Jacob having got nothing but what Esau had sold him, when he sold him his birthright; so that it is plain, dominion, if these words signify it, was not understood to belong to the birthright.

Section 114. And that in those days of the patriarchs, dominion was not understood to be the right of the heir, but only a greater portion of goods is plain from Gen. xxi. 10. for Sarah, taking Isaac to be heir, says, Cast out this bondwoman and her son, for the son of this bondwoman shall not be heir with my son: whereby could be meant nothing, but that he should not have a pretence to an equal share of his father's estate after his death, but should have his portion presently, and be gone. Accordingly we read, Gen. xxv. 5, 6. that Abraham gave all that he had unto Isaac, but unto the sons of the concubines which Abraham had, Abraham gave gifts, and sent them away from Isaac his son, while he yet lived. That is, Abraham having given portions to all his other sons, and sent them away, that which he had reserved, being the greatest part of his substance, Isaac as heir possessed after his death: but by being heir, he had no right to be lord over his brethren; for if he had, why should Sarah endeavor to rob him of one of his subjects, or lessen the number of his slaves, by desiring to have Ishmael sent away?

Section 115. Thus, as under the law, the privilege of birthright was nothing but a double portion: so we see that before Moses, in the patriarchs time, from whence our author pretends to take his model, there was no knowledge, no thought, that birthright gave rule or empire, paternal or kingly authority, to anyone over his brethren. If this be not plain enough in the story of Isaac and Ishmael, he that will look into 1 Chron. v. 12. may there read these words: Reuben was the first-born; but forasmuch as he defiled his father's bed, his birthright was given unto the sons of Joseph, the son of Israel: and the genealogy is not to be reckoned after the birthright; for Judah prevailed above his brethren, and of him came the chief ruler; but the birthright was Joseph's. What this birthright was, Jacob blessing Joseph, Gen. xlviii. 22. tells us in these words, Moreover I have given you one portion above your brethren, which I took out of the hand of the Amorite, with my sword and with my bow. Whereby it is not only plain, that the birthright was nothing but a double portion; but the text in Chronicles is express against our author's doctrine, and shows that dominion was no part of the birthright; for it tells us, that Joseph had the birthright, but Judah the dominion. One would think our author were very fond of the very name of birthright, when he brings this instance of Jacob and Esau, to prove that dominion belongs to the heir over his brethren.

Section 116. 1. Because it will be but an ill example to prove, that dominion by God's ordination belonged to the eldest son, because Jacob the youngest here had it, let him come by it how he would: for if it prove anything, it can only prove, against our author, that the assignment of dominion to the eldest is not by divine institution, which would then be unalterable: for if by the law of God, or nature, absolute power and empire belongs to the eldest son and his heirs, so that they are supreme monarchs, and all the rest of their brethren slaves, our author gives us reason to doubt whether the eldest son has a power to part with it, to the prejudice of his posterity, since he tells us, Observations, 158. That in grants and gifts that have their original from God or nature, no inferior power of man can limit, or make any law of prescription against them.

Section 117. 2. Because this place, Gen. xxvii. 29. brought by our author, concerns not at all the dominion of one brother over the other, nor the subjection of Esau to Jacob: for it is plain in the history, that Esau was never subject to Jacob, but lived apart in mount Seir, where he founded a distinct people and government, and was himself prince over them, as much as Jacob was in his own family. This text, if considered, can never be understood of Esau himself, or the personal dominion of Jacob over him: for the words brethren and sons of your mother, could not be used literally by Isaac, who knew Jacob had only one brother; and these words are so far from being true in a literal sense, or establishing any dominion in Jacob over Esau, that in the story we find the quite contrary, for Gen. xxxii. Jacob several times calls Esau lord, and himself his servant; and Gen. xxxiii. he bowed himself seven times to the ground to Esau. Whether Esau then were a subject and vassal (nay, as our author tells us, all subjects are slaves) to Jacob, and Jacob his sovereign prince by birthright, I leave the reader to judge; and to believe if he can, that these words of Isaac, Be lord over your brethren, and let your mother's sons bow down to you, confirmed Jacob in a sovereignty over Esau, upon the account of the birthright he had got from him.

Section 118. He that reads the story of Jacob and Esau, will find there was never any jurisdiction or authority, that either of them had over the other after their father's death: they lived with the friendship and equality of brethren, neither lord, neither slave to his brother; but independent each of other, were both heads of their distinct families, where they received no laws from one another, but lived separately, and were the roots out of which sprang two distinct people under two distinct governments. This blessing then of Isaac, whereon our author would build the dominion of the elder brother, signifies no more, but what Rebecca had been told from God, Gen. xxv. 23. Two nations are in your womb, and two manners of people shall be separated from your bowels, and the one people shall be stronger than the other people, and the elder shall serve the younger; and so Jacob blessed Judah, Gen. xlix. and gave him the scepter and dominion, from whence our author might have argued as well, that jurisdiction and dominion belongs to the third son over his brethren, as well as from this blessing of Isaac, that it belonged to Jacob: both these places contain only predictions of what should long after happen to their posterities, and not any declaration of the right of inheritance to dominion in either. And thus we have our author's two great and only arguments to prove, that heirs are lords over their brethren.

1. Because God tells Cain, Gen. iv. that however sin might set upon him, he ought or might be master of it: for the most learned interpreters understood the words of sin, and not of Abel, and give so strong reasons for it, that nothing can convincingly be inferred, from so doubtful a text, to our author's purpose.

2. Because in this of Gen. xxvii. Isaac foretells that the Israelites, the posterity of Jacob, should have dominion over the Edomites, the posterity of Esau; therefore says our author, heirs are lords of their brethren: I leave anyone to judge of the conclusion.

Section 119. And now we see how our author has provided for the descending, and conveyance down of Adam's monarchical power, or paternal dominion to posterity, by the inheritance of his heir, succeeding to all his father's authority, and becoming upon his death as much lord as his father was, not only over his own children, but over his brethren, and all descended from his father, and so in infinitum. But yet who this heir is, he does not once tell us; and all the light we have from him in this so fundamental a point, is only, that in his instance of Jacob, by using the word birthright, as that which passed from Esau to Jacob, he leaves us to guess, that by heir, he means the eldest son; though I do not remember he anywhere mentions expressly the title of the first-born, but all along keeps himself under the shelter of the indefinite term heir. But taking it to be his meaning, that the eldest son is heir, (for if the eldest be not, there will be no pretence why the sons should not be all heirs alike) and so by right of primogeniture has dominion over his brethren; this is but one step towards the settlement of succession, and the difficulties remain still as much as ever, till he can show us who is meant by right heir, in all those cases which may happen where the present possessor has no son. This he silently passes over, and perhaps wisely too: for what can be wiser, after one has affirmed, that the person having that power, as well as the power and form of government, is the ordinance of God, and by divine institution, Observations, 254. p. 12. than to be careful, not to stare any question concerning the person, the resolution whereof will certainly lead him into a confession, that God and nature has determined nothing about him? And if our author cannot show who by right of nature, or a clear positive law of God, has the next right to inherit the dominion of this natural monarch he has been at such pains about, when he died without a son, he might have spared his pains in all the rest, it being more necessary for the settling men's consciences, and determining their subjection and allegiance, to show them who by original right, superior and antecedent to the will, or any act of men, has a title to this paternal jurisdiction, than it is to show that by nature there was such a jurisdiction; it being to no purpose for me to know there is such a paternal power, which I ought, and am disposed to obey, unless, where there are many pretenders, I also know the person that is rightfully invested and endowed with it.

Section 120. For the main matter in question being concerning the duty of my obedience, and the obligation of conscience I am under to pay it to him that is of right my lord and ruler, I must know the person that this right of paternal power resides in, and so empowers him to claim obedience from me: for let it be true what he says, p. 12. That civil power not only in general is by divine institution, but even the assignment of it specially to the eldest parents; and Observations, 254. That not only the power or right of government, but the form of the power of governing, and the person having that power, are all the ordinance of God; yet unless he show us in all cases who is this person, ordained by God, who is this eldest parent; all his abstract notions of monarchical power will signify just nothing, when they are to be reduced to practice, and men are conscientiously to pay their obedience: for paternal jurisdiction being not the thing to be obeyed, because it cannot command, but is only that which gives one man a right which another has not, and if it come by inheritance, another man cannot have, to command and be obeyed; it is ridiculous to say, I pay obedience to the paternal power, when I obey him, to whom paternal power gives no right to my obedience: for he can have no divine right to my obedience, who cannot show his divine right to the power of ruling over me, as well as that by divine right there is such a power in the world.

Section 121. And hence not being able to make out any prince's title to government, as heir to Adam, which therefore is of no use, and had been better let alone, he is fain to resolve all into present possession, and makes civil obedience as due to an usurper, as to a lawful king; and thereby the usurper's title as good. His words are, Observations, 253. and they deserve to be remembered: If a usurper dispossesses the true heir, the subject's obedience to the fatherly power must go along, and wait upon God's providence. But I shall leave his title of usurpers to be examined in its due place, and desire my sober reader to consider what thanks princes owe such politics as this, which can suppose paternal power (i.e.) a right to government in the hands of a Cade, or a Cromwell; and so all obedience being due to paternal power, the obedience of subjects will be due to them, by the same right, and upon as good grounds, as it is to lawful princes; and yet this, as dangerous a doctrine as it is, must necessarily follow from making all political power to be nothing else, but Adam's paternal power by right and divine institution, descending from him without being able to show to whom it descended, or who is heir to it.

Section 122. To settle government in the world, and to lay obligations to obedience on any man's conscience, it is as necessary (supposing with our author that all power be nothing but the being possessed of Adam's fatherhood) to satisfy him, who has a right to this power, this fatherhood, when the possessor dies without sons to succeed immediately to it, as it was to tell him, that upon the death of the father, the eldest son had a right to it: for it is still to be remembered, that the great question is, (and that which our author would be thought to contend for, if he did not sometimes forget it) what persons have a right to be obeyed, and not whether there be a power in the world, which is to be called paternal, without knowing in whom it resides: for so it be a power, i.e. right to govern, it matters not, whether it be termed paternal or regal, natural or acquired; whether you call it supreme fatherhood, or supreme brotherhood, will be all one, provided we know who has it.

Section 123. I go on then to ask, whether in the inheriting of this paternal power, this supreme fatherhood, the grandson by a daughter has a right before a nephew by a brother? Whether the grandson by the eldest son, being an infant, before the younger son, a man and able? Whether the daughter before the uncle? or any other man, descended by a male line? Whether a grandson by a younger daughter, before a grand-daughter by an elder daughter? Whether the elder son by a concubine, before a younger son by a wife? From whence also will arise many questions of legitimacy, and what in nature is the difference between a wife and a concubine? for as to the municipal or positive laws of men, they can signify nothing here. It may further be asked, whether the eldest son, being a fool, shall inherit this paternal power, before the younger, a wise man? and what degree of folly it must be that shall exclude him? and who shall be judge of it? Whether the son of a fool, excluded for his folly, before the son of his wise brother who reigned? Who has the paternal power while the widow-queen is with child by the deceased king, and nobody knows whether it will be a son or a daughter? Which shall be heir of the two male-twins, who by the dissection of the mother were laid open to the world? Whether a sister by the half blood, before a brother's daughter by the whole blood?

Section 124. These, and many more such doubts, might be proposed about the titles of succession, and the right of inheritance; and that not as idle speculations, but such as in history we shall find have concerned the inheritance of crowns and kingdoms; and if ours want them, we need not go father for famous examples of it, than the other kingdom in this very island, which having been fully related by the ingenious and learned author of Patriarcha non Monarcha, I need say no more of. Until our author has resolved all the doubts that may arise about the next heir, and showed that they are plainly determined by the law of nature, or the revealed law of God, all his suppositions of a monarchical, absolute, supreme, paternal power in Adam, and the descent of that power to his heirs, would not be of the least use to establish the authority, or make out the title, of anyone prince now on earth; but would rather unsettle and bring all into question: for let our author tell us as long as he pleases, and let all men believe it too, that Adam had a paternal, and thereby a monarchical power; that this (the only power in the world) descended to his heirs; and that there is no other power in the world but this: let this be all as clear demonstration, as it is manifest error, yet if it be not past doubt, to whom this paternal power descends, and whose now it is, nobody can be under any obligation of obedience, unless anyone will say, that I am bound to pay obedience to paternal power in a man who has no more paternal power than I myself; which is all one as to say, I obey a man, because he has a right to govern; and if I be asked, how I know he has a right to govern, I should answer, it cannot be known, that he has any at all: for that cannot be the reason of my obedience, which I know not to be so; much less can that be a reason of my obedience, which nobody at all can know to be so.

Section 125. And therefore all this ado about Adam's fatherhood, the greatness of its power, and the necessity of its supposal, helps nothing to establish the power of those that govern, or to determine the obedience of subjects who are to obey, if they cannot tell whom they are to obey, or it cannot be known who are to govern, and who to obey. In the state the world is now, it is irrecoverably ignorant, who is Adam's heir. This fatherhood, this monarchical power of Adam, descending to his heirs, would be of no more use to the government of mankind, than it would be to the quieting of men's consciences, or securing their health, if our author had assured them, that Adam had a power to forgive sins, or cure diseases, which by divine institution descended to his heir, while this heir is impossible to be known. And should not he do as rationally, who upon this assurance of our author went and confessed his sins, and expected a good absolution; or took physic with expectation of health, from anyone who had taken on himself the name of priest or physician, or thrust himself into those employments, saying, I acquiesce in the absolving power descending from Adam, or I shall be cured by the medicinal power descending from Adam; as he who says, I submit to and obey the paternal power descending from Adam, when it is confessed all these powers descend only to his single heir, and that heir is unknown?

Section 126. It is true, the civil lawyers have pretended to determine some of these cases concerning the succession of princes; but by our author's principles, they have meddled in a matter that belongs not to them: for if all political power be derived only from Adam, and be to descend only to his successive heirs, by the ordinance of God and divine institution, this is a right antecedent and paramount to all government; and therefore the positive laws of men cannot determine that, which is itself the foundation of all law and government, and is to receive its rule only from the law of God and nature. And that being silent in the case, I am apt to think there is no such right to be conveyed this way: I am sure it would be to no purpose if there were, and men would be more at a loss concerning government, and obedience to governors, than if there were no such right; since by positive laws and compact, which divine institution (if there be any) shuts out, all these endless inextricable doubts can be safely provided against: but it can never be understood, how a divine natural right, and that of such moment as is all order and peace in the world, should be conveyed down to posterity, without any plain natural or divine rule concerning it. And there would be an end of all civil government, if the assignment of civil power were by divine institution to the heir, and yet by that divine institution the person of the heir could not be known. This paternal regal power being by divine right only his, it leaves no room for human prudence, or consent, to place it anywhere else; for if only one man has a divine right to the obedience of mankind, nobody can claim that obedience, but he that can show that right; nor can men's consciences by any other pretence be obliged to it. And thus this doctrine cuts up all government by the roots.

Section 127. Thus we see how our author, laying it for a sure foundation, that the very person that is to rule, is the ordinance of God, and by divine institution, tells us at large, only that this person is the heir, but who this heir is, he leaves us to guess; and so this divine institution, which assigns it to a person whom we have no rule to know, is just as good as an assignment to nobody at all. But whatever our author does, divine institution makes no such ridiculous assignments: nor can God be supposed to make it a sacred law, that one certain person should have a right to something, and yet not give rules to mark out, and know that person by, or give an heir a divine right to power, and yet not point out who that heir is. It is rather to be thought, that an heir had no such right by divine institution, than that God should give such a right to the heir, but yet leave it doubtful and undeterminable who such heir is.

Section 128. If God had given the land of Canaan to Abraham, and in general terms to somebody after him, without naming his seed, whereby it might be known who that somebody was, it would have been as good and useful an assignment, to determine the right to the land of Canaan, as it would be the determining the right of crowns, to give empire to Adam and his successive heirs after him, without telling who his heir is: for the word heir, without a rule to know who it is, signifies no more than some body, I know not whom. God making it a divine institution, that men should not marry those who were near of kin, thinks it not enough to say, none of you shall approach to any that is near of kin to him, to uncover their nakedness; but moreover, gives rules to know who are those near of kin, forbidden by divine institution; or else that law would have been of no use, it being to no purpose to lay restraint, or give privileges to men, in such general terms, as the particular person concerned cannot be known by. But God not having anywhere said, the next heir shall inherit all his father's estate or dominion, we are not to wonder, that he has nowhere appointed who that heir should be; for never having intended any such thing, never designed any heir in that sense, we cannot expect he should anywhere nominate, or appoint any person to it, as we might, had it been otherwise. And therefore in Scripture, though the word heir occurs, yet there is no such thing as heir in our author's sense, one that was by right of nature to inherit all that his father had, exclusive of his brethren. Hence Sarah supposes, that if Ishmael staid in the house, to share in Abraham's estate after his death, this son of a bond-woman might be heir with Isaac; and therefore, says she, cast out this bond-woman and her son, for the son of this bond-woman shall not be heir with my son: but this cannot excuse our author, who telling us there is, in every number of men, one who is right and next heir to Adam, ought to have told us what the laws of descent are: but he having been so sparing to instruct us by rules, how to know who is heir, let us see in the next place, what his history out of Scripture, on which he pretends wholly to build his government, gives us in this necessary and fundamental point.

Section 129. Our author, to make good the title of his book, p. 13. begins his history of the descent of Adam's regal power, p. 13. in these words: This lordship which Adam by command had over the whole world, and by right descending from him, the patriarchs did enjoy, was a large, etc. How does he prove that the patriarchs by descent did enjoy it? For dominion of life and death, says he, we find Judah the father pronounced sentence of death against Tamar his daughter in law for playing the harlot, p. 13. How does this prove that Judah had absolute and sovereign authority? He pronounced sentence of death. The pronouncing of sentence of death is not a certain mark of sovereignty, but usually the office of inferior magistrates. The power of making laws of life and death is indeed a mark of sovereignty, but pronouncing the sentence according to those laws may be done by others, and therefore this will but ill prove that he had sovereign authority: as if one should say, Judge Jefferies pronounced sentence of death in the late times, therefore Judge Jefferies had sovereign authority. But it will be said, Judah did it not by commission from another, and therefore did it in his own right. Who knows whether he had any right at all? Heat of passion might carry him to do that which he had no authority to do. Judah had dominion of life and death: how does that appear? He exercised it, he pronounced sentence of death against Tamar: our author thinks it is very good proof, that because he did it, therefore he had a right to do it: he lay with her also; by the same way of proof, he had a right to do that too. If the consequence be good from doing to a right of doing, Absalom too may be reckoned among our author's sovereigns, for he pronounced such a sentence of death against his brother Amnon, and much upon a like occasion, and had it executed too, if that be sufficient to prove a dominion of life and death.

But allowing this all to be clear demonstration of sovereign power, who was it that had this lordship by right descending to him from Adam, as large and ample as the most absolute dominion of any monarch? Judah, says our author, Judah a younger son of Jacob, his father and elder brethren living; so that if our author's own proof be to be taken, a younger brother may, in the life of his father and elder brothers, by right of descent, enjoy Adam's monarchical power; and if one so qualified may be monarch by descent, why may not every man? if Judah, his father and elder brother living, were one of Adam's heirs, I know not who can be excluded from this inheritance; all men by inheritance may be monarchs as well as Judah.

Section 130. Touching war, we see that Abraham commanded an army of 318 soldiers of his own family, and Esau met his brother Jacob with 400 men at arms. For matter of peace, Abraham made a league with Abimelech, etc. p. 13. Is it not possible for a man to have 318 men in his family, without being heir to Adam? A planter in the West Indies has more, and might, if he pleased, (who doubts?) muster them up and lead them out against the Indians, to seek reparation upon any injury received from them; and all this without the absolute dominion of a monarch, descending to him from Adam. Would it not be an admirable argument to prove, that all power by God's institution descended from Adam by inheritance, and that the very person and power of this planter were the ordinance of God, because he had power in his family over servants, born in his house, and bought with his money? For this was just Abraham's case;

those who were rich in the patriarch's days, as in the West Indies now, bought men and maid servants, and by their increase, as well as purchasing of new, came to have large and numerous families, which though they made use of in war or peace, can it be thought the power they had over them was an inheritance descended from Adam, when it was the purchase of their money? A man's riding in an expedition against an enemy, his horse bought in a fair would be as good a proof that the owner enjoyed the lordship which Adam by command had over the whole world, by right descending to him, as Abraham's leading out the servants of his family is, that the patriarchs enjoyed this lordship by descent from Adam: since the title to the power, the master had in both cases, whether over slaves or horses, was only from his purchase; and the getting a dominion over anything by bargain and money, is a new way of proving one had it by descent and inheritance.

Section 131. But making war and peace are marks of sovereignty. Let it be so in politic societies: may not therefore a man in the West Indies, who has with him sons of his own, friends, or companions, soldiers under pay, or slaves bought with money, or perhaps a band made up of all these, make war and peace, if there should be occasion, and ratify the articles too with an oath, without being a sovereign, an absolute king over those who went with him? He that says he cannot must then allow many masters of ships, many private planters, to be absolute monarchs, for as much as this they have done. War and peace cannot be made for politic societies, but by the supreme power of such societies; because war and peace, giving a different motion to the force of such a politic body, none can make war or peace, but that which has the direction of the force of the whole body, and that in politic societies is only the supreme power. In voluntary societies for the time, he that has such a power by consent may make war and peace, and so may a single man for himself, the state of war not consisting in the number of partisans, but the enmity of the parties, where they have no superior to appeal to.

Section 132. The actual making of war or peace is no proof of any other power, but only of disposing those to exercise or cease acts of enmity for whom he makes it; and this power in many cases anyone may have without any politic supremacy: and therefore the making of war or peace will not prove that everyone that does so is a politic ruler, much less a king; for then commonwealths must be kings too, for they do as certainly make war and peace as monarchical government.

Section 133. But granting this a mark of sovereignty in Abraham, is it a proof of the descent to him of Adam's sovereignty over the whole world? If it be, it will surely be as good a proof of the descent of Adam's lordship to others too. And then commonwealths, as well as Abraham, will be heirs of Adam, for they make war and peace, as well as he. If you say, that the lordship of Adam does not by right descend to commonwealths, though they make war and peace, the same say I of Abraham, and then there is an end of your argument: if you stand to your argument, and say those that do make war and peace, as commonwealths do without doubt, do inherit Adam's lordship, there is an end of your monarchy, unless you will say, that commonwealths by descent enjoying Adam's lordship are monarchies; and that indeed would be a new way of making all the governments in the world monarchical.

Section 134. To give our author the honor of this new invention, for I confess it is not I have first found it out by tracing his principles, and so charged it on him, it is fit my readers know that (as absurd as it may seem) he teaches it himself, p. 23. where he ingenuously says, In all kingdoms and commonwealths in the world, whether the prince be the supreme father of the people, or but the true heir to such a father, or come to the crown by usurpation or election, or whether some few or a multitude govern the commonwealth; yet still the authority that is in anyone, or in many, or in all these, is the only right, and natural authority of a supreme father; which right of fatherhood, he often tells us, is regal and royal authority; as particularly, p. 12. the page immediately preceding this instance of Abraham. This regal authority, he says, those that govern commonwealths have; and if it be true, that regal and royal authority be in those that govern commonwealths, it is as true that commonwealths are governed by kings; for if regal authority be in him that governs, he that governs must needs be a king, and so all commonwealths are nothing but down-right monarchies; and then what need any more ado about the matter? The governments of the world are as they should be; there is nothing but monarchy in it. This, without doubt, was the surest way our author could have found, to turn all other governments, but monarchical, out of the world.

Section 135. But all this scarce proves Abraham to have been a king as heir to Adam. If by inheritance he had been king, Lot, who was of the same family, must needs have been his subject, by that title, before the servants in his family; but we see they lived as friends and equals, and when their herdsmen could not agree, there was no pretence of jurisdiction or superiority between them, but they parted by consent, Gen. xiii. hence he is called both by Abraham, and by the text, Abraham's brother, the name of friendship and equality, and not of jurisdiction and authority, though he was really but his nephew. And if our author knows that Abraham was Adam's heir, and a king, it was more, it seems, than Abraham himself knew, or his servant whom he sent a wooing for his son; for when he sets out the advantages of the match, xxiv. Gen. 35. thereby to prevail with the young woman and her friends, he says, I am Abraham's servant, and the lord has blessed my master greatly, and he is become great; and he has given him flocks and herds, and silver and gold, and men-servants and maid-servants, and camels and asses; and Sarah, my master's wife, bare a son to my master when she was old, and unto him has he given all he has. Can one think that a discreet servant, that was thus particular to set out his master's greatness, would have omitted the crown Isaac was to have, if he had known of any such? Can it be imagined he should have neglected to have told them on such an occasion as this, that Abraham was a king, a name well known at that time, for he had nine of them his neighbors, if he or his master had thought any such thing, the likeliest matter of all the rest, to make his errand successful?

Section 136. But this discovery it seems was reserved for our author to make 2 or 3000 years after, and let him enjoy the credit of it; only he should have taken care that some of Adam's land should have descended to this his heir, as well as all Adam's lordship: for though this lordship which Abraham, (if we may believe our author) as well as the other patriarchs, by right descending to him, did enjoy, was as large and ample as the most absolute dominion of any monarch which has been since the creation; yet his estate, his territories, his dominions were very narrow and scanty, for he had not the possession of a foot of land, until he bought a field and a cave of the sons of Heth to bury Sarah in.

Section 137. The instance of Esau joined with this of Abraham, to prove that the lordship which Adam had over the whole world, by right descending from him, the patriarchs did enjoy, is yet more pleasant than the former. Esau met his brother Jacob with 400 men at arms; he therefore was a king by right of heir to Adam. Four hundred armed men then, however got together, are enough to prove him that leads them, to be a king and Adam's heir. There have been Tories in Ireland, (whatever there are in other countries) who would have thanked our author for so honorable an opinion of them, especially if there had been nobody near with a better title of 500 armed men, to question their royal authority of 400. It is a shame for men to trifle so, to say no worse of it, in so serious an argument. Here Esau is brought as a proof that Adam's lordship, Adam's absolute dominion, as large as that of any monarch, descended by right to the patriarchs, and in this very Chapter p. 19. Jacob is brought as an instance of one that by birthright was lord over his brethren. So we have here two brothers absolute monarchs by the same title, and at the same time heirs to Adam; the eldest, heir to Adam, because he met his brother with 400 men; and the youngest, heir to Adam by birthright: Esau enjoyed the lordship which Adam had over the whole world by right descending to him, in as large and ample manner, as the most absolute dominion of any monarch; and at the same time, Jacob lord over him, by the right heirs have to be lords over their brethren. *Risum teneatis?* I never, I confess, met with any man of parts so dexterous as Sir Robert at this way of arguing: but it was his misfortune to light upon an hypothesis, that could not be accommodated to the nature of things, and human affairs; his principles could not be made to agree with that constitution and order, which God had settled in the world, and therefore must needs often clash with common sense and experience.

Section 138. In the next section, he tells us, this Patriarchal power continued not only until the flood, but after it, as the name patriarch does in part prove. The word patriarch does more than in part prove, that Patriarchal power continued in the world as long as there were patriarchs, for it is necessary that Patriarchal power should be while there are patriarchs; as it is necessary there should be paternal or conjugal power while there are fathers or husbands; but this is but playing with names. That which he would fallaciously insinuate is the thing in question to be proved, that is that the lordship which Adam had over the world, the supposed absolute universal dominion of Adam by right descending from him, the patriarchs did enjoy. If he affirms such an absolute monarchy continued to the flood, in the world, I would be glad to know what records he has it from; for I confess I cannot find a word of it in my Bible: if by Patriarchal power he means anything else, it is nothing to the matter in hand. And how the name patriarch in some part proves, that those, who are called by that name, had absolute monarchical power, I confess, I do not see, and therefore I think needs no answer till the argument from it be made out a little clearer.

Section 139. The three sons of Noah had the world, says our author, divided among them by their father, from them was the whole world overspread, p. 14. The world might be overspread by the offspring of Noah's sons, though he never divided the world among them; for the earth might be replenished without being divided: so that all our author's argument here proves no such division. However, I allow it to him, and then ask, the world being divided among them, which of the three was Adam's heir? If Adam's lordship, Adam's monarchy, by right descended only to the eldest, then the other two could be but his subjects, his slaves: if by right it descended to all three brothers, by the same right, it will descend to all mankind; and then it will be impossible what he says, p. 19. that heirs are lords of their brethren, should be true; but all brothers, and consequently all men, will be equal and independent, all heirs to Adam's monarchy, and consequently all monarchs too, one as much as another. But it will be said, Noah their father divided the world among them; so that our author will allow more to Noah, than he will to God almighty, for Observations, 211. he thought it hard, that God himself should give the world to Noah and his sons, to the prejudice of Noah's birthright: his words are, Noah was left sole heir to the world: why should it be thought that God would disinherit him of his birthright, and make him, of all men in the world, the only tenant in common with his children? and yet here he thinks it fit that Noah should disinherit Shem of his birthright, and divide the world between him and his brethren; so that this birthright, when our author pleases, must, and when he pleases must not, be sacred and inviolable.

Section 140. If Noah did divide the world between his sons, and his assignment of dominions to them were good, there is an end of divine institution; all our author's discourse of Adam's heir, with whatsoever he builds on it, is quite out of doors; the natural power of kings falls to the ground; and then the form of the power governing, and the person having that power, will not be (as he says they are, Observations, 254.) the ordinance of God, but they will be ordinances of man: for if the right of the heir be the ordinance of God, a divine right, no man, father or not father, can alter it: if it be not a divine right, it is only human, depending on the will of man: and so where human institution gives it not, the first-born has no right at all above his brethren; and men may put government into what hands, and under what form, they please.

Section 141. He goes on, Most of the civilest nations of the earth labor to fetch their original from some of the sons, or nephews of Noah, p. 14. How many do most of the civilest nations amount to? and who are they? I fear the Chinese, a very great and civil people, as well as several other people of the East, West, North and South, trouble not themselves much about this matter. All that believe the Bible, which I believe are our author's most of the civilest nations, must necessarily derive themselves from Noah; but for the rest of the world, they think little of his sons or nephews. But if the heralds and antiquaries of all nations, for it is these men generally that labor to find out the originals of nations, or all the nations themselves, should labor to fetch their original from some of the sons or nephews of Noah, what would this be to prove, that the lordship which Adam had over the whole world, by right descended to the patriarchs? Whoever, nations, or races of men, labor to fetch their original from, may be concluded to be thought by them, men of renown, famous to posterity, for the greatness of their virtues and actions; but beyond these they look not, nor consider who they were heirs to, but look on them as such as raised themselves, by their own virtue, to a degree that would give a luster to those who in future ages could pretend to derive themselves from them. But if it were Ogyges, Hercules, Brama, Tamerlane, Pharamond; nay, if Jupiter and Saturn were the names, from whence diverse races of men, both ancient and modern, have labored to derive their original; will that prove, that those men enjoyed the lordship of Adam, by right descending to them? If not, this is but a flourish of our author's to mislead his reader that in itself signifies nothing.

Section 142. To as much purpose is what he tells us, p. 15. concerning this division of the world, That some say it was by Lot, and others that Noah sailed round the Mediterranean in ten years, and divided the world into Asia, Africa and Europe, portions for his three sons. America then, it seems, was left to be his that could catch it. Why our author takes such pains to prove the division of the world by Noah to his sons, and will not leave out an imagination, though no better than a dream, that he can find anywhere to favor it, is hard to guess, since such a division, if it prove anything, must necessarily take away the title of Adam's heir; unless three brothers can all together be heirs of Adam; and therefore the following words, Howsoever the manner of this division be uncertain, yet it is most certain the division itself was by families from Noah and his children, over which the parents were heads and princes, p. 15. if allowed him to be true, and of any source to prove, that all the power in the world is nothing but the lordship of Adam's descending by right, they will only prove, that the fathers of the children are all heirs to this lordship of Adam: for if in those days Cham and Japheth, and other parents, besides the eldest son, were heads and princes over their families, and had a right to divide the earth by families, what hinders younger brothers, being fathers of families, from having the same right? If Cham and Japheth were princes by right descending to them, notwithstanding any title of heir in their eldest brother, younger brothers by the same right descending to them are princes now; and so all our author's natural power of kings will reach no farther than their own children, and no kingdom, by this natural right, can be bigger than a family: for either this lordship of Adam over the whole world, by right descends only to the eldest son, and then there can be but one heir, as our author says, p. 19. or else, it by right descends to all the sons equally, and then every father of a family will have it, as well as the three sons of Noah: take which you will, it destroys the present governments and kingdoms, that are now in the world, since whoever has this natural power of a king, by right descending to him, must have it, either as our author tells us Cain had it, and be lord over his brethren, and so be alone king of the whole world; or else, as he tells us here, Shem, Cham and Japheth had it, three brothers, and so be only prince of his own family, and all families independent one of another: all the world must be only one empire by the right of the next heir, or else every family be a distinct government of itself, by the lordship of Adam's descending to parents of families.

Section 143. And to this only tend all the proofs he here gives us of the descent of Adam's lordship: for continuing his story of this descent, he says, in the dispersion of Babel, we must certainly find the establishment of royal power, throughout the kingdoms of the world, p. 14. If you must find it, pray do, and you will help us to a new piece of history: but you must show it us before we shall be bound to believe, that regal power was established in the world upon your principles: for, that regal power was established in the kingdoms of the world, I think nobody will dispute; but that there should be kingdoms in the world, whose several kings enjoyed their crowns, by right descending to them from Adam, that we think not only apocryphal, but also utterly impossible. If our author has no better foundation for his monarchy than a supposition of what was done at the dispersion of Babel, the monarchy he erects thereon, whose top is to reach to heaven to unite mankind, will serve only to divide and scatter them as that tower did; and, instead of establishing civil government and order in the world, will produce nothing but confusion.

Section 144. For he tells us, the nations they were divided into, were distinct families, which had fathers for rulers over them; whereby it appears, that even in the confusion, God was careful to preserve the fatherly authority, by distributing the diversity of languages according to the diversity of families, p. 14. It would have been a hard matter for anyone but our author to have found out so plainly, in the text he here brings, that all the nations in that dispersion were governed by fathers, and that God was careful to preserve the fatherly authority. The words of the text are; These are the sons of Shem after their families, after their tongues in their lands, after their nations; and the same thing is said of Cham and Japheth, after an enumeration of their posterities; in all which there is not one word said of their governors, or forms of government; of fathers, or fatherly authority. But our author, who is very quick sighted to spy out fatherhood, where nobody else could see any the least glimpses of it, tells us positively their rulers were fathers, and God was careful to preserve the fatherly authority; and why? Because those of the same family spoke the same language, and so of necessity in the division kept together. Just as if one should argue thus: Hannibal in his army, consisting of divers nations, kept those of the same language together; therefore fathers were captains of each band, and Hannibal was careful of the fatherly authority: or in peopling of Carolina, the English, French, Scotch and Welch that are there, plant themselves together, and by them the country is divided in their lands after their tongues, after their families, after their nations; therefore care was taken of the fatherly authority: or because, in many parts of America, every little tribe was a distinct people, with a different language, one should infer, that therefore God was careful to preserve the fatherly authority, or that therefore their rulers enjoyed Adam's lordship by right descending to them, though we know not who were their governors, nor what their form of government, but only that they were divided into little independent societies, speaking different languages.

Section 145. The Scripture says not a word of their rulers or forms of government, but only gives an account, how mankind came to be divided into distinct languages and nations; and therefore it is not to argue from the authority of Scripture, to tell us positively, fathers were their rulers, when the Scripture says no such thing; but to set up fancies of one's own brain, when we confidently aver matter of fact, where records are utterly silent. Upon a like ground, i.e. none at all, he says, That they were not confused multitudes without heads and governors, and at liberty to choose what governors or governments they pleased.

Section 146. For I demand, when mankind were all yet of one language, all congregated in the plain of Shinar, were they then all under one monarch, who enjoyed the lordship of Adam by right descending to him? If they were not, there were then no thoughts, it is plain, of Adam's heir, no right to government known then upon that title; no care taken, by God or man, of Adam's fatherly authority. If when mankind were but one people, dwelt all together, and were of one language, and were upon building a city together; and when it was plain, they could not but know the right heir, for Shem lived till Isaac's time, a long while after the division at Babel; if then, I say, they were not under the monarchical government of Adam's fatherhood, by right descending to the heir, it is plain there was no regard had to the fatherhood, no monarchy acknowledged due to Adam's heir, no empire of Shem's in Asia, and consequently no such division of the world by Noah, as our author has talked of. As far as we can conclude anything from Scripture in this matter, it seems from this place, that if they had any government, it was rather a commonwealth than an absolute monarchy: for the Scripture tells us, Gen. xi. They said: it was not a prince commanded the building of this city and tower, it was not by the command of one monarch, but by the consultation of many, a free people; let us build a city: they built it for themselves as free-men, not as slaves for their lord and master: that we be not scattered abroad; having a city once built, and fixed habitations to settle our abodes and families. This was the consultation and design of a people, that were at liberty to part asunder, but desired to keep in one body, and could not have been either necessary or likely in men tied together under the government of one monarch, who if they had been, as our author tells us, all slaves under the absolute dominion of a monarch, needed not have taken such care to hinder themselves from wandering out of the reach of his dominion. I demand whether this be not plainer in Scripture than anything of Adam's heir or fatherly authority?

Section 147. But if being, as God says, Gen. xi. 6. one people, they had one ruler, one king by natural right, absolute and supreme over them, what care had God to preserve the paternal authority of the supreme fatherhood, if on a sudden he suffer 72 (for so many our author talks of) distinct nations to be erected out of it, under distinct governors, and at once to withdraw themselves from the obedience of their sovereign? This is to entitle God's care how, and to what we please. Can it be sense to say, that God was careful to preserve the fatherly authority in those who had it not? for if these were subjects under a supreme prince, what authority had they? Was it an instance of God's care to preserve the fatherly authority, when he took away the true supreme fatherhood of the natural monarch? Can it be reason to say, that God, for the preservation of fatherly authority, lets several new governments with their governors stare up, who could not all have fatherly authority? And is it not as much reason to say, that God is careful to destroy fatherly authority, when he suffers one, who is in possession of it, to have his government torn in pieces, and shared by several of his subjects? Would it not be an argument just like this, for monarchical government, to say, when any monarchy was shattered to pieces, and divided among revolted subjects, that God was careful to preserve monarchical power, by rending a settled empire into a multitude of little governments? If anyone will say, that what happens in providence to be preserved, God is careful to preserve as a thing therefore to be esteemed by men as necessary or useful, it is a peculiar propriety of speech, which everyone will not think fit to imitate: but this I am sure is impossible to be either proper, or true speaking, that Shem, for example, (for he was then alive,) should have fatherly authority, or sovereignty by right of fatherhood, over that one people at Babel, and that the next moment, Shem yet living, 72 others should have fatherly authority, or sovereignty by right of fatherhood, over the same people, divided into so many distinct governments: either these 72 fathers actually were rulers, just before the confusion, and then they were not one people, but that God himself says they were; or else they were a commonwealth, and then where was monarchy? or else these 72 fathers had fatherly authority, but knew it not. Strange! that fatherly authority should be the only original of government among men, and yet all mankind not know it; and stranger yet, that the confusion of tongues should reveal it to them all of a sudden, that in an instant these 72 should know that they had fatherly power, and all others know that they were to obey it in them, and everyone know that particular fatherly authority to which he was a subject. He that can think this arguing from Scripture, may from thence make out what model of an Utopia will best suit with his fancy or interest; and this fatherhood, thus disposed of, will justify both a prince who claims an universal monarchy, and his subjects, who, being fathers of families, shall quit all subjection to him, and canton his empire into less governments for themselves; for it will always remain a doubt in which of these the fatherly authority resided, till our author resolves us, whether Shem, who was then alive, or these 72 new princes, beginning so many new empires in his dominions, and over his subjects, had right to govern, since our author tells us, that both one and the other had fatherly, which is supreme authority, and are brought in by him as instances of those who did enjoy the lordships of Adam by right descending to them, which was as large and ample as the most absolute dominion of any monarch. This at least is unavoidable, that if God was careful to preserve the fatherly authority, in the 72 new-erected nations, it necessarily follows, that he was as careful to destroy all pretences of Adam's heir; since he took care, and therefore did preserve the fatherly authority in so many, at least 71, that could not possibly be Adam's heirs, when the right heir (if God had ever ordained any such inheritance) could not but be known, Shem then living, and they being all one people.

Section 148. Nimrod is his next instance of enjoying this Patriarchal power, p. 16. but I know not for what reason our author seems a little unkind to him, and says, that he against right enlarged his empire, by seizing violently on the rights of other lords of families. These lords of families here were called fathers of families, in his account of the dispersion at Babel: but it matters not how they were called, so we know who they are; for this fatherly authority must be in them, either as heirs to Adam, and so there could not be 72, nor above one at once; or else as natural parents over their children, and so every father will have paternal authority over his children by the same right, and in as large extent as those 72 had, and so be independent princes over their own offspring. Taking his lords of families in this later sense, (as it is hard to give those words any other sense in this place) he gives us a very pretty account of the original of monarchy, in these following words, p. 16. And in this sense he may be said to be the author and founder of monarchy, that is

As against right seizing violently on the rights of fathers over their children; which paternal authority, if it be in them, by right of nature, (for else how could those 72 come by it?) nobody can take from them without their own consents; and then I desire our author and his friends to consider, how far this will concern other princes, and whether it will not, according to his conclusion of that paragraph, resolve all regal power of those, whose dominions extend beyond their families, either into tyranny and usurpation, or election and consent of fathers of families, which will differ very little from consent of the people.

Section 149. All his instances, in the next section, p. 17. of the 12 dukes of Edom, the nine kings in a little corner of Asia in Abraham's days, the 31 kings in Canaan destroyed by Joshua, and the care he takes to prove that these were all sovereign princes, and that every town in those days had a king, are so many direct proofs against him, that it was not the lordship of Adam by right descending to them, that made kings: for if they had held their royalties by that title, either there must have been but one sovereign over them all, or else every father of a family had been as good a prince, and had as good a claim to royalty, as these: for if all the sons of Esau had each of them, the younger as well as the eldest, the right of fatherhood, and so were sovereign princes after their father's death, the same right had their sons after them, and so on to all posterity; which will limit all the natural power of fatherhood, only to be over the issue of their own bodies, and their descendents; which power of fatherhood dies with the head of each family, and makes way for the like power of fatherhood to take place in each of his sons over their respective posterities: whereby the power of fatherhood will be preserved indeed, and is intelligible, but will not be at all to our author's purpose. None of the instances he brings are proofs of any power they had, as heirs of Adam's paternal authority by the title of his fatherhood descending to them; no, nor of any power they had by virtue of their own: for Adam's fatherhood being over all mankind, it could descend but to one at once, and from him to his right heir only, and so there could by that title be but one king in the world at a time: and by right of fatherhood, not descending from Adam, it must be only as they themselves were fathers, and so could be over none but their own posterity. So that if those 12 dukes of Edom; if Abraham and the nine kings his neighbors; if Jacob and Esau, and the 31 kings in Canaan, the 72 kings mutilated by Adonibeseck, the 32 kings that came to Benhadad, the 70 kings of Greece making war at Troy, were, as our author contends, all of them sovereign princes; it is evident that kings derived their power from some other original than fatherhood, since some of these had power over more than their own posterity; and it is demonstration, they could not be all heirs to Adam: for I challenge any man to make any pretence to power by right of fatherhood, either intelligible or possible in anyone, otherwise, than either as Adam's heir, or as progenitor over his own descendents, naturally sprung from him. And if our author could show that anyone of these princes, of which he gives us here so large a catalogue, had his authority by either of these titles, I think I might yield him the cause; though it is manifest they are all impertinent, and directly contrary to what he brings them to prove, that is That the lordship which Adam had over the world by right descended to the patriarchs.

Section 150. Having told us, p. 16, That the Patriarchal government continued in Abraham, Isaac, and Jacob, until the Egyptian bondage, p. 17. he tells us, By manifest footsteps we may trace this paternal government unto the Israelites coming into Egypt, where the exercise of supreme Patriarchal government was intermitted, because they were in subjection to a stronger prince. What these footsteps are of paternal government, in our author's sense, i.e. of absolute monarchical power descending from Adam, and exercised by right of fatherhood, we have seen, that is for 2290 years no footsteps at all; since in all that time he cannot produce anyone example of any person who claimed or exercised regal authority by right of fatherhood; or show anyone who being a king was Adam's heir: all that his proofs amount to, is only this, that there were fathers, patriarchs and kings, in that age of the world; but that the fathers and patriarchs had any absolute arbitrary power, or by what titles those kings had theirs, and of what extent it was, the Scripture is wholly silent; it is manifest by right of fatherhood they neither did, nor could claim any title to dominion and empire.

Section 151. To say, that the exercise of supreme Patriarchal government was intermitted, because they were in subjection to a stronger prince, proves nothing but what I before suspected, that is That Patriarchal jurisdiction or government is a fallacious expression, and does not in our author signify (what he would yet insinuate by it) paternal and regal power, such an absolute sovereignty as he supposes was in Adam.

Section 152. For how can he say that Patriarchal jurisdiction was intermitted in Egypt, where there was a king, under whose regal government the Israelites were, if Patriarchal were absolute monarchical jurisdiction? And if it were not, but something else, why does he make such ado about a power not in question, and nothing to the purpose? The exercise of Patriarchal jurisdiction, if Patriarchal be regal, was not intermitted while the Israelites were in Egypt. It is true, the exercise of regal power was not then in the hands of any of the promised seed of Abraham, nor before neither that I know; but what is that to the intermission of regal authority, as descending from Adam, unless our author will have it, that this chosen line of Abraham had the right of inheritance to Adam's lordship? and then to what purpose are his instances of the 72 rulers, in whom the fatherly authority was preserved in the confusion at Babel? Why does he bring the 12 princes sons of Ishmael; and the dukes of Edom, and join them with Abraham, Isaac, and Jacob, as examples of the exercise of true Patriarchal government, if the exercise of Patriarchal jurisdiction were intermitted in the world, whenever the heirs of Jacob had not supreme power? I fear, supreme Patriarchal jurisdiction was not only intermitted, but from the time of the Egyptian bondage quite lost in the world, since it will be hard to find, from that time downwards, anyone who exercised it as an inheritance descending to him from the patriarchs Abraham, Isaac, and Jacob. I imagined monarchical government would have served his turn in the hands of Pharaoh, or anybody. But one cannot easily discover in all places what his discourse tends to, as particularly in this place it is not obvious to guess what he drives at, when he says, the exercise of supreme Patriarchal jurisdiction in Egypt, or how this serves to make out the descent of Adam's lordship to the patriarchs, or anybody else.

Section 153. For I thought he had been giving us out of Scripture, proofs and examples of monarchical government, founded on paternal authority, descending from Adam; and not an history of the Jews: among whom yet we find no kings, until many years after they were a people: and when kings were their rulers, there is not the least mention or room for a pretence that they were heirs to Adam, or kings by paternal authority. I expected, talking so much as he does of Scripture, that he would have produced thence a series of monarchs, whose titles were clear to Adam's fatherhood, and who, as heirs to him, owned and exercised paternal jurisdiction over their subjects, and that this was the true patriarchical government; whereas he neither proves, that the patriarchs were kings; nor that either kings or patriarchs were heirs to Adam, or so much as pretended to it: and one may as well prove, that the patriarchs were all absolute monarchs; that the power both of patriarchs and kings was only paternal; and that this power descended to them from Adam: I say all these propositions may be as well proved by a confused account of a multitude of little kings in the West Indies, out of Ferdinando Soto, or any of our late histories of the Northern America, or by our author's 70 kings of Greece, out of Homer, as by anything he brings out of Scripture, in that multitude of kings he has reckoned up.

Section 154. And methinks he should have let Homer and his wars of Troy alone, since his great zeal to truth or monarchy carried him to such a pitch of transport against philosophers and poets, that he tells us in his preface, that there are too many in these days, who please themselves in running after the opinions of philosophers and poets, to find out such an original of government, as might promise them some title to liberty, to the great scandal of Christianity, and bringing in of atheism. And yet these heathens, philosopher Aristotle, and poet Homer, are not rejected by our zealous Christian politician, whenever they offer anything that seems to serve his turn; whether to the great scandal of Christianity and bringing in of atheism, let him look. This I cannot but observe, in authors who it is visible write not for truth, how ready zeal for interest and party is to entitle Christianity to their designs, and to charge atheism on those who will not without examining submit to their doctrines, and blindly swallow their nonsense.

But to return to his Scripture history, our author further tells us, p. 18. that after the return of the Israelites out of bondage, God, out of a special care of them, chose Moses and Joshua successively to govern as princes in the place and stead of the supreme fathers. If it be true, that they returned out of bondage, it must be into a state of freedom, and must imply, that both before and after this bondage they were free, unless our author will say, that changing of masters is returning out of bondage; or that a slave returns out of bondage, when he is removed from one galley to another. If then they returned out of bondage, it is plain that in those days, whatever our author in his preface says to the contrary, there were difference between a son, a subject, and a slave; and that neither the patriarchs before, nor their rulers after this Egyptian bondage, numbered their sons or subjects among their possessions, and disposed of them with as absolute a dominion, as they did their other goods.

Section 155. This is evident in Jacob, to whom Reuben offered his two sons as pledges; and Judah was at last surety for Benjamin's safe return out of Egypt: which all had been vain, superfluous, and but a sort of mockery, if Jacob had had the same power over everyone of his family, as he had over his ox or his ass, as an owner over his substance; and the offers that Reuben or Judah made had been such a security for returning of Benjamin, as if a man should take two lambs out of his lord's flock, and offer one as security, that he will safely restore the other.

Section 156. When they were out of this bondage, what then? God out of a special care of them, the Israelites. It is well that once in his book he will allow God to have any care of the people; for in other places he speaks of mankind, as if God had no care of any part of them, but only of their monarchs, and that the rest of the people, the societies of men, were made as so many herds of cattle, only for the service, use, and pleasure of their princes.

Section 157. God chose Moses and Joshua successively to govern as princes; a shrewd argument our author has found out to prove God's care of the fatherly authority, and Adam's heirs, that here, as an expression of his care of his own people, he chooses those for princes over them, that had not the least pretence to either. The persons chosen were, Moses of the tribe of Levi, and Joshua of the tribe of Ephraim, neither of which had any title of fatherhood. But says our author, they were in the place and stead of the supreme fathers. If God had anywhere as plainly declared his choice of such fathers to be rulers, as he did of Moses and Joshua, we might believe Moses and Joshua were in their place and stead: but that being the question in debate, until that be better proved, Moses being chosen by God to be ruler of his people, will no more prove that government belonged to Adam's heir, or to the fatherhood, than God's choosing Aaron of the tribe of Levi to be priest, will prove that the priesthood belonged to Adam's heir, or the prime fathers; since God would choose Aaron to be priest, and Moses ruler in Israel, though neither of those offices were settled on Adam's heir, or the fatherhood.

Section 158. Our author goes on, and after them likewise for a time he raised up judges, to defend his people in time of peril, p. 18. This proves fatherly authority to be the original of government, and that it descended from Adam to his heirs, just as well as what went before: only here our author seems to confess, that these judges, who were all the governors they then had, were only men of valor, whom they made their generals to defend them in time of peril; and cannot God raise up such men, unless fatherhood have a title to government? But says our author, when God gave the Israelites kings, he re-established the ancient and prime right of lineal succession to paternal government, p. 18.

Section 160. How did God re-establish it? by a law, a positive command? We find no such thing. Our author means then, that when God gave them a king, in giving them a king, he re-established the right, etc. To re-establish *de facto* the right of lineal succession to paternal government, is to put a man in possession of that government which his fathers did enjoy, and he by lineal succession had a right to: for, first, if it were another government than what his ancestors had, it was not succeeding to an ancient right, but beginning a new one: for if a prince should give a man, besides his ancient patrimony, which for some ages his family had been diseased of, an additional estate, never before in the possession of his ancestors, he could not be said to re-establish the right of lineal succession to any more than what had been formerly enjoyed by his ancestors. If therefore the power the kings of Israel had, were anything more than Isaac or Jacob had, it was not the re-establishing in them the right of succession to a power, but giving them a new power, however you please to call it, paternal or not: and whether Isaac and Jacob had the same power that the kings of Israel had, I desire anyone, by what has been above said, to consider; and I do not think they will find, that either Abraham, Isaac, or Jacob, had any regal power at all.

Section 161. Next, there can be no re-establishment of the prime and ancient right of lineal succession to anything, unless he, that is put in possession of it, has the right to succeed, and be the true and next heir to him he succeeds to. Can that be a re-establishment, which begins in a new family? Or that the re-establishment of an ancient right of lineal succession, when a crown is given to one, who has no right of succession to it, and who, if the lineal succession had gone on, had been out of all possibility of pretence to it? Saul, the first king God gave the Israelites, was of the tribe of Benjamin. Was the ancient and prime right of lineal succession re-established in him? The next was David, the youngest son of Jesse, of the posterity of Judah, Jacob's third son. Was the ancient and prime right of lineal succession to paternal government re-established in him? or in Solomon, his younger son and successor in the throne? or in Jeroboam over the ten tribes? or in Athaliah, a woman who reigned six years an utter stranger to the royal blood? If the ancient and prime right of lineal succession to paternal government were re-established in any of these or their posterity, the ancient and prime right of lineal succession to paternal government belongs to younger brothers as well as elder, and may be re-established in any man living; for whatever younger brothers, by ancient and prime right of lineal succession, may have as well as the elder, that every man living may have a right to, by lineal succession, and Sir Robert as well as any other. And so what a brave right of lineal succession, to his paternal or regal government, our author has re-established, for the securing the rights and inheritance of crowns, where everyone may have it, let the world consider.

Section 162. But says our author however, p. 19. whensoever God made choice of any special person to be king, he intended that the issue also should have benefit thereof, as being comprehended sufficiently in the person of the father, although the father was only named in the grant. This yet will not help out succession; for if, as our author says, the benefit of the grant be intended to the issue of the grantee, this will not direct the succession; since, if God give anything to a man and his issue in general, the claim cannot be to anyone of that issue in particular; everyone that is of his race will have an equal right. If it be said, our author meant heir, I believe our author was as willing as anybody to have used that word, if it would have served his turn: but Solomon, who succeeded David in the throne, being no more his heir than Jeroboam, who succeeded him in the government of the ten tribes, was his issue, our author had reason to avoid saying, That God intended it to the heirs, when that would not hold in a succession, which our author could not except against; and so he has left his succession as undetermined, as if he had said nothing about it: for if the regal power be given by God to a man and his issue, as the land of Canaan was to Abraham and his seed, must they not all have a title to it, all share in it? And one may as well say that by God's grant to Abraham and his seed, the land of Canaan was to belong only to one of his seed exclusive of all others, as by God's grant of dominion to a man and his issue, this dominion was to belong in peculiar to one of his issue exclusive of all others.

Section 163. But how will our author prove that whensoever God made choice of any special person to be a king, he intended that the (I suppose he means his) issue also should have benefit thereof? Has he so soon forgotten Moses and Joshua, whom in this very section, he says, God out of a special care chose to govern as princes and the judges that God raised up? Had not these princes, having the authority of the supreme fatherhood, the same power that the kings had; and being specially chosen by God himself, should not their issue have the benefit of that choice, as well as David's or Solomon's? If these had the paternal authority put into their hands immediately by God, why had not their issue the benefit of this grant in a succession to this power? or if they had it as Adam's heirs, why did not their heirs enjoy it after them by right descending to them? for they could not be heirs to one another. Was the power the same, and from the same original, in Moses, Joshua and the Judges, as it was in David and the Kings; and was it inheritable in one, and not in the other? If it was not paternal authority, then God's own people were governed by those that had not paternal authority, and those governors did well enough without it: if it were paternal authority, and God chose the persons that were to exercise it, our author's rule fails, that whensoever God makes choice of any person to be supreme ruler (for I suppose the name king has no spell in it, it is not the title, but the power makes the difference) he intends that the issue also should have the benefit of it, since from their coming out of Egypt to David's time, 400 years, the issue was never so sufficiently comprehended in the person of the father, as that any son, after the death of his father, succeeded to the government among all those judges that judged Israel. If, to avoid this, it be said, God always chose the person of the successor, and so, transferring the fatherly authority to him, excluded his issue from succeeding to it, that is manifestly not so in the story of Jephtha, where he reconciled with the people, and they made him judge over them, as is plain, Judg. 11.

Section 164. It is in vain then to say, that whensoever God chooses any special person to have the exercise of paternal authority, (for if that be not to be king, I desire to know the difference between a king and one having the exercise of paternal authority) he intends the issue also should have the benefit of it, since we find the authority, the judges had, ended with them, and descended not to their issue; and if the judges had not paternal authority, I fear it will trouble our author, or any of the friends to his principles, to tell who had then the paternal authority, that is, the government and supreme power among the Israelites; and I suspect they must confess that the chosen people of God continued a people several hundreds of years, without any knowledge or thought of this paternal authority, or any appearance of monarchical government at all.

Section 165. To be satisfied of this, he need but read the story of the Levite, and the war thereupon with the Benjamites, in the three last chapters of Judges; and when he finds, that the Levite appeals to the people for justice that it was the tribes and the congregation, that debated, resolved, and directed all that was done on that occasion; he must conclude, either that God was not careful to preserve the fatherly authority among his own chosen people; or else that the fatherly authority may be preserved, where there is no monarchical government: if the latter, then it will follow, that though fatherly authority be never so well proved, yet it will not infer a necessity of monarchical government; if the former, it will seem very strange and improbable, that God should ordain fatherly authority to be so sacred among the sons of men, that there could be no power, or government without it, and yet that among his own people, even while he is providing a government for them, and therein prescribes rules to the several states and relations of men, this great and fundamental one, this most material and necessary of all the rest, should be concealed, and lie neglected for 400 years after.

Section 166. Before I leave this, I must ask how our author knows that whensoever God makes choice of any special person to be king, he intends that the issue should have the benefit thereof? Does God by the law of nature or revelation say so? By the same law also he must say, which of his issue must enjoy the crown in succession, and so point out the heir, or else leave his issue to divide or scramble for the government: both alike absurd, and such as will destroy the benefit of such grant to the issue. When any such declaration of God's intention is produced, it will be our duty to believe God intends it so; but till that be done, our author must show us some better warrant, before we shall be obliged to receive him as the authentic revealer of God's intentions.

Section 167. The issue, says our author, is comprehended sufficiently in the person of the father, although the father only was named in the grant: and yet God, when he gave the land of Canaan to Abraham, Gen. xiii. 15. thought fit to put his seed into the grant too: so the priesthood was given to Aaron and his seed; and the crown God gave not only to David, but his seed also: and however our author assures us that God intends, that the issue should have the benefit of it, when he chooses any person to be king, yet we see that the kingdom which he gave to Saul, without mentioning his seed after him, never came to any of his issue: and why, when God chose a person to be king, he should intend, that his issue should have the benefit of it, more than when he chose one to be judge in Israel, I would fain know a reason; or why does a grant of fatherly authority to a king more comprehend the issue, than when a like grant is made to a judge? Is paternal authority by right to descend to the issue of one, and not of the other? There will need some reason to be shown of this difference, more than the name, when the thing given is the same fatherly authority, and the manner of giving it, God's choice of the person, the same too; for I suppose our author, when he says, God raised up judges, will by no means allow, they were chosen by the people.

Section 168. But since our author has so confidently assured us of the care of God to preserve the fatherhood, and pretends to build all he says upon the authority of the Scripture, we may well expect that that people, whose law, constitution and history is chiefly contained in the Scripture, should furnish him with the clearest instances of God's care of preserving the fatherly authority, in that people who it is agreed he had a most peculiar care of. Let us see then what state this paternal authority or government was in among the Jews, from their beginning to be a people. It was omitted, by our author's confession, from their coming into Egypt, until their return out of that bondage, above 200 years: from thence until God gave the Israelites a king, about 400 years more, our author gives but a very slender account of it; nor indeed all that time are there the least footsteps of paternal or regal government among them. But then says our author, God re-established the ancient and prime right of lineal succession to paternal government.

Section 169. What a lineal succession to paternal government was then established, we have already seen. I only now consider how long this lasted, and that was to their captivity, about 500 years: from thence to their destruction by the Romans, above 650 years after, the ancient and prime right of lineal succession to paternal government was again lost, and they continued a people in the promised land without it. So that of 1750 years that they were God's peculiar people, they had hereditary kingly government among them not one third of the time; and of that time there is not the least footstep of one moment of paternal government, nor the re-establishment of the ancient and prime right of lineal succession to it, whether we suppose it to be derived, as from its fountain, from David, Saul, Abraham, or, which upon our author's principles is the only true, from Adam.

OF CIVIL-GOVERNMENT

BOOK II

CHAPTER I.

Section 1. It having been shown in the foregoing discourse,

1. That Adam had not, either by natural right of fatherhood, or by positive donation from God, any such authority over his children, or dominion over the world, as is pretended:

2. That if he had, his heirs, yet, had no right to it:

3. That if his heirs had, there being no law of nature nor positive law of God that determines which is the right heir in all cases that may arise, the right of succession, and consequently of bearing rule, could not have been certainly determined:

4. That if even that had been determined, yet the knowledge of which is the eldest line of Adam's posterity, being so long since utterly lost, that in the races of mankind and families of the world, there remains not to one above another, the least pretence to be the eldest house, and to have the right of inheritance:

All these premises having, as I think, been clearly made out, it is impossible that the rulers now on earth should make any benefit, or derive any the least shadow of authority from that, which is held to be the fountain of all power, Adam's private dominion and paternal jurisdiction; so that he that will not give just occasion to think that all government in the world is the product only of force and violence, and that men live together by no other rules but that of beasts, where the strongest carries it, and so lay a foundation for perpetual disorder and mischief, tumult, sedition and rebellion, (things that the followers of that hypothesis so loudly cry out against) must of necessity find out another rise of government, another original of political power, and another way of designing and knowing the persons that have it, than what Sir Robert Filmer has taught us.

Section 2. To this purpose, I think it may not be amiss, to set down what I take to be political power; that the power of a magistrate over a subject may be distinguished from that of a father over his children, a master over his servant, a husband over his wife, and a lord over his slave. All which distinct powers happening sometimes together in the same man, if he be considered under these different relations, it may help us to distinguish these powers one from another, and show the difference between a ruler of a commonwealth, a father of a family, and a captain of a galley.

Section 3. Political power, then, I take to be a right of making laws with penalties of death, and consequently all less penalties, for the regulating and preserving of property, and of employing the force of the community, in the execution of such laws, and in the defense of the commonwealth from foreign injury; and all this only for the public good.

CHAPTER II.

Of the State of Nature.

Section 4. To understand political power right, and derive it from its original, we must consider, what state all men are naturally in, and that is, a state of perfect freedom to order their actions, and dispose of their possessions and persons, as they think fit, within the bounds of the law of nature, without asking leave, or depending upon the will of any other man.

A state also of equality, wherein all the power and jurisdiction is reciprocal, no one having more than another; there being nothing more evident, than that creatures of the same species and rank, promiscuously born to all the same advantages of nature, and the use of the same faculties, should also be equal one among another without subordination or subjection, unless the lord and master of them all should, by any manifest declaration of his will, set one above another, and confer on him, by an evident and clear appointment, an undoubted right to dominion and sovereignty.

Section 5. This equality of men by nature, the judicious Hooker looks upon as so evident in itself, and beyond all question, that he makes it the foundation of that obligation to mutual love among men, on which he builds the duties they owe one another, and from whence he derives the great maxims of justice and charity. His words are,

The like natural inducement has brought men to know that it is no less their duty, to love others than themselves; for seeing those things which are equal, must needs all have one measure; if I cannot but wish to receive good, even as much at every man's hands, as any man can wish unto his own soul, how should I look to have any part of my desire herein satisfied, unless myself be careful to satisfy the like desire, which is undoubtedly in other men, being of one and the same nature? To have anything offered them repugnant to this desire, must needs in all respects grieve them as much as me; so that if I do harm, I must look to suffer, there being no reason that others should show greater measure of love to me, than they have by me showed unto them: my desire therefore to be loved of my equals in nature, as much as possible may be, impose upon me a natural duty of bearing to them-ward fully the like affection; from which relation of equality between ourselves and them that are as ourselves, what several rules and canons natural reason has drawn, for direction of life, no man is ignorant. Eccl. Pol. Lib. 1.

Section 6. But though this is a state of liberty, yet it is not a state of license: though man in that state have an uncontrollable liberty to dispose of his person or possessions, yet he has not liberty to destroy himself, or so much as any creature in his possession, but where some nobler use than its bare preservation calls for it. The state of nature has a law of nature to govern it, which obliges everyone: and reason, which is that law, teaches all mankind, who will but consult it, that being all equal and independent, no one ought to harm another in his life, health, liberty, or possessions: for men being all the workmanship of one omnipotent, and infinitely wise maker; all the servants of one sovereign master, sent into the world by his order, and about his business; they are his property, whose workmanship they are, made to last during his, not one another's pleasure: and being furnished with like faculties, sharing all in one community of nature, there cannot be supposed any such subordination among us, that may authorize us to destroy one another, as if we were made for one another's uses, as the inferior ranks of creatures are for ours. Everyone, as he is bound to preserve himself, and not to quit his station willfully, so by the like reason, when his own preservation comes not in competition, ought he, as much as he can, to preserve the rest of mankind, and may not, unless it be to do justice on an offender, take away, or impair the life, or what tends to the preservation of the life, the liberty, health, limb, or goods of another.

Section 7. And that all men may be restrained from invading others rights, and from doing hurt to one another, and the law of nature be observed, which wills the peace and preservation of all mankind, the execution of the law of nature is, in that state, put into every man's hands, whereby everyone has a right to punish the transgressors of that law to such a degree, as may hinder its violation: for the law of nature would, as all other laws that concern men in this world, be in vain, if there were nobody that in the state of nature had a power to execute that law, and thereby preserve the innocent and restrain offenders. And if anyone in the state of nature may punish another for any evil he has done, everyone may do so: for in that state of perfect equality, where naturally there is no superiority or jurisdiction of one over another, what any may do in prosecution of that law, everyone must needs have a right to do.

Section 8. And thus, in the state of nature, one man comes by a power over another; but yet no absolute or arbitrary power, to use a criminal, when he has got him in his hands, according to the passionate heats, or boundless extravagancy of his own will; but only to punish to him, so far as calm reason and conscience dictate, what is proportionate to his transgression, which is so much as may serve for reparation and restraint: for these two are the only reasons, why one man may lawfully do harm to another, which is that we call punishment. In transgressing the law of nature, the offender declares himself to live by another rule than that of reason and common equity, which is that measure God has set to the actions of men, for their mutual security; and so he becomes dangerous to mankind, the tie, which is to secure them from injury and violence, being slighted and broken by him. Which being a trespass against the whole species, and the peace and safety of it, provided for by the law of nature, every man upon this score, by the right he has to preserve mankind in general, may restrain, or where it is necessary, destroy things noxious to them, and so may bring such evil on anyone, who has transgressed that law, as may make him repent the doing of it, and thereby deter him, and by his example others, from doing the like mischief. And in this case, and upon this ground, every man has a right to punish the offender, and be executioner of the law of nature.

Section 9. I doubt not but this will seem a very strange doctrine to some men: but before they condemn it, I desire them to resolve me, by what right any prince or state can put to death, or punish an alien, for any crime he commits in their country. It is certain their laws, by virtue of any sanction they receive from the promulgated will of the legislative, reach not a stranger: they speak not to him, nor, if they did, is he bound to hearken to them. The legislative authority, by which they are in force over the subjects of that commonwealth, has no power over him. Those who have the supreme power of making laws in England, France or Holland, are to an Indian, but like the rest of the world, men without authority: and therefore, if by the law of nature every man has not a power to punish offences against it, as he soberly judges the case to require, I see not how the magistrates of any community can punish an alien of another country; since, in reference to him, they can have no more power than what every man naturally may have over another.

Section 10. Besides the crime which consists in violating the law, and varying from the right rule of reason, whereby a man so far becomes degenerate, and declares himself to quit the principles of human nature, and to be a noxious creature, there is commonly injury done to some person or other, and some other man receives damage by his transgression: in which case he who has received any damage, has, besides the right of punishment common to him with other men, a particular right to seek reparation from him that has done it: and any other person, who finds it just, may also join with him that is injured, and assist him in recovering from the offender so much as may make satisfaction for the harm he has suffered.

Section 11. From these two distinct rights, the one of punishing the crime for restraint, and preventing the like offence, which right of punishing is in everybody; the other of taking reparation, which belongs only to the injured party, comes it to pass that the magistrate, who by being magistrate has the common right of punishing put into his hands, can often, where the public good demands not the execution of the law, remit the punishment of criminal offences by his own authority, but yet cannot remit the satisfaction due to any private man for the damage he has received. That, he who has suffered the damage has a right to demand in his own name, and he alone can remit: the damned person has this power of appropriating to himself the goods or service of the offender, by right of self-preservation, as every man has a power to punish the crime, to prevent its being committed again, by the right he has of preserving all mankind, and doing all reasonable things he can in order to that end: and thus it is, that every man, in the state of nature, has a power to kill a murderer, both to deter others from doing the like injury, which no reparation can compensate, by the example of the punishment that attends it from everybody, and also to secure men from the attempts of a criminal, who having renounced reason, the common rule and measure God has given to mankind, has, by the unjust violence and slaughter he has committed upon one, declared war against all mankind, and therefore may be destroyed as a lion or a tiger, one of those wild savage beasts, with whom men can have no society nor security: and upon this is grounded that great law of nature, Whoso sheds man's blood, by man shall his blood be shed. And Cain was so fully convinced that everyone had a right to destroy such a criminal, that after the murder of his brother, he cries out, Everyone that finds shall slay me; so plain was it written in the hearing of all mankind.

Section 12. By the same reason may a man in the state of nature punish the lesser breaches of that law? It will perhaps be demanded, with death? I answer, each transgression may be punished to that degree, and with so much severity, as will suffice to make it an ill bargain to the offender, give him cause to repent, and terrify others from doing the like. Every offence, that can be committed in the state of nature, may in the state of nature be also punished equally, and as far as it may, in a commonwealth: for though it would be besides my present purpose, to enter here into the specifics of the law of nature, or its measures of punishment; yet, it is certain there is such a law, and that too, as intelligible and plain to a rational creature, and a studier of that law, as the positive laws of commonwealths; nay, possibly plainer; as much as reason is easier to be understood, than the fancies and intricate contrivances of men, following contrary and hidden interests put into words; for so truly are a great part of the municipal laws of countries, which are only so far right, as they are founded on the law of nature, by which they are to be regulated and interpreted.

Section 13. To this strange doctrine, that is That in the state of nature everyone has the executive power of the law of nature, I doubt not but it will be objected, that it is unreasonable for men to be judges in their own cases, that self-love will make men partial to themselves and their friends: and on the other side, that ill nature, passion and revenge will carry them too far in punishing others; and hence nothing but confusion and disorder will follow, and that therefore God has certainly appointed government to restrain the partiality and violence of men. I easily grant, that civil government is the proper remedy for the inconveniencies of the state of nature, which must certainly be great, where men may be judges in their own case, since it is easy to be imagined, that he who was so unjust as to do his brother an injury, will scarce be so just as to condemn himself for it: but I shall desire those who make this objection, to remember, that absolute monarchs are but men; and if government is to be the remedy of those evils, which necessarily follow from men's being judges in their own cases, and the state of nature is therefore not to be endured, I desire to know what kind of government that is, and how much better it is than the state of nature, where one man, commanding a multitude, has the liberty to be judge in his own case, and may do to all his subjects whatever he pleases, without the least liberty to anyone to question or control those who execute his pleasure? and in whatsoever he does, whether led by reason, mistake or passion, must be submitted to? much better it is in the state of nature, wherein men are not bound to submit to the unjust will of another: and if he that judges, judges amiss in his own, or any other case, he is answerable for it to the rest of mankind.

Section 14. It is often asked as a mighty objection, where are, or ever were there any men in such a state of nature? To which it may suffice as an answer at present, that since all princes and rulers of independent governments all through the world, are in a state of nature, it is plain the world never was, nor ever will be, without numbers of men in that state. I have named all governors of independent communities, whether they are, or are not, in league with others: for it is not every compact that puts an end to the state of nature between men, but only this one of agreeing together mutually to enter into one community, and make one body politic; other promises, and compacts, men may make one with another, and yet still be in the state of nature. The promises and bargains for truck, etc. between the two men in the desert island, mentioned by Garcilasso de la Vega, in his history of Peru; or between a Swiss and an Indian, in the woods of America, are binding to them, though they are perfectly in a state of nature, in reference to one another: for truth and keeping of faith belongs to men, as men, and not as members of society.

Section 15. To those that say, there were never any men in the state of nature, I will not only oppose the authority of the judicious Hooker, Eccl. Pol. lib. i. sect. 10. where he says, The laws which have been hitherto mentioned, i.e. the laws of nature, do bind men absolutely, even as they are men, although they have never any settled fellowship, never any solemn agreement among themselves what to do, or not to do: but forasmuch as we are not by ourselves sufficient to furnish ourselves with competent store of things, needful for such a life as our nature does desire, a life fit for the dignity of man; therefore to supply those defects and imperfections which are in us, as living single and solely by ourselves, we are naturally induced to seek communion and fellowship with others: this was the cause of men's uniting themselves at first in politic societies. But I moreover affirm, that all men are naturally in that state, and remain so, till by their own consents they make themselves members of some politic society; and I doubt not in the sequel of this discourse, to make it very clear.

CHAPTER III.

Of the State of War.

Section 16. The state of war is a state of enmity and destruction: and therefore declaring by word or action, not a passionate, but a sedate settled design upon another man's life, puts him in a state of war with him against whom he has declared such an intention, and so has exposed his life to the other's power to be taken away by him, or anyone that joins with him in his defense, and espouses his quarrel; it being reasonable and just, I should have a right to destroy that which threatens me with destruction: for, by the fundamental law of nature, man being to be preserved as much as possible, when all cannot be preserved, the safety of the innocent is to be preferred: and one may destroy a man who makes war upon him, or has discovered an enmity to his being, for the same reason that he may kill a wolf or a lion; because such men are not under the ties of the common-law of reason, have no other rule, but that of force and violence, and so may be treated as beasts of prey, those dangerous and noxious creatures, that will be sure to destroy him whenever he falls into their power.

Section 17. And hence it is, that he who attempts to get another man into his absolute power, does thereby put himself into a state of war with him; it being to be understood as a declaration of a design upon his life: for I have reason to conclude, that he who would get me into his power without my consent, would use me as he pleased when he had got me there, and destroy me too when he had a fancy to it; for nobody can desire to have me in his absolute power, unless it be to compel me by force to that which is against the right of my freedom, i.e. make me a slave. To be free from such force is the only security of my preservation; and reason bids me look on him, as an enemy to my preservation, who would take away that freedom which is the fence to it; so that he who makes an attempt to enslave me, thereby puts himself into a state of war with me. He that, in the state of nature, would take away the freedom that belongs to anyone in that state, must necessarily be supposed to have a design to take away everything else, that freedom being the foundation of all the rest; as he that, in the state of society, would take away the freedom belonging to those of that society or commonwealth, must be supposed to design to take away from them everything else, and so be looked on as in a state of war.

Section 18. This makes it lawful for a man to kill a thief, who has not in the least hurt him, nor declared any design upon his life, any further than, by the use of force, so to get him in his power, as to take away his money, or what he pleases, from him; because using force, where he has no right, to get me into his power, let his pretence be what it will, I have no reason to suppose, that he, who would take away my liberty, would not, when he had me in his power, take away everything else. And therefore it is lawful for me to treat him as one who has put himself into a state of war with me, i.e. kill him if I can; for to that hazard does he justly expose himself, whoever introduces a state of war, and is aggressor in it.

Section 19. And here we have the plain difference between the state of nature and the state of war, which however some men have confounded, are as far distant, as a state of peace, good will, mutual assistance and preservation, and a state of enmity, malice, violence and mutual destruction, are one from another. Men living together according to reason, without a common superior on earth with authority to judge between them, is properly the state of nature. But force, or a declared design of force, upon the person of another, where there is no common superior on earth to appeal to for relief, is the state of war: and it is the want of such an appeal gives a man the right of war even against an aggressor, though he be in society and a fellow subject. Thus a thief, whom I cannot harm, but by appeal to the law, for having stolen all that I am worth, I may kill, when he sets on me to rob me but of my horse or coat; because the law, which was made for my preservation, where it cannot interpose to secure my life from present force, which, if lost, is capable of no reparation, permits me my own defense, and the right of war, a liberty to kill the aggressor, because the aggressor allows not time to appeal to our common judge, nor the decision of the law, for remedy in a case where the mischief may be irreparable. Want of a common judge with authority, puts all men in a state of nature: force without right, upon a man's person, makes a state of war, both where there is, and is not, a common judge.

Section 20. But when the actual force is over, the state of war ceases between those that are in society, and are equally on both sides subjected to the fair determination of the law; because then there lies open the remedy of appeal for the past injury, and to prevent future harm: but where no such appeal is, as in the state of nature, for want of positive laws, and judges with authority to appeal to, the state of war once begun, continues, with a right to the innocent party to destroy the other whenever he can, until the aggressor offers peace, and desires reconciliation on such terms as may repair any wrongs he has already done, and secure the innocent for the future; nay, where an appeal to the law, and constituted judges, lies open, but the remedy is denied by a manifest perverting of justice, and a barefaced wresting of the laws to protect or indemnify the violence or injuries of some men, or party of men, there it is hard to imagine anything but a state of war: for wherever violence is used, and injury done, though by hands appointed to administer justice, it is still violence and injury, however colored with the name, pretences, or forms of law, the end whereof being to protect and redress the innocent, by an unbiased application of it, to all who are under it; wherever that is not bona fide done, war is made upon the sufferers, who having no appeal on earth to right them, they are left to the only remedy in such cases, an appeal to heaven.

Section 21. To avoid this state of war (wherein there is no appeal but to heaven, and wherein every the least difference is apt to end, where there is no authority to decide between the contenders) is one great reason of men's putting themselves into society, and quitting the state of nature: for where there is an authority, a power on earth, from which relief can be had by appeal, there the continuance of the state of war is excluded, and the controversy is decided by that power. Had there been any such court, any superior jurisdiction on earth, to determine the right between Jephtha and the Ammonites, they had never come to a state of war: but we see he was forced to appeal to heaven. The Lord the Judge (says he) be judge this day between the children of Israel and the children of Ammon, Judg. xi. 27. and then prosecuting, and relying on his appeal, he leads out his army to battle: and therefore in such controversies, where the question is put, who shall be judge? It cannot be meant, who shall decide the controversy; everyone knows what Jephtha here tells us, that the Lord the Judge shall judge. Where there is no judge on earth, the appeal lies to God in heaven. That question then cannot mean, who shall judge, whether another has put himself in a state of war with me, and whether I may, as Jephtha did, appeal to heaven in it? of that I myself can only be judge in my own conscience, as I will answer it, at the great day, to the supreme judge of all men.

CHAPTER IV.

Of Slavery.

Section 22. The natural liberty of man is to be free from any superior power on earth, and not to be under the will or legislative authority of man, but to have only the law of nature for his rule. The liberty of man, in society, is to be under no other legislative power, but that established, by consent, in the commonwealth; nor under the dominion of any will, or restraint of any law, but what that legislative shall enact, according to the trust put in it. Freedom then is not what Sir Robert Filmer tells us, Observations, A. 55. a liberty for everyone to do what he lists, to live as he pleases, and not to be tied by any laws: but freedom of men under government is, to have a standing rule to live by, common to everyone of that society, and made by the legislative power erected in it; a liberty to follow my own will in all things, where the rule prescribes not; and not to be subject to the inconstant, uncertain, unknown, arbitrary will of another man: as freedom of nature is, to be under no other restraint but the law of nature.

Section 23. This freedom from absolute, arbitrary power, is so necessary to, and closely joined with a man's preservation, that he cannot part with it, but by what forfeits his preservation and life together: for a man, not having the power of his own life, cannot, by compact, or his own consent, enslave himself to anyone, nor put himself under the absolute, arbitrary power of another, to take away his life, when he pleases. Nobody can give more power than he has himself; and he that cannot take away his own life, cannot give another power over it. Indeed, having by his fault forfeited his own life, by some act that deserves death; he, to whom he has forfeited it, may (when he has him in his power) delay to take it, and make use of him to his own service, and he does him no injury by it: for, whenever he finds the hardship of his slavery outweigh the value of his life, it is in his power, by resisting the will of his master, to draw on himself the death he desires.

Section 24. This is the perfect condition of slavery, which is nothing else, but the state of war continued, between a lawful conqueror and a captive: for, if once compact enter between them, and make an agreement for a limited power on the one side, and obedience on the other, the state of war and slavery ceases, as long as the compact endures: for, as has been said, no man can, by agreement, pass over to another that which he has not in himself, a power over his own life.

I confess, we find among the Jews, as well as other nations, that men did sell themselves; but, it is plain, this was only to drudgery, not to slavery: for, it is evident, the person sold was not under an absolute, arbitrary, despotical power: for the master could not have power to kill him, at any time, whom, at a certain time, he was obliged to let go free out of his service; and the master of such a servant was so far from having an arbitrary power over his life, that he could not, at pleasure, so much as maim him, but the loss of an eye, or tooth, set him free, Exod. xxi.

CHAPTER V.

Of Property.

Section 25. Whether we consider natural reason, which tells us, that men, being once born, have a right to their preservation, and consequently to meat and drink, and such other things as nature affords for their subsistence: or revelation, which gives us an account of those grants God made of the world to Adam, and to Noah, and his sons, it is very clear, that God, as king David says, Psalm. CXV. 16. has given the earth to the children of men; given it to mankind in common. But this being supposed, it seems to some a very great difficulty, how anyone should ever come to have a property in anything: I will not content myself to answer, that if it be difficult to make out property, upon a supposition that God gave the world to Adam, and his posterity in common, it is impossible that any man, but one universal monarch, should have any property upon a supposition, that God gave the world to Adam, and his heirs in succession, exclusive of all the rest of his posterity. But I shall endeavor to show, how men might come to have a property in several parts of that which God gave to mankind in common, and that without any express compact of all the commoners.

Section 26. God, who has given the world to men in common, has also given them reason to make use of it to the best advantage of life, and convenience. The earth, and all that is therein, is given to men for the support and comfort of their being. And though all the fruits it naturally produces, and beasts it feeds, belong to mankind in common, as they are produced by the spontaneous hand of nature; and nobody has originally a private dominion, exclusive of the rest of mankind, in any of them, as they are thus in their natural state: yet being given for the use of men, there must of necessity be a means to appropriate them some way or other, before they can be of any use, or at all beneficial to any particular man. The fruit, or venison, which nourishes the wild Indian, who knows no enclosure, and is still a tenant in common, must be his, and so his, i.e. a part of him, that another can no longer have any right to it, before it can do him any good for the support of his life.

Section 27. Though the earth, and all inferior creatures, be common to all men, yet every man has a property in his own person: this nobody has any right to but himself. The labors of his body, and the work of his hands, we may say, are properly his. Whatsoever then he removes out of the state that nature has provided, and left it in, he has mixed his labor with, and joined to it something that is his own, and thereby makes it his property. It being by him removed from the common state nature has placed it in, it has by this labor something annexed to it, that excludes the common right of other men: for this labor being the unquestionable property of the laborer, no man but he can have a right to what that is once joined to, at least where there is enough, and as good, left in common for others.

Section 28. He that is nourished by the acorns he picked up under an oak, or the apples he gathered from the trees in the wood, has certainly appropriated them to himself. Nobody can deny but the nourishment is his. I ask then, when did they begin to be his? when he digested? or when he eats? or when he boiled? or when he brought them home? or when he picked them up? and it is plain, if the first gathering made them not his, nothing else could. That labor put a distinction between them and common: that added something to them more than nature, the common mother of all, had done; and so they became his private right. And will anyone say, he had no right to those acorns or apples, he thus appropriated, because he had not the consent of all mankind to make them his? Was it a robbery thus to assume to himself what belonged to all in common? If such consent as that was necessary, man had starved, notwithstanding the plenty God had given him. We see in commons, which remain so by compact, that it is the taking any part of what is common, and removing it out of the state nature leaves it in, which begins the property; without which the common is of no use. And the taking of this or that part does not depend on the express consent of all the commoners. Thus the grass my horse has bit; the turfs my servant has cut; and the ore I have dug in any place, where I have a right to them in common with others, become my property, without the assignation or consent of anybody. The labor that was mine, removing them out of that common state they were in, has fixed my property in them.

Section 29. By making an explicit consent of every commoner, necessary to anyone's appropriating to himself any part of what is given in common, children or servants could not cut the meat, which their father or master had provided for them in common, without assigning to everyone his peculiar part. Though the water running in the fountain is everyone's, yet who can doubt, but that in the pitcher is his only who drew it out? His labor has taken it out of the hands of nature, where it was common, and belonged equally to all her children, and has thereby appropriated it to himself.

Section 30. Thus this law of reason makes the deer that Indian's who has killed it; it is allowed to be his goods, who has bestowed his labor upon it, though before it was the common right of everyone. And among those who are counted the civilized part of mankind, who have made and multiplied positive laws to determine property, this original law of nature, for the beginning of property, in what was before common, still takes place; and by virtue thereof, what fish anyone catches in the ocean, that great and still remaining common of mankind; or what ambergris anyone takes up here, is by the labor that removes it out of that common state nature left it in, made his property, who takes that pains about it. And even among us, the hare that anyone is hunting, is thought his who pursues her during the chase: for being a beast that is still looked upon as common, and no man's private possession; whoever has employed so much labor about any of that kind, as to find and pursue her, has thereby removed her from the state of nature, wherein she was common, and has begun a property.

Section 31. It will perhaps be objected to this, that if gathering the acorns, or other fruits of the earth, etc. makes a right to them, then anyone may engross as much as he will. To which I answer, Not so. The same law of nature, that does by this means give us property, does also bound that property too. God has given us all things richly, 1 Tim. vi. 12. is the voice of reason confirmed by inspiration? But how far has he given it us? To enjoy. As much as anyone can make use of to any advantage of life before it spoils, so much he may by his labor fix a property in: whatever is beyond this, is more than his share, and belongs to others. Nothing was made by God for man to spoil or destroy. And thus, considering the plenty of natural provisions there was a long time in the world, and the few spenders; and to how small a part of that provision the industry of one man could extend itself, and engross it to the prejudice of others; especially keeping within the bounds, set by reason, of what might serve for his use; there could be then little room for quarrels or contentions about property so established.

Section 32. But the chief matter of property being now not the fruits of the earth, and the beasts that subsist on it, but the earth itself; as that which takes in and carries with it all the rest; I think it is plain, that property in that too is acquired as the former. As much land as a man tills, plants, improves, cultivates, and can use the product of, so much is his property. He by his labor does, as it were, enclose it from the common. Nor will it invalidate his right, to say everybody else has an equal title to it; and therefore he cannot appropriate, he cannot enclose, without the consent of all his fellow-commoners, all mankind. God, when he gave the world in common to all mankind, commanded man also to labor, and the penury of his condition required it of him. God and his reason commanded him to subdue the earth, i.e. improve it for the benefit of life, and therein lay out something upon it that was his own, his labor. He that in obedience to this command of God, subdued, tilled and sowed any part of it, thereby annexed to it something that was his property, which another had no title to, nor could without injury take from him.

Section 33. Nor was this appropriation of any parcel of land, by improving it, any prejudice to any other man, since there was still enough and as good left; and more than the yet unprovided could use. So that, in effect, there was never the less left for others because of his enclosure for himself: for he that leaves as much as another can make use of, does as good as take nothing at all. Nobody could think himself injured by the drinking of another man, though he took a good draught, who had a whole river of the same water left him to quench his thirst: and the case of land and water, where there is enough of both, is perfectly the same.

Section 34. God gave the world to men in common; but since he gave it them for their benefit, and the greatest conveniences of life they were capable to draw from it, it cannot be supposed he meant it should always remain common and uncultivated. He gave it to the use of the industrious and rational, (and labor was to be his title to it) not to the fancy or covetousness of the quarrelsome and contentious. He that had as good left for his improvement, as was already taken up, needed not complain, ought not to meddle with what was already improved by another's labor: if he did, it is plain he desired the benefit of another's pains, which he had no right to, and not the ground which God had given him in common with others to labor on, and whereof there was as good left, as that already possessed, and more than he knew what to do with, or his industry could reach to.

Section 35. It is true, in land that is common in England, or any other country, where there is plenty of people under government, who have money and commerce, no one can enclose or appropriate any part, without the consent of all his fellow-commoners; because this is left common by compact, i.e. by the law of the land, which is not to be violated. And though it be common, in respect of some men, it is not so to all mankind; but is the joint property of this country, or this parish. Besides, the remainder, after such enclosure, would not be as good to the rest of the commoners, as the whole was when they could all make use of the whole; whereas in the beginning and first peopling of the great common of the world, it was quite otherwise. The law man was under, was rather for appropriating. God commanded, and his wants forced him to labor. That was his property which could not be taken from him wherever he had fixed it. And hence subduing or cultivating the earth, and having dominion, we see are joined together. The one gave title to the other. So that God, by commanding to subdue, gave authority so far to appropriate: and the condition of human life, which requires labor and materials to work on, necessarily introduces private possessions.

Section 36. The measure of property nature has well set by the extent of men's labor and the conveniences of life: no man's labor could subdue, or appropriate all; nor could his enjoyment consume more than a small part; so that it was impossible for any man, this way, to entrench upon the right of another, or acquire to himself a property, to the prejudice of his neighbor, who would still have room for as good, and as large a possession (after the other had taken out his) as before it was appropriated. This measure did confine every man's possession to a very moderate proportion, and such as he might appropriate to himself, without injury to anybody, in the first ages of the world, when men were more in danger to be lost, by wandering from their company, in the then vast wilderness of the earth, than to be straitened for want of room to plant in. And the same measure may be allowed still without prejudice to anybody, as full as the world seems: for supposing a man, or family, in the state they were at first peopling of the world by the children of Adam, or Noah; let him plant in some in-land, vacant places of America, we shall find that the possessions he could make himself, upon the measures we have given, would not be very large, nor, even to this day, prejudice the rest of mankind, or give them reason to complain, or think themselves injured by this man's encroachment, though the race of men have now spread themselves to all the corners of the world, and do infinitely exceed the small number was at the beginning. Nay, the extent of ground is of so little value, without labor, that I have heard it affirmed, that in Spain itself a man may be permitted to plough, sow and reap, without being disturbed, upon land he has no other title to, but only his making use of it. But, on the contrary, the inhabitants think themselves beholden to him, who, by his industry on neglected, and consequently were land, has increased the stock of corn, which they wanted. But be this as it will, which I lay no stress on; this I dare boldly affirm, that the same rule of propriety, (that is) that every man should have as much as he could make use of, would hold still in the world, without straitening anybody; since there is land enough in the world to suffice double the inhabitants, had not the invention of money, and the tacit agreement of men to put a value on it, introduced (by consent) larger possessions, and a right to them; which, how it has done, I shall by and by show more at large.

Section 37. This is certain, that in the beginning, before the desire of having more than man needed had altered the intrinsic value of things, which depends only on their usefulness to the life of man; or had agreed, that a little piece of yellow metal, which would keep without wearing or decay, should be worth a great piece of flesh, or a whole heap of corn; though men had a right to appropriate, by their labor, each one to himself, as much of the things of nature, as he could use: yet this could not be much, nor to the prejudice of others, where the same plenty was still left to those who would use the same industry. To which let me add, that he who appropriates land to himself by his labor, does not lessen, but increase the common stock of mankind: for the provisions serving to the support of human life, produced by one acre of enclosed and cultivated land, are (to speak much within compass) ten times more than those which are yielded by an acre of land of an equal richness lying were in common. And therefore he that encloses land, and has a greater plenty of the conveniences of life from ten acres, than he could have from an hundred left to nature, may truly be said to give ninety acres to mankind: for his labor now supplies him with provisions out of ten acres, which were but the product of an hundred lying in common. I have here rated the improved land very low, in making its product but as ten to one, when it is much nearer an hundred to one: for I ask, whether in the wild woods and uncultivated were of America, left to nature, without any improvement, tillage or husbandry, a thousand acres yield the needy and wretched inhabitants as many conveniences of life, as ten acres of equally fertile land do in Devonshire, where they are well cultivated?

Before the appropriation of land, he who gathered as much of the wild fruit, killed, caught, or tamed, as many of the beasts, as he could; he that so employed his pains about any of the spontaneous products of nature, as any way to alter them from the state which nature put them in, by placing any of his labor on them, did thereby acquire a propriety in them: but if they perished, in his possession, without their due use; if the fruits rotted, or the venison putrefied, before he could spend it, he offended against the common law of nature, and was liable to be punished; he invaded his neighbor's share, for he had no right, father than his use called for any of them, and they might serve to afford him conveniences of life.

Section 38. The same measures governed the possession of land too: whatsoever he tilled and reaped, laid up and made use of, before it spoiled, that was his peculiar right; whatsoever he enclosed, and could feed, and make use of, the cattle and product was also his. But if either the grass of his enclosure rotted on the ground, or the fruit of his planting perished without gathering, and laying up, this part of the earth, notwithstanding his enclosure, was still to be looked on as were, and might be the possession of any other. Thus, at the beginning, Cain might take as much ground as he could till, and make it his own land, and yet leave enough to Abel's sheep to feed on; a few acres would serve for both their possessions. But as families increased, and industry enlarged their stocks, their possessions enlarged with the need of them; but yet it was commonly without any fixed property in the ground they made use of, till they incorporated, settled themselves together, and built cities; and then, by consent, they came in time, to set out the bounds of their distinct territories, and agree on limits between them and their neighbors; and by laws within themselves, settled the properties of those of the same society: for we see, that in that part of the world which was first inhabited, and therefore like to be best peopled, even as low down as Abraham's time, they wandered with their flocks, and their herds, which was their substance, freely up and down; and this Abraham did, in a country where he was a stranger. Whence it is plain, that at least a great part of the land lay in common; that the inhabitants valued it not, nor claimed property in any more than they made use of. But when there was not room enough in the same place, for their herds to feed together, they by consent, as Abraham and Lot did, Gen. xiii. 5. separated and enlarged their pasture, where it best liked them. And for the same reason Esau went from his father, and his brother, and planted in mount Seir, Gen. xxxvi. 6.

Section 39. And thus, without supposing any private dominion, and property in Adam, over all the world, exclusive of all other men, which can no way be proved, nor anyone's property be made out from it; but supposing the world given, as it was, to the children of men in common, we see how labor could make men distinct titles to several parcels of it, for their private uses; wherein there could be no doubt of right, no room for quarrel.

Section 40. Nor is it so strange, as perhaps before consideration it may appear, that the property of labor should be able to over-balance the community of land: for it is labor indeed that puts the difference of value on everything; and let anyone consider what the difference is between an acre of land planted with tobacco or sugar, sown with wheat or barley, and an acre of the same land lying in common, without any husbandry upon it, and he will find, that the improvement of labor makes the far greater part of the value. I think it will be but a very modest computation to say, that of the products of the earth useful to the life of man nine tenths are the effects of labor: nay, if we will rightly estimate things as they come to our use, and cast up the several expenses about them, what in them is purely owing to nature, and what to labor, we shall find, that in most of them ninety-nine hundredths are wholly to be put on the account of labor.

Section 41. There cannot be a clearer demonstration of anything, than several nations of the Americans are of this, who are rich in land, and poor in all the comforts of life; whom nature having furnished as liberally as any other people, with the materials of plenty, i.e. a fruitful soil, apt to produce in abundance, what might serve for food, raiment, and delight; yet for want of improving it by labor, have not one hundredth part of the conveniences we enjoy: and a king of a large and fruitful territory there, feeds, lodges, and is clad worse than a day-laborer in England.

Section 42. To make this a little clearer, let us but trace some of the ordinary provisions of life, through their several progresses, before they come to our use, and see how much they receive of their value from human industry. Bread, wine and cloth, are things of daily use, and great plenty; yet notwithstanding, acorns, water and leaves, or skins, must be our bread, drink and clothing, did not labor furnish us with these more useful commodities: for whatever bread is more worth than acorns, wine than water, and cloth or silk, than leaves, skins or moss, that is wholly owing to labor and industry; the one of these being the food and raiment which unassisted nature furnishes us with; the other, provisions which our industry and pains prepare for us, which how much they exceed the other in value, when anyone has computed, he will then see how much labor makes the far greatest part of the value of things we enjoy in this world: and the ground which produces the materials, is scarce to be reckoned in, as any, or at most, but a very small part of it; so little, that even among us, land that is left wholly to nature, that has no improvement of pasturage, tillage, or planting, is called, as indeed it is, were; and we shall find the benefit of it amount to little more than nothing.

This shows how much numbers of men are to be preferred to largeness of dominions; and that the increase of lands, and the right employing of them, is the great are of government: and that prince, who shall be so wise and godlike, as by established laws of liberty to secure protection and encouragement to the honest industry of mankind, against the oppression of power and narrowness of party, will quickly be too hard for his neighbors: but this by the by. To return to the argument in hand,

Section 43. An acre of land, that bears here twenty bushels of wheat, and another in America, which, with the same husbandry, would do the like, are, without doubt, of the same natural intrinsic value: but yet the benefit mankind receives from the one in a year, is worth 5:1, and from the other possibly not worth a penny, if all the profit an Indian received from it were to be valued, and sold here; at least, I may truly say, not one thousandth. It is labor then which puts the greatest part of value upon land, without which it would scarcely be worth anything: it is to that we owe the greatest part of all its useful products; for all that the straw, bran, bread, of that acre of wheat, is more worth than the product of an acre of as good land, which lies were, is all the effect of labor: for it is not barely the plough-man's pains, the reaper's and thresher's toil, and the baker's sweat, is to be counted into the bread we eat; the labor of those who broke the oxen, who dug and wrought the iron and stones, who felled and framed the timber employed about the plough, mill, oven, or any other utensils, which are a vast number, requisite to this corn, from its being seed to be sown to its being made bread, must all be charged on the account of labor, and received as an effect of that: nature and the earth furnished only the almost worthless materials, as in themselves. It would be a strange catalogue of things, that industry provided and made use of, about every loaf of bread, before it came to our use, if we could trace them; iron, wood, leather, bark, timber, stone, bricks, coals, lime, cloth, dying drugs, pitch, tar, masts, ropes, and all the materials made use of in the ship, that brought any of the commodities made use of by any of the workmen, to any part of the work; all which it would be almost impossible, at least too long, to reckon up.

Section 44. From all which it is evident, that though the things of nature are given in common, yet man, by being master of himself, and proprietor of his own person, and the actions or labor of it, had still in himself the great foundation of property; and that, which made up the great part of what he applied to the support or comfort of his being, when invention and arts had improved the conveniences of life, was perfectly his own, and did not belong in common to others.

Section 45. Thus labor, in the beginning, gave a right of property, wherever anyone was pleased to employ it upon what was common, which remained a long while the far greater part, and is yet more than mankind makes use of. Men, at first, for the most part, contented themselves with what unassisted nature offered to their necessities: and though afterwards, in some parts of the world, (where the increase of people and stock, with the use of money, had made land scarce, and so of some value) the several communities settled the bounds of their distinct territories, and by laws within themselves regulated the properties of the private men of their society, and so, by compact and agreement, settled the property which labor and industry began; and the leagues that have been made between several states and kingdoms, either expressly or tacitly disowning all claim and right to the land in the others possession, have, by common consent, given up their pretences to their natural common right, which originally they had to those countries, and so have, by positive agreement, settled a property among themselves, in distinct parts and parcels of the earth; yet there are still great tracts of ground to be found, which (the inhabitants thereof not having joined with the rest of mankind, in the consent of the use of their common money) lie were, and are more than the people who dwell on it do, or can make use of, and so still lie in common; though this can scarce happen among that part of mankind that have consented to the use of money.

Section 46. The greatest part of things really useful to the life of man, and such as the necessity of subsisting made the first commoners of the world look after, as it does the Americans now, are generally things of short duration; such as, if they are not consumed by use, will decay and perish of themselves: gold, silver and diamonds, are things that fancy or agreement has put the value on, more than real use, and the necessary support of life. Now of those good things which nature has provided in common, everyone had a right (as has been said) to as much as he could use, and property in all that he could effect with his labor; all that his industry could extend to, to alter from the state nature had put it in, was his. He that gathered a hundred bushels of acorns or apples, had thereby a property in them, they were his goods as soon as gathered. He was only to look, that he used them before they spoiled, else he took more than his share, and robbed others. And indeed it was a foolish thing, as well as dishonest, to hoard up more than he could make use of. If he gave away a part to anybody else, so that it perished not uselessly in his possession, these he also made use of. And if he also bartered away plums, that would have rotted in a week, for nuts that would last good for his eating a whole year, he did no injury; he wearied not the common stock; destroyed no part of the portion of goods that belonged to others, so long as nothing perished uselessly in his hands. Again, if he would give his nuts for a piece of metal, pleased with its color; or exchange his sheep for shells, or wool for a sparkling pebble or a diamond, and keep those by him all his life, he invaded not the right of others, he might heap up as much of these durable things as he pleased; the exceeding of the bounds of his just property not lying in the largeness of his possession, but the perishing of anything uselessly in it.

Section 47. And thus came in the use of money, some lasting thing that men might keep without spoiling, and that by mutual consent men would take in exchange for the truly useful, but perishable supports of life.

Section 48. And as different degrees of industry were apt to give men possessions in different proportions, so this invention of money gave them the opportunity to continue and enlarge them: for supposing an island, separate from all possible commerce with the rest of the world, wherein there were but an hundred families, but there were sheep, horses and cows, with other useful animals, wholesome fruits, and land enough for corn for a hundred thousand times as many, but nothing in the island, either because of its commonness, or perishableness, fit to supply the place of money; what reason could anyone have there to enlarge his possessions beyond the use of his family, and a plentiful supply to its consumption, either in what their own industry produced, or they could barter for like perishable, useful commodities, with others? Where there is not something, both lasting and scarce, and so valuable to be hoarded up, there men will be apt to enlarge their possessions of land, were it never so rich, never so free for them to take: for I ask, what would a man value ten thousand, or an hundred thousand acres of excellent land, ready cultivated, and well stocked too with cattle, in the middle of the inland parts of America, where he had no hopes of commerce with other parts of the world, to draw money to him by the sale of the product? It would not be worth the inclosing, and we should see him give up again to the wild common of nature, whatever was more than would supply the conveniences of life to be had there for him and his family.

Section 49. Thus in the beginning all the world was America, and more so than that is now; for no such thing as money was anywhere known. Find out something that has the use and value of money among his neighbors, you shall see the same man will begin presently to enlarge his possessions.

Section 50. But since gold and silver, being little useful to the life of man in proportion to food, clothing, and shelter, has its value only from the consent of men, whereof labor yet makes, in great part, the measure, it is plain, that men have agreed to a disproportionate and unequal possession of the earth, they having, by a tacit and voluntary consent, found out a way how a man may fairly possess more land than he himself can use the product of, by receiving in exchange for the surplus gold and silver, which may be hoarded up without injury to anyone; these metals not spoiling or decaying in the hands of the possessor. This parting of things in an inequality of private possessions, men have made practicable out of the bounds of society, and without compact, only by putting a value on gold and silver, and tacitly agreeing in the use of money: for in governments, the laws regulate the right of property, and the possession of land is determined by positive constitutions.

Section 51. And thus, I think, it is very easy to conceive, without any difficulty, how labor could at first begin a title of property in the common things of nature, and how the spending it upon our uses bounded it. So that there could then be no reason of quarrelling about title, or any doubt about the largeness of possession it gave. Right and convenience went together; for as a man had a right to all he could employ his labor upon, so he had no temptation to labor for more than he could make use of. This left no room for controversy about the title, nor for encroachment on the right of others; what portion a man carved to himself, was easily seen; and it was useless, as well as dishonest, to carve himself too much, or take more than he needed.

CHAPTER VI.

Of Paternal Power.

Section 52. It may perhaps be censured as an impertinent criticism, in a discourse of this nature, to find fault with words and names, that have obtained in the world: and yet possibly it may not be amiss to offer new ones, when the old are apt to lead men into mistakes, as this of paternal power probably has done, which seems so to place the power of parents over their children wholly in the father, as if the mother had no share in it; whereas, if we consult reason or revelation, we shall find, she has an equal title. This may give one reason to ask, whether this might not be more properly called parental power? for whatever obligation nature and the right of generation lays on children, it must certainly bind them equal to both the concurrent causes of it. And accordingly we see the positive law of God everywhere joins them together, without distinction, when it commands the obedience of children, Honor your father and your mother, Exod. xx. 12. Whosoever curses his father or his mother, Lev. xx. 9. You shall fear every man his mother and his father, Lev. xix. 3. Children, obey your parents, etc. Eph. vi. 1. is the style of the Old and New Testament.

Section 53. Had but this one thing been well considered, without looking any deeper into the matter, it might perhaps have kept men from running into those gross mistakes, they have made, about this power of parents; which, however it might, without any great harshness, bear the name of absolute dominion, and regal authority, when under the title of paternal power it seemed appropriated to the father, would yet have sounded but oddly, and in the very name shown the absurdity, if this supposed absolute power over children had been called parental; and thereby have discovered, that it belonged to the mother too: for it will but very ill serve the turn of those men, who contend so much for the absolute power and authority of the fatherhood, as they call it, that the mother should have any share in it; and it would have but ill supported the monarchy they contend for, when by the very name it appeared, that that fundamental authority, from whence they would derive their government of a single person only, was not placed in one, but two persons jointly. But to let this of names pass.

Section 54. Though I have said above, Chapter II, that all men by nature are equal, I cannot be supposed to understand all sorts of equality: age or virtue may give men a just precedence: excellency of parts and merit may place others above the common level: birth may subject some, and alliance or benefits others, to pay an observance to those to whom nature, gratitude, or other respects, may have made it due: and yet all this consists with the equality, which all men are in, in respect of jurisdiction or dominion one over another; which was the equality I there spoke of, as proper to the business in hand, being that equal right, that every man has, to his natural freedom, without being subjected to the will or authority of any other man.

Section 55. Children, I confess, are not born in this full state of equality, though they are born to it. Their parents have a sort of rule and jurisdiction over them, when they come into the world and for some time after; but it is but a temporary one. The bonds of this subjection are like the swaddling clothes they are wrapped up in, and supported by, in the weakness of their infancy: age and reason as they grow up, loosen them, till at length they drop quite off, and leave a man at his own free disposal.

Section 56. Adam was created a perfect man, his body and mind in full possession of their strength and reason, and so was capable, from the first instant of his being to provide for his own support and preservation, and govern his actions according to the dictates of the law of reason which God had implanted in him. From him the world is peopled with his descendants, who are all born infants, weak and helpless, without knowledge or understanding: but to supply the defects of this imperfect state, till the improvement of growth and age has removed them, Adam and Eve, and after them all parents were, by the law of nature, under an obligation to preserve, nourish, and educate the children they had begotten; not as their own workmanship, but the workmanship of their own maker, the Almighty, to whom they were to be accountable for them.

Section 57. The law, that was to govern Adam, was the same that was to govern all his posterity, the law of reason. But his offspring having another way of entrance into the world, different from him, by a natural birth, that produced them ignorant and without the use of reason, they were not presently under that law; for nobody can be under a law, which is not promulgated to him; and this law being promulgated or made known by reason only, he that is not come to the use of his reason, cannot be said to be under this law; and Adam's children, being not presently as soon as born under this law of reason, were not presently free: for law, in its true notion, is not so much the limitation as the direction of a free and intelligent agent to his proper interest, and prescribes no farther than is for the general good of those under that law: could they be happier without it, the law, as an useless thing, would of itself vanish; and that ill deserves the name of confinement which hedges us in only from bogs and precipices. So that, however it may be mistaken, the end of law is not to abolish or restrain, but to preserve and enlarge freedom: for in all the states of created beings capable of laws, where there is no law, there is no freedom: for liberty is, to be free from restraint and violence from others; which cannot be, where there is no law: but freedom is not, as we are told, a liberty for every man to do what he lists: (for who could be free, when every other man's humor might domineer over him?) but a liberty to dispose, and order as he lists, his person, actions, possessions, and his whole property, within the allowance of those laws under which he is, and therein not to be subject to the arbitrary will of another, but freely follow his own.

Section 58. The power, then, that parents have over their children, arises from that duty which is incumbent on them, to take care of their off-spring, during the imperfect state of childhood. To inform the mind, and govern the actions of their yet ignorant non-age, till reason shall take its place, and ease them of that trouble, is what the children want, and the parents are bound to: for God having given man an understanding to direct his actions, has allowed him a freedom of will, and liberty of acting, as properly belonging thereunto, within the bounds of that law he is under. But while he is in an estate, wherein he has not understanding of his own to direct his will, he is not to have any will of his own to follow: he that understands for him, must will for him too; he must prescribe to his will, and regulate his actions; but when he comes to the estate that made his father a freeman, the son is a freeman too.

Section 59. This holds in all the laws a man is under, whether natural or civil. Is a man under the law of nature? What made him free of that law? what gave him a free disposing of his property, according to his own will, within the compass of that law? I answer, a state of maturity wherein he might be supposed capable to know that law, that so he might keep his actions within the bounds of it. When he has acquired that state, he is presumed to know how far that law is to be his guide, and how far he may make use of his freedom, and so comes to have it; till then, somebody else must guide him, who is presumed to know how far the law allows a liberty. If such a state of reason, such an age of discretion made him free, the same shall make his son free too. Is a man under the law of England? What made him free of that law? that is, to have the liberty to dispose of his actions and possessions according to his own will, within the permission of that law? A capacity of knowing that law; which is supposed by that law, at the age of one and twenty years, and in some cases sooner. If this made the father free, it shall make the son free too. Until then we see the law allows the son to have no will, but he is to be guided by the will of his father or guardian, who is to understand for him. And if the father die, and fail to substitute a deputy in his trust; if he has not provided a tutor, to govern his son, during his minority, during his want of understanding, the law takes care to do it; some other must govern him, and be a will to him, till he has attained to a state of freedom, and his understanding be fit to take the government of his will. But after that, the father and son are equally free as much as tutor and pupil after nonage; equally subjects of the same law together, without any dominion left in the father over the life, liberty, or estate of his son, whether they be only in the state and under the law of nature, or under the positive laws of an established government.

Section 60. But if, through defects that may happen out of the ordinary course of nature, anyone comes not to such a degree of reason, wherein he might be supposed capable of knowing the law, and so living within the rules of it, he is never capable of being a free man, he is never let loose to the disposure of his own will (because he knows no bounds to it, has not understanding, its proper guide) but is continued under the tuition and government of others, all the time his own understanding is incapable of that charge. And so lunatics and idiots are never set free from the government of their parents; children, who are not as yet come unto those years whereat they may have; and innocents which are excluded by a natural defect from ever having; thirdly, madmen, which for the present cannot possibly have the use of right reason to guide themselves, have for their guide, the reason that guided other men which are tutors over them, to seek and procure their good for them, says Hooker, Eccl. Pol. lib. i. sect. 7. All which seems no more than that duty, which God and nature has laid on man, as well as other creatures, to preserve their offspring, till they can be able to shift for themselves, and will scarce amount to an instance or proof of parents' regal authority.

Section 61. Thus we are born free, as we are born rational; not that we have actually the exercise of either: age, that brings one, brings with it the other too. And thus we see how natural freedom and subjection to parents may consist together, and are both founded on the same principle. A child is free by his father's title, by his father's understanding, which is to govern him till he has it of his own. The freedom of a man at years of discretion, and the subjection of a child to his parents, while yet short of that age, are so consistent, and so distinguishable, that the most blinded contenders for monarchy, by right of fatherhood, cannot miss this difference; the most obstinate cannot but allow their consistency: for were their doctrine all true, were the right heir of Adam now known, and by that title settled a monarch in his throne, invested with all the absolute unlimited power Sir Robert Filmer talks of; if he should die as soon as his heir were born, must not the child, notwithstanding he were never so free, never so much sovereign, be in subjection to his mother and nurse, to tutors and governors, until age and education brought him reason and ability to govern himself and others? The necessities of his life, the health of his body, and the information of his mind, would require him to be directed by the will of others, and not his own; and yet will anyone think, that this restraint and subjection were inconsistent with, or spoiled him of that liberty or sovereignty he had a right to, or gave away his empire to those who had the government of his nonage? This government over him only prepared him the better and sooner for it. If anybody should ask me, when my son is of age to be free? I shall answer, just when his monarch is of age to govern. But at what time, says the judicious Hooker, Eccl. Pol. l. i. sect. 6. a man may be said to have attained so far forth the use of reason, as sufficed to make him capable of those laws whereby he is then bound to guide his actions: this is a great deal easier for sense to discern, than for anyone by skill and learning to determine.

Section 62. Commonwealths themselves take notice of, and allow, that there is a time when men are to begin to act like free men, and therefore till that time require not oaths of fealty, or allegiance, or other public owning of, or submission to the government of their countries.

Section 63. The freedom then of man, and liberty of acting according to his own will, is grounded on his having reason, which is able to instruct him in that law he is to govern himself by, and make him know how far he is left to the freedom of his own will. To turn him loose to an unrestrained liberty, before he has reason to guide him, is not the allowing him the privilege of his nature to be free; but to thrust him out among brutes, and abandon him to a state as wretched, and as much beneath that of a man, as theirs. This is that which puts the authority into the parent's hands to govern the minority of their children. God has made it their business to employ this care on their off-spring, and has placed in them suitable inclinations of tenderness and concern to temper this power, to apply it, as his wisdom designed it, to the children's good, as long as they should need to be under it.

Section 64. But what reason can hence advance this care of the parents due to their off-spring into an absolute arbitrary dominion of the father, whose power reaches no father, than by such a discipline, as he finds most effectual, to give such strength and health to their bodies, such vigor and rectitude to their minds, as may best fit his children to be most useful to themselves and others; and, if it be necessary to his condition, to make them work, when they are able, for their own subsistence. But in this power the mother too has her share with the father.

Section 65. Nay, this power so little belongs to the father by any peculiar right of nature, but only as he is guardian of his children, that when he quits his care of them, he loses his power over them, which goes along with their nourishment and education, to which it is inseparably annexed; and it belongs as much to the foster-father of an exposed child, as to the natural father of another. So little power does the bare act of begetting give a man over his issue; if all his care ends there, and this be all the title he has to the name and authority of a father. And what will become of this paternal power in that part of the world, where one woman has more than one husband at a time? or in those parts of America, where, when the husband and wife part, which happens frequently, the children are all left to the mother, follow her, and are wholly under her care and provision? If the father die while the children are young, do they not naturally everywhere owe the same obedience to their mother, during their minority, as to their father were he alive? and will anyone say that the mother has a legislative power over her children? that she can make standing rules, which shall be of perpetual obligation, by which they ought to regulate all the concerns of their property, and bound their liberty all the course of their lives? or can she enforce the observation of them with capital punishments? for this is the proper power of the magistrate, of which the father has not so much as the shadow. His command over his children is but temporary, and reaches not their life or property: it is but a help to the weakness and imperfection of their nonage, a discipline necessary to their education: and though a father may dispose of his own possessions as he pleases, when his children are out of danger of perishing for want, yet his power extends not to the lives or goods, which either their own industry, or another's bounty has made theirs; nor to their liberty neither, when they are once arrived to the enfranchisement of the years of discretion. The father's empire then ceases, and he can from thence forwards no more dispose of the liberty of his son, than that of any other man: and it must be far from an absolute or perpetual jurisdiction, from which a man may withdraw himself, having license from divine authority to leave father and mother, and cleave to his wife.

Section 66. But though there be a time when a child comes to be as free from subjection to the will and command of his father, as the father himself is free from subjection to the will of anybody else, and they are each under no other restraint, but that which is common to them both, whether it be the law of nature, or municipal law of their country; yet this freedom exempts not a son from that honor which he ought, by the law of God and nature, to pay his parents. God having made the parents instruments in his great design of continuing the race of mankind, and the occasions of life to their children; as he has laid on them an obligation to nourish, preserve, and bring up their offspring; so he has laid on the children a perpetual obligation of honoring their parents, which containing in it an inward esteem and reverence to be shown by all outward expressions, ties up the child from anything that may ever injure or affront, disturb or endanger, the happiness or life of those from whom he received his; and engages him in all actions of defense, relief, assistance and comfort of those, by whose means he entered into being, and has been made capable of any enjoyments of life: from this obligation no state, no freedom can absolve children. But this is very far from giving parents a power of command over their children, or an authority to make laws and dispose as they please of their lives or liberties. It is one thing to owe honor, respect, gratitude and assistance; another to require an absolute obedience and submission. The honor due to parents, a monarch in his throne owes his mother; and yet this lessens not his authority, nor subjects him to her government.

Section 67. The subjection of a minor places in the father a temporary government, which terminates with the minority of the child: and the honor due from a child, places in the parents a perpetual right to respect, reverence, support and compliance too, more or less, as the father's care, cost, and kindness in his education, has been more or less. This ends not with minority, but holds in all parts and conditions of a man's life. The want of distinguishing these two powers, that is that which the father has in the right of tuition, during minority, and the right of honor all his life, may perhaps have caused a great part of the mistakes about this matter: for to speak properly of them, the first of these is rather the privilege of children, and duty of parents, than any prerogative of paternal power. The nourishment and education of their children is a charge so incumbent on parents for their children's good, that nothing can absolve them from taking care of it: and though the power of commanding and chastising them go along with it, yet God has woven into the principles of human nature such a tenderness for their off-spring, that there is little fear that parents should use their power with too much rigor; the excess is seldom on the severe side, the strong bias of nature drawing the other way. And therefore God almighty when he would express his gentle dealing with the Israelites, he tells them, that though he chastened them, he chastened them as a man chastens his son, Deut. viii. 5. i.e. with tenderness and affection, and kept them under no severer discipline than what was absolutely best for them, and had been less kindness to have slackened. This is that power to which children are commanded obedience, that the pains and care of their parents may not be increased, or ill rewarded.

Section 68. On the other side, honor and support, all that which gratitude requires returning for the benefits received by and from them, is the indispensible duty of the child, and the proper privilege of the parents. This is intended for the parents advantage, as the other is for the child's; though education, the parents duty, seems to have most power, because the ignorance and infirmities of childhood stand in need of restraint and correction; which is a visible exercise of rule, and a kind of dominion. And that duty which is comprehended in the word honor, requires less obedience, though the obligation be stronger on grown, than younger children: for who can think the command, Children obey your parents, requires in a man, that has children of his own, the same submission to his father, as it does in his yet young children to him; and that by this precept he were bound to obey all his father's commands, if, out of a conceit of authority, he should have the indiscretion to treat him still as a boy?

Section 69. The first part then of paternal power, or rather duty, which is education, belongs so to the father, that it terminates at a certain season; when the business of education is over, it ceases of itself, and is also alienable before: for a man may put the tuition of his son in other hands; and he that has made his son an apprentice to another, has discharged him, during that time, of a great part of his obedience both to himself and to his mother. But all the duty of honor, the other part, remains never the less entire to them; nothing can cancel that: it is so inseparable from them both, that the father's authority cannot dispossess the mother of this right, nor can any man discharge his son from honoring her that bore him. But both these are very far from a power to make laws, and enforcing them with penalties, that may reach estate, liberty, limbs and life. The power of commanding ends with nonage; and though, after that, honor and respect, support and defense, and whatsoever gratitude can oblige a man to, for the highest benefits he is naturally capable of, be always due from a son to his parents; yet all this puts no scepter into the father's hand, no sovereign power of commanding. He has no dominion over his son's property, or actions; nor any right, that his will should prescribe to his son's in all things; however it may become his son in many things, not very inconvenient to him and his family, to pay deference to it.

Section 70. A man may owe honor and respect to an ancient, or wise man; deference to his child or friend; relief and support to the distressed; and gratitude to a benefactor, to such a degree, that all he has, all he can do, cannot sufficiently pay it: but all these give no authority, no right to anyone, of making laws over him from whom they are owing. And it is plain, all this is due not only to the bare title of father; not only because, as has been said, it is owing to the mother too; but because these obligations to parents, and the degrees of what is required of children, may be varied by the different care and kindness, trouble and expense, which is often employed upon one child more than another.

Section 71. This shows the reason how it comes to pass, that parents in societies, where they themselves are subjects, retain a power over their children, and have as much right to their subjection, as those who are in the state of nature. Which could not possibly be, if all political power were only paternal, and that in truth they were one and the same thing: for then, all paternal power being in the prince, the subject could naturally have none of it. But these two powers, political and paternal, are so perfectly distinct and separate; are built upon so different foundations, and given to so different ends, that every subject that is a father, has as much a paternal power over his children, as the prince has over his: and every prince, that has parents, owes them as much filial duty and obedience, as the meanest of his subjects do to theirs; and can therefore contain not any part or degree of that kind of dominion, which a prince or magistrate has over his subject.

Section 72. Though the obligation on the parents to bring up their children, and the obligation on children to honor their parents, contain all the power on the one hand, and submission on the other, which are proper to this relation, yet there is another power ordinarily in the father, whereby he has a tie on the obedience of his children; which though it be common to him with other men, yet the occasions of showing it, almost constantly happening to fathers in their private families, and the instances of it elsewhere being rare, and less taken notice of, it passes in the world for a part of paternal jurisdiction. And this is the power men generally have to bestow their estates on those who please them best; the possession of the father being the expectation and inheritance of the children, ordinarily in certain proportions, according to the law and custom of each country; yet it is commonly in the father's power to bestow it with a more sparing or liberal hand, according as the behavior of this or that child has comported with his will and humor.

Section 73. This is no small tie on the obedience of children: and there being always annexed to the enjoyment of land, a submission to the government of the country, of which that land is a part; it has been commonly supposed, that a father could oblige his posterity to that government, of which he himself was a subject, and that his compact held them; whereas, it being only a necessary condition annexed to the land, and the inheritance of an estate which is under that government, reaches only those who will take it on that condition, and so is no natural tie or engagement, but a voluntary submission: for every man's children being by nature as free as himself, or any of his ancestors ever were, may, while they are in that freedom, choose what society they will join themselves to, what commonwealth they will put themselves under. But if they will enjoy the inheritance of their ancestors, they must take it on the same terms their ancestors had it, and submit to all the conditions annexed to such a possession. By this power indeed fathers oblige their children to obedience to themselves, even when they are past minority, and most commonly too subject them to this or that political power: but neither of these by any peculiar right of fatherhood, but by the reward they have in their hands to enforce and recompense such a compliance; and is no more power than what a French man has over an English man, who by the hopes of an estate he will leave him, will certainly have a strong tie on his obedience: and if, when it is left him, he will enjoy it, he must certainly take it upon the conditions annexed to the possession of land in that country where it lies, whether it be France or England.

Section 74. To conclude then, though the father's power of commanding extends no farther than the minority of his children, and to a degree only fit for the discipline and government of that age; and though that honor and respect, and all that which the Latins called piety, which they indispensably owe to their parents all their life-time, and in all estates, with all that support and defense is due to them, gives the father no power of governing, i.e. making laws and enacting penalties on his children; though by all this he has no dominion over the property or actions of his son: yet it is obvious to conceive how easy it was, in the first ages of the world, and in places still, where the thinness of people gives families leave to separate into unpossessed quarters, and they have room to remove or plant themselves in yet vacant habitations, for the father of the family to become the prince of it; he had been a ruler from the beginning of the infancy of his children: and since without some government it would be hard for them to live together, it was likeliest it should, by the express or tacit consent of the children when they were grown up, be in the father, where it seemed without any change barely to continue; when indeed nothing more was required to it, than the permitting the father to exercise alone, in his family, that executive power of the law of nature, which every free man naturally has, and by that permission resigning up to him a monarchical power, while they remained in it. But that this was not by any paternal right, but only by the consent of his children, is evident from hence, that nobody doubts, but if a stranger, whom chance or business had brought to his family, had there killed any of his children, or committed any other fact, he might condemn and put him to death, or otherwise have punished him, as well as any of his children; which it was impossible he should do by virtue of any paternal authority over one who was not his child, but by virtue of that executive power of the law of nature, which, as a man, he had a right to: and he alone could punish him in his family, where the respect of his children had laid by the exercise of such a power, to give way to the dignity and authority they were willing should remain in him, above the rest of his family.

Section 75. Thus it was easy and almost natural for children, by a tacit and scarce avoidable consent, to make way for the father's authority and government. They had been accustomed in their childhood to follow his direction and to refer their little differences to him; and when they were men, who fitter to rule them? Their little properties, and less covetousness, seldom afforded greater controversies; and when any should arise, where could they have a fitter umpire than he, by whose care they had everyone been sustained and brought up, and who had a tenderness for them all? It is no wonder that they made no distinction between minority and full age; nor looked after one and twenty, or any other age that might make them the free disposers of themselves and fortunes, when they could have no desire to be out of their pupilage: the government they had been under, during it, continued still to be more their protection than restraint; and they could nowhere find a greater security to their peace, liberties, and fortunes, than in the rule of a father.

Section 76. Thus the natural fathers of families, by an insensible change, became the politic monarchs of them too: and as they chanced to live long, and leave able and worthy heirs, for several successions, or otherwise; so they laid the foundations of hereditary, or elective kingdoms, under several constitutions and manners, according as chance, contrivance, or occasions happened to mould them. But if princes have their titles in their fathers right, and it be a sufficient proof of the natural right of fathers to political authority, because they commonly were those in whose hands we find, de facto, the exercise of government: I say, if this argument be good, it will as strongly prove, that all princes, nay princes only, ought to be priests, since it is as certain, that in the beginning, the father of the family was priest, as that he was ruler n his own household.

CHAPTER VII.

Of Political or Civil Society.

Section 77. God having made man such a creature, that in his own judgment, it was not good for him to be alone, put him under strong obligations of necessity, convenience, and inclination to drive him into society, as well as fitted him with understanding and language to continue and enjoy it. The first society was between man and wife, which gave beginning to that between parents and children; to which, in time, that between master and servant came to be added: and though all these might, and commonly did meet together, and make up but one family, wherein the master or mistress of it had some sort of rule proper to a family; each of these, or all together, came short of political society, as we shall see, if we consider the different ends, ties, and bounds of each of these.

Section 78. Conjugal society is made by a voluntary compact between man and woman; and though it consist chiefly in such a communion and right in one another's bodies as is necessary to its chief end, procreation; yet it draws with it mutual support and assistance, and a communion of interests too, as necessary not only to unite their care and affection, but also necessary to their common off-spring, who have a right to be nourished, and maintained by them, till they are able to provide for themselves.

Section 79. For the end of conjunction, between male and female, being not barely procreation, but the continuation of the species; this conjunction between male and female ought to last, even after procreation, so long as is necessary to the nourishment and support of the young ones, who are to be sustained by those that got them, until they are able to shift and provide for themselves. This rule, which the infinite wise maker has set to the works of his hands, we find the inferior creatures steadily obey. In those viviparous animals which feed on grass, the conjunction between male and female lasts no longer than the very act of copulation; because the teat of the dam being sufficient to nourish the young, until it be able to feed on grass, the male only begets, but concerns not himself for the female or young, to whose sustenance he can contribute nothing. But in beasts of prey the conjunction lasts longer: because the dam not being able well to subsist herself, and nourish her numerous off-spring by her own prey alone, a more laborious, as well as more dangerous way of living, than by feeding on grass, the assistance of the male is necessary to the maintenance of their common family, which cannot subsist till they are able to prey for themselves, but by the joint care of male and female. The same is to be observed in all birds, (except some domestic ones, where plenty of food excuses the cock from feeding, and taking care of the young brood) whose young needing food in the nest, the cock and hen continue mates, till the young are able to use their wing, and provide for themselves.

Section 80. And herein I think lies the chief, if not the only reason, why the male and female in mankind are tied to a longer conjunction than other creatures, that is because the female is capable of conceiving, and de facto is commonly with child again, and brings forth to a new birth, long before the former is out of a dependency for support on his parents help, and able to shift for himself, and has all the assistance is due to him from his parents: whereby the father, who is bound to take care for those he has begot, is under an obligation to continue in conjugal society with the same woman longer than other creatures, whose young being able to subsist of themselves, before the time of procreation returns again, the conjugal bond dissolves of itself, and they are at liberty, till Hymen at his usual anniversary season summons them again to choose new mates. Wherein one cannot but admire the wisdom of the great Creator, who having given to man foresight, and an ability to lay up for the future, as well as to supply the present necessity, has made it necessary, that society of man and wife should be more lasting, than of male and female among other creatures; that so their industry might be encouraged, and their interest better united, to make provision and lay up goods for their common issue, which uncertain mixture, or easy and frequent solutions of conjugal society would mightily disturb.

Section 81. But though these are ties upon mankind, which make the conjugal bonds more firm and lasting in man, than the other species of animals; yet it would give one reason to enquire, why this compact, where procreation and education are secured, and inheritance taken care for, may not be made determinable, either by consent, or at a certain time, or upon certain conditions, as well as any other voluntary compacts, there being no necessity in the nature of the thing, nor to the ends of it, that it should always be for life; I mean, to such as are under no restraint of any positive law, which ordains all such contracts to be perpetual.

Section 82. But the husband and wife, though they have but one common concern, yet having different understandings, will unavoidably sometimes have different wills too; it therefore being necessary that the last determination, i.e. the rule, should be placed somewhere; it naturally falls to the man's share, as the abler and the stronger. But this reaching but to the things of their common interest and property, leaves the wife in the full and free possession of what by contract is her peculiar right, and gives the husband no more power over her life than she has over his; the power of the husband being so far from that of an absolute monarch, that the wife has in many cases a liberty to separate from him, where natural right, or their contract allows it; whether that contract be made by themselves in the state of nature, or by the customs or laws of the country they live in; and the children upon such separation fall to the father or mother's lot, as such contract does determine.

Section 83. For all the ends of marriage being to be obtained under politic government, as well as in the state of nature, the civil magistrate does not abridge the right or power of either naturally necessary to those ends, that is procreation and mutual support and assistance while they are together; but only decides any controversy that may arise between man and wife about them. If it were otherwise, and that absolute sovereignty and power of life and death naturally belonged to the husband, and were necessary to the society between man and wife, there could be no matrimony in any of those countries where the husband is allowed no such absolute authority. But the ends of matrimony requiring no such power in the husband, the condition of conjugal society put it not in him, it being not at all necessary to that state. Conjugal society could subsist and attain its ends without it; nay, community of goods, and the power over them, mutual assistance and maintenance, and other things belonging to conjugal society, might be varied and regulated by that contract which unites man and wife in that society, as far as may consist with procreation and the bringing up of children till they could shift for themselves; nothing being necessary to any society, that is not necessary to the ends for which it is made.

Section 84. The society between parents and children, and the distinct rights and powers belonging respectively to them, I have treated of so largely, in the foregoing chapter that I shall not here need to say anything of it. And I think it is plain, that it is far different from a politic society.

Section 85. Master and servant are names as old as history, but given to those of far different condition; for a freeman makes himself a servant to another, by selling him, for a certain time, the service he undertakes to do, in exchange for wages he is to receive: and though this commonly puts him into the family of his master, and under the ordinary discipline thereof; yet it gives the master but a temporary power over him, and no greater than what is contained in the contract between them. But there is another sort of servants, who by a peculiar name we call slaves, who being captives taken in a just war, are by the right of nature subjected to the absolute dominion and arbitrary power of their masters. These men having, as I say, forfeited their lives, and with it their liberties, and lost their estates; and being in the state of slavery, not capable of any property, cannot in that state be considered as any part of civil society; the chief end whereof is the preservation of property.

Section 86. Let us therefore consider a master of a family with all these subordinate relations of wife, children, servants, and slaves, united under the domestic rule of a family; which, what resemblance soever it may have in its order, offices, and number too, with a little commonwealth, yet is very far from it, both in its constitution, power and end: or if it must be thought a monarchy, and the paterfamilias the absolute monarch in it, absolute monarchy will have but a very shattered and short power, when it is plain, by what has been said before, that the master of the family has a very distinct and differently limited power, both as to time and extent, over those several persons that are in it; for excepting the slave (and the family is as much a family, and his power as paterfamilias as great, whether there be any slaves in his family or no) he has no legislative power of life and death over any of them, and none too but what a mistress of a family may have as well as he. And he certainly can have no absolute power over the whole family, who has but a very limited one over every individual in it. But how a family, or any other society of men, differ from that which is properly political society, we shall best see, by considering wherein political society itself consists.

Section 87. Man being born, as has been proved, with a title to perfect freedom, and an uncontrolled enjoyment of all the rights and privileges of the law of nature, equally with any other man, or number of men in the world, has by nature a power, not only to preserve his property, that is, his life, liberty and estate, against the injuries and attempts of other men; but to judge of, and punish the breaches of that law in others, as he is persuaded the offence deserves, even with death itself, in crimes where the heinousness of the fact, in his opinion, requires it. But because no political society can be, nor subsist, without having in itself the power to preserve the property, and in order thereunto, punish the offences of all those of that society; there, and there only is political society, where everyone of the members has quitted this natural power, resigned it up into the hands of the community in all cases that exclude him not from appealing for protection to the law established by it. And thus all private judgment of every particular member being excluded, the community comes to be umpire, by settled standing rules, indifferent, and the same to all parties; and by men having authority from the community, for the execution of those rules, decides all the differences that may happen between any members of that society concerning any matter of right; and punishes those offences which any member has committed against the society, with such penalties as the law has established: whereby it is easy to discern, who are, and who are not, in political society together. Those who are united into one body, and have a common established law and judicature to appeal to, with authority to decide controversies between them, and punish offenders, are in civil society one with another: but those who have no such common people, I mean on earth, are still in the state of nature, each being, where there is no other, judge for himself, and executioner; which is, as I have before showed it, the perfect state of nature.

Section 88. And thus the commonwealth comes by a power to set down what punishment shall belong to the several transgressions which they think worthy of it, committed among the members of that society, (which is the power of making laws) as well as it has the power to punish any injury done unto any of its members, by anyone that is not of it, (which is the power of war and peace;) and all this for the preservation of the property of all the members of that society, as far as is possible. But though every man who has entered into civil society, and is become a member of any commonwealth, has thereby quitted his power to punish offences, against the law of nature, in prosecution of his own private judgment, yet with the judgment of offences, which he has given up to the legislative in all cases, where he can appeal to the magistrate, he has given a right to the commonwealth to employ his force, for the execution of the judgments of the commonwealth, whenever he shall be called to it; which indeed are his own judgments, they being made by himself, or his representative. And herein we have the original of the legislative and executive power of civil society, which is to judge by standing laws, how far offences are to be punished, when committed within the commonwealth; and also to determine, by occasional judgments founded on the present circumstances of the fact, how far injuries from without are to be vindicated; and in both these to employ all the force of all the members, when there shall be need.

Section 89. Wherever therefore any number of men are so united into one society, as to quit everyone his executive power of the law of nature, and to resign it to the public, there and there only is a political or civil society. And this is done, wherever any number of men, in the state of nature, enter into society to make one people, one body politic, under one supreme government; or else when anyone joins himself to, and incorporates with any government already made: for hereby he authorizes the society, or which is all one, the legislative thereof, to make laws for him, as the public good of the society shall require; to the execution whereof, his own assistance (as to his own decrees) is due. And this puts men out of a state of nature into that of a commonwealth, by setting up a judge on earth, with authority to determine all the controversies, and redress the injuries that may happen to any member of the commonwealth; which judge is the legislative, or magistrates appointed by it. And wherever there are any numbers of men, however associated, that have no such decisive power to appeal to, there they are still in the state of nature.

Section 90. Hence it is evident, that absolute monarchy, which by some men is counted the only government in the world, is indeed inconsistent with civil society, and so can be no form of civil-government at all: for the end of civil society, being to avoid, and remedy those inconveniencies of the state of nature, which necessarily follow from every man's being judge in his own case, by setting up a known authority, to which everyone of that society may appeal upon any injury received, or controversy that may arise, and which everyone of the society ought to obey; wherever any persons are, who have not such an authority to appeal to, for the decision of any difference between them, there those persons are still in the state of nature; and so is every absolute prince, in respect of those who are under his dominion.

Section 91. For he being supposed to have all, both legislative and executive power in himself alone, there is no judge to be found, no appeal lies open to anyone, who may fairly, and indifferently, and with authority decide, and from whose decision relief and redress may be expected of any injury or inconvenience, that may be suffered from the prince, or by his order: so that such a man, however entitled, Czar, or Grand Seignior, or how you please, is as much in the state of nature, with all under his dominion, as he is with the rest of mankind: for wherever any two men are, who have no standing rule, and common judge to appeal to on earth, for the determination of controversies of right between them, there they are still in the state of nature, and under all the inconveniencies of it, with only this woeful difference to the subject, or rather slave of an absolute prince: that whereas, in the ordinary state of nature, he has a liberty to judge of his right, and according to the best of his power, to maintain it; now, whenever his property is invaded by the will and order of his monarch, he has not only no appeal, as those in society ought to have, but as if he were degraded from the common state of rational creatures, is denied a liberty to judge of, or to defend his right; and so is exposed to all the misery and inconveniencies, that a man can fear from one, who being in the unrestrained state of nature, is yet corrupted with flattery, and armed with power.

Section 92. For he that thinks absolute power purifies men's blood, and corrects the baseness of human nature, need read but the history of this, or any other age, to be convinced of the contrary. He that would have been insolent and injurious in the woods of America, would not probably be much better in a throne; where perhaps learning and religion shall be found out to justify all that he shall do to his subjects, and the sword presently silence all those that dare question it: for what the protection of absolute monarchy is, what kind of fathers of their countries it makes princes to be, and to what a degree of happiness and security it carries civil society, where this sort of government is grown to perfection, he that will look into the late relation of Ceylon, may easily see.

Section 93. In absolute monarchies indeed, as well as other governments of the world, the subjects have an appeal to the law, and judges to decide any controversies, and restrain any violence that may happen between the subjects themselves, one among another. This everyone thinks necessary, and believes he deserves to be thought a declared enemy to society and mankind, who should go about to take it away. But whether this be from a true love of mankind and society, and such a charity as we owe all one to another, there is reason to doubt: for this is no more than what every man, who loves his own power, profit, or greatness, may and naturally must do, keep those animals from hurting, or destroying one another, who labor and drudge only for his pleasure and advantage; and so are taken care of, not out of any love the master has for them, but love of himself, and the profit they bring him: for if it be asked, what security, what fence is there, in such a state, against the violence and oppression of this absolute ruler? the very question can scarce be borne. They are ready to tell you, that it deserves death only to ask after safety.

Between subject and subject, they will grant, there must be measures, laws and judges, for their mutual peace and security: but as for the ruler, he ought to be absolute, and is above all such circumstances; because he has power to do more hurt and wrong, it is right when he does it. To ask how you may be guarded from harm, or injury, on that side where the strongest hand is to do it, is presently the voice of faction and rebellion: as if when men quitting the state of nature entered into society, they agreed that all of them but one, should be under the restraint of laws, but that he should still retain all the liberty of the state of nature, increased with power, and made licentious by impunity. This is to think, that men are so foolish, that they take care to avoid what mischiefs may be done them by pole-cats, or foxes; but are content, nay, think it safety, to be devoured by lions.

Section 94. But whatever flatterers may talk to amuse people's understandings, it hinders not men from feeling; and when they perceive, that any man, in what station soever, is out of the bounds of the civil society which they are of, and that they have no appeal on earth against any harm, they may receive from him, they are apt to think themselves in the state of nature, in respect of him whom they find to be so; and to take care, as soon as they can, to have that safety and security in civil society, for which it was first instituted, and for which only they entered into it. And therefore, though perhaps at first, (as shall be showed more at large hereafter in the following part of this discourse) someone good and excellent man having got a pre-eminency among the rest, had this deference paid to his goodness and virtue, as to a kind of natural authority, that the chief rule, with arbitration of their differences, by a tacit consent devolved into his hands, without any other caution, but the assurance they had of his uprightness and wisdom; yet when time, giving authority, and (as some men would persuade us) sacredness of customs, which the negligent, and unforeseen innocence of the first ages began, had brought in successors of another stamp, the people finding their properties not secure under the government, as then it was, (whereas government has no other end but the preservation of property) could never be safe nor at rest, nor think themselves in civil society, until the legislature was placed in collective bodies of men, call them senate, parliament, or what you please. By which means every single person became subject, equally with other the meanest men, to those laws, which he himself, as part of the legislative, had established; nor could anyone, by his own authority, avoid the force of the law, when once made; nor by any pretence of superiority plead exemption, thereby to license his own, or the miscarriages of any of his dependents. †No man in civil society can be exempted from the laws of it: for if any man may do what he thinks fit, and there be no appeal on earth, for redress or security against any harm he shall do; I ask, whether he be not perfectly still in the state of nature, and so can be no part or member of that civil society; unless anyone will say, the state of nature and civil society are one and the same thing, which I have never yet found anyone so great a patron of anarchy as to affirm.

CHAPTER VIII.

Of the Beginning of Political Societies.

Section 95. Men being, as has been said, by nature, all free, equal, and independent, no one can be put out of this estate, and subjected to the political power of another, without his own consent. The only way whereby anyone divests himself of his natural liberty, and puts on the bonds of civil society, is by agreeing with other men to join and unite into a community, for their comfortable, safe, and peaceable living one among another, in a secure enjoyment of their properties, and a greater security against any, that are not of it. This any number of men may do, because it injures not the freedom of the rest; they are left as they were in the liberty of the state of nature. When any numbers of men have so consented to make one community or government, they are thereby presently incorporated, and make one body politic, wherein the majority has a right to act and conclude the rest.

Section 96. For when any number of men have, by the consent of every individual, made a community, they have thereby made that community one body, with a power to act as one body, which is only by the will and determination of the majority: for that which acts any community, being only the consent of the individuals of it, and it being necessary to that which is one body to move one way; it is necessary the body should move that way whither the greater force carries it, which is the consent of the majority: or else it is impossible it should act or continue one body, one community, which the consent of every individual that united into it, agreed that it should; and so everyone is bound by that consent to be concluded by the majority. And therefore we see, that in assemblies, empowered to act by positive laws, where no number is set by that positive law which empowers them, the act of the majority passes for the act of the whole, and of course determines, as having, by the law of nature and reason, the power of the whole.

Section 97. And thus every man, by consenting with others to make one body politic under one government, puts himself under an obligation, to everyone of that society, to submit to the determination of the majority, and to be concluded by it; or else this original compact, whereby he with others incorporates into one society, would signify nothing, and be no compact, if he be left free, and under no other ties than he was in before in the state of nature. For what appearance would there be of any compact? what new engagement if he were no father tied by any decrees of the society, than he himself thought fit, and did actually consent to? This would be still as great a liberty, as he himself had before his compact, or anyone else in the state of nature has, who may submit himself, and consent to any acts of it if he thinks fit.

Section 98. For if the consent of the majority shall not, in reason, be received as the act of the whole, and conclude every individual; nothing but the consent of every individual can make anything to be the act of the whole: but such a consent is next to impossible ever to be had, if we consider the infirmities of health, and avocations of business, which in a number, though much less than that of a commonwealth, will necessarily keep many away from the public assembly. To which if we add the variety of opinions, and contrariety of interests, which unavoidably happen in all collections of men, the coming into society upon such terms would be only like Cato's coming into the theatre, only to go out again. Such a constitution as this would make the mighty Leviathan of a shorter duration, than the feeblest creatures, and not let it outlast the day it was born in: which cannot be supposed, till we can think, that rational creatures should desire and constitute societies only to be dissolved: for where the majority cannot conclude the rest, there they cannot act as one body, and consequently will be immediately dissolved again.

Section 99. Whosoever therefore out of a state of nature unite into a community, must be understood to give up all the power, necessary to the ends for which they unite into society, to the majority of the community, unless they expressly agreed in any number greater than the majority. And this is done by barely agreeing to unite into one political society, which is the entire compact that is, or needs be, between the individuals, that enter into, or make up a commonwealth. And thus that, which begins and actually constitutes any political society, is nothing but the consent of any number of freemen capable of a majority to unite and incorporate into such a society. And this is that and that only, which did, or could give beginning to any lawful government in the world.

Section 100. To this I find two objections made.

- First, that there are no instances to be found in history, of a company of men independent, and equal one among another, that met together, and in this way began and set up a government.

- Secondly, it is impossible that men should do so, because all men being born under government, they are to submit to that, and are not at liberty to begin a new one.

Section 101. To the first there is this to answer, that it is not at all to be wondered, that history gives us but a very little account of men that lived together in the state of nature. The inconveniences of that condition, and the love and want of society, no sooner brought any number of them together, but they presently united and incorporated, if they designed to continue together. And if we may not suppose men ever to have been in the state of nature, because we hear not much of them in such a state, we may as well suppose the armies of Salmanasser or Xerxes were never children, because we hear little of them, until they were men, and embodied in armies. Government is everywhere antecedent to records, and letters seldom come in among a people until a long continuation of civil society has, by other more necessary areas, provided for their safety, ease, and plenty: and then they begin to look after the history of their founders, and search into their original, when they have outlived the memory of it: for it is with commonwealths as with particular persons, they are commonly ignorant of their own births and infancies: and if they know anything of their original, they are beholden for it, to the accidental records that others have kept of it. And those that we have, of the beginning of any polities in the world, excepting that of the Jews, where God himself immediately interposed, and which favors not at all paternal dominion, are all either plain instances of such a beginning as I have mentioned, or at least have manifest footsteps of it.

Section 102. He must show a strange inclination to deny evident matter of fact, when it agrees not with his hypothesis, who will not allow, that the beginning of Rome and Venice were by the uniting together of several men free and independent one of another, among whom there was no natural superiority or subjection. And if Josephus Acosta's word may be taken, he tells us, that in many parts of America there was no government at all. There are great and apparent conjectures, says he, that these men, speaking of those of Peru, for a long time had neither kings nor commonwealths, but lived in troops, as they do this day in Florida, the Cheriquanas, those of Brazil, and many other nations, which have no certain kings, but as occasion is offered, in peace or war, they choose their captains as they please, l. i. c. 25. If it be said, that every man there was born subject to his father or the head of his family; that the subjection due from a child to a father took not away his freedom of uniting into what political society he thought fit, has been already proved. But be that as it will, these men, it is evident, were actually free; and whatever superiority some politicians now would place in any of them, they themselves claimed it not, but by consent were all equal, till by the same consent they set rulers over themselves. So that their politic societies all began from a voluntary union, and the mutual agreement of men freely acting in the choice of their governors, and forms of government.

Section 103. And I hope those who went away from Sparea with Palantus, mentioned by Justin, l. iii. c. 4. will be allowed to have been freemen independent one of another, and to have set up a government over themselves, by their own consent. Thus I have given several examples, out of history, of people free and in the state of nature that being met together incorporated and began a commonwealth. And if the want of such instances be an argument to prove that government were not, nor could not be so begun, I suppose the contenders for paternal empire were better let it alone, than urge it against natural liberty: for if they can give so many instances, out of history, of governments begun upon paternal right, I think (though at best an argument from what has been, to what should of right be, has no great force) one might, without any great danger, yield them the cause. But if I might advise them in the case, they would do well not to search too much into the original of governments, as they have begun de facto, lest they should find, at the foundation of most of them, something very little favorable to the design they promote, and such a power as they contend for.

Section 104. But to conclude, reason being plain on our side, that men are naturally free, and the examples of history showing, that the governments of the world, that were begun in peace, had their beginning laid on that foundation, and were made by the consent of the people; there can be little room for doubt, either where the right is, or what has been the opinion, or practice of mankind, about the first erecting of governments.

Section 105. I will not deny that if we look back as far as history will direct us, towards the original of commonwealths, we shall generally find them under the government and administration of one man. And I am also apt to believe, that where a family was numerous enough to subsist by itself, and continued entire together, without mixing with others, as it often happens, where there is much land, and few people, the government commonly began in the father: for the father having, by the law of nature, the same power with every man else to punish, as he thought fit, any offences against that law, might thereby punish his transgressing children, even when they were men, and out of their pupilage; and they were very likely to submit to his punishment, and all join with him against the offender, in their turns, giving him thereby power to execute his sentence against any transgression, and so in effect make him the law-maker, and governor over all that remained in conjunction with his family. He was fittest to be trusted; paternal affection secured their property and interest under his care; and the custom of obeying him, in their childhood, made it easier to submit to him, rather than to any other. If therefore they must have one to rule them, as government is hardly to be avoided among men that live together; who so likely to be the man as he that was their common father; unless negligence, cruelty, or any other defect of mind or body made him unfit for it? But when either the father died, and left his next heir, for want of age, wisdom, courage, or any other qualities, less fit for rule; or where several families met, and consented to continue together; there, it is not to be doubted, but they used their natural freedom, to set up him, whom they judged the ablest, and most likely, to rule well over them. Conformable hereunto we find the people of America, who (living out of the reach of the conquering swords, and spreading domination of the two great empires of Peru and Mexico) enjoyed their own natural freedom, though, cæteris paribus, they commonly prefer the heir of their deceased king; yet if they find him any way weak, or incapable, they pass him by, and set up the stoutest and bravest man for their ruler.

Section 106. Thus, though looking back as far as records give us any account of peopling the world, and the history of nations, we commonly find the government to be in one hand; yet it destroys not that which I affirm, that is that the beginning of politic society depends upon the consent of the individuals, to join into, and make one society; who, when they are thus incorporated, might set up what form of government they thought fit. But this having given occasion to men to mistake, and think, that by nature government was monarchical, and belonged to the father, it may not be amiss here to consider, why people in the beginning generally pitched upon this form, which though perhaps the father's pre-eminence might, in the first institution of some commonwealths, give a rise to, and place in the beginning, the power in one hand; yet it is plain that the reason, that continued the form of government in a single person, was not any regard, or respect to paternal authority; since all petty monarchies, that is, almost all monarchies, near their original, have been commonly, at least upon occasion, elective.

Section 107. First then, in the beginning of things, the father's government of the childhood of those sprung from him, having accustomed them to the rule of one man, and taught them that where it was exercised with care and skill, with affection and love to those under it, it was sufficient to procure and preserve to men all the political happiness they sought for in society. It was no wonder that they should pitch upon, and naturally run into that form of government, which from their infancy they had been all accustomed to; and which, by experience, they had found both easy and safe. To which, if we add, that monarchy being simple, and most obvious to men, whom neither experience had instructed in forms of government, nor the ambition or insolence of empire had taught to beware of the encroachments of prerogative, or the inconveniencies of absolute power, which monarchy in succession was apt to lay claim to, and bring upon them; it was not at all strange, that they should not much trouble themselves to think of methods of restraining any exorbitances of those to whom they had given the authority over them, and of balancing the power of government, by placing several parts of it in different hands. They had neither felt the oppression of tyrannical dominion, nor did the fashion of the age, nor their possessions, or way of living, (which afforded little matter for covetousness or ambition) give them any reason to apprehend or provide against it; and therefore it is no wonder they put themselves into such a frame of government, as was not only, as I said, most obvious and simple, but also best suited to their present state and condition; which stood more in need of defense against foreign invasions and injuries, than of multiplicity of laws. The equality of a simple poor way of living, confining their desires within the narrow bounds of each man's small property, made few controversies, and so no need of many laws to decide them, or variety of officers to superintend the process, or look after the execution of justice, where there were but few trespasses, and few offenders. Since then those, who liked one another so well as to join into society, cannot but be supposed to have some acquaintance and friendship together, and some trust one in another; they could not but have greater apprehensions of others, than of one another: and therefore their first care and thought cannot but be supposed to be, how to secure themselves against foreign force. It was natural for them to put themselves under a frame of government which might best serve to that end, and choose the wisest and bravest man to conduct them in their wars, and lead them out against their enemies, and in this chiefly be their ruler.

Section 108. Thus we see, that the kings of the Indians in America, which is still a pattern of the first ages in Asia and Europe, while the inhabitants were too few for the country, and want of people and money gave men no temptation to enlarge their possessions of land, or contest for wider extent of ground, are little more than generals of their armies; and though they command absolutely in war, yet at home and in time of peace they exercise very little dominion, and have but a very moderate sovereignty, the resolutions of peace and war being ordinarily either in the people, or in a council. Though the war itself, which admits not of plurality of governors, naturally devolves the command into the king's sole authority.

Section 109. And thus in Israel itself, the chief business of their judges, and first kings, seems to have been to be captains in war, and leaders of their armies; which (besides what is signified by going out and in before the people, which was, to march forth to war, and home again in the heads of their forces) appears plainly in the story of Jephtha. The Ammonites making war upon Israel, the Gileadites in fear send to Jephtha, a bastard of their family whom they had cast off, and reconcile with him, if he will assist them against the Ammonites, to make him their ruler; which they do in these words, And the people made him head and captain over them, Judg. xi. 11. which was, as it seems, all one as to be judge. And he judged Israel, Judg. xii. 7. that is, was their captain-general six years. So when Jotham upbraids the Shechemites with the obligation they had to Gideon, who had been their judge and ruler, he tells them, He fought for you, and adventured his life far, and delivered you out of the hands of Midian, Judg. ix. 17. Nothing mentioned of him, but what he did as a general: and indeed that is all is found in his history, or in any of the rest of the judges. And Abimelech particularly is called king, though at most he was but their general. And when, being weary of the ill conduct of Samuel's sons, the children of Israel desired a king, like all the nations to judge them, and to go out before them, and to fight their battles, 1 Sam. viii. 20. God granting their desire says to Samuel, I will send you a man, and you shall anoint him to be captain over my people Israel, that he may save my people out of the hands of the Philistines, ix. 16. As if the only business of a king had been to lead out their armies, and fight in their defense; and accordingly at his inauguration pouring a vial of oil upon him, declares to Saul, that the Lord had anointed him to be captain over his inheritance, x. 1. And therefore those, who after Saul's being solemnly chosen and saluted king by the tribes at Mispah, were unwilling to have him their king, made no other objection but this, How shall this man save us? v. 27. as if they should have said, this man is unfit to be our king, not having skill and conduct enough in war, to be able to defend us. And when God resolved to transfer the government to David, it is in these words, But now your kingdom shall not continue: the Lord has sought him a man after his own heart, and the Lord has commanded him to be captain over his people, xiii. 14. As if the whole kingly authority were nothing else but to be their general: and therefore the tribes who had stuck to Saul's family, and opposed David's reign, when they came to Hebron with terms of submission to him, they tell him, among other arguments they had to submit to him as to their king, that he was in effect their king in Saul's time, and therefore they had no reason but to receive him as their king now. Also (say they) in time past, when Saul was king over us, you were he that let out and brought in Israel, and the Lord said unto you, You shall feed my people Israel, and you shall be a captain over Israel.

Section 110. Thus, whether a family by degrees grew up into a commonwealth, and the fatherly authority being continued on to the elder son, everyone in his turn growing up under it, tacitly submitted to it, and the easiness and equality of it not offending anyone, everyone acquiesced, till time seemed to have confirmed it, and settled a right of succession by prescription: or whether several families, or the descendants of several families, whom chance, neighborhood, or business brought together, uniting into society, the need of a general, whose conduct might defend them against their enemies in war, and the great confidence the innocence and sincerity of that poor but virtuous age, (such as are almost all those which begin governments, that ever come to last in the world) gave men one of another, made the first beginners of commonwealths generally put the rule into one man's hand, without any other express limitation or restraint, but what the nature of the thing, and the end of government required: whichever of those it was that at first put the rule into the hands of a single person, certain it is nobody was entrusted with it but for the public good and safety, and to those ends, in the infancies of commonwealths, those who had it commonly used it. And unless they had done so, young societies could not have subsisted; without such nursing fathers tender and careful of the public weal, all governments would have sunk under the weakness and infirmities of their infancy, and the prince and the people had soon perished together.

Section 111. But though the golden age (before vain ambition, and *amor sceleratus habendi*, evil concupiscence, had corrupted men's minds into a mistake of true power and honor) had more virtue, and consequently better governors, as well as less vicious subjects; and there was then no stretching prerogative on the one side, to oppress the people; nor consequently on the other, any dispute about privilege, to lessen or restrain the power of the magistrate, and so no contest between rulers and people about governors or government: yet, when ambition and luxury in future ages would retain and increase the power, without doing the business for which it was given; and aided by flattery, taught princes to have distinct and separate interests from their people, men found it necessary to examine more carefully the original and rights of government; and to find out ways to restrain the exorbitances, and prevent the abuses of that power, which they having entrusted in another's hands only for their own good, they found was made use of to hurt them.

Section 112. Thus we may see how probable it is, that people that were naturally free, and by their own consent either submitted to the government of their father, or united together out of different families to make a government, should generally put the rule into one man's hands, and choose to be under the conduct of a single person, without so much as by express conditions limiting or regulating his power, which they thought safe enough in his honesty and prudence; though they never dreamed of monarchy being Jure Divino, which we never heard of among mankind, till it was revealed to us by the divinity of this last age; nor ever allowed paternal power to have a right to dominion, or to be the foundation of all government. And thus much may suffice to show, that as far as we have any light from history, we have reason to conclude, that all peaceful beginnings of government have been laid in the consent of the people. I say peaceful, because I shall have occasion in another place to speak of conquest, which some esteem a way of beginning of governments.

Section 113. The other objection I find urged against the beginning of polities, in the way I have mentioned, is this, that is: that all men being born under government, some or other, it is impossible any of them should ever be free, and at liberty to unite together, and begin a new one, or ever be able to erect a lawful government.

If this argument be good; I ask, how came so many lawful monarchies into the world? for if anybody, upon this supposition, can show me anyone man in any age of the world free to begin a lawful monarchy, I will be bound to show him ten other freemen at liberty, at the same time to unite and begin a new government under a regal, or any other form; it being demonstration, that if anyone, born under the dominion of another, may be so free as to have a right to command others in a new and distinct empire, everyone that is born under the dominion of another may be so free too, and may become a ruler, or subject, of a distinct separate government. And so by this their own principles, either all men, however born, are free, or else there is but one lawful prince, one lawful government in the world. And then they have nothing to do, but barely to show us which that is; which when they have done, I doubt not but all mankind will easily agree to pay obedience to him.

Section 114. Though it is a sufficient answer to their objection, to show that it involves them in the same difficulties that it does those they use it against; yet I shall endeavor to discover the weakness of this argument a little further.

All men, say they, are born under government, and therefore they cannot be at liberty to begin a new one. Everyone is born a subject to his father, or his prince, and is therefore under the perpetual tie of subjection and allegiance. It is plain mankind never owned nor considered any such natural subjection that they were born in, to one or to the other that tied them, without their own consents, to a subjection to them and their heirs.

Section 115. For there are no examples so frequent in history, both sacred and profane, as those of men withdrawing themselves, and their obedience, from the jurisdiction they were born under, and the family or community they were bred up in, and setting up new governments in other places; from whence sprang all that number of petty commonwealths in the beginning of ages, and which always multiplied, as long as there was room enough, until the stronger, or more fortunate, swallowed the weaker; and those great ones again breaking to pieces, dissolved into lesser dominions. All which are so many testimonies against paternal sovereignty, and plainly prove, that it was not the natural right of the father descending to his heirs, that made governments in the beginning, since it was impossible, upon that ground, there should have been so many little kingdoms; all must have been but only one universal monarchy, if men had not been at liberty to separate themselves from their families, and the government, be it what it will, that was set up in it, and go and make distinct commonwealths and other governments, as they thought fit.

Section 116. This has been the practice of the world from its first beginning to this day; nor is it now any more hindrance to the freedom of mankind, that they are born under constituted and ancient polities, that have established laws, and set forms of government, than if they were born in the woods, among the unconfined inhabitants, that run loose in them: for those, who would persuade us, that by being born under any government, we are naturally subjects to it, and have no more any title or pretence to the freedom of the state of nature, have no other reason (other than that of paternal power, which we have already answered) to produce for it, but only, because our fathers or progenitors passed away their natural liberty, and thereby bound up themselves and their posterity to a perpetual subjection to the government, which they themselves submitted to. It is true, that whatever engagements or promises anyone has made for himself, he is under the obligation of them, but cannot, by any compact whatsoever, bind his children or posterity: for his son, when a man, being altogether as free as the father, any act of the father can no more give away the liberty of the son, than it can of anybody else: he may indeed annex such conditions to the land, he enjoyed as a subject of any commonwealth, as may oblige his son to be of that community, if he will enjoy those possessions which were his father's; because that estate being his father's property, he may dispose, or settle it, as he pleases.

Section 117. And this has generally given the occasion to mistake in this matter; because commonwealths not permitting any part of their dominions to be dismembered, nor to be enjoyed by any but those of their community, the son cannot ordinarily enjoy the possessions of his father, but under the same terms his father did, by becoming a member of the society; whereby he puts himself presently under the government he finds there established, as much as any other subject of that commonwealth. And thus the consent of freemen, born under government, which only makes them members of it, being given separately in their turns, as each comes to be of age, and not in a multitude together; people take no notice of it, and thinking it not done at all, or not necessary, conclude they are naturally subjects as they are men.

Section 118. But, it is plain, governments themselves understand it otherwise; they claim no power over the son, because of that they had over the father; nor look on children as being their subjects, by their fathers being so. If a subject of England has a child, by an English woman in France, whose subject is he? Not the king of England's; for he must have leave to be admitted to the privileges of it: nor the king of France's; for how then has his father a liberty to bring him away, and breed him as he pleases? and who ever was judged as a traitor or deserter, if he left, or warred against a country, for being barely born in it of parents that were aliens there? It is plain then, by the practice of governments themselves, as well as by the law of right reason, that a child is born a subject of no country or government. He is under his father's tuition and authority, until he comes to age of discretion; and then he is a freeman, at liberty what government he will put himself under, what body politic he will unite himself to: for if an Englishman's son, born in France, be at liberty, and may do so, it is evident there is no tie upon him by his father's being a subject of this kingdom; nor is he bound up by any compact of his ancestors. And why then has not his son, by the same reason, the same liberty, though he is born anywhere else? Since the power that a father has naturally over his children, is the same, wherever they be born, and the ties of natural obligations, are not bounded by the positive limits of kingdoms and commonwealths.

Section 119. Every man being, as has been showed, naturally free, and nothing being able to put him into subjection to any earthly power, but only his own consent; it is to be considered, what shall be understood to be a sufficient declaration of a man's consent, to make him subject to the laws of any government. There is a common distinction of an express and a tacit consent, which will concern our present case. Nobody doubts but an express consent, of any man entering into any society, makes him a perfect member of that society, a subject of that government. The difficulty is, what ought to be looked upon as a tacit consent, and how far it binds, i.e. how far anyone shall be looked on to have consented, and thereby submitted to any government, where he has made no expressions of it at all. And to this I say, that every man, that has any possessions, or enjoyment, of any part of the dominions of any government, does thereby give his tacit consent, and is as far forth obliged to obedience to the laws of that government, during such enjoyment, as anyone under it; whether this his possession be of land, to him and his heirs forever, or a lodging only for a week; or whether it be barely travelling freely on the highway; and in effect, it reaches as far as the very being of anyone within the territories of that government.

Section 120. To understand this the better, it is fit to consider, that every man, when he at first incorporates himself into any commonwealth, he, by his uniting himself thereunto, annexed also, and submits to the community, those possessions, which he has, or shall acquire, that do not already belong to any other government: for it would be a direct contradiction, for anyone to enter into society with others for the securing and regulating of property; and yet to suppose his land, whose property is to be regulated by the laws of the society, should be exempt from the jurisdiction of that government, to which he himself, the proprietor of the land, is a subject. By the same act therefore, whereby anyone unites his person, which was before free, to any commonwealth; by the same he unites his possessions, which were before free, to it also; and they become, both of them, person and possession, subject to the government and dominion of that commonwealth, as long as it has a being. Whoever therefore, from thenceforth, by inheritance, purchase, permission, or other ways, enjoys any part of the land, so annexed to, and under the government of that commonwealth, must take it with the condition it is under; that is, of submitting to the government of the commonwealth, under whose jurisdiction it is, as far as any subject of it.

Section 121. But since the government has a direct jurisdiction only over the land, and reaches the possessor of it, (before he has actually incorporated himself in the society) only as he dwells upon, and enjoys that; the obligation anyone is under, by virtue of such enjoyment, to submit to the government, begins and ends with the enjoyment; so that whenever the owner, who has given nothing but such a tacit consent to the government, will, by donation, sale, or otherwise, quit the said possession, he is at liberty to go and incorporate himself into any other commonwealth; or to agree with others to begin a new one, in vacuis locis, in any part of the world, they can find free and unpossessed: whereas he, that has once, by actual agreement, and any express declaration, given his consent to be of any commonwealth, is, perpetually and indispensably obliged to be, and remain unalterably a subject to it, and can never be again in the liberty of the state of nature; unless, by any calamity, the government he was under comes to be dissolved; or else by some public act cuts him off from being any longer a member of it.

Section 122. But submitting to the laws of any country, living quietly, and enjoying privileges and protection under them, makes not a man a member of that society: this is only a local protection and homage due to and from all those, who, not being in a state of war, come within the territories belonging to any government, to all parts whereof the force of its laws extends. But this no more makes a man a member of that society, a perpetual subject of that commonwealth, than it would make a man a subject to another, in whose family he found it convenient to abide for some time; though, while he continued in it, he were obliged to comply with the laws, and submit to the government he found there. And thus we see, that foreigners, by living all their lives under another government, and enjoying the privileges and protection of it, though they are bound, even in conscience, to submit to its administration, as far north as any area; yet do not thereby come to be subjects or members of that commonwealth. Nothing can make any man so, but his actually entering into it by positive engagement, and express promise and compact. This is that, which I think, concerning the beginning of political societies, and that consent which makes anyone a member of any commonwealth.

CHAPTER IX.

Of the Ends of Political Society and Government.

Section 123. If man in the state of nature be so free, as has been said; if he be absolute lord of his own person and possessions, equal to the greatest, and subject to nobody, why will he part with his freedom? why will he give up this empire, and subject himself to the dominion and control of any other power? To which it is obvious to answer, that though in the state of nature he has such a right, yet the enjoyment of it is very uncertain, and constantly exposed to the invasion of others: for all being kings as much as he, every man his equal, and the greater part no strict observers of equity and justice, the enjoyment of the property he has in this state is very unsafe, very unsecure. This makes him willing to quit a condition, which, however free, is full of fears and continual dangers: and it is not without reason, that he seeks out, and is willing to join in society with others, who are already united, or have a mind to unite, for the mutual preservation of their lives, liberties and estates, which I call by the general name, property.

Section 124. The great and chief end, therefore, of men's uniting into commonwealths, and putting themselves under government, is the preservation of their property. To which in the state of nature there are many things wanting.

First, there must be an established, settled, known law, received and allowed by common consent to be the standard of right and wrong, and the common measure to decide all controversies between them: for though the law of nature be plain and intelligible to all rational creatures; yet men being biased by their interest, as well as ignorant for want of study of it, are not apt to allow of it as a law binding to them in the application of it to their particular cases.

Section 125. Secondly, In the state of nature there wants a known and indifferent judge, with authority to determine all differences according to the established law: for everyone in that state being both judge and executioner of the law of nature, men being partial to themselves, passion and revenge is very apt to carry them too far, and with too much heat, in their own cases; as well as negligence, and lack of concern, to make them too remiss in other men's.

Section 126. Thirdly, In the state of nature there often wants power to back and support the sentence when right, and to give it due execution. They who by any injustice offended, will seldom fail, where they are able, by force to make good their injustice; such resistance many times makes the punishment dangerous, and frequently destructive, to those who attempt it.

Section 127. Thus mankind, notwithstanding all the privileges of the state of nature, being but in an ill condition, while they remain in it, are quickly driven into society. Hence it comes to pass, that we seldom find any number of men live any time together in this state. The inconveniencies that they are therein exposed to, by the irregular and uncertain exercise of the power every man has of punishing the transgressions of others, make them take sanctuary under the established laws of government, and therein seek the preservation of their property. It is this makes them so willingly give up everyone his single power of punishing, to be exercised by such alone, as shall be appointed to it among them; and by such rules as the community, or those authorized by them to that purpose, shall agree on. And in this we have the original right and rise of both the legislative and executive power, as well as of the governments and societies themselves.

Section 128. For in the state of nature, to omit the liberty he has of innocent delights, a man has two powers. The first is to do whatsoever he thinks fit for the preservation of himself, and others within the permission of the law of nature: by which law, common to them all, he and all the rest of mankind are one community, make up one society, distinct from all other creatures. And were it not for the corruption and virtuousness of degenerate men, there would be no need of any other; no necessity that men should separate from this great and natural community, and by positive agreements combine into smaller and divided associations.

The other power a man has in the state of nature is the power to punish the crimes committed against that law. Both these he gives up, when he joins in a private, if I may so call it, or particular politic society, and incorporates into any commonwealth, separate from the rest of mankind.

Section 129. The first power, that is of doing whatsoever be thought for the preservation of himself, and the rest of mankind, he gives up to be regulated by laws made by the society, so far forth as the preservation of himself, and the rest of that society shall require; which laws of the society in many things confine the liberty he had by the law of nature.

Section 130. Secondly, The power of punishing he wholly gives up, and engages his natural force, (which he might before employ in the execution of the law of nature, by his own single authority, as he thought fit) to assist the executive power of the society, as the law thereof shall require: for being now in a new state, wherein he is to enjoy many conveniences, from the labor, assistance, and society of others in the same community, as well as protection from its whole strength; he is to part also with as much of his natural liberty, in providing for himself, as the good, prosperity, and safety of the society shall require; which is not only necessary, but just, since the other members of the society do the like.

Section 131. But though men, when they enter into society, give up the equality, liberty, and executive power they had in the state of nature, into the hands of the society, to be so far disposed of by the legislative, as the good of the society shall require; yet it being only with an intention in everyone the better to preserve himself, his liberty and property; (for no rational creature can be supposed to change his condition with an intention to be worse) the power of the society, or legislative constituted by them, can never be supposed to extend father, than the common good; but is obliged to secure everyone's property, by providing against those three defects above mentioned, that made the state of nature so unsafe and uneasy. And so whoever has the legislative or supreme power of any commonwealth, is bound to govern by established standing laws, promulgated and known to the people, and not by extemporary decrees; by indifferent and upright judges, who are to decide controversies by those laws; and to employ the force of the community at home, only in the execution of such laws, or abroad to prevent or redress foreign injuries, and secure the community from inroads and invasion. And all this to be directed to no other end, but the peace, safety, and public good of the people.

CHAPTER X.

Of the Forms of a Commonwealth.

Section 132. The majority having, as has been showed, upon men's first uniting into society, the whole power of the community naturally in them, may employ all that power in making laws for the community from time to time, and executing those laws by officers of their own appointing; and then the form of the government is a perfect democracy: or else may put the power of making laws into the hands of a few select men, and their heirs or successors; and then it is an oligarchy: or else into the hands of one man, and then it is a monarchy: if to him and his heirs, it is an hereditary monarchy: if to him only for life, but upon his death the power only of nominating a successor to return to them; an elective monarchy. And so accordingly of these the community may make compounded and mixed forms of government, as they think good. And if the legislative power be at first given by the majority to one or more persons only for their lives, or any limited time, and then the supreme power to revert to them again; when it is so reverted, the community may dispose of it again anew into what hands they please, and so constitute a new form of government: for the form of government depending upon the placing the supreme power, which is the legislative, it being impossible to conceive that an inferior power should prescribe to a superior, or any but the supreme make laws, according as the power of making laws is placed, such is the form of the commonwealth.

Section 133. By commonwealth, I must be understood all along to mean, not a democracy, or any form of government, but any independent community, which the Latins signified by the word civitas, to which the word which best answers in our language, is commonwealth, and most properly expresses such a society of men, which community or city in English does not; for there may be subordinate communities in a government; and city among us has a quite different notion from commonwealth: and therefore, to avoid ambiguity, I crave leave to use the word commonwealth in that sense, in which I find it used by king James the first; and I take it to be its genuine signification; which if anybody dislike, I consent with him to change it for a better.

CHAPTER XI.

Of the Extent of the Legislative Power.

Section 134. The great end of men's entering into society, being the enjoyment of their properties in peace and safety, and the great instrument and means of that being the laws established in that society; the first and fundamental positive law of all commonwealths is the establishing of the legislative power; as the first and fundamental natural law, which is to govern even the legislative itself, is the preservation of the society, and (as far as will consist with the public good) of every person in it. This legislative is not only the supreme power of the commonwealth, but sacred and unalterable in the hands where the community have once placed it; nor can any edict of anybody else, in what form soever conceived, or by what power soever backed, have the force and obligation of a law, which has not its sanction from that legislative which the public has chosen and appointed: for without this the law could not have that, which is absolutely necessary to its being a law, the consent of the society, over whom nobody can have a power to make laws, but by their own consent, and by authority received from them; and therefore all the obedience, which by the most solemn ties anyone can be obliged to pay, ultimately terminates in this supreme power, and is directed by those laws which it enacts: nor can any oaths to any foreign power whatsoever, or any domestic subordinate power, discharge any member of the society from his obedience to the legislative, acting pursuant to their trust; nor oblige him to any obedience contrary to the laws so enacted, or father than they do allow; it being ridiculous to imagine one can be tied ultimately to obey any power in the society, which is not the supreme.

Section 135. Though the legislative, whether placed in one or more, whether it be always in being, or only by intervals, though it be the supreme power in every commonwealth; yet,

First, It is not, nor can possibly be absolutely arbitrary over the lives and fortunes of the people: for it being but the joint power of every member of the society given up to that person, or assembly, which is legislator; it can be no more than those persons had in a state of nature before they entered into society, and gave up to the community: for nobody can transfer to another more power than he has in himself; and nobody has an absolute arbitrary power over himself, or over any other, to destroy his own life, or take away the life or property of another. A man, as has been proved, cannot subject himself to the arbitrary power of another; and having in the state of nature no arbitrary power over the life, liberty, or possession of another, but only so much as the law of nature gave him for the preservation of himself, and the rest of mankind; this is all he does, or can give up to the commonwealth, and by it to the legislative power, so that the legislative can have no more than this. Their power, in the utmost bounds of it, is limited to the public good of the society. It is a power that has no other end but preservation, and therefore can never have a right to destroy, enslave, or designedly to impoverish the subjects. The obligations of the law of nature cease not in society, but only in many cases are drawn closer, and have by human laws known penalties annexed to them, to enforce their observation. Thus the law of nature stands as an eternal rule to all men, legislators as well as others. The rules that they make for other men's actions, must, as well as their own and other men's actions, be conformable to the law of nature, i.e. to the will of God, of which that is a declaration, and the fundamental law of nature being the preservation of mankind, no human sanction can be good, or valid against it.

Section 136. Secondly, The legislative, or supreme authority, cannot assume to its self a power to rule by extemporary arbitrary decrees, but is bound to dispense justice, and decide the rights of the subject by promulgated standing laws, and known authorized judges: for the law of nature being unwritten, and so nowhere to be found but in the minds of men, they who through passion or interest shall misapply it cannot so easily be convinced of their mistake where there is no established judge: and so it serves not, as it ought, to determine the rights, and fence the properties of those that live under it, especially where everyone is judge, interpreter, and executioner of it too, and that in his own case: and he that has right on his side, having ordinarily but his own single strength, has not force enough to defend himself from injuries, or to punish delinquents. To avoid these inconveniencies, which disorder men's properties in the state of nature, men unite into societies, that they may have the united strength of the whole society to secure and defend their properties, and may have standing rules to bound it, by which everyone may know what is his. To this end it is that men give up all their natural power to the society which they enter into, and the community put the legislative power into such hands as they think fit, with this trust, that they shall be governed by declared laws, or else their peace, quiet, and property will still be at the same uncertainty, as it was in the state of nature.

Section 137. Absolute arbitrary power, or governing without settled standing laws, can neither of them consist with the ends of society and government, which men would not quit the freedom of the state of nature for, and tie themselves up under, were it not to preserve their lives, liberties and fortunes, and by stated rules of right and property to secure their peace and quiet. It cannot be supposed that they should intend, had they a power so to do, to give to anyone, or more, an absolute arbitrary power over their persons and estates, and put a force into the magistrate's hand to execute his unlimited will arbitrarily upon them. This were to put themselves into a worse condition than the state of nature, wherein they had a liberty to defend their right against the injuries of others, and were upon equal terms of force to maintain it, whether invaded by a single man, or many in combination. Whereas by supposing they have given up themselves to the absolute arbitrary power and will of a legislator, they have disarmed themselves, and armed him, to make a prey of them when he pleases; he being in a much worse condition, who is exposed to the arbitrary power of one man, who has the command of 100,000, than he that is exposed to the arbitrary power of 100,000 single men; nobody being secure, that his will, who has such a command, is better than that of other men, though his force be 100,000 times stronger. And therefore, whatever form the commonwealth is under, the ruling power ought to govern by declared and received laws, and nor by extemporary dictates and undetermined resolutions: for then mankind will be in a far worse condition than in the state of nature, if they shall have armed one, or a few men with the joint power of a multitude, to force them to obey at pleasure the exorbitant and unlimited decrees of their sudden thoughts, or unrestrained, and until that moment unknown wills, without having any measures set down which may guide and justify their actions: for all the power the government has, being only for the good of the society, as it ought not to be arbitrary and at pleasure, so it ought to be exercised by established and promulgated laws; that both the people may know their duty, and be safe and secure within the limits of the law; and the rulers too kept within their bounds, and not be tempted, by the power they have in their hands, to employ it to such purposes, and by such measures, as they would not have known, and own not willingly.

Section 138. Thirdly, The supreme power cannot take from any man any part of his property without his own consent: for the preservation of property being the end of government, and that for which men enter into society, it necessarily supposes and requires, that the people should have property, without which they must be supposed to lose that, by entering into society, which was the end for which they entered into it; too gross an absurdity for any man to own. Men therefore in society having property, they have such a right to the goods, which by the law of the community are theirs, that nobody has a right to take their substance or any part of it from them, without their own consent: without this they have no property at all; for I have truly no property in that, which another can by right take from me, when he pleases, against my consent. Hence it is a mistake to think, that the supreme or legislative power of any commonwealth, can do what it will, and dispose of the estates of the subject arbitrarily, or take any part of them at pleasure. This is not much to be feared in governments where the legislative consists, wholly or in part, in assemblies which are variable, whose members, upon the dissolution of the assembly, are subjects under the common laws of their country, equally with the rest. But in governments, where the legislative is in one lasting assembly always in being, or in one man, as in absolute monarchies, there is danger still, that they will think themselves to have a distinct interest from the rest of the community; and so will be apt to increase their own riches and power, by taking what they think fit from the people: for a man's property is not at all secure, though there be good and equitable laws to set the bounds of it between him and his fellow subjects, if he who commands those subjects have power to take from any private man, what part he pleases of his property, and use and dispose of it as he thinks good.

Section 139. But government, into whatsoever hands it is put, being, as I have before showed, entrusted with this condition, and for thousand, that men might have and secure their properties; the prince, or senate, however it may have power to make laws, for the regulating of property between the subjects one among another, yet can never have a power to take to themselves the whole, or any part of the subjects property, without their own consent: for this would be in effect to leave them no property at all. And to let us see, that even absolute power, where it is necessary, is not arbitrary by being absolute, but is still limited by that reason, and confined to those ends, which required it in some cases to be absolute, we need look no farther than the common practice of martial discipline: for the preservation of the army, and in it of the whole commonwealth, requires an absolute obedience to the command of every superior officer, and it is justly death to disobey or dispute the most dangerous or unreasonable of them; but yet we see, that neither the sergeant, that could command a soldier to march up to the mouth of a cannon, or stand in a breach, where he is almost sure to perish, can command that soldier to give him one penny of his money; nor the general, that can condemn him to death for deserting his post, or for not obeying the most desperate orders, can yet, with all his absolute power of life and death, dispose of one farthing of that soldier's estate, or seize one jot of his goods; whom yet he can command anything, and hang for the least disobedience; because such a blind obedience is necessary to that end, for which the commander has his power, that is the preservation of the rest; but the disposing of his goods has nothing to do with it.

Section 140. It is true, governments cannot be supported without great charge, and it is fit everyone who enjoys his share of the protection, should pay out of his estate his proportion for the maintenance of it. But still it must be with his own consent, i.e. the consent of the majority, giving it either by themselves, or their representatives chosen by them: for if anyone shall claim a power to lay and levy taxes on the people, by his own authority, and without such consent of the people, he thereby invades the fundamental law of property, and subverts the end of government: for what property have I, that another may by right take, when he pleases, to himself?

Section 141. Fourthly, The legislative cannot transfer the power of making laws to any other hands: for it being but a delegated power from the people, they who have it cannot pass it over to others. The people alone can appoint the form of the commonwealth, which is by constituting the legislative, and appointing in whose hands that shall be. And when the people have said, We will submit to rules, and be governed by laws made by such men, and in such forms, nobody else can say other men shall make laws for them; nor can the people be bound by any laws, but such as are enacted by those whom they have chosen, and authorized to make laws for them. The power of the legislative, being derived from the people by a positive voluntary grant and institution, can be no other than what that positive grant conveyed, which being only to make laws, and not to make legislators, the legislative can have no power to transfer their authority of making laws, and place it in other hands.

Section 142. These are the bounds which the trust, which is put in them by the society, and the law of God and nature, have set to the legislative power of every commonwealth, in all forms of government.

First, They are to govern by promulgated established laws, not to be varied in particular cases, but to have one rule for rich and poor, for the favorite at court, and the country man at plough.

Secondly, These laws also ought to be designed for no other end ultimately, but the good of the people.

Thirdly, They must not raise taxes on the property of the people, without the consent of the people, given by themselves, or their deputies. And this properly concerns only such governments where the legislative is always in being, or at least where the people have not reserved any part of the legislative to deputies, to be from time to time chosen by themselves.

Fourthly, The legislative neither must nor can transfer the power of making laws to anybody else, or place it anywhere, but where the people have.

CHAPTER XII.

Of the Legislative, Executive, and Federative Power of the Commonwealth.

Section 143. The legislative power is that, which has a right to direct how the force of the commonwealth shall be employed for preserving the community and the members of it. But because those laws which are constantly to be executed, and whose force is always to continue, may be made in a little time; therefore there is no need, that the legislative should be always in being, not having always business to do. And because it may be too great a temptation to human frailty, apt to grasp at power, for the same persons, who have the power of making laws, to have also in their hands the power to execute them, whereby they may exempt themselves from obedience to the laws they make, and suit the law, both in its making, and execution, to their own private advantage, and thereby come to have a distinct interest from the rest of the community, contrary to the end of society and government: therefore in well-ordered commonwealths, where the good of the whole is so considered, as it ought, the legislative power is put into the hands of divers persons, who duly assembled, have by themselves, or jointly with others, a power to make laws, which when they have done, being separated again, they are themselves subject to the laws they have made; which is a new and near tie upon them, to take care, that they make them for the public good.

Section 144. But because the laws, that are at once, and in a short time made, have a constant and lasting force, and need a perpetual execution, or an attendance thereunto; therefore it is necessary there should be a power always in being, which should see to the execution of the laws that are made, and remain in force. And thus the legislative and executive powers come often to be separated.

Section 145. There is another power in every commonwealth, which one may call natural, because it is that which answers to the power every man naturally had before he entered into society: for though in a commonwealth the members of it are distinct persons still in reference to one another, and as such are governed by the laws of the society; yet in reference to the rest of mankind, they make one body, which is, as every member of it before was, still in the state of nature with the rest of mankind. Hence it is that the controversies that happen between any men of the society with those that are out of it, are managed by the public; and an injury done to a member of their body, and engages the whole in the reparation of it. So that under this consideration, the whole community is one body in the state of nature, in respect of all other states or persons out of its community.

Section 146. This therefore contains the power of war and peace, leagues and alliances, and all the transactions, with all persons and communities without the commonwealth, and may be called federative, if anyone pleases. So the thing be understood, I am indifferent as to the name.

Section 147. These two powers, executive and federative, though they be really distinct in themselves, yet one comprehending the execution of the municipal laws of the society within its self, upon all that are parts of it; the other the management of the security and interest of the public without, with all those that it may receive benefit or damage from, yet they are always almost united. And though this federative power in the well or ill management of it be of great moment to the commonwealth, yet it is much less capable to be directed by antecedent, standing, positive laws, than the executive; and so must necessarily be left to the prudence and wisdom of those, whose hands it is in, to be managed for the public good: for the laws that concern subjects one among another, being to direct their actions, may well enough precede them. But what is to be done in reference to foreigners, depending much upon their actions, and the variation of designs and interests, must be left in great part to the prudence of those, who have this power committed to them, to be managed by the best of their skill, for the advantage of the commonwealth.

Section 148. Though, as I said, the executive and federative power of every community be really distinct in themselves, yet they are hardly to be separated, and placed at the same time, in the hands of distinct persons: for both of them requiring the force of the society for their exercise, it is almost impracticable to place the force of the commonwealth in distinct, and not subordinate hands; or that the executive and federative power should be placed in persons, that might act separately, whereby the force of the public would be under different commands: which would be apt some time or other to cause disorder and ruin.

CHAPTER XIII.

Of the Subordination of the Powers of the Commonwealth.

Section 149. Though in a constituted commonwealth, standing upon its own basis, and acting according to its own nature, that is, acting for the preservation of the community, there can be but one supreme power, which is the legislative, to which all the rest are and must be subordinate, yet the legislative being only a fiduciary power to act for certain ends, there remains still in the people a supreme power to remove or alter the legislative, when they find the legislative act contrary to the trust reposed in them: for all power given with trust for the attaining an end, being limited by that end, whenever that end is manifestly neglected, or opposed, the trust must necessarily be forfeited, and the power devolve into the hands of those that gave it, who may place it anew where they shall think best for their safety and security. And thus the community perpetually retains a supreme power of saving themselves from the attempts and designs of anybody, even of their legislators, whenever they shall be so foolish, or so wicked, as to lay and carry on designs against the liberties and properties of the subject: for no man or society of men, having a power to deliver up their preservation, or consequently the means of it, to the absolute will and arbitrary dominion of another; whenever anyone shall go about to bring them into such a slavish condition, they will always have a right to preserve, what they have not a power to part with; and to rid themselves of those, who invade this fundamental, sacred, and unalterable law of self-preservation, for which they entered into society. And thus the community may be said in this respect to be always the supreme power, but not as considered under any form of government, because this power of the people can never take place till the government is dissolved.

Section 150. In all cases, while the government subsists, the legislative is the supreme power: for what can give laws to another, must needs be superior to him; and since the legislative is no otherwise legislative of the society, but by the right it has to make laws for all the parts, and for every member of the society, prescribing rules to their actions, and giving power of execution, where they are transgressed, the legislative must needs be the supreme, and all other powers, in any members or parts of the society, derived from and subordinate to it.

Section 151. In some commonwealths, where the legislative is not always in being, and the executive is vested in a single person, who has also a share in the legislative; there that single person in a very tolerable sense may also be called supreme: not that he has in himself all the supreme power, which is that of law-making; but because he has in him the supreme execution, from whom all inferior magistrates derive all their several subordinate powers, or at least the greatest part of them: having also no legislative superior to him, there being no law to be made without his consent, which cannot be expected should ever subject him to the other part of the legislative, be is properly enough in this sense supreme. But yet it is to be observed, that though oaths of allegiance and fealty are taken to him, it is not to him as supreme legislator, but as supreme executor of the law, made by a joint power of him with others; allegiance being nothing but an obedience according to law, which when he violates, he has no right to obedience, nor can claim it otherwise than as the public person vested with the power of the law, and so is to be considered as the image, phantom, or representative of the commonwealth, acted by the will of the society, declared in its laws; and thus he has no will, no power, but that of the law. But when he quits this representation, this public will, and acts by his own private will, he degrades himself, and is but a single private person without power, and without will, that has any right to obedience; the members owing no obedience but to the public will of the society.

Section 152. The executive power, placed anywhere but in a person that has also a share in the legislative, is visibly subordinate and accountable to it, and may be at pleasure changed and displaced; so that it is not the supreme executive power, that is exempt from subordination, but the supreme executive power vested in one, who having a share in the legislative, has no distinct superior legislative to be subordinate and accountable to, father than he himself shall join and consent; so that he is no more subordinate than he himself shall think fit, which one may certainly conclude will be but very little. Of other ministerial and subordinate powers in a commonwealth, we need not speak, they being so multiplied with infinite variety, in the different customs and constitutions of distinct commonwealths, that it is impossible to give a particular account of them all. Only thus much, which is necessary to our present purpose, we may take notice of concerning them, that they have no manner of authority, any of them, beyond what is by positive grant and commission delegated to them, and are all of them accountable to some other power in the commonwealth.

Section 153. It is not necessary, no, nor so much as convenient, that the legislative should be always in being; but absolutely necessary that the executive power should, because there is not always need of new laws to be made, but always need of execution of the laws that are made. When the legislative has put the execution of the laws, they make, into other hands; they have a power still to resume it out of those hands, when they find cause, and to punish for any mal-administration against the laws. The same holds also in regard of the federative power, that and the executive being both ministerial and subordinate to the legislative, which, as has been showed, in a constituted commonwealth is the supreme. The legislative also in this case being supposed to consist of several persons, (for if it be a single person, it cannot but be always in being, and so will, as supreme, naturally have the supreme executive power, together with the legislative) may assemble, and exercise their legislature, at the times that either their original constitution, or their own adjournment, appoints, or when they please; if neither of these has appointed any time, or there be no other way prescribed to convoke them: for the supreme power being placed in them by the people, it is always in them, and they may exercise it when they please, unless by their original constitution they are limited to certain seasons, or by an act of their supreme power they have adjourned to a certain time; and when that time comes, they have a right to assemble and act again.

Section 154. If the legislative, or any part of it, be made up of representatives chosen for that time by the people, which afterwards return into the ordinary state of subjects, and have no share in the legislature but upon a new choice, this power of choosing must also be exercised by the people, either at certain appointed seasons, or else when they are summoned to it; and in this latter case, the power of convoking the legislative is ordinarily placed in the executive, and has one of these two limitations in respect of time: that either the original constitution requires their assembling and acting at certain intervals, and then the executive power does nothing but ministerially issue directions for their electing and assembling, according to due forms; or else it is left to his prudence to call them by new elections, when the occasions or exigencies of the public require the amendment of old, or making of new laws, or the redress or prevention of any inconveniencies, that lie on, or threaten the people.

Section 155. It may be demanded here, What if the executive power, being possessed of the force of the commonwealth, shall make use of that force to hinder the meeting and acting of the legislative, when the original constitution, or the public exigencies require it? I say, using force upon the people without authority, and contrary to the trust put in him that does so, is a state of war with the people, who have a right to reinstate their legislative in the exercise of their power: for having erected a legislative, with an intent they should exercise the power of making laws, either at certain set times, or when there is need of it, when they are hindered by any force from what is so necessary to the society, and wherein the safety and preservation of the people consists, the people have a right to remove it by force. In all states and conditions, the true remedy of force without authority, is to oppose force to it. The use of force without authority always puts him that uses it into a state of war, as the aggressor, and renders him liable to be treated accordingly.

Section 156. The power of assembling and dismissing the legislative, placed in the executive, gives not the executive a superiority over it, but is a fiduciary trust placed in him, for the safety of the people, in a case where the uncertainty and variableness of human affairs could not bear a steady fixed rule: for it not being possible, that the first framers of the government should, by any foresight, be so much masters of future events, as to be able to prefix so just periods of return and duration to the assemblies of the legislative, in all times to come, that might exactly answer all the exigencies of the commonwealth; the best remedy could be found for this defect, was to trust this to the prudence of one who was always to be present, and whose business it was to watch over the public good. Constant frequent meetings of the legislative, and long continuations of their assemblies, without necessary occasion, could not but be burdensome to the people, and must necessarily in time produce more dangerous inconveniencies, and yet the quick turn of affairs might be sometimes such as to need their present help: any delay of their convening might endanger the public; and sometimes too their business might be so great, that the limited time of their sitting might be too short for their work, and rob the public of that benefit which could be had only from their mature deliberation. What then could be done in this case to prevent the community from being exposed some time or other to eminent hazard, on one side or the other, by fixed intervals and periods, set to the meeting and acting of the legislative, but to entrust it to the prudence of some, who being present, and acquainted with the state of public affairs, might make use of this prerogative for the public good? and where else could this be so well placed as in his hands, who was entrusted with the execution of the laws for the same end? Thus supposing the regulation of times for the assembling and sitting of the legislative, not settled by the original constitution, it naturally fell into the hands of the executive, not as an arbitrary power depending on his good pleasure, but with this trust always to have it exercised only for the public weal, as the occurrences of times and change of affairs might require. Whether settled periods of their convening, or a liberty left to the prince for convoking the legislative, or perhaps a mixture of both, has the least inconvenience attending it, it is not my business here to inquire, but only to show, that though the executive power may have the prerogative of convoking and dissolving such conventions of the legislative, yet it is not thereby superior to it.

Section 157. Things of this world are in so constant a flux that nothing remains long in the same state. Thus people, riches, trade, power, change their stations, flourishing mighty cities come to ruin, and prove in times neglected desolate corners, while other unfrequented places grow into populous countries, filled with wealth and inhabitants. But things not always changing equally, and private interest often keeping up customs and privileges, when the reasons of them are ceased, it often comes to pass, that in governments, where part of the legislative consists of representatives chosen by the people, that in tract of time this representation becomes very unequal and disproportionate to the reasons it was at first established upon. To what gross absurdities the following of custom, when reason has left it, may lead, we may be satisfied, when we see the bare name of a town, of which there remains not so much as the ruins, where scarce so much housing as a sheepcote, or more inhabitants than a shepherd is to be found, sends as many representatives to the grand assembly of law-makers, as a whole county numerous in people, and powerful in riches. This strangers stand amazed at, and everyone must confess needs a remedy; though most think it hard to find one, because the constitution of the legislative being the original and supreme act of the society, antecedent to all positive laws in it, and depending wholly on the people, no inferior power can alter it. And therefore the people, when the legislative is once constituted, having, in such a government as we have been speaking of, no power to act as long as the government stands; this inconvenience is thought incapable of a remedy.

Section 158. *Salus populi suprema lex* is certainly so just and fundamental a rule, that he, who sincerely follows it, cannot dangerously err. If therefore the executive, who has the power of convoking the legislative, observing rather the true proportion, than fashion of representation, regulates, not by old custom, but true reason, the number of members, in all places that have a right to be distinctly represented, which no part of the people however incorporated can pretend to, but in proportion to the assistance which it affords to the public, it cannot be judged to have set up a new legislative, but to have restored the old and true one, and to have rectified the disorders which succession of time had insensibly, as well as inevitably introduced: For it being the interest as well as intention of the people, to have a fair and equal representative; whoever brings it nearest to that, is an undoubted friend to, and establisher of the government, and cannot miss the consent and approbation of the community; prerogative being nothing but a power, in the hands of the prince, to provide for the public good, in such cases, which depending upon unforeseen and uncertain occurrences, certain and unalterable laws could not safely direct; whatsoever shall be done manifestly for the good of the people, and the establishing the government upon its true foundations, is, and always will be, just prerogative. The power of erecting new corporations, and therewith new representatives, carries with it a supposition, that in time the measures of representation might vary, and those places have a just right to be represented which before had none; and by the same reason, those cease to have a right, and be too inconsiderable for such a privilege, which before had it. it is not a change from the present state, which perhaps corruption or decay has introduced, that makes an inroad upon the government, but the tendency of it to injure or oppress the people, and to set up one part or party, with a distinction from, and an unequal subjection of the rest. Whatsoever cannot but be acknowledged to be of advantage to the society, and people in general, upon just and lasting measures, will always, when done, justify itself; and whenever the people shall choose their representatives upon just and undeniably equal measures, suitable to the original frame of the government, it cannot be doubted to be the will and act of the society, whoever permitted or caused them so to do.

CHAPTER XIV.

Of Prerogative.

Section 159. Where the legislative and executive power are in distinct hands, (as they are in all moderated monarchies, and well-framed governments) there the good of the society requires, that several things should be left to the discretion of him that has the executive power: for the legislators not being able to foresee, and provide by laws, for all that may be useful to the community, the executor of the laws, having the power in his hands, has by the common law of nature a right to make use of it for the good of the society, in many cases, where the municipal law has given no direction, till the legislative can conveniently be assembled to provide for it. Many things there are, which the law can by no means provide for; and those must necessarily be left to the discretion of him that has the executive power in his hands, to be ordered by him as the public good and advantage shall require: nay, it is fit that the laws themselves should in some cases give way to the executive power, or rather to this fundamental law of nature and government, that is That as much as may be, all the members of the society are to be preserved: for since many accidents may happen, wherein a strict and rigid observation of the laws may do harm; (as not to pull down an innocent man's house to stop the fire, when the next to it is burning) and a man may come sometimes within the reach of the law, which makes no distinction of persons, by an action that may deserve reward and pardon; it is fit the ruler should have a power, in many cases, to mitigate the severity of the law, and pardon some offenders: for the end of government being the preservation of all, as much as may be, even the guilty are to be spared, where it can prove no prejudice to the innocent.

Section 160. This power to act according to discretion, for the public good, without the prescription of the law, and sometimes even against it, is that which is called prerogative: for since in some governments the lawmaking power is not always in being, and is usually too numerous, and so too slow, for the dispatch requisite to execution; and because also it is impossible to foresee, and so by laws to provide for, all accidents and necessities that may concern the public, or to make such laws as will do no harm, if they are executed with an inflexible rigor, on all occasions, and upon all persons that may come in their way; therefore there is a latitude left to the executive power, to do many things of choice which the laws do not prescribe.

Section 161. This power, while employed for the benefit of the community, and suitably to the trust and ends of the government, is undoubted prerogative, and never is questioned: for the people are very seldom or never scrupulous or nice in the point; they are far from examining prerogative, while it is in any tolerable degree employed for the use it was meant, that is, for the good of the people, and not manifestly against it: but if there comes to be a question between the executive power and the people, about a thing claimed as a prerogative; the tendency of the exercise of such prerogative to the good or hurt of the people, will easily decide that question.

Section 162. It is easy to conceive, that in the infancy of governments, when commonwealths differed little from families in number of people, they differed from them too but little in number of laws: and the governors, being as the fathers of them, watching over them for their good, the government was almost all prerogative. A few established laws served the turn, and the discretion and care of the ruler supplied the rest. But when mistake or flattery prevailed with weak princes to make use of this power for private ends of their own, and not for the public good, the people were fain by express laws to get prerogative determined in those points wherein they found disadvantage from it: and thus declared limitations of prerogative were by the people found necessary in cases which they and their ancestors had left, in the utmost latitude, to the wisdom of those princes who made no other but a right use of it, that is, for the good of their people.

Section 163. And therefore they have a very wrong notion of government, who say, that the people have encroached upon the prerogative, when they have got any part of it to be defined by positive laws: for in so doing they have not pulled from the prince anything that of right belonged to him, but only declared, that that power which they indefinitely left in his or his ancestors hands, to be exercised for their good, was not a thing which they intended him when he used it otherwise: for the end of government being the good of the community, whatsoever alterations are made in it, tending to that end, cannot be an encroachment upon anybody, since nobody in government can have a right tending to any other end: and those only are encroachments which prejudice or hinder the public good. Those who say otherwise speak as if the prince had a distinct and separate interest from the good of the community, and was not made for it; the root and source from which spring almost all those evils and disorders which happen in kingly governments. And indeed, if that be so, the people under his government are not a society of rational creatures, entered into a community for their mutual good; they are not such as have set rulers over themselves, to guard, and promote that good; but are to be looked on as an herd of inferior creatures under the dominion of a master, who keeps them and works them for his own pleasure or profit. If men were so void of reason, and brutish, as to enter into society upon such terms, prerogative might indeed be, what some men would have it, an arbitrary power to do things hurtful to the people.

Section 164. But since a rational creature cannot be supposed, when free, to put himself into subjection to another, for his own harm; (though, where he finds a good and wise ruler, he may not perhaps think it either necessary or useful to set precise bounds to his power in all things) prerogative can be nothing but the people's permitting their rulers to do several things, of their own free choice, where the law was silent, and sometimes too against the direct letter of the law, for the public good; and their acquiescing in it when so done: for as a good prince, who is mindful of the trust put into his hands, and careful of the good of his people, cannot have too much prerogative, that is, power to do good; so a weak and ill prince, who would claim that power which his predecessors exercised without the direction of the law, as a prerogative belonging to him by right of his office, which he may exercise at his pleasure, to make or promote an interest distinct from that of the public, gives the people an occasion to claim their right, and limit that power, which, while it was exercised for their good, they were content should be tacitly allowed.

Section 165. And therefore he that will look into the history of England, will find, that prerogative was always largest in the hands of our wisest and best princes; because the people, observing the whole tendency of their actions to be the public good, contested not what was done without law to that end: or, if any human frailty or mistake (for princes are but men, made as others) appeared in some small declinations from that end; yet 'twas visible, the main of their conduct tended to nothing but the care of the public. The people therefore, finding reason to be satisfied with these princes, whenever they acted without, or contrary to the letter of the law, acquiesced in what they did, and, without the least complaint, let them enlarge their prerogative as they pleased, judging rightly, that they did nothing herein to the prejudice of their laws, since they acted conformable to the foundation and end of all laws, the public good.

Section 166. Such godly princes indeed had some title to arbitrary power by that argument, that would prove absolute monarchy the best government, as that which God himself governs the universe by; because such kings partake of his wisdom and goodness. Upon this is founded that saying, That the reigns of good princes have been always most dangerous to the liberties of their people: for when their successors, managing the government with different thoughts, would draw the actions of those good rulers into precedent, and make them the standard of their prerogative, as if what had been done only for the good of the people was a right in them to do, for the harm of the people, if they so pleased; it has often occasioned contest, and sometimes public disorders, before the people could recover their original right, and get that to be declared not to be prerogative, which truly was never so; since it is impossible that anybody in the society should ever have a right to do the people harm; though it be very possible, and reasonable, that the people should not go about to set any bounds to the prerogative of those kings, or rulers, who themselves transgressed not the bounds of the public good: for prerogative is nothing but the power of doing public good without a rule.

Section 167. The power of calling parliaments in England, as to precise time, place, and duration, is certainly a prerogative of the king, but still with this trust, that it shall be made use of for the good of the nation, as the exigencies of the times, and variety of occasions, shall require: for it being impossible to foresee which should always be the fittest place for them to assemble in, and what the best season; the choice of these was left with the executive power, as might be most subservient to the public good, and best suit the ends of parliaments.

Section 168. The old question will be asked in this matter of prerogative, But who shall be judge when this power is made a right use of? I answer: between an executive power in being, with such a prerogative, and a legislative that depends upon his will for their convening, there can be no judge on earth; as there can be none between the legislative and the people, should either the executive, or the legislative, when they have got the power in their hands, design, or go about to enslave or destroy them. The people have no other remedy in this, as in all other cases where they have no judge on earth, but to appeal to heaven: for the rulers, in such attempts, exercising a power the people never put into their hands, (who can never be supposed to consent that anybody should rule over them for their harm) do that which they have not a right to do. And where the body of the people, or any single man, is deprived of their right, or is under the exercise of a power without right, and have no appeal on earth, then they have a liberty to appeal to heaven, whenever they judge the cause of sufficient moment. And therefore, though the people cannot be judge, so as to have, by the constitution of that society, any superior power, to determine and give effective sentence in the case; yet they have, by a law antecedent and paramount to all positive laws of men, reserved that ultimate determination to themselves which belongs to all mankind, where there lies no appeal on earth, that is to judge, whether they have just cause to make their appeal to heaven. And this judgment they cannot part with, it being out of a man's power so to submit himself to another, as to give him a liberty to destroy him; God and nature never allowing a man so to abandon himself, as to neglect his own preservation: and since he cannot take away his own life, neither can he give another power to take it. Nor let anyone think, this lays a perpetual foundation for disorder; for this operates not, till the inconveniency is so great, that the majority feel it, and are weary of it, and find a necessity to have it amended. But this executive power, or wise princes, never need come in the danger of: and it is the thing, of all others, they have most need to avoid, as of all others the most perilous.

CHAPTER XV.

Of Paternal, Political, and Despotical Power, considered together.

Section 169. Though I have had occasion to speak of these separately before, yet the great mistakes of late about government, having, as I suppose, arisen from confounding these distinct powers one with another, it may not, perhaps, be amiss to consider them here together.

Section 170. First, then, Paternal or parental power is nothing but that which parents have over their children, to govern them for the children's good, till they come to the use of reason, or a state of knowledge, wherein they may be supposed capable to understand that rule, whether it be the law of nature, or the municipal law of their country, they are to govern themselves by: capable, I say, to know it, as well as several others, who live as freemen under that law. The affection and tenderness which God has planted in the breast of parents towards their children, makes it evident, that this is not intended to be a severe arbitrary government, but only for the help, instruction, and preservation of their offspring. But happen it as it will, there is, as I have proved, no reason why it should be thought to extend to life and death, at any time, over their children, more than over anybody else; neither can there be any pretence why this parental power should keep the child, when grown to a man, in subjection to the will of his parents, any father than having received life and education from his parents, obliges him to respect, honor, gratitude, assistance and support, all his life, to both father and mother. And thus, it is true, the paternal is a natural government, but not at all extending itself to the ends and jurisdictions of that which is political. The power of the father does not reach at all to the property of the child, which is only in his own disposing.

Section 171. Secondly, Political power is that power, which every man having in the state of nature, has given up into the hands of the society, and therein to the governors, whom the society has set over itself, with this express or tacit trust, that it shall be employed for their good, and the preservation of their property: now this power, which every man has in the state of nature, and which he parts with to the society in all such cases where the society can secure him, is to use such means, for the preserving of his own property, as he thinks good, and nature allows him; and to punish the breach of the law of nature in others, so as (according to the best of his reason) may most conduce to the preservation of himself, and the rest of mankind. So that the end and measure of this power, when in every man's hands in the state of nature, being the preservation of all of his society, that is, all mankind in general, it can have no other end or measure, when in the hands of the magistrate, but to preserve the members of that society in their lives, liberties, and possessions; and so cannot be an absolute, arbitrary power over their lives and fortunes, which are as much as possible to be preserved; but a power to make laws, and annex such penalties to them, as may tend to the preservation of the whole, by cutting off those parts, and those only, which are so corrupt, that they threaten the sound and healthy, without which no severity is lawful. And this power has its original only from compact and agreement, and the mutual consent of those who make up the community.

Section 172. Thirdly, Despotical power is an absolute, arbitrary power one man has over another, to take away his life, whenever he pleases. This is a power, which neither nature gives, for it has made no such distinction between one man and another; nor compact can convey: for man not having such an arbitrary power over his own life, cannot give another man such a power over it; but it is the effect only of forfeiture, which the aggressor makes of his own life, when he puts himself into the state of war with another: for having quitted reason, which God has given to be the rule between man and man, and the common bond whereby human kind is united into one fellowship and society; and having renounced the way of peace which that teaches, and made use of the force of war, to compass his unjust ends upon another, where he has no right; and so revolting from his own kind to that of beasts, by making force, which is theirs, to be his rule of right, he renders himself liable to be destroyed by the injured person, and the rest of mankind, that will join with him in the execution of justice, as any other wild beast, or noxious brute, with whom mankind can have neither society nor security . And thus captives, taken in a just and lawful war, and such only, are subject to a despotical power, which, as it arises not from compact, so neither is it capable of any, but is the state of war continued: for what compact can be made with a man that is not master of his own life? what condition can he perform? and if he be once allowed to be master of his own life, the despotical, arbitrary power of his master ceases. He that is master of himself, and his own life, has a right too to the means of preserving it; so that as soon as a compact enters, slavery ceases, and he so far quits his absolute power, and puts an end to the state of war, who enters into conditions with his captive.

Section 173. Nature gives the first of these, that is paternal power to parents for the benefit of their children during their minority, to supply their want of ability, and understanding how to manage their property. (By property I must be understood here, as in other places, to mean that property which men have in their persons as well as goods.) Voluntary agreement gives the second, that is political power to governors for the benefit of their subjects, to secure them in the possession and use of their properties. And forfeiture gives the third despotical power to lords for their own benefit, over those who are stripped of all property.

Section 174. He, that shall consider the distinct rise and extent, and the different ends of these several powers, will plainly see, that paternal power comes as far short of that of the magistrate, as despotical exceeds it; and that absolute dominion, however placed, is so far from being one kind of civil society, that it is as inconsistent with it, as slavery is with property. Paternal power is only where minority makes the child incapable to manage his property; political, where men have property in their own disposal; and despotical, over such as have no property at all.

CHAPTER XVI.

Of Conquest.

Section 175. Though governments can originally have no other rise than that before mentioned, nor polities be founded on anything but the consent of the people; yet such have been the disorders ambition has filled the world with, that in the noise of war, which makes so great a part of the history of mankind, this consent is little taken notice of: and therefore many have mistaken the force of arms for the consent of the people, and reckon conquest as one of the originals of government. But conquest is as far from setting up any government, as demolishing a house is from building a new one in the place. Indeed, it often makes way for a new frame of a commonwealth, by destroying the former; but, without the consent of the people, can never erect a new one.

Section 176. That the aggressor, who puts himself into the state of war with another, and unjustly invades another man's right, can, by such an unjust war, never come to have a right over the conquered, will be easily agreed by all men, who will not think, that robbers and pirates have a right of empire over whomsoever they have force enough to master; or that men are bound by promises, which unlawful force extorts from them. Should a robber break into my house, and with a dagger at my throat make me seal deeds to convey my estate to him, would this give him any true title? Just such a title, by his sword, has an unjust conqueror, who forces me into submission. The injury and the crime are equal, whether committed by the wearer of a crown, or some petty villain. The title of the offender, and the number of his followers, make no difference in the offence, unless it is to aggravate it. The only difference is, great robbers punish little ones, to keep them in their obedience; but the great ones are rewarded with laurels and triumphs, because they are too big for the weak hands of justice in this world, and have the power in their own possession, which should punish offenders. What is my remedy against a robber, that so broke into my house? Appeal to the law for justice. But perhaps justice is denied, or I am crippled and cannot stir, robbed and have not the means to do it. If God has taken away all means of seeking remedy, there is nothing left but patience. But my son, when able, may seek the relief of the law, which I am denied: he or his son may renew his appeal, until he recovers his right. But the conquered, or their children, have no court, no arbitrator on earth to appeal to. Then they may appeal, as Jephtha did, to heaven, and repeat their appeal till they have recovered the native right of their ancestors, which was, to have such a legislative over them, as the majority should approve, and freely acquiesce in. If it be objected, This would cause endless trouble; I answer, no more than justice does, where she lies open to all that appeal to her. He that troubles his neighbor without a cause, is punished for it by the justice of the court he appeals to: and he that appeals to heaven must be sure he has right on his side; and a right to that is worth the trouble and cost of the appeal, as he will answer at a tribunal that cannot be deceived, and will be sure to punish everyone according to the mischiefs he has created to his fellow subjects; that is, any part of mankind: from whence it is plain, that he that conquers in an unjust war can thereby have no title to the subjection and obedience of the conquered.

Section 177.   But supposing victory favors the right side, let us consider a conqueror in a lawful war, and see what power he gets, and over whom.   First, It is plain he gets no power by his conquest over those that conquered with him. They that fought on his side cannot suffer by the conquest, but must at least be as much freemen as they were before. And most commonly they serve upon terms, and on condition to share with their leader, and enjoy a part of the spoil, and other advantages that attend the conquering sword; or at least have a part of the subdued country bestowed upon them. And the conquering people are not, I hope, to be slaves by conquest, and wear their laurels only to show they are sacrifices to their leaders triumph. They that found absolute monarchy upon the title of the sword, make their heroes, who are the founders of such monarchies, arrant Draw-can-sirs, and forget they had any officers and soldiers that fought on their side in the battles they won, or assisted them in the subduing, or shared in possessing, the countries they mastered. We are told by some, that the English monarchy is founded in the Norman conquest, and that our princes have thereby a title to absolute dominion: which if it were true, (as by the history it appears otherwise) and that William had a right to make war on this island; yet his dominion by conquest could reach no farther than to the Saxons and Britons, that were then inhabitants of this country. The Normans that came with him, and helped to conquer, and all descended from them, are freemen, and no subjects by conquest; let that give what dominion it will. And if I, or anybody else, shall claim freedom, as derived from them, it will be very hard to prove the contrary: and it is plain, the law, that has made no distinction between the one and the other, intends not there should be any difference in their freedom or privileges.

Section 178.   But supposing, which seldom happens, that the conquerors and conquered never incorporate into one people, under the same laws and freedom; let us see next what power a lawful conqueror has over the subdued: and that I say is purely despotical. He has an absolute power over the lives of those who by an unjust war have forfeited them; but not over the lives or fortunes of those who engaged not in the war, nor over the possessions even of those who were actually engaged in it.

Section 179.   Secondly, I say then the conqueror gets no power but only over those who have actually assisted, concurred, or consented to that unjust force that is used against him: for the people having given to their governors no power to do an unjust thing, such as is to make an unjust war, (for they never had such a power in themselves) they ought not to be charged as guilty of the violence and injustice that is committed in an unjust war, any father than they actually abet it; no more than they are to be thought guilty of any violence or oppression their governors should use upon the people themselves, or any part of their fellow subjects, they having empowered them no more to the one than to the other. Conquerors, it is true, seldom trouble themselves to make the distinction, but they willingly permit the confusion of war to sweep all together: but yet this alters not the right; for the conquerors power over the lives of the conquered, being only because they have used force to do, or maintain an injustice, he can have that power only over those who have concurred in that force; all the rest are innocent; and he has no more title over the people of that country, who have done him no injury, and so have made no forfeiture of their lives, than he has over any other, who, without any injuries or provocations, have lived upon fair terms with him.

Section 180. Thirdly, The power a conqueror gets over those he overcomes in a just war, is perfectly despotical: he has an absolute power over the lives of those, who, by putting themselves in a state of war, have forfeited them; but he has not thereby a right and title to their possessions. This I doubt not, but at first sight will seem a strange doctrine, it being so quite contrary to the practice of the world; there being nothing more familiar in speaking of the dominion of countries, than to say such a one conquered it; as if conquest, without any more ado, conveyed a right of possession. But when we consider, that the practice of the strong and powerful, how universal soever it may be, is seldom the rule of right, however it be one part of the subjection of the conquered, not to argue against the conditions cut out to them by the conquering sword.

Section 181. Though in all war there be usually a complication of force and damage, and the aggressor seldom fails to harm the estate, when he uses force against the persons of those he makes war upon; yet it is the use of force only that puts a man into the state of war: for whether by force he begins the injury, or else having quietly, and by fraud, done the injury, he refuses to make reparation, and by force maintains it, (which is the same thing, as at first to have done it by force) it is the unjust use of force that makes the war: for he that breaks open my house, and violently turns me out of doors; or having peaceably got in, by force keeps me out, does in effect the same thing; supposing we are in such a state, that we have no common judge on earth, whom I may appeal to, and to whom we are both obliged to submit: for of such I am now speaking. It is the unjust use of force then, that puts a man into the state of war with another; and thereby he that is guilty of it makes a forfeiture of his life: for quitting reason, which is the rule given between man and man, and using force, the way of beasts, he becomes liable to be destroyed by him he uses force against, as any savage ravenous beast, that is dangerous to his being.

Section 182. But because the miscarriages of the father are no faults of the children, and they may be rational and peaceable, notwithstanding the brutishness and injustice of the father; the father, by his miscarriages and violence, can forfeit but his own life, but involves not his children in his guilt or destruction. His goods, which nature, that wills the preservation of all mankind as much as is possible, has made to belong to the children to keep them from perishing, do still continue to belong to his children: for supposing them not to have joined in the war, either through infancy, absence, or choice, they have done nothing to forfeit them: nor has the conqueror any right to take them away, by the bare title of having subdued him that by force attempted his destruction; though perhaps he may have some right to them, to repair the damages he has sustained by the war, and the defense of his own right; which how far it reaches to the possessions of the conquered, we shall see by and by. So that he that by conquest has a right over a man's person to destroy him if he pleases, has not thereby a right over his estate to possess and enjoy it: for it is the brutal force the aggressor has used, that gives his adversary a right to take away his life, and destroy him if he pleases, as a noxious creature; but it is damage sustained that alone gives him title to another man's goods: for though I may kill a thief that sets on me in the high-way, yet I may not (which seems less) take away his money, and let him go: this would be robbery on my side. His force and the state of war he put himself in, made him forfeit his life, but gave me no title to his goods. The right then of conquest extends only to the lives of those who joined in the war, not to their estates, but only in order to make reparation for the damages received, and the charges of the war, and that too with reservation of the right of the innocent wife and children.

Section 183. Let the conqueror have as much justice on his side, as could be supposed, he has no right to seize more than the vanquished could forfeit: his life is at the victor's mercy; and his service and goods he may appropriate, to make himself reparation; but he cannot take the goods of his wife and children; they too had a title to the goods he enjoyed, and their shares in the estate he possessed: for example, I in the state of nature (and all commonwealths are in the state of nature one with another) have injured another man, and refusing to give satisfaction, it comes to a state of war, wherein my defending by force what I had gotten unjustly, makes me the aggressor. I am conquered: my life, it is true, as forfeit, is at mercy, but not my wife's and children's. They made not the war, nor assisted in it. I could not forfeit their lives; they were not mine to forfeit. My wife had a share in my estate; that neither could I forfeit. And my children also, being born of me, had a right to be maintained out of my labor or substance. Here then is the case: the conqueror has a title to reparation for damages received, and the children have a title to their father's estate for their subsistence: for as to the wife's share, whether her own labor, or compact, gave her title to it, it is plain; her husband could not forfeit what was hers. What must be done in the case? I answer; the fundamental law of nature being, that all, as much as may be, should be preserved, it follows, that if there be not enough fully to satisfy both, that is for the conqueror's losses, and children's maintenance, he that has, and to spare, must remit something of his full satisfaction, and give way to the pressing and preferable title of those who are in danger to perish without it.

Section 184. But supposing the charge and damages of the war are to be made up to the conqueror, to the utmost farthing; and that the children of the vanquished, spoiled of all their father's goods, are to be left to starve and perish; yet the satisfying of what shall, on this score, be due to the conqueror, will scarce give him a title to any country be shall conquer: for the damages of war can scarce amount to the value of any considerable tract of land, in any part of the world, where all the land is possessed, and none lies fallow. And if I have not taken away the conqueror's land, which, being vanquished, it is impossible I should; scarce any other spoil I have done him can amount to the value of mine, supposing it equally cultivated, and of an extent any way coming near what I had over-run of his. The destruction of a year's product or two (for it seldom reaches four or five) is the utmost spoil that usually can be done: for as to money, and such riches and treasure taken away, these are none of nature's goods, they have but a fantastical imaginary value: nature has put no such upon them: they are of no more account by her standard, than the wampompeke of the Americans to an European prince, or the silver money of Europe would have been formerly to an American. And five years product is not worth the perpetual inheritance of land, where all is possessed, and none remains fallow, to be taken up by him that is dispossessed: which will be easily granted, if one do but take away the imaginary value of money, the disproportion being more than between five and five hundred; though, at the same time, half a year's product is more worth than the inheritance, where there being more land than the inhabitants possess and make use of, anyone has liberty to make use of the unused: but there conquerors take little care to possess themselves of the lands of the vanquished. No damage therefore, that men in the state of nature (as all princes and governments are in reference to one another) suffer from one another, can give a conqueror power to dispossess the posterity of the vanquished, and turn them out of that inheritance, which ought to be the possession of them and their descendants to all generations. The conqueror indeed will be apt to think himself master: and it is the very condition of the subdued not to be able to dispute their right. But if that be all, it gives no other title than what bare force gives to the stronger over the weaker: and, by this reason, he that is strongest will have a right to whatever he pleases to seize on.

Section 185. Over those then that joined with him in the war, and over those of the subdued country that opposed him not, and the posterity even of those that did, the conqueror, even in a just war, has, by his conquest, no right of dominion: they are free from any subjection to him, and if their former government be dissolved, they are at liberty to begin and erect another to themselves.

Section 186. The conqueror, it is true, usually, by the force he has over them, compels them, with a sword at their breasts, to stoop to his conditions, and submit to such a government as he pleases to afford them; but the enquiry is, what right he has to do so? If it be said, they submit by their own consent, then this allows their own consent to be necessary to give the conqueror a title to rule over them. It remains only to be considered, whether promises extorted by force, without right, can be thought consent, and how far they bind. To which I shall say, they bind not at all; because whatsoever another gets from me by force, I still retain the right of, and he is obliged presently to restore. He that forces my horse from me ought presently to restore him, and I have still a right to retake him. By the same reason, he that forced a promise from me, ought presently to restore it, i.e. quit me of the obligation of it; or I may resume it myself, i.e. choose whether I will perform it: for the law of nature laying an obligation on me only by the rules the prescribes, cannot oblige me by the violation of her rules: such is the extorting anything from me by force. Nor does it at all alter the case to say, I gave my promise, no more than it excuses the force, and passes the right, when I put my hand in my pocket, and deliver my purse myself to a thief, who demands it with a pistol at my breast.

Section 187. From all which it follows, that the government of a conqueror, imposed by force on the subdued, against whom he had no right of war, or who joined not in the war against him, where he had right, has no obligation upon them.

Section 188. But let us suppose, that all the men of that community, being all members of the same body politic, may be taken to have joined in that unjust war wherein they are subdued, and so their lives are at the mercy of the conqueror.

Section 189. I say, this concerns not their children who are in their minority: for since a father has not, in himself, a power over the life or liberty of his child, no act of his can possibly forfeit it. So that the children, whatever may have happened to the fathers, are freemen, and the absolute power of the conqueror reaches no farther than the persons of the men that were subdued by him, and dies with them: and should he govern them as slaves, subjected to his absolute arbitrary power, he has no such right of dominion over their children. He can have no power over them but by their own consent, whatever he may drive them to say or do; and he has no lawful authority, while force, and not choice, compels them to submission.

Section 190. Every man is born with a double right: first, a right of freedom to his person, which no other man has a power over, but the free disposal of it lies in himself. Secondly, a right, before any other man, to inherit with his brethren his father's goods.

Section 191. By the first of these, a man is naturally free from subjection to any government, though he be born in a place under its jurisdiction; but if he disclaim the lawful government of the country he was born in, he must also quit the right that belonged to him by the laws of it, and the possessions there descending to him from his ancestors, if it were a government made by their consent.

Section 192. By the second, the inhabitants of any country, who are descended, and derive a title to their estates from those who are subdued, and had a government forced upon them against their free consents, retain a right to the possession of their ancestors, though they consent not freely to the government, whose hard conditions were by force imposed on the possessors of that country: for the first conqueror never having had a title to the land of that country, the people who are the descendants of, or claim under those who were forced to submit to the yoke of a government by constraint, have always a right to shake it off, and free themselves from the usurpation or tyranny which the sword has brought in upon them, till their rulers put them under such a frame of government as they willingly and of choice consent to. Who doubts but the Grecian Christians, descendants of the ancient possessors of that country, may justly cast off the Turkish yoke, which they have so long groaned under, whenever they have an opportunity to do it? For no government can have a right to obedience from a people who have not freely consented to it; which they can never be supposed to do, until either they are put in a full state of liberty to choose their government and governors, or at least until they have such standing laws, to which they have by themselves or their representatives given their free consent, and also till they are allowed their due property, which is so to be proprietors of what they have, that nobody can take away any part of it without their own consent, without which, men under any government are not in the state of freemen, but are direct slaves under the force of war.

Section 193. But granting that the conqueror in a just war has a right to the estates, as well as power over the persons, of the conquered; which, it is plain, he has not: nothing of absolute power will follow from hence, in the continuance of the government; because the descendants of these being all freemen, if he grants them estates and possessions to inhabit his country, (without which it would be worth nothing) whatsoever he grants them, they have, so far as it is granted, property in. The nature whereof is, that without a man's own consent it cannot be taken from him.

Section 194. Their persons are free by a native right, and their properties, be they more or less, are their own, and at their own dispose, and not at his; or else it is no property. Supposing the conqueror gives to one man a thousand acres, to him and his heirs forever, to another he lets a thousand acres for his life, under the rent of £50. or £500. per annum has not the one of these a right to his thousand acres for ever, and the other, during his life, paying the said rent? and has not the tenant for life a property in all that he gets over and above his rent, by his labor and industry during the said term, supposing it be double the rent? Can anyone say, the king, or conqueror, after his grant, may by his power of conqueror take away all, or part of the land from the heirs of one, or from the other during his life, he paying the rent? or can he take away from either the goods or money they have got upon the said land, at his pleasure? If he can, then all free and voluntary contracts cease, and are void in the world; there needs nothing to dissolve them at any time, but power enough: and all the grants and promises of men in power are but mockery and collusion: for can there be anything more ridiculous than to say, I give you and yours this forever, and that in the surest and most solemn way of conveyance can be devised; and yet it is to be understood, that I have right, if I please, to take it away from you again tomorrow?

Section 195. I will not dispute now whether princes are exempt from the laws of their country; but this I am sure, they owe subjection to the laws of God and nature, Nobody, no power, can exempt them from the obligations of that eternal law. Those are so great, and so strong, in the case of promises, that omnipotence itself can be tied by them. Grants, promises, and oaths, are bonds that hold the Almighty: whatever some flatterers say to princes of the world, who all together, with all their people joined to them, are, in comparison of the great God, but as a drop of the bucket, or a dust on the balance, inconsiderable, nothing!

Section 196. The short of the case in conquest is this: the conqueror, if he have a just cause, has a despotical right over the persons of all, that actually aided, and concurred in the war against him, and a right to make up his damage and cost out of their labor and estates, so he injure not the right of any other. Over the rest of the people, if there were any that consented not to the war, and over the children of the captives themselves, or the possessions of either, he has no power; and so can have, by virtue of conquest, no lawful title himself to dominion over them, or derive it to his posterity; but is an aggressor, if he attempts upon their properties, and thereby puts himself in a state of war against them, and has no better a right of principality, he, nor any of his successors, than Hingar, or Hubba, the Danes, had here in England; or Spartacus, had he conquered Italy, would have had; which is to have their yoke cast off, as soon as God shall give those under their subjection courage and opportunity to do it. Thus, notwithstanding whatever title the kings of Assyria had over Judah, by the sword, God assisted Hezekiah to throw off the dominion of that conquering empire. And the lord was with Hezekiah, and he prospered; wherefore he went forth, and he rebelled against the king of Assyria, and served him not, 2 Kings xviii. 7. Whence it is plain, that shaking off a power, which force, and not right, has set over anyone, though it has the name of rebellion, yet is no offence before God, but is that which he allows and countenances, though even promises and covenants, when obtained by force, have intervened: for it is very probable, to anyone that reads the story of Ahaz and Hezekiah attentively, that the Assyrians subdued Ahaz, and deposed him, and made Hezekiah king in his father's lifetime; and that Hezekiah by agreement had done him homage, and paid him tribute all this time.

CHAPTER XVII.

Of Usurpation.

Section 197. As conquest may be called a foreign usurpation, so usurpation is a kind of domestic conquest, with this difference, that an usurper can never have right on his side, it being no usurpation, but where one is got into the possession of what another has right to. This, so far as it is usurpation, is a change only of persons, but not of the forms and rules of the government: for if the usurper extends his power beyond what of right belonged to the lawful princes, or governors of the commonwealth, it is tyranny added to usurpation.

Section 198. In all lawful governments, the designation of the persons, who are to bear rule, is as natural and necessary a part as the form of the government itself, and is that which had its establishment originally from the people; the anarchy being much alike, to have no form of government at all; or to agree, that it shall be monarchical, but to appoint no way to design the person that shall have the power, and be the monarch. Hence all commonwealths, with the form of government established, have rules also of appointing those who are to have any share in the public authority, and settled methods of conveying the right to them: for the anarchy is much alike, to have no form of government at all; or to agree that it shall be monarchical, but to appoint no way to know or design the person that shall have the power, and be the monarch. Whoever gets into the exercise of any part of the power, by other ways than what the laws of the community have prescribed, has no right to be obeyed, though the form of the commonwealth is still preserved; since he is not the person the laws have appointed, and consequently not the person the people have consented to. Nor can such a usurper, or any deriving from him, ever have a title, till the people are both at liberty to consent, and have actually consented to allow, and confirm in him the power he has till then usurped.

CHAPTER XVIII.

Of Tyranny.

Section 199. As usurpation is the exercise of power, which another has a right to; so tyranny is the exercise of power beyond right, which nobody can have a right to. And this is making use of the power anyone has in his hands, not for the good of those who are under it, but for his own private separate advantage. When the governor, however entitled, makes not the law, but his will, the rule; and his commands and actions are not directed to the preservation of the properties of his people, but the satisfaction of his own ambition, revenge, covetousness, or any other irregular passion.

Section 200. If one can doubt this to be truth, or reason, because it comes from the obscure hand of a subject, I hope the authority of a king will make it pass with him. King James the first, in his speech to the parliament, 1603, tells them thus, I will ever prefer the weal of the public, and of the whole commonwealth, in making of good laws and constitutions, to any particular and private ends of mine; thinking ever the wealth and weal of the commonwealth to be my greatest weal and worldly felicity; a point wherein a lawful king does directly differ from a tyrant: for I do acknowledge, that the special and greatest point of difference that is between a rightful king and an usurping tyrant, is this, that whereas the proud and ambitious tyrant does think his kingdom and people are only ordained for satisfaction of his desires and unreasonable appetites, the righteous and just king does by the contrary acknowledge himself to be ordained for the procuring of the wealth and property of his people. And again, in his speech to the parliament, 1609, he has these words, The king binds himself by a double oath, to the observation of the fundamental laws of his kingdom; tacitly, as by being a king, and so bound to protect as well the people, as the laws of his kingdom; and expressly, by his oath at his coronation; so as every just king, in a settled kingdom, is bound to observe that pact made to his people, by his laws, in framing his government agreeable thereunto, according to that pact which God made with Noah after the deluge. Hereafter, seed-time and harvest, and cold and heat, and summer and winter, and day and night, shall not cease while the earth remains. And therefore a king governing in a settled kingdom, leaves to be a king, and degenerates into a tyrant, as soon as he leaves off to rule according to his laws. And a little after, therefore all kings that are not tyrants, or perjured, will be glad to bind themselves within the limits of their laws; and they that persuade them the contrary, are vipers, and pests both against them and the commonwealth. Thus that learned king, who well understood the notion of things, makes the difference between a king and a tyrant to consist only in this, that one makes the laws the bounds of his power, and the good of the public, the end of his government; the other makes all give way to his own will and appetite.

Section 201. It is a mistake, to think this fault is proper only to monarchies; other forms of government are liable to it, as well as that: for wherever the power, that is put in any hands for the government of the people, and the preservation of their properties, is applied to other ends, and made use of to impoverish, harass, or subdue them to the arbitrary and irregular commands of those that have it; there it presently becomes tyranny, whether those that thus use it are one or many. Thus we read of the thirty tyrants at Athens, as well as one at Syracuse; and the intolerable dominion of the Decemvirate at Rome was nothing better.

Section 202. Wherever law ends, tyranny begins, if the law be transgressed to another's harm; and whosoever in authority exceeds the power given him by the law, and makes use of the force he has under his command, to compass that upon the subject, which the law allows not, ceases in that to be a magistrate; and, acting without authority, may be opposed, as any other man, who by force invades the right of another. This is acknowledged in subordinate magistrates. He that has authority to seize my person in the street, may be opposed as a thief and a robber, if he endeavors to break into my house to execute a writ, notwithstanding that I know he has such a warrant, and such a legal authority, as will empower him to arrest me abroad. And why this should not hold in the highest, as well as in the most inferior magistrate, I would gladly be informed. Is it reasonable, that the eldest brother, because he has the greatest part of his father's estate, should thereby have a right to take away any of his younger brothers portions? or that a rich man, who possessed a whole country, should from thence have a right to seize, when he pleased, the cottage and garden of his poor neighbor? The being rightfully possessed of great power and riches, exceedingly beyond the greatest part of the sons of Adam, is so far from being an excuse, much less a reason, for rapine and oppression, which the damaging of another without authority is, that it is a great aggravation of it: for the exceeding the bounds of authority is no more a right in a great, than in a petty officer; no more justifiable in a king than a constable; but is so much the worse in him, in that he has more trust put in him, has already a much greater share than the rest of his brethren, and is supposed, from the advantages of his education, employment, and counselors, to be more knowing in the measures of right and wrong.

Section 203. May the commands then of a prince be opposed? may he be resisted as often as anyone shall find himself aggrieved, and but imagine he has not right done him? This will unhinge and overturn all polities, and, instead of government and order, leave nothing but anarchy and confusion.

Section 204. To this I answer, that force is to be opposed to nothing, but to unjust and unlawful force; whoever makes any opposition in any other case, draws on himself a just condemnation both from God and man; and so no such danger or confusion will follow, as is often suggested: for,

Section 205. First, As, in some countries, the person of the prince by the law is sacred; and so, whatever he commands or does, his person is still free from all question or violence, not liable to force, or any judicial censure or condemnation. But yet opposition may be made to the illegal acts of any inferior officer, or other commissioned by him; unless he will, by actually putting himself into a state of war with his people, dissolve the government, and leave them to that defense which belongs to everyone in the state of nature: for of such things who can tell what the end will be? and a neighbor kingdom has showed the world an odd example. In all other cases the sacredness of the person exempts him from all inconveniencies, whereby he is secure, while the government stands, from all violence and harm whatsoever; than which there cannot be a wiser constitution: for the harm he can do in his own person not being likely to happen often, nor to extend itself far; nor being able by his single strength to subvert the laws, nor oppress the body of the people, should any prince have so much weakness, and ill nature as to be willing to do it, the inconveniency of some particular mischiefs, that may happen sometimes, when a heady prince comes to the throne, are well recompensed by the peace of the public, and security of the government, in the person of the chief magistrate, thus set out of the reach of danger: it being safer for the body, that some few private men should be sometimes in danger to suffer, than that the head of the republic should be easily, and upon slight occasions, exposed.

Section 206. Secondly, But this privilege, belonging only to the king's person, hinders not, but they may be questioned, opposed, and resisted, who use unjust force, though they pretend a commission from him, which the law authorizes not; as is plain in the case of him that has the king's writ to arrest a man, which is a full commission from the king; and yet he that has it cannot break open a man's house to do it, nor execute this command of the king upon certain days, nor in certain places, though this commission have no such exception in it; but they are the limitations of the law, which if anyone transgress, the king's commission excuses him not: for the king's authority being given him only by the law, he cannot empower anyone to act against the law, or justify him, by his commission, in so doing; the commission, or command of any magistrate, where he has no authority, being as void and insignificant, as that of any private man; the difference between the one and the other, being that the magistrate has some authority so far, and to such ends, and the private man has none at all: for it is not the commission, but the authority, that gives the right of acting; and against the laws there can be no authority. But, notwithstanding such resistance, the king's person and authority are still both secured, and so no danger to governor or government.

Section 207. Thirdly, Supposing a government wherein the person of the chief magistrate is not thus sacred; yet this doctrine of the lawfulness of resisting all unlawful exercises of his power, will not upon every slight occasion endanger him, or embroil the government: for where the injured party may be relieved, and his damages repaired by appeal to the law, there can be no pretence for force, which is only to be used where a man is intercepted from appealing to the law: for nothing is to be accounted hostile force, but where it leaves not the remedy of such an appeal; and it is such force alone, that puts him that uses it into a state of war, and makes it lawful to resist him. A man with a sword in his hand demands my purse in the high-way, when perhaps I have not twelve pence in my pocket: this man I may lawfully kill. To another I deliver £100 to hold only while I alight, which he refuses to restore me, when I am got up again, but draws his sword to defend the possession of it by force, if I endeavor to retake it. The mischief this man does me is a hundred, or possibly a thousand times more than the other perhaps intended me (whom I killed before he really did me any); and yet I might lawfully kill the one, and cannot so much as hurt the other lawfully. The reason whereof is plain; because the one using force, which threatened my life, I could not have time to appeal to the law to secure it: and when it was gone, it was too late to appeal. The law could not restore life to my dead carcass: the loss was irreparable; which to prevent, the law of nature gave me a right to destroy him, who had put himself into a state of war with me, and threatened my destruction. But in the other case, my life not being in danger, I may have the benefit of appealing to the law, and have reparation for my £100 that way.

Section 208. Fourthly, But if the unlawful acts done by the magistrate be maintained (by the power he has got), and the remedy which is due by law, be by the same power obstructed; yet the right of resisting, even in such manifest acts of tyranny, will not suddenly, or on slight occasions, disturb the government: for if it reach no farther than some private men's cases, though they have a right to defend themselves, and to recover by force what by unlawful force is taken from them; yet the right to do so will not easily engage them in a contest, wherein they are sure to perish; it being as impossible for one, or a few oppressed men to disturb the government, where the body of the people do not think themselves concerned in it, as for a raving mad-man, or heady mal-content to overturn a well-settled state; the people being as little apt to follow the one, as the other.

Section 209. But if either these illegal acts have extended to the majority of the people; or if the mischief and oppression has lighted only on some few, but in such cases, as the precedent, and consequences seem to threaten all; and they are persuaded in their consciences, that their laws, and with them their estates, liberties, and lives are in danger, and perhaps their religion too; how they will be hindered from resisting illegal force, used against them, I cannot tell. This is an inconvenience, I confess, that attends all governments whatsoever, when the governors have brought it to this pass, to be generally suspected of their people; the most dangerous state which they can possibly put themselves in; wherein they are the less to be pitied, because it is so easy to be avoided; it being as impossible for a governor, if he really means the good of his people, and the preservation of them, and their laws together, not to make them see and feel it, as it is for the father of a family, not to let his children see he loves, and takes care of them.

Section 210. But if all the world shall observe pretences of one kind, and actions of another; arts used to elude the law, and the trust of prerogative (which is an arbitrary power in some things left in the prince's hand to do good, not harm to the people) employed contrary to the end for which it was given: if the people shall find the ministers and subordinate magistrates chosen suitable to such ends, and favored, or laid by, proportionally as they promote or oppose them: if they see several experiments made of arbitrary power, and that religion underhand favored, (though publicly proclaimed against) which is readiest to introduce it; and the operators in it supported, as much as may be; and when that cannot be done, yet approved still, and liked the better: if a long train of actions show the councils all tending that way; how can a man any more hinder himself from being persuaded in his own mind, which way things are going; or from casting about how to save himself, than he could from believing the captain of the ship he was in, was carrying him, and the rest of the company, to Algiers, when he found him always steering that course, though cross winds, leaks in his ship, and want of men and provisions did often force him to turn his course another way for some time, which he steadily returned to again, as soon as the wind, weather, and other circumstances would let him?

CHAPTER XIX.

Of the Dissolution of Government.

Section 211. He that will with any clearness speak of the dissolution of government ought in the first place to distinguish between the dissolution of the society and the dissolution of the government. That which makes the community, and brings men out of the loose state of nature, into one politic society, is the agreement which everyone has with the rest to incorporate, and act as one body, and so be one distinct commonwealth. The usual, and almost only way whereby this union is dissolved, is the inroad of foreign force making a conquest upon them: for in that case, (not being able to maintain and support themselves, as one entire and independent body) the union belonging to that body which consisted therein, must necessarily cease, and so everyone return to the state he was in before, with a liberty to shift for himself, and provide for his own safety, as he thinks fit, in some other society. Whenever the society is dissolved, it is certain the government of that society cannot remain. Thus conquerors swords often cut up governments by the roots, and mangle societies to pieces, separating the subdued or scattered multitude from the protection of, and dependence on, that society which ought to have preserved them from violence. The world is too well instructed in, and too forward to allow for this way of dissolving of governments, to need any more to be said of it; and there wants not much argument to prove, that where the society is dissolved, the government cannot remain; that being as impossible, as for the frame of an house to subsist when the materials of it are scattered and dissipated by a whirl-wind, or jumbled into a confused heap by an earthquake.

Section 212. Besides this over-turning from without, governments are dissolved from within,

First, When the legislative is altered. Civil society being a state of peace, among those who are of it, from whom the state of war is excluded by the umpirage, which they have provided in their legislative, for the ending all differences that may arise among any of them, it is in their legislative, that the members of a commonwealth are united, and combined together into one coherent living body. This is the soul that gives form, life, and unity, to the commonwealth: from hence the several members have their mutual influence, sympathy, and connection: and therefore, when the legislative is broken, or dissolved, dissolution and death follows: for the essence and union of the society consisting in having one will, the legislative, when once established by the majority, has the declaring, and as it were keeping of that will. The constitution of the legislative is the first and fundamental act of society, whereby provision is made for the continuation of their union, under the direction of persons, and bonds of laws, made by persons authorized thereunto, by the consent and appointment of the people, without which no one man, or number of men, among them, can have authority of making laws that shall be binding to the rest. When anyone, or more, shall take upon them to make laws, whom the people have not appointed so to do, they make laws without authority, which the people are not therefore bound to obey; by which means they come again to be out of subjection, and may constitute to themselves a new legislative, as they think best, being in full liberty to resist the force of those, who without authority would impose anything upon them. Everyone is at the disposure of his own will, when those who had, by the delegation of the society, the declaring of the public will, are excluded from it, and others usurp the place, who have no such authority or delegation.

Section 213. This being usually brought about by such in the commonwealth who misuse the power they have; it is hard to consider it aright, and know at whose door to lay it, without knowing the form of government in which it happens. Let us suppose then the legislative placed in the concurrence of three distinct persons.

1. A single hereditary person, having the constant, supreme, executive power, and with it the power of convoking and dissolving the other two within certain periods of time.

2. An assembly of hereditary nobility.

3. An assembly of representatives chosen, pro tempore, by the people. Such a form of government supposed, it is evident,

Section 214. First, that when such a single person, or prince, sets up his own arbitrary will in place of the laws, which are the will of the society, declared by the legislative, then the legislative is changed: for that being in effect the legislative, whose rules and laws are put in execution, and required to be obeyed; when other laws are set up, and other rules pretended, and enforced, than what the legislative, constituted by the society, have enacted, it is plain that the legislative is changed. Whoever introduces new laws, not being thereunto authorized by the fundamental appointment of the society, or subverts the old, disowns and overturns the power by which they were made, and so sets up a new legislative.

Section 215. Secondly, when the prince hinders the legislative from assembling in its due time, or from acting freely, pursuant to those ends for which it was constituted, the legislative is altered: for it is not a certain number of men, no, nor their meeting, unless they have also freedom of debating, and leisure of perfecting, what is for the good of the society, wherein the legislative consists: when these are taken away or altered, so as to deprive the society of the due exercise of their power, the legislative is truly altered; for it is not names that constitute governments, but the use and exercise of those powers that were intended to accompany them; so that he, who takes away the freedom, or hinders the acting of the legislative in its due seasons, in effect takes away the legislative, and puts an end to the government.

Section 216. Thirdly, when, by the arbitrary power of the prince, the electors, or ways of election, are altered, without the consent, and contrary to the common interest of the people, there also the legislative is altered: for, if others than those whom the society has authorized thereunto, do choose, or in another way than what the society has prescribed, those chosen are not the legislative appointed by the people.

Section 217. Fourthly, The delivery also of the people into the subjection of a foreign power, either by the prince, or by the legislative, is certainly a change of the legislative, and so a dissolution of the government: for the end why people entered into society being to be preserved one entire, free, independent society, to be governed by its own laws; this is lost, whenever they are given up into the power of another.

Section 218. Why, in such a constitution as this, the dissolution of the government in these cases is to be imputed to the prince, is evident; because he, having the force, treasure and offices of the state to employ, and often persuading himself, or being flattered by others, that as supreme magistrate he is incapable of control; he alone is in a condition to make great advances toward such changes, under pretence of lawful authority, and has it in his hands to terrify or suppress opposers, as factious, seditious, and enemies to the government: whereas no other part of the legislative, or people, is capable by themselves to attempt any alteration of the legislative, without open and visible rebellion, apt enough to be taken notice of, which, when it prevails, produces effects very little different from foreign conquest. Besides, the prince in such a form of government, having the power of dissolving the other parts of the legislative, and thereby rendering them private persons, they can never in opposition to him, or without his concurrence, alter the legislative by a law, his consent being necessary to give any of their decrees that sanction. But yet, so far as the other parts of the legislative any way contribute to any attempt upon the government, and do either promote, or not, what lies in them, hinder such designs, they are guilty, and partake in this, which is certainly the greatest crime men can be guilty of one towards another.

Section 219. There is one way more whereby such a government may be dissolved, and that is, when he who has the supreme executive power, neglects and abandons that charge, so that the laws already made can no longer be put in execution. This is demonstratively to reduce all to anarchy, and so effectually to dissolve the government: for laws not being made for themselves, but to be, by their execution, the bonds of the society, to keep every part of the body politic in its due place and function; when that totally ceases, the government visibly ceases, and the people become a confused multitude, without order or connection. Where there is no longer the administration of justice, for the securing of men's rights, nor any remaining power within the community to direct the force, or provide for the necessities of the public, there certainly is no government left. Where the laws cannot be executed, it is all one as if there were no laws; and a government without laws is, I suppose, a mystery in politics, unconceivable to human capacity, and inconsistent with human society.

Section 220. In these and the like cases, when the government is dissolved, the people are at liberty to provide for themselves, by erecting a new legislative, differing from the other, by the change of persons, or form, or both, as they shall find it most for their safety and good: for the society can never, by the fault of another, lose the native and original right it has to preserve itself, which can only be done by a settled legislative, and a fair and impartial execution of the laws made by it. But the state of mankind is not so miserable that they are not capable of using this remedy, till it is too late to look for any. To tell people they may provide for themselves, by erecting a new legislative, when by oppression, artifice, or being delivered over to a foreign power, their old one is gone, is only to tell them, they may expect relief when it is too late, and the evil is past cure. This is in effect no more than to bid them first be slaves, and then to take care of their liberty; and when their chains are on, tell them, they may act like freemen. This, if barely so, is rather mockery than relief; and men can never be secure from tyranny, if there be no means to escape it till they are perfectly under it: and therefore it is, that they have not only a right to get out of it, but to prevent it.

Section 221. There is therefore, secondly, another way whereby governments are dissolved, and that is, when the legislative, or the prince, either of them, act contrary to their trust.

First, The legislative acts against the trust reposed in them, when they endeavor to invade the property of the subject, and to make themselves, or any part of the community, masters, or arbitrary disposers of the lives, liberties, or fortunes of the people.

Section 222. The reason why men enter into society, is the preservation of their property; and the end why they choose and authorize a legislative, is, that there may be laws made, and rules set, as guards and fences to the properties of all the members of the society, to limit the power, and moderate the dominion, of every part and member of the society: for since it can never be supposed to be the will of the society, that the legislative should have a power to destroy that which everyone designs to secure, by entering into society, and for which the people submitted themselves to legislators of their own making; whenever the legislators endeavor to take away, and destroy the property of the people, or to reduce them to slavery under arbitrary power, they put themselves into a state of war with the people, who are thereupon absolved from any father obedience, and are left to the common refuge, which God has provided for all men, against force and violence. Whensoever therefore the legislative shall transgress this fundamental rule of society; and either by ambition, fear, folly or corruption, endeavor to grasp themselves, or put into the hands of any other, an absolute power over the lives, liberties, and estates of the people; by this breach of trust they forfeit the power the people had put into their hands for quite contrary ends, and it devolves to the people, who have a right to resume their original liberty, and, by the establishment of a new legislative, (such as they shall think fit) provide for their own safety and security, which is the end for which they are in society. What I have said here, concerning the legislative in general, holds true also concerning the supreme executor, who having a double trust put in him, both to have a part in the legislative, and the supreme execution of the law, acts against both, when he goes about to set up his own arbitrary will as the law of the society. He acts also contrary to his trust, when he either employs the force, treasure, and offices of the society, to corrupt the representatives, and gain them to his purposes; or openly pre-engages the electors, and prescribes to their choice, such, whom he has, by solicitations, threats, promises, or otherwise, won to his designs; and employs them to bring in such, who have promised before-hand what to vote, and what to enact. Thus to regulate candidates and electors, and new-model the ways of election, what is it but to cut up the government by the roots, and poison the very fountain of public security? for the people having reserved to themselves the choice of their representatives, as the fence to their properties, could do it for no other end, but that they might always be freely chosen, and so chosen, freely act, and advise, as the necessity of the commonwealth, and the public good should, upon examination, and mature debate, be judged to require. These, those who give their votes before they hear the debate, and have weighed the reasons on all sides, are not capable of doing. To prepare such an assembly as this, and endeavor to set up the declared abettors of his own will, for the true representatives of the people, and the law-makers of the society, is certainly as great a breach of trust, and as perfect a declaration of a design to subvert the government, as is possible to be met with. To which, if one shall add rewards and punishments visibly employed to the same end, and all the arts of perverted law made use of, to take off and destroy all that stand in the way of such a design, and will not comply and consent to betray the liberties of their country, it will be past doubt what is doing. What power they ought to have in the society, who thus employ it contrary to the trust went along with it in its first institution, is easy to determine; and one cannot but see, that he, who has once attempted any such thing as this, cannot any longer be trusted.

Section 223. To this perhaps it will be said, that the people being ignorant, and always discontented, to lay the foundation of government in the unsteady opinion and uncertain humor of the people, is to expose it to certain ruin; and no government will be able long to subsist, if the people may set up a new legislative, whenever they take offence at the old one. To this I answer, Quite the contrary. People are not so easily got out of their old forms, as some are apt to suggest. They are hardly to be prevailed with to amend the acknowledged faults in the frame they have been accustomed to. And if there be any original defects, or adventitious ones introduced by time, or corruption; it is not an easy thing to get them changed, even when the entire world sees there is an opportunity for it. This slowness and aversion in the people to quite their old constitutions, has, in the many revolutions which have been seen in this kingdom, in this and former ages, still kept us to, or, after some interval of fruitless attempts, still brought us back again to our old legislative of king, lords and commons: and whatever provocations have made the crown be taken from some of our princes heads, they never carried the people so far as to place it in another line.

Section 224.   But it will be said, this hypothesis lays a ferment for frequent rebellion. To which I answer: First, no more than any other hypothesis: for when the people are made miserable, and find themselves exposed to the ill usage of arbitrary power, cry up their governors, as much as you will, for sons of Jupiter; let them be sacred and divine, descended, or authorized from heaven; give them out for whom or what you please, the same will happen. The people generally ill treated, and contrary to right, will be ready upon any occasion to ease themselves of a burden that sits heavy upon them. They will wish, and seek for the opportunity, which in the change, weakness and accidents of human affairs, seldom delays long to offer itself. He must have lived but a little while in the world, who has not seen examples of this in his time; and he must have read very little, who cannot produce examples of it in all sorts of governments in the world.

Section 225.   Secondly, I answer, such revolutions happen not upon every little mismanagement in public affairs. Great mistakes in the ruling part, many wrong and inconvenient laws, and all the slips of human frailty, will be borne by the people without mutiny or murmur. But if a long train of abuses, prevarications and artifices, all tending the same way, make the design visible to the people, and they cannot but feel what they lie under, and see where they are going; it is not to be wondered, that they should then rouse themselves, and endeavor to put the rule into such hands which may secure to them the ends for which government was at first erected; and without which, ancient names, and specious forms, are so far from being better, that they are much worse, than the state of nature, or pure anarchy; the inconveniencies being all as great and as near, but the remedy father off and more difficult.

Section 226.   Thirdly, I answer, that this doctrine of a power in the people of providing for their safety a-new, by a new legislative, when their legislators have acted contrary to their trust, by invading their property, is the best fence against rebellion, and the probable means to hinder it: for rebellion being an opposition, not to persons, but authority, which is founded only in the constitutions and laws of the government; those, whoever they be, who by force break through, and by force justify their violation of them, are truly and properly rebels: for when men, by entering into society and civil-government, have excluded force, and introduced laws for the preservation of property, peace, and unity among themselves, those who set up force again in opposition to the laws, do rebel are, that is, bring back again the state of war, and are properly rebels: which they who are in power, (by the pretence they have to authority, the temptation of force they have in their hands, and the flattery of those about them) being likeliest to do; the properest way to prevent the evil, is to show them the danger and injustice of it, who are under the greatest temptation to run into it.

Section 227.   In both the fore-mentioned cases, when either the legislative is changed, or the legislators act contrary to the end for which they were constituted; those who are guilty are guilty of rebellion: for if anyone by force takes away the established legislative of any society, and the laws by them made, pursuant to their trust, he thereby takes away the umpirage, which everyone had consented to, for a peaceable decision of all their controversies, and a bar to the state of war among them. They, who remove, or change the legislative, take away this decisive power, which nobody can have, but by the appointment and consent of the people; and so destroying the authority which the people did, and nobody else can set up, and introducing a power which the people has not authorized, they actually introduce a state of war, which is that of force without authority: and thus, by removing the legislative established by the society, (in whose decisions the people acquiesced and united, as to that of their own will) they untie the knot, and expose the people a-new to the state of war. And if those, who by force take away the legislative, are rebels, the legislators themselves, as has been shown, can be no less esteemed so; when they, who were set up for the protection, and preservation of the people, their liberties and properties, shall by force invade and endeavor to take them away; and so they putting themselves into a state of war with those who made them the protectors and guardians of their peace, are properly, and with the greatest aggravation, rebels.

Section 228. But if they, who say it lays a foundation for rebellion, mean that it may occasion civil wars, or intestine broils, to tell the people they are absolved from obedience when illegal attempts are made upon their liberties or properties, and may oppose the unlawful violence of those who were their magistrates, when they invade their properties contrary to the trust put in them; and that therefore this doctrine is not to be allowed, being so destructive to the peace of the world: they may as well say, upon the same ground, that honest men may not oppose robbers or pirates, because this may occasion disorder or bloodshed. If any mischief comes in such cases, it is not to be charged upon him who defends his own right, but on him that invades his neighbors. If the innocent honest man must quietly quit all he has, for peace sake, to him who will lay violent hands upon it, I desire it may be considered, what a kind of peace there will be in the world, which consists only in violence and rapine; and which is to be maintained only for the benefit of robbers and oppressors. Who would not think it an admirable peace between the mighty and the mean, when the lamb, without resistance, yielded his throat to be torn by the imperious wolf? Polyphemus's den gives us a perfect pattern of such a peace, and such a government, wherein Ulysses and his companions had nothing to do, but quietly to suffer themselves to be devoured. And no doubt Ulysses, who was a prudent man, preached up passive obedience, and exhorted them to a quiet submission, by representing to them of what concernment peace was to mankind; and by showing the inconveniences might happen, if they should offer to resist Polyphemus, who had now the power over them.

Section 229. The end of government is the good of mankind; and which is best for mankind, that the people should be always exposed to the boundless will of tyranny, or that the rulers should be sometimes liable to be opposed, when they grow exorbitant in the use of their power, and employ it for the destruction, and not the preservation of the properties of their people?

Section 230. Nor let anyone say, that mischief can arise from hence, as often as it shall please a busy head, or turbulent spirit, to desire the alteration of the government. It is true, such men may stir, whenever they please; but it will be only to their own just ruin and perdition: for till the mischief be grown general, and the ill designs of the rulers become visible, or their attempts sensible to the greater part, the people, who are more disposed to suffer than right themselves by resistance, are not apt to stir. The examples of particular injustice or oppression of here and there an unfortunate man, moves them not. But if they universally have a persuasion, grounded upon manifest evidence, that designs are carrying on against their liberties, and the general course and tendency of things cannot but give them strong suspicions of the evil intention of their governors, who is to be blamed for it? Who can help it, if they, who might avoid it, bring themselves into this suspicion? Are the people to be blamed, if they have the sense of rational creatures, and can think of things no otherwise than as they find and feel them? And is it not rather their fault, who put things into such a posture, that they would not have them thought to be as they are? I grant that the pride, ambition, and turbulence of private men have sometimes caused great disorders in commonwealths, and factions have been fatal to states and kingdoms. But whether the mischief has oftener begun in the people's wantonness, and a desire to cast off the lawful authority of their rulers, or in the rulers insolence, and endeavors to get and exercise an arbitrary power over their people; whether oppression, or disobedience, gave the first rise to the disorder, I leave it to impartial history to determine. This I am sure, whoever, either ruler or subject, by force goes about to invade the rights of either prince or people, and lays the foundation for overturning the constitution and frame of any just government, is highly guilty of the greatest crime, I think, a man is capable of, being to answer for all those mischiefs of blood, rapine, and desolation, which the breaking to pieces of governments bring on a country. And he who does it, is justly to be esteemed the common enemy and pest of mankind, and is to be treated accordingly.

Section 231. That subjects or foreigners, attempting by force on the properties of any people, may be resisted with force, is agreed on all hands. But that magistrates, doing the same thing, may be resisted, has of late been denied: as if those who had the greatest privileges and advantages by the law, had thereby a power to break those laws, by which alone they were set in a better place than their brethren: whereas their offence is thereby the greater, both as being ungrateful for the greater share they have by the law, and breaking also that trust, which is put into their hands by their brethren.

Section 232. Whosoever uses force without right, as everyone does in society, who does it without law, puts himself into a state of war with those against whom he so uses it; and in that state all former ties are cancelled, all other rights cease, and everyone has a right to defend himself, and to resist the aggressor. This is so evident, that Barclay himself, that great assertor of the power and sacredness of kings, is forced to confess, That it is lawful for the people, in some cases, to resist their king; and that too in a chapter, wherein he pretends to show, that the divine law shuts up the people from all manner of rebellion. Whereby it is evident, even by his own doctrine that, since they may in some cases resist, all resisting of princes is not rebellion. His words are these. *Quod siquis dicat, Ergone populus tyrannicæ crudelitati & furori jugulum semper præbehit? Ergone multitudo civitates suas fame, ferro, & flammâ vastari, seque, conjuges, & liberos fortunæ ludibrio & tyranni libidini exponi, inque omnia vitæ pericula omnesque miserias & molestias á rege deduci patientur? Num illis quod omni animantium generi est á naturâ tributum, denegari debet, ut sc. vim vi repellant, seseq; ab injuriâ tueantur? Huic breviter responsum sit, Populo universo negari defensionem, quæ juris naturalis est, neque ultionem quæ præter naturam est adversus regem concedi debere. Quapropter si rex non in singulares tantum personas aliquot privatum odium exerceat, sed corpus etiam reipublicæ, cujus ipse caput est, i.e. totum populum, vel insignem aliquam ejus partem immani & intolerandâ seu tyrannide divexet; populo, quidem hoc casu resistendi ac tuendi se ab injuriâ potestas competit, sed tuendise tantum, non enim in principem invadendi: & restituendæ injuriæ illatæ, non recedendi à debitâ reverentiâ propter acceptam injuriam. Præsentem denique impetum propulsandi non vim præteritam ulciscenti jus habet. Horum enim alterum à naturâ est, ut vitam scilicet corpusque tueamur. Alterum vero contra naturam, ut inferior de superiori supplicium sumat. Quod itaque populus malum, antequam factum sit, impedire potest, ne fiat, id postquam factum est, in regem authorem sceleris vindicare non potest: populus igitur hoc ampliùs quam privatus quispiam habet: quod huic, vel ipsis adversariis judicibus, excepto Buchanano, nullum nisi in patientia remedium superest. Cùm ille si intolerabilis tyrannus est (modicum enim ferre omnino debet) resistere cum reverentiâ possit, Barclay contra Monarchom. l. iii. c. 8.*

In English thus:

Section 233. But if anyone should ask, Must the people then always lay themselves open to the cruelty and rage of tyranny? Must they see their cities pillaged, and laid in ashes, their wives and children exposed to the tyrant's lust and fury, and themselves and families reduced by their king to ruin, and all the miseries of want and oppression, and yet sit still? Must men alone be debarred the common privilege of opposing force with force, which nature allows so freely to all other creatures for their preservation from injury? I answer: Self-defense is a part of the law of nature; nor can it be denied the community, even against the king himself: but to revenge themselves upon him, must by no means be allowed them: it being not agreeable to that law. Wherefore if the king shall show an hatred, not only to some particular persons, but sets himself against the body of the commonwealth, whereof he is the head, and shall, with intolerable ill usage, cruelly tyrannize over the whole, or a considerable part of the people, in this case the people have a right to resist and defend themselves from injury: but it must be with this caution, that they only defend themselves, but do not attack their prince: they may repair the damages received, but must not for any provocation exceed the bounds of due reverence and respect. They may repulse the present attempt, but must not revenge past violence: for it is natural for us to defend life and limb, but that an inferior should punish a superior, is against nature. The mischief which is designed them, the people may prevent before it is done; but when it is done, they must not revenge it on the king, though author of the villainy. This therefore is the privilege of the people in general, above what any private person has; that particular men are allowed by our adversaries themselves (Buchanan only excepted) to have no other remedy but patience;

but the body of the people may with respect resist intolerable tyranny; for when it is but moderate, they ought to endure it.

Section 234. Thus far that great advocate of monarchical power allows of resistance.

Section 235. It is true, he has annexed two limitations to it, to no purpose:

First, he says, it must be with reverence.

Secondly, it must be without retribution, or punishment; and the reason he gives is, because an inferior cannot punish a superior.

First, how to resist force without striking again, or how to strike with reverence, will need some skill to make intelligible. He that shall oppose an assault only with a shield to receive the blows, or in any more respectful posture, without a sword in his hand, to abate the confidence and force of the assailant, will quickly be at an end of his resistance, and will find such a defense serve only to draw on himself the worse usage. This is as ridiculous a way of resisting, as Juvenal thought it of fighting; *ubi tu pulsas, ego vapulo tantum.* And the success of the combat will be unavoidably the same he there describes it:

- *—Libertas pauperis hæc est:*

- *Pulsatus rogat, & pugnis concisus, adorat,*

- *Ut liceat paucis cum dentibus inde reverti.*

This will always be the event of such an imaginary resistance, where men may not strike again. He therefore who may resist, must be allowed to strike. And then let our author, or anybody else, join a knock on the head, or a cut on the face, with as much reverence and respect as he thinks fit. He that can reconcile blows and reverence, may, for aught I know, desire for his pains, a civil, respectful cudgeling wherever he can meet with it.

Secondly, as to his second, an inferior cannot punish a superior; that is true, generally speaking, while he is his superior. But to resist force with force, being the state of war that levels the parties, cancels all former relation of reverence, respect, and superiority: and then the odds that remains, is, that he, who opposes the unjust aggressor, has this superiority over him, that he has a right, when he prevails, to punish the offender, both for the breach of the peace, and all the evils that followed upon it. Barclay therefore, in another place, more coherently to himself, denies it to be lawful to resist a king in any case. But he there assigns two cases, whereby a king may un-king himself. His words are,

Quid ergo, nulline casus incidere possunt quibus populo sese erigere atque in regem impotentius dominantem arma capere & invadere jure suo suáque authoritate liceat? Nulli certe quamdiu rex manet. Semper enim ex divinis id obstat, Regem honorificato; & qui potestati resistit, Dei ordinationi resistit: non aliàs igitur in eum populo potestas est quam si id committat propter quod ipso jure rex esse desinat. Tunc enim se ipse principatu exuit atque in privatis constituit liber: hoc modo populus & superior efficitur, reverso ad eum sc. jure illo quod ante regem inauguratum in interregno habuit. At sunt paucorum generum commissa ejusmodi quæ hunc effectum pariunt. At ego cum plurima animo perlustrem, duo tantum invenio, duos, inquam, casus quibus rex ipso facto ex rege non regem se facit & omni honore & dignitate regali atque in subditos potestate destituit; quorum etiam meminit Winzerus. Horum unus est, Si regnum disperdat, quemadmodum de Nerone fertur, quod is nempe senatum populumque Romanum, atque adeo urbem ipsam ferro flammaque vastare, ac novas sibi sedes quærere decrevisset. Et de Caligula, quod palam denunciarit se neque civem neque principem senatui amplius fore, inque animo habuerit interempto utriusque ordinis electissimo quoque Alexandriam commigrare, ac ut populum uno ictu interimeret, unam ei cervicem optavit. Talia cum rex aliquis meditatur & molitur serio, omnem regnandi curam & animum ilico abjicit, ac proinde imperium in subditos amittit, ut dominus servi pro derelicto habiti dominium.

Section 236. Alter casus est, Si rex in alicujus clientelam se contulit; ac regnum quod liberum à majoribus & populo traditum accepit, alienæ ditioni mancipavit. Nam tunc quamvis forte non eâ mente id agit populo plane ut incommodet: tamen

quia quod præcipuum est regiæ dignitatis amisit, ut summus scilicet in regno secundum Deum sit, & solo Deo inferior, atque populum etiam totum ignorantem vel invitum, cujus libertatem saream & tectam conservare debuit, in alterius gentis ditionem & potestatem dedidit; hâc velut quadam regni ab alienatione effecit, ut nec quod ipse in regno imperium habuit retineat, nec in eum cui collatum voluit, juris quicquam transferat; atque ita eo facto liberum jam & suæ potestatis populum relinquit, cujus rei exemplum unum annales Scotici suppeditant. Barclay contra Monarchom. l. iii. c. 16.

Which in English runs thus.

Section 237. What then, can there no case happen wherein the people may of right, and by their own authority, help themselves, take arms, and set upon their king, imperiously domineering over them? None at all, while he remains a king. Honor the king, and he that resists the power, resists the ordinance of God; are divine oracles that will never permit it. The people therefore can never come by a power over him, unless he does something that makes him cease to be a king: for then he divests himself of his crown and dignity, and returns to the state of a private man, and the people become free and superior, the power which they had in the interregnum, before they crowned him king, devolving to them again. But there are but few miscarriages which bring the matter to this state. After considering it well on all sides, I can find but two. Two cases there are, I say, whereby a king, ipso facto, becomes no king, and loses all power and regal authority over his people; which are also taken notice of by Winzerus.

The first is, If he endeavor to overturn the government, that is, if he have a purpose and design to ruin the kingdom and commonwealth, as it is recorded of Nero, that he resolved to cut off the senate and people of Rome, lay the city fallow with fire and sword, and then remove to some other place. And of Caligula, that he openly declared, that he would be no longer a head to the people or senate, and that he had it in his thoughts to cut off the worthiest men of both ranks, and then retire to Alexandria: and he wished that the people had but one neck, that he might dispatch them all at a blow. Such designs as these, when any king harbors in his thoughts, and seriously promotes, he immediately gives up all care and thought of the commonwealth; and consequently forfeits the power of governing his subjects, as a master does the dominion over his slaves whom he has abandoned.

Section 238. The other case is, when a king makes himself the dependent of another, and subjects his kingdom which his ancestors left him, and the people put free into his hands, to the dominion of another: for however perhaps it may not be his intention to prejudice the people; yet because he has hereby lost the principal part of regal dignity, that is to be next and immediately under God, supreme in his kingdom; and also because he betrayed or forced his people, whose liberty he ought to have carefully preserved, into the power and dominion of a foreign nation. By this, as it were, alienation of his kingdom, he himself loses the power he had in it before, without transferring any the least right to those on whom he would have bestowed it; and so by this act sets the people free, and leaves them at their own disposal. One example of this is to be found in the Scotch Annals.

Section 239. In these cases Barclay, the great champion of absolute monarchy, is forced to allow, that a king may be resisted, and ceases to be a king. That is, in short, not to multiply cases, in whatsoever he has no authority, there he is no king, and may be resisted: for wheresoever the authority ceases, the king ceases too, and becomes like other men who have no authority. And these two cases he instances in, differ little from those above mentioned, to be destructive to governments, only that he has omitted the principle from which his doctrine flows; and that is, the breach of trust, in not preserving the form of government agreed on, and in not intending the end of government itself, which is the public good and preservation of property. When a king has dethroned himself, and put himself in a state of war with his people, what shall hinder them from prosecuting him who is no king, as they would any other man, who has put himself into a state of war with them; Barclay, and those of his opinion, would do well to tell us. This father I desire may be taken notice of out of Barclay, that he says, The mischief that is designed them, the people may prevent before it be done: whereby he allows resistance when tyranny is but in design. Such designs as these (says he) when any king harbors in his thoughts and seriously promotes, he immediately gives up all care and thought of the commonwealth; so that, according to him, the neglect of the public good is to be taken as an evidence of such design, or at least for a sufficient cause of resistance. And the reason of all, he gives in these words, because he betrayed or forced his people, whose liberty he ought carefully to have preserved. What he adds, into the power and dominion of a foreign nation, signifies nothing, the fault and forfeiture lying in the loss of their liberty, which he ought to have preserved, and not in any distinction of the persons to whose dominion they were subjected. The peoples right is equally invaded, and their liberty lost, whether they are made slaves to any of their own, or a foreign nation; and in this lies the injury, and against this only have they the right of defense. And there are instances to be found in all countries, which show, that it is not the change of nations in the persons of their governors, but the change of government, that gives the offence. Bilson, a bishop of our church, and a great stickler for the power and prerogative of princes, does, if I mistake not, in his treatise of Christian subjection, acknowledge, that princes may forfeit their power, and their title to the obedience of their subjects; and if there needed authority in a case where reason is so plain, I could send my reader to Bracton, Fortescue, and the author of the Mirrour, and others, writers that cannot be suspected to be ignorant of our government, or enemies to it. But I thought Hooker alone might be enough to satisfy those men, who relying on him for their ecclesiastical polity, are by a strange fate carried to deny those principles upon which he builds it. Whether they are herein made the tools of cunning workmen, to pull down their own fabric, they were best look. This I am sure, their civil policy is so new, so dangerous, and so destructive to both rulers and people, that as former ages never could bear the broaching of it; so it may be hoped, those to come, redeemed from the impositions of these Egyptian under-task-masters, will abhor the memory of such servile flatterers, who, while it seemed to serve their turn, resolved all government into absolute tyranny, and would have all men born to, what their mean souls fitted them for, slavery.

Section 240. Here, it is like, the common question will be made, who shall be judge, whether the prince or legislative act contrary to their trust? This, perhaps, ill-affected and factious men may spread among the people, when the prince only makes use of his due prerogative. To this I reply, the people shall be judge; for who shall be judge whether his trustee or deputy acts well, and according to the trust reposed in him, but he who deputes him, and must, by having deputed him, have still a power to discard him, when he fails in his trust? If this be reasonable in particular cases of private men, why should it be otherwise in that of the greatest moment, where the welfare of millions is concerned, and also where the evil, if not prevented, is greater, and the redress very difficult, dear, and dangerous?

Section 241. But father, this question, (Who shall be judge?) cannot mean that there is no judge at all: for where there is no judicature on earth, to decide controversies among men, God in heaven is judge. He alone, it is true, is judge of the right. But every man is judge for himself, as in all other cases, so in this, whether another has put himself into a state of war with him, and whether he should appeal to the Supreme Judge, as Jephtha did.

Section 242. If a controversy arise between a prince and some of the people, in a matter where the law is silent, or doubtful, and the thing be of great consequence, I should think the proper umpire, in such a case, should be the body of the people: for in cases where the prince has a trust reposed in him, and is dispensed from the common ordinary rules of the law; there, if any men find themselves aggrieved, and think the prince acts contrary to, or beyond that trust, who so proper to judge as the body of the people, (who, at first, lodged that trust in him) how far they meant it should extend? But if the prince, or whoever they be in the administration, decline that way of determination, the appeal then lies nowhere but to heaven; force between either persons, who have no known superior on earth, or which permits no appeal to a judge on earth, being properly a state of war, wherein the appeal lies only to heaven; and in that state the injured party must judge for himself, when he will think fit to make use of that appeal, and put himself upon it.

Section 243. To conclude, The power that every individual gave the society, when he entered into it, can never revert to the individuals again, as long as the society lasts, but will always remain in the community; because without this there can be no community, no commonwealth, which is contrary to the original agreement: so also when the society has placed the legislative in any assembly of men, to continue in them and their successors, with direction and authority for providing such successors, the legislative can never revert to the people while that government lasts; because having provided a legislative with power to continue forever, they have given up their political power to the legislative, and cannot resume it. But if they have set limits to the duration of their legislative, and made this supreme power in any person, or assembly, only temporary; or else, when by the miscarriages of those in authority, it is forfeited; upon the forfeiture, or at the determination of the time set, it reverts to the society, and the people have a right to act as supreme, and continue the legislative in themselves; or erect a new form, or under the old form place it in new hands, as they think good.

FINIS.

APPENDIX

The Text of Magna Charta
1215

JOHN, by the grace of God King of England, Lord of Ireland, Duke of Normandy and Aquitaine, and Count of Anjou, to his archbishops, bishops, abbots, earls, barons, justices, foresters, sheriffs, stewards, servants, and to all his officials and loyal subjects,

Greetings,

KNOW THAT BEFORE GOD, for the health of our soul and those of our ancestors and heirs, to the honor of God, the exaltation of the holy Church, and the better ordering of our kingdom, at the advice of our reverend fathers Stephen, archbishop of Canterbury, primate of all England, and cardinal of the holy Roman Church, Henry archbishop of Dublin, William bishop of London, Peter bishop of Winchester, Jocelin bishop of Bath and Glastonbury, Hugh bishop of Lincoln, Walter Bishop of Worcester, William bishop of Coventry, Benedict bishop of Rochester, Master Pandulf subdeacon and member of the papal household, Brother Aymeric master of the knighthood of the Temple in England, William Marshal earl of Pembroke, William earl of Salisbury, William earl of Warren, William earl of Arundel, Alan de Galloway constable of Scotland, Warin Fitz Gerald, Peter Fitz Herbert, Hubert de Burgh seneschal of Poitou, Hugh de Neville, Matthew Fitz Herbert, Thomas Basset, Alan Basset, Philip Daubeny, Robert de Roppeley, John Marshal, John Fitz Hugh, and other loyal subjects:

(1) FIRST, THAT WE HAVE GRANTED TO GOD, and by this present charter have confirmed for us and our heirs in perpetuity, that the English Church shall be free, and shall have its rights undiminished, and its liberties unimpaired. That we wish this so to be observed, appears from the fact that of our own free will, before the outbreak of the present dispute between us and our barons, we granted and confirmed by charter the freedom of the Church's elections - a right reckoned to be of the greatest necessity and importance to it - and caused this to be confirmed by Pope Innocent III. This freedom we shall observe ourselves, and desire to be observed in good faith by our heirs in perpetuity.

TO ALL FREE MEN OF OUR KINGDOM we have also granted, for us and our heirs forever, all the liberties written out below, to have and to keep for them and their heirs, of us and our heirs:

(2) If any earl, baron, or other person that holds lands directly of the Crown, for military service, shall die, and at his death his heir shall be of full age and owe a 'relief', the heir shall have his inheritance on payment of the ancient scale of 'relief'. That is to say, the heir or heirs of an earl shall pay 100s for the entire earl's barony, the heir or heirs of a knight 100s. at most for the entire knight's 'fee', and any man that owes less shall pay less, in accordance with the ancient usage of 'fees'

(3) But if the heir of such a person is under age and a ward, when he comes of age he shall have his inheritance without 'relief' or fine.

(4) The guardian of the land of an heir who is under age shall take from it only reasonable revenues, customary dues, and feudal services. He shall do this without destruction or damage to men or property. If we have given the guardianship of the land to a sheriff, or to any person answerable to us for the revenues,

and he commits destruction or damage, we will exact compensation from him, and the land shall be entrusted to two worthy and prudent men of the same 'fee', who shall be answerable to us for the revenues, or to the person to whom we have assigned them. If we have given or sold to anyone the guardianship of such land, and he causes destruction or damage, he shall lose the guardianship of it, and it shall be handed over to two worthy and prudent men of the same 'fee', who shall be similarly answerable to us.

(5) For so long as a guardian has guardianship of such land, he shall maintain the houses, parks, fish preserves, ponds, mills, and everything else pertaining to it, from the revenues of the land itself. When the heir comes of age, he shall restore the whole land to him, stocked with plough teams and such implements of husbandry as the season demands and the revenues from the land can reasonably bear.

(6) Heirs may be given in marriage, but not to someone of lower social standing. Before a marriage takes place, it shall be made known to the heir's next-of-kin.

(7) At her husband's death, a widow may have her marriage portion and inheritance at once and without trouble. She shall pay nothing for her dower, marriage portion, or any inheritance that she and her husband held jointly on the day of his death. She may remain in her husband's house for forty days after his death, and within this period her dower shall be assigned to her.

(8) No widow shall be compelled to marry, so long as she wishes to remain without a husband. But she must give security that she will not marry without royal consent, if she holds her lands of the Crown, or without the consent of whatever other lord she may hold them for.

(9) Neither we nor our officials will seize any land or rent in payment of a debt, so long as the debtor has movable goods sufficient to discharge the debt. A debtor's sureties shall not be distrained upon so long as the debtor himself can discharge his debt. If, for lack of means, the debtor is unable to discharge his debt, his sureties shall be answerable for it. If they so desire, they may have the debtor's lands and rents until they have received satisfaction for the debt that they paid for him, unless the debtor can show that he has settled his obligations to them.

(10) If anyone who has borrowed a sum of money from Jews dies before the debt has been repaid, his heir shall pay no interest on the debt for so long as he remains under age, irrespective of whom he holds his lands. If such a debt falls into the hands of the Crown, it will take nothing except the principal sum specified in the bond.

(11) If a man dies owing money to Jews, his wife may have her dower and pay nothing towards the debt from it. If he leaves children that are under age, their needs may also be provided for on a scale appropriate to the size of his holding of lands. The debt is to be paid out of the residue, reserving the service due to his feudal lords. Debts owed to persons other than Jews are to be dealt with similarly.

(12) No 'scutage' or 'aid' may be levied in our kingdom without its general consent, unless it is for the ransom of our person, to make our eldest son a knight, and (once) to marry our eldest daughter. For these purposes only a reasonable 'aid' may be levied. 'Aids' from the city of London are to be treated similarly.

(13) The city of London shall enjoy all its ancient liberties and free customs, both by land and by water. We also will and grant that all other cities, boroughs, towns, and ports shall enjoy all their liberties and free customs.

(14) To obtain the general consent of the realm for the assessment of an 'aid' - except in the three cases specified above - or a 'scutage', we will cause the archbishops, bishops, abbots, earls, and greater barons to be summoned individually by letter. To those who hold lands directly for us we will cause a general summons to be issued, through the sheriffs and other officials, to come together on a fixed day (of which at least forty days notice shall be given) and at a fixed place. In all letters of summons, the cause of the summons will be stated. When a summons has been issued, the business appointed for the day shall go forward in accordance with the resolution of those present, even if not all those who were summoned have appeared.

(15) In future we will allow no one to levy an 'aid' from his free men, except to ransom his person, to make his eldest son a knight, and (once) to marry his eldest daughter. For these purposes only a reasonable 'aid' may be levied.

(16) No man shall be forced to perform more service for a knight's 'fee', or other free holding of land, than is due from it.

(17) Ordinary lawsuits shall not follow the royal court around, but shall be held in a fixed place.

(18) Inquests of *novel disseisin*, *mort d'ancestor*, and *darrein presentment* shall be taken only in their proper county court. We ourselves, or in our absence abroad our chief justice, will send two justices to each county four times a year, and these justices, with four knights of the county elected by the county itself, shall hold the assizes in the county court, on the day and in the place where the court meets.

(19) If any assizes cannot be taken on the day of the county court, as many knights and freeholders shall afterwards remain behind, of those who have attended the court, as will suffice for the administration of justice, having regard to the volume of business to be done.

(20) For a trivial offence, a free man shall be fined only in proportion to the degree of his offence, and for a serious offence correspondingly, but not so heavily as to deprive him of his livelihood. In the same way, a merchant shall be spared his merchandise, and a husbandman the implements of his husbandry, if they fall upon the mercy of a royal court. None of these fines shall be imposed except by the assessment on oath of reputable men of the neighborhood.

(21) Earls and barons shall be fined only by their equals, and in proportion to the gravity of their offence.

(22) A fine imposed upon the lay property of a clerk in holy orders shall be assessed upon the same principles, without reference to the value of his ecclesiastical benefice.

(23) No town or person shall be forced to build bridges over rivers except those with an ancient obligation to do so.

(24) No sheriff, constable, coroners, or other royal officials are to hold lawsuits that should be held by the royal justices.

(25) Every county, hundred, wapentake, and tithing shall remain at its ancient rent, without increase, except the royal demesne manors.

(26) If at the death of a man who holds a lay 'fee' of the Crown, a sheriff or royal official produces royal letters patent of summons for a debt due to the Crown, it shall be lawful for them to seize and list movable goods found in the lay 'fee' of the dead man to the value of the debt, as assessed by worthy men. Nothing shall be removed until the whole debt is paid, when the residue shall be given over to the executors to carry out the dead man's will. If no debt is due to the Crown, all the movable goods shall be regarded as the property of the dead man, except the reasonable shares of his wife and children.

(27) If a free man dies intestate, his movable goods are to be distributed by his next-of-kin and friends, under the supervision of the Church. The rights of his debtors are to be preserved.

(28) No constable or other royal official shall take corn or other movable goods from any man without immediate payment, unless the seller voluntarily offers postponement of this.

(29) No constable may compel a knight to pay money for castle-guard if the knight is willing to undertake the guard in person or with reasonable excuse to supply some other fit man to do it. A knight taken or sent on military service shall be excused from castle-guard for the period of this service.

(30) No sheriff, royal official, or other person shall take horses or cares for transport from any free man, without his consent.

(31) Neither we nor any royal official will take wood for our castle, or for any other purpose, without the consent of the owner.

(32) We will not keep the lands of people convicted of felony in our hand for longer than a year and a day, after which they shall be returned to the lords of the 'fees' concerned.

(33) All fish-weirs shall be removed from the Thames, the Medway, and throughout the whole of England, except on the sea coast.

(34) The writ called precipe shall not in future be issued to anyone in respect of any holding of land, if a free man could thereby be deprived of the right of trial in his own lord's court.

(35) There shall be standard measures of wine, ale, and corn (the London quareer), throughout the kingdom. There shall also be a standard width of dyed cloth, russett, and haberject, namely two ells within the selvedges. Weights are to be standardized similarly.

(36) In future nothing shall be paid or accepted for the issue of a writ of inquisition of life or limbs. It shall be given gratis, and not refused.

(37) If a man holds land of the Crown by 'fee-farm', 'socage', or 'burgage', and also holds land of someone else for knight's service, we will not have guardianship of his heir, nor of the land that belongs to the other person's 'fee', by virtue of the 'fee-farm', 'socage', or 'burgage', unless the 'fee-farm' owes knight's service. We will not have the guardianship of a man's heir, or of land that he holds of someone else, by reason of any small property that he may hold of the Crown for a service of knives, arrows, or the like.

(38) In future no official shall place a man on trial upon his own unsupported statement, without producing credible witnesses to the truth of it.

(39) No free man shall be seized or imprisoned, or stripped of his rights or possessions, or outlawed or exiled, or deprived of his standing in any other way, nor will we proceed with force against him, or send others to do so, except by the lawful judgment of his equals or by the law of the land.

(40) To no one will we sell, to no one deny or delay right or justice.

(41) All merchants may enter or leave England unharmed and without fear, and may stay or travel within it, by land or water, for purposes of trade, free from all illegal exactions, in accordance with ancient and lawful customs. This, however, does not apply in time of war to merchants from a country that is at war with us. Any such merchants found in our country at the outbreak of war shall be detained without injury to their persons or property, until we or our chief justice have discovered how our own merchants are being treated in the country at war with us. If our own merchants are safe they shall be safe too.

(42) In future it shall be lawful for any man to leave and return to our kingdom unharmed and without fear, by land or water, preserving his allegiance to us, except in time of war, for some short period, for the common benefit of the realm. People that have been imprisoned or outlawed in accordance with the law of the land, people from a country that is at war with us, and merchants - who shall be dealt with as stated above - are excepted from this provision.

(43) If a man holds lands of any 'escheat' such as the 'honor' of Wallingford, Nottingham, Boulogne, Lancaster, or of other 'escheats' in our hand that are baronies, at his death his heir shall give us only the 'relief' and service that he would have made to the baron, had the barony been in the baron's hand. We will hold the 'escheat' in the same manner as the baron held it.

(44) People who live outside the forest need not in future appear before the royal justices of the forest in answer to general summonses, unless they are actually involved in proceedings or are sureties for someone who has been seized for a forest offence.

(45) We will appoint as justices, constables, sheriffs, or other officials, only men that know the law of the realm and are minded to keep it well.

(46) All barons who have founded abbeys, and have charters of English kings or ancient tenure as evidence of this, may have guardianship of them when there is no abbot, as is their due.

(47) All forests that have been created in our reign shall at once be disafforested. River-banks that have been enclosed in our reign shall be treated similarly.

(48) All evil customs relating to forests and warrens, foresters, warreners, sheriffs and their servants, or river-banks and their wardens, are at once to be investigated in every county by twelve sworn knights of the county, and within forty days of their enquiry the evil customs are to be abolished completely and irrevocably. But we, or our chief justice if we are not in England, are first to be informed.

(49) We will at once return all hostages and charters delivered up to us by Englishmen as security for peace or for loyal service. We will remove completely from their offices the kinsmen of Gerard de Ath, Peter, Guy, and Andrew de Chanceaux, Guy de Cigogne, and in future they shall hold no offices in England. The people in question are Engelard de Cigogn, Geoffrey de Mareigny and his brothers, Philip Marc and his brothers, with Geoffrey his nephew, and all their followers. As soon as peace is restored, we will remove from the kingdom all the foreign knights, bowmen, their attendants, and the mercenaries that have come to

it, to its harm, with horses and arms. To any man whom we have deprived or dispossessed of lands, castles, liberties, or rights, without the lawful judgment of his equals, we will at once restore these. In cases of dispute the matter shall be resolved by the judgment of the twenty-five barons referred to below in the clause for securing the peace. In cases, however, where a man was deprived or dispossessed of something without the lawful judgment of his equals by our father King Henry or our brother King Richard, and it remains in our hands or is held by others under our warranty, we shall have respite for the period commonly allowed to Crusaders, unless a lawsuit had been begun, or an enquiry had been made at our order, before we took the Cross as a Crusader. On our return from the Crusade, or if we abandon it, we will at once render justice in full. We shall have similar respite in rendering justice in connection with forests that are to be disafforested, or to remain forests, when these were first afforested by our father Henry or our brother Richard; with the guardianship of lands in another person's fee, when we have hitherto had this by virtue of a fee held of us for knights service by a third party; and with abbeys founded in another person's fee, in which the lord of the fee claims to own a right. On our return from the Crusade, or if we abandon it, we will at once do full justice to complaints about these matters. No one shall be arrested or imprisoned on the appeal of a woman for the death of any person except her husband. All fines that have been given to us unjustly and against the law of the land, and all fines that we have exacted unjustly, shall be entirely remitted or the matter decided by a majority judgment of the twenty-five barons referred to below in the clause for securing the peace together with Stephen, archbishop of Canterbury, if he can be present, and such others as he wishes to bring with him. If the archbishop cannot be present, proceedings shall continue without him, provided that if any of the twenty-five barons has been involved in a similar suit himself, his judgment shall be set aside, and someone else chosen and sworn in his place, as a substitute for the single occasion, by the rest of the twenty-five. If we have deprived or dispossessed any Welshmen of lands, liberties, or anything else in England or in Wales, without the lawful judgment of their equals, these are at once to be returned to them. A dispute on this point shall be determined in the Marches by the judgment of equals. English law shall apply to holdings of land in England, Welsh law to those in Wales, and the law of the Marches to those in the Marches. The Welsh shall treat us and ours in the same way. In cases where a Welshman was deprived or dispossessed of anything, without the lawful judgment of his equals, by our father King Henry or our brother King Richard, and it remains in our hands or is held by others under our warranty, we shall have respite for the period commonly allowed to Crusaders, unless a lawsuit had been begun, or an enquiry had been made at our order, before we took the Cross as a Crusader. But on our return from the Crusade, or if we abandon it, we will at once do full justice according to the laws of Wales and the said regions. We will at once return the son of Llywelyn, all Welsh hostages, and the charters delivered to us as security for the peace. With regard to the return of the sisters and hostages of Alexander, king of Scotland, his liberties and his rights, we will treat him in the same way as our other barons of England, unless it appears from the charters that we hold from his father William, formerly king of Scotland, that he should be treated otherwise. This matter shall be resolved by the judgment of his equals in our court. All these customs and liberties that we have granted shall be observed in our kingdom in so far as concerns our own relations with our subjects. Let all men of our kingdom, whether clergy or laymen, observe them similarly in their relations with their own men. Strange characters may have ended here.

SINCE WE HAVE GRANTED ALL THESE THINGS for God, for the better ordering of our kingdom, and to allay the discord that has arisen between us and our barons, and since we desire that they shall be enjoyed in their entirety, with lasting strength, forever, we give and grant to the barons the following security: The barons shall elect twenty-five of their number to keep, and cause to be observed with all their might, the peace and liberties granted and confirmed to them by this charter. If we, our chief justice, our officials, or any of our servants offend in any respect against any man, or transgress any of the articles of the peace or of this security, and the offence is made known to four of the said twenty-five barons, they shall come to us - or in our absence from the kingdom to the chief justice - to declare it and claim immediate redress. If we, or in our absence abroad the chief justice, make no redress within forty days, reckoning from the day on which the offence was declared to us or to him, the four barons shall refer the matter to the rest of the twenty-five barons, who may distrain upon and assail us in every way possible, with the support of the whole community of the land, by seizing our castles, lands, possessions, or anything else saving only our own person and those of the queen and our children, until they have secured such redress as they have determined upon. Having secured the redress, they may then resume their normal obedience to us. Any man who so desires may take an oath to obey the commands of the twenty-five barons for the achievement of these ends, and to join with them in assailing us to the utmost of his power. We give public and free permission to take this oath to any man who so desires, and at no time will we prohibit any man from taking it. Indeed, we will compel any of our subjects who are unwilling to take it to swear it at our command. If-one of the twenty-five barons dies or leaves the country, or is prevented in any other way from discharging his duties, the rest of them shall choose another baron in his place, at their discretion, who shall be duly sworn in as they were. In the event of disagreement among the twenty-five barons on any matter referred to them for decision, the verdict of the majority present shall have the same validity as a unanimous verdict of the whole twenty-five, whether these were all present or some of those summoned were unwilling or unable to appear. The twenty-five barons shall swear to obey all the above articles faithfully, and shall cause them to be obeyed by others to the best of their power. We will not seek to procure from anyone, either by our own efforts or those of a third party, anything by which any part of these concessions or liberties might be revoked or diminished. Should such a thing be procured, it shall be null and void and we will at no time make use of it, either ourselves or through a third party.

We have remitted and pardoned fully to all men any ill-will, hurt, or grudges that have arisen between us and our subjects, whether clergy or laymen, since the beginning of the dispute. We have in addition remitted fully, and for our own part have also pardoned, to all clergy and laymen any offences committed as a result of the said dispute between Easter 1215 AD and the restoration of peace.

In addition we have caused letters patent to be made for the barons, bearing witness to this security and to the concessions set out above, over the seals of Stephen archbishop of Canterbury, Henry archbishop of Dublin, the other bishops named above, and Master Pandulf.

IT IS ACCORDINGLY OUR WISH AND COMMAND that the English Church shall be free, and that men in our kingdom shall have and keep all these liberties, rights, and concessions, well and peaceably in their fullness and entirety for them and their heirs, of us and our heirs, in all things and all places for ever.

Both we and the barons have sworn that all this shall be observed in good faith and without deceit. Witness the above mentioned people and many others.

Given by our hand in the meadow that is called Runnymede, between Windsor and Staines, on the fifteenth day of June in the seventeenth year of our reign.

A LETTER CONCERNING TOLERATION

by John Locke
1689

---HONORED SIR,

--Since you are pleased to inquire what are my thoughts about the mutual toleration of Christians in their different professions of religion, I must answer you freely that I esteem that toleration to be the chief characteristic mark of the true Church. For whatsoever some people boast of the antiquity of places and names, or of the pomp of their outward worship; others, of the reformation of their discipline; all, of the orthodoxy of their faith- for everyone is orthodox to himself- these things, and all others of this nature, are much rather marks of men striving for power and empire over one another than of the Church of Christ. Let anyone have never so true a claim to all these things, yet if he be destitute of charity, meekness, and good-will in general towards all mankind, even to those that are not Christians, he is certainly yet short of being a true Christian himself. "The kings of the Gentiles exercise leadership over them," said our Savior to his disciples, "but you shall not be so." The business of true religion is quite another thing. It is not instituted in order to the erecting of an external pomp, nor to the obtaining of ecclesiastical dominion, nor to the exercising of compulsive force, but to the regulating of men's lives, according to the rules of virtue and piety. Whosoever will list himself under the banner of Christ, must, in the first place and above all things make war upon his own lusts and vices. It is in vain for any man to usurp the name of Christian, without holiness of life, purity of manners, benignity and meekness of spirit. "Let everyone that names the name of Christ, depart from iniquity."(2) "You, when you are converted, strengthen your brethren," said our Lord to Peter.(3) It would, indeed, be very hard for one that appears careless about his own salvation to persuade me that he were extremely concerned for mine. For it is impossible that those should sincerely and heartily apply themselves to make other people Christians, who have not really embraced the Christian religion in their own hearts. If the Gospel and the apostles may be credited, no man can be a Christian without charity and without that faith which works, not by force, but by love. Now, I appeal to the consciences of those that persecute, torment, destroy, and kill other men upon pretence of religion, whether they do it out of friendship and kindness towards them or no? And I shall then indeed, and not until then, believe they do so, when I shall see those fiery zealots correcting, in the same manner, their friends and familiar acquaintance for the manifest sins they commit against the precepts of the Gospel; when I shall see them persecute with fire and sword the members of their own communion that are tainted with enormous vices and without amendment are in danger of eternal perdition; and when I shall see them thus express their love and desire of the salvation of their souls by the infliction of torments and exercise of all manner of cruelties. For if it be out of a principle of charity, as they pretend, and love to men's souls that they deprive them of their estates, maim them with corporal punishments, starve and torment them in noisome prisons, and in the end even take away their lives- I say, if all this be done merely to make men Christians and procure their salvation, why then do they suffer whoredom, fraud, malice, and such-like enormities, which (according to the apostle)(4) manifestly relish of heathenish corruption, to predominate so much and abound among their flocks and people? These, and such-like things, are certainly more contrary to the glory of God, to the purity of the Church, and to the salvation of souls, than any conscientious dissent from ecclesiastical decisions, or separation from public worship, while accompanied with innocence of life. Why, then, does this burning zeal for God, for the Church, and for the salvation of souls- burning I say, literally, with fire and wood- pass by those moral vices and wickedness, without any chastisement, which are acknowledged by all men to be diametrically opposite to the profession of Christianity, and bend all its nerves either to the introducing of ceremonies, or to the establishment of opinions, which for the most part are about nice and intricate matters, that exceed the capacity of ordinary understandings? Which of the parties contending about these things is in the right, which of them is guilty of schism or heresy, whether those that domineer or those that suffer, will then at last be manifest when the causes of their separation comes to be judged of He, certainly, that follows Christ, embraces His doctrine, and bears His yoke, though he forsake both father and mother, separate from the public assemblies and ceremonies of his country, or whomsoever or whatsoever else he relinquishes, will not then be judged a heretic.

- Luke 22. 25.

-(2) II Tim. 2. 19.

-(3) Luke 22. 32.

-(4) Rom. 1.

--Now, though the divisions that are among sects should be allowed to be never so obstructive of the salvation of souls; yet, nevertheless, adultery, fornication, uncleanliness, lasciviousness, idolatry, and such-like things, cannot be denied to be works of the flesh, concerning which the apostle has expressly declared that "they who do them shall not inherit the Kingdom of God." Whosoever, therefore, is sincerely solicitous about the Kingdom of God and thinks it his duty to endeavor the enlargement of it among men, ought to apply himself with no less care and industry to the rooting out of these immoralities than to the destruction of sects. But if anyone do otherwise, and while he is cruel and implacable towards those that differ from him in opinion, he be indulgent to such iniquities and immoralities as are unbecoming the name of a Christian, let such a one talk never so much of the Church, he plainly demonstrates by his actions that it is another kingdom he aims at, and not the advancement of the Kingdom of God.

- Gal. 5.

--That any man should think fit to cause another man- whose salvation he heartily desires- to die in torments, and that even in an unconverted state, would, I confess, seem very strange to me, and I think, to any other also. But nobody, surely, will ever believe that such a carriage can proceed from charity, love, or goodwill. If anyone maintains that men ought to be compelled by fire and sword to profess certain doctrines, and conform to this or that exterior worship, without any regard had unto their morals; if anyone endeavor to convert those that are erroneous unto the faith, by forcing them to profess things that they do not believe and allowing them to practice things that the Gospel does not permit, it cannot be doubted indeed but such a one is desirous to have a numerous assembly joined in the same profession with himself; but that he principally intends by those means to compose a truly Christian Church is altogether incredible. It is not, therefore, to be wondered at if those who do not really contend for the advancement of the true religion, and of the Church of Christ, make use of arms that do not belong to the Christian warfare. If, like the Captain of our salvation, they sincerely desired the good of souls, they would tread in the steps and follow the perfect example of that Prince of Peace, who sent out His soldiers to the subduing of nations, and gathering them into His Church, not armed with the sword, or other instruments of force, but prepared with the Gospel of peace and with the exemplary holiness of their lives. This was His method. Though if infidels were to be converted by force, if those that are either blind or obstinate were to be drawn off from their errors by armed soldiers, we know very well that it was much more easy for Him to do it with armies of heavenly legions than for any son of the Church, howsoever potent, with all his platoons.

--The toleration of those that differ from others in matters of religion is so agreeable to the Gospel of Jesus Christ, and to the genuine reason of mankind, that it seems monstrous for men to be so blind as not to perceive the necessity and advantage of it in so clear a light. I will not here tax the pride and ambition of some, the passion and uncharitable zeal of others. These are faults from which human affairs can perhaps scarce ever be perfectly freed; but yet such as nobody will bear the plain imputation of, without covering them with some specious color; and so pretend to commendation, while they are carried away by their own irregular passions. But, however, that some may not color their spirit of persecution and unchristian cruelty with a pretence of care of the public good and observation of the laws; and that others, under pretence of religion, may not seek impunity for their libertinism and licentiousness; in a word, that none may impose either upon himself or others, by the pretences of loyalty and obedience to the prince, or of tenderness and sincerity in the worship of God; I esteem it above all things necessary to distinguish exactly the business of civil government from that of religion and to settle the just bounds that lie between the one and the other. If this be not done, there can be no end put to the controversies that will be always arising between those that have, or at least pretend to have, on the one side, a concernment for the interest of men's souls, and, on the other side, a care of the commonwealth.

--The commonwealth seems to me to be a society of men constituted only for the procuring, preserving, and advancing their own civil interests.

--Civil interests I call life, liberty, health, and care of body; and the possession of outward things, such as money, lands, houses, furniture, and the like.

--It is the duty of the civil magistrate, by the impartial execution of equal laws, to secure unto all the people in general, and to every one of his subjects in particular, the just possession of these things belonging to this life. If anyone presumes to violate the laws of public justice and equity, established for the preservation of those things, his presumption is to be checked by the fear of punishment, consisting of the deprivation or diminution of those civil interests, or goods, which otherwise he might and ought to enjoy. But seeing no man does willingly suffer himself to be punished by the deprivation of any part of his goods, and much less of his liberty or life, therefore, is the magistrate armed with the force and strength of all his subjects, in order to the punishment of those that violate any other man's rights.

--Now that the whole jurisdiction of the magistrate reaches only to these civil concernments, and that all civil power, right and dominion, is bounded and confined to the only care of promoting these things; and that it neither can nor ought in any manner to be extended to the salvation of souls, these following considerations seem unto me abundantly to demonstrate:

--First, because the care of souls is not committed to the civil magistrate, any more than to other men. It is not committed unto him, I say, by God; because it appears not that God has ever given any such authority to one man over another as to compel anyone to his religion. Nor can any such power be vested in the magistrate by the consent of the people, because no man can so far abandon the care of his own salvation as blindly to leave to the choice of any other, whether prince or subject, to prescribe to him what faith or worship he shall embrace. For no man can, if he would, conform his faith to the dictates of another. All the life and power of true religion consist in the inward and full persuasion of the mind; and faith is not faith without believing. Whatever profession we make, to whatever outward worship we conform, if we are not fully satisfied in our own mind that the one is true and the other well pleasing unto God, such profession and such practice, far from being any furtherance, are indeed great obstacles to our salvation. For in this manner, instead of expiating other sins by the exercise of religion, I say, in offering thus unto God Almighty such a worship as we esteem to be displeasing unto Him, we add unto the number of our other sins those also of hypocrisy and contempt of His Divine Majesty.

--In the second place, the care of souls cannot belong to the civil magistrate, because his power consists only in outward force; but true and saving religion consists in the inward persuasion of the mind, without which nothing can be acceptable to God. And such is the nature of the understanding, that it cannot be compelled to the belief of anything by outward force. Confiscation of estate, imprisonment, torments, nothing of that nature can have any such efficacy as to make men change the inward judgment that they have framed of things.

--It may indeed be alleged that the magistrate may make use of arguments, and, thereby; draw the heterodox into the way of truth, and procure their salvation. I grant it; but this is common to him with other men. In teaching, instructing, and redressing the erroneous by reason, he may certainly do what becomes any good man to do. Being part of the civil government does not oblige him to put off either humanity or Christianity; but it is one thing to persuade, another to command; one thing to press with arguments, another with penalties. This civil power alone has a right to do; to the other, goodwill is authority enough. Every man has commission to admonish, exhort, convince another of error, and, by reasoning, to draw him into truth; but to give laws, receive obedience, and compel with the sword, belongs to none but the magistrate. And, upon this ground, I affirm that the magistrate's power extends not to the establishing of any articles of faith, or forms of worship, by the force of his laws. For laws are of no force at all without penalties, and penalties in this case are absolutely impertinent, because they are not proper to convince the mind. Neither the profession of any articles of faith, nor the conformity to any outward form of worship (as has been already said), can be available to the salvation of souls, unless the truth of the one and the acceptableness of the other unto God be thoroughly believed by those that so profess and practice. But penalties are no way capable to produce such belief. It is only light and evidence that can work a change in men's opinions; which light can in no manner proceed from corporal sufferings, or any other outward penalties.

--In the third place, the care of the salvation of men's souls cannot belong to the magistrate; because, though the rigor of laws and the force of penalties were capable to convince and change men's minds, yet would not that help at all to the salvation of their souls. For there being but one truth, one way to heaven, what hope is there that more men would be led into it if they had no rule but the religion of the court and were put under the necessity to quit the light of their own reason, and oppose the dictates of their own consciences, and blindly to resign themselves up to the will of their governors and to the religion which either ignorance, ambition, or superstition had chanced to establish in the countries where they were born? In the variety and contradiction of opinions in religion, wherein the princes of the world are as much divided as in their secular interests, the narrow way would be much straitened; one country alone would be in the right, and all the rest of the world put under an obligation of following their princes in the ways that lead to destruction; and that which heightens the absurdity, and very ill suits the notion of a Deity, men would owe their eternal happiness or misery to the places of their nativity.

--These considerations, to omit many others that might have been urged to the same purpose, seem to me sufficient to conclude that all the power of civil government relates only to men's civil interests, is confined to the care of the things of this world, and has nothing to do with the world to come.

--Let us now consider what a church is. A church, then, I take to be a voluntary society of men and women, joining themselves together of their own accord for the public worshipping of God in such manner as they judge acceptable to Him, and effectual to the salvation of their souls.

--I say it is a free and voluntary society. Nobody is born a member of any church; otherwise the religion of parents would descend unto children by the same right of inheritance as their temporal estates, and everyone would hold his faith by the same tenure he does his lands, than which nothing can be imagined more absurd. Thus, therefore, that matter stands. No man by nature is bound unto any particular church or sect, but everyone joins himself voluntarily to that society in which he believes he has found that profession and worship which is truly acceptable to God. The hope of salvation, as it was the only cause of his entrance into that communion, so it can be the only reason of his stay there. For if afterwards he discover anything either erroneous in the doctrine or incongruous in the worship of that society to which he has joined himself, why should it not be as free for him to go out as it was to enter? No member of a religious society can be tied with any other bonds but what proceed from the certain expectation of eternal life. A church, then, is a society of members voluntarily uniting to that end.

--It follows now that we consider what is the power of this church and unto what laws it is subject.

--Forasmuch as no society, howsoever free, or upon whatsoever slight occasion instituted, whether of philosophers for learning, of merchants for commerce, or of men of leisure for mutual conversation and discourse, no church or company, I say, can in the least subsist and hold together, but will presently dissolve and break in pieces, unless it be regulated by some laws, and the members all consent to observe some order. Place and time of meeting must be agreed on; rules for admitting and excluding members must be established; distinction of officers, and putting things into a regular course, and suchlike, cannot be omitted. But since the joining together of several members into this church-society, as has already been demonstrated, is absolutely free and spontaneous, it necessarily follows that the right of making its laws can belong to none but the society itself; or, at least (which is the same thing), to those whom the society by common consent has authorized thereunto.

--Some, perhaps, may object that no such society can be said to be a true church unless it have in it a bishop or presbyter, with ruling authority derived from the very apostles, and continued down to the present times by an uninterrupted succession.

--To these I answer: In the first place, let them show me the edict by which Christ has imposed that law upon His Church. And let not any man think me impertinent, if in a thing of this consequence I require that the terms of that edict be very express and positive; for the promise He has made us, that "wheresoever two or three are gathered together" in His name, He will be in the midst of them, seems to imply the contrary. Whether such an assembly wants anything necessary to a true church, pray do you consider. Certain I am that nothing can be there wanting unto the salvation of souls, which is sufficient to our purpose.

- Matt. 18. 20.

--Next, pray observe how great have always been the divisions among even those who lay so much stress upon the Divine institution and continued succession of a certain order of rulers in the Church. Now, their very dissension unavoidably puts us upon a necessity of deliberating and, consequently, allows a liberty of choosing that which upon consideration we prefer.

--And, in the last place, I consent that these men have a ruler in their church, established by such a long series of succession as they judge necessary, provided I may have liberty at the same time to join myself to that society in which I am persuaded those things are to be found which are necessary to the salvation of my soul. In this manner ecclesiastical liberty will be preserved on all sides, and no man will have a legislator imposed upon him but whom himself has chosen.

--But since men are so solicitous about the true church, I would only ask them here, by the way, if it be not more agreeable to the Church of Christ to make the conditions of her communion consist in such things, and such things only, as the Holy Spirit has in the Holy Scriptures declared, in express words, to be necessary to salvation; I ask, I say, whether this be not more agreeable to the Church of Christ than for men to impose their own inventions and interpretations upon others as if they were of Divine authority, and to establish by ecclesiastical laws, as absolutely necessary to the profession of Christianity, such things as the Holy Scriptures do either not mention, or at least not expressly command? Whosoever requires those things in order to have ecclesiastical communion, which Christ does not require in order to life eternal, he may, perhaps, indeed constitute a society accommodated to his own opinion and his own advantage; but how that can be called the Church of Christ which is established upon laws that are not His, and which excludes such persons from its communion as He will one day receive into the Kingdom of Heaven, I understand not. But this being not a proper place to inquire into the marks of the true church, I will only mind those that contend so earnestly for the decrees of their own society, and that cry out continually, "The Church! the Church!" with as much noise, and perhaps upon the same principle, as the Ephesian silversmiths did for their Diana; this, I say, I desire to mind them of, that the Gospel frequently declares that the true disciples of Christ must suffer persecution; but that the Church of Christ should persecute others, and force others by fire and sword to embrace her faith and doctrine, I could never yet find in any of the books of the New Testament.

--The end of a religious society (as has already been said) is the public worship of God and, by means thereof, the acquisition of eternal life. All discipline ought, therefore, to tend to that end, and all ecclesiastical laws to be thereunto confined. Nothing ought nor can be transacted in this society relating to the possession of civil and worldly goods. No force is here to be made use of upon any occasion whatsoever. For force belongs wholly to the civil magistrate, and the possession of all outward goods is subject to his jurisdiction.

--But, it may be asked, by what means then shall ecclesiastical laws be established, if they must be thus destitute of all compulsive power? I answer: They must be established by means suitable to the nature of such things, whereof the external profession and observation- if not proceeding from a thorough conviction and approbation of the mind- is altogether useless and unprofitable. The arms by which the members of this society are to be kept within their duty are exhortations, admonitions, and advices. If by these means the offenders will not be reclaimed, and the erroneous convinced, there remains nothing further to be done but that such stubborn and obstinate persons, who give no ground to hope for their reformation, should be cast out and separated from the society. This is the last and utmost force of ecclesiastical authority. No other punishment can thereby be inflicted than that, the relation ceasing between the body and the member who is cut off. The person so condemned ceases to be a part of that church.

--These things being thus determined let us inquire, in the next place: How far the duty of toleration extends, and what is required from everyone by it?

--And, first, I hold that no church is bound, by the duty of toleration, to retain any such person in her bosom as, after admonition, continues obstinately to offend against the laws of the society. For, these being the condition of communion and the bond of the society, if the breach of them were permitted without any discipline, the society would immediately be thereby dissolved. But, nevertheless, in all such cases care is to be taken that the sentence of excommunication, and the execution thereof, carry with it no rough usage of word or action whereby the ejected person may any wise be damned in body or estate. For all such force (as has often been said) belongs only to the magistrate, nor should any private persons at any time to use force, unless it is in self-defense against unjust violence. Excommunication neither does, nor can, deprive the excommunicated person of any of those civil goods that he formerly possessed. All those things are the domain of the civil government and are under the magistrate's protection. The whole force of excommunication consists only in this: that, the resolution of the society in that respect being declared, the union that was between the body and some member comes thereby to be dissolved; and, that relation ceasing, the participation of some certain things which the society communicated to its members, and unto which no man has any civil right, comes also to cease. For there is no civil injury done unto the excommunicated person by the church minister's refusing him that bread and wine, in the celebration of the Lord's Supper, which was not bought with his but other men's money.

--Secondly, no private person has any right in any manner to prejudice another person in his civil enjoyments because he is of another church or religion. All the rights and franchises that belong to him as a man, or as a denizen, are inviolably to be preserved to him. These are not the business of religion. Neither violence nor injury is to be offered him, whether he is Christian or Pagan. Nay, we must not content ourselves with the narrow measures of bare justice; charity, bounty, and liberality must be added to it. This the Gospel enjoins, this reason directs, and this that natural fellowship we are born into requires of us. If any man errs from the right way, it is his own misfortune, no injury to you; nor therefore are you to punish him in the things of this life because you suppose he will be miserable in that which is to come.

--What I say concerning the mutual toleration of private persons differing from one another in religion, I understand also of particular churches which stand, as it were, in the same relation to each other as private persons among themselves: nor has anyone of them any manner of jurisdiction over any other; no, not even when the civil magistrate (as it sometimes happens) comes to be of this or the other communion. For the civil government can give no new right to the church, nor the church to the civil government. So that, whether the magistrate join himself to any church, or separate from it, the church remains always as it was before- a free and voluntary society. It neither requires the power of the sword by the magistrate's coming to it, nor does it lose the right of instruction and excommunication by his going from it. This is the fundamental and immutable right of a spontaneous society- that it has power to remove any of its members who transgress the rules of its institution; but it cannot, by the accession of any new members, acquire any right of jurisdiction over those that are not joined with it. And therefore peace, equity, and friendship are always mutually to be observed by particular churches, in the same manner as by private persons, without any pretence of superiority or jurisdiction over one another.

--That the thing may be made clearer by an example, let us suppose two churches -- the one of Arminians, the other of Calvinists- residing in the city of Constantinople. Will anyone say that either of these churches has right to deprive the members of the other of their estates and liberty (as we see practiced elsewhere) because of their differing from it in some doctrines and ceremonies, while the Turks, in the meanwhile, silently stand by and *laugh* to see with what inhuman cruelty Christians thus rage against Christians? But if one of these churches has this power of treating the other ill, I ask which of them it is to whom that power belongs, and by what right? It will be answered, undoubtedly, that it is the orthodox church which has the right of authority over the erroneous or heretical. This is, in great and specious words, to say just nothing at all. For every church is orthodox to itself; to others, erroneous or heretical. For whatsoever any church believes, it believes to be true and the contrary unto those things it pronounces to be error. So that the controversy between these churches about the truth of their doctrines and the purity of their worship is on both sides equal; nor is there any judge, either at Constantinople or elsewhere upon earth, by whose sentence it can be determined. The decision of that question belongs only to the Supreme Judge of all men, to who also alone belongs the punishment of the erroneous. In the meanwhile, let those men consider how heinously they sin, who, adding injustice, if not to their error, yet certainly to their pride, do rashly and arrogantly take upon them to misuse the servants of another master, who are not at all accountable to them.

--Nay, further: if it could be manifest which of these two dissenting churches was in the right, there would not accrue thereby unto the orthodox any right of destroying the other. For churches have neither any jurisdiction in worldly matters, nor are fire and sword any proper instruments wherewith to convince men's minds of error, and inform them of the truth. Let us suppose, nevertheless, that the civil magistrate inclined to favor one of them and to put his sword into their hands that (by his consent) they might chastise the dissenters as they pleased. Will any man say that any right can be derived unto a Christian church over its brethren from a Turkish emperor? An *infidel*, who has himself no authority to punish Christians for the articles of their faith, cannot confer such an authority upon any society of Christians, nor give unto them a right which he has not himself. This would be the case at Constantinople; and the reason of the thing is the same in any Christian kingdom. The civil power is the same in every place. Nor can that power, in the hands of a Christian prince, confer any greater authority upon the Church than in the hands of a heathen; which is to say, just none at all.

--Nevertheless, it is worthy to be observed and lamented that the most violent of these defenders of the truth, the opposers of errors, the exclaimers against schism do hardly ever let loose this their zeal for God, with which they are so warmed and inflamed, unless where they have the civil magistrate on their side. But so soon as ever court favor has given them the better end of the staff, and they begin to feel themselves the stronger, then presently peace and charity are to be laid aside. Otherwise they are religiously to be observed. Where they have not the power to carry on persecution and to become masters, there they desire to live upon fair terms and preach up toleration. When they are not strengthened with the civil power, then they can bear most patiently and unmovedly the contagion of idolatry, superstition, and heresy in their neighborhood; of which on other occasions the interest of religion makes them to be extremely apprehensive. They do not forwardly attack those errors which are in fashion at court or are countenanced by the government. Here they can be content to spare their arguments; which yet (with their leave) is the only right method of propagating truth, which has no such way of prevailing as when strong arguments and good reason are joined with the softness of civility and good usage.

--Nobody, therefore, in total, neither single persons nor churches, nay, nor even commonwealths, have any just title to invade the civil rights and worldly goods of each other upon pretence of religion. Those that are of another opinion would do well to consider with themselves how pernicious a seed of discord and war, how powerful a provocation to endless hatreds, rapines, and slaughters they thereby furnish unto mankind. No peace and security, no, not so much as common friendship, can ever be established or preserved among men so long as this opinion prevails, that dominion is founded in grace and that religion is to be propagated by force of arms.

--In the third place, let us see what the duty of toleration requires from those who are distinguished from the rest of mankind (from the laity, as they please to call us) by some ecclesiastical character and office; whether they be bishops, priests, presbyters, ministers, or however else dignified or distinguished. It is not my business to inquire here into the original of the power or dignity of the clergy. This only I say, that, whencesoever their authority is sprung, since it is ecclesiastical, it ought to be confined within the bounds of the Church, nor can it in any manner be extended to civil affairs, because the Church itself is a thing absolutely separate and distinct from the commonwealth. The boundaries on both sides are fixed and immovable. He jumbles heaven and earth together, the things most remote and opposite, who mixes these two societies, which are in their original, end, business, and in everything perfectly distinct and infinitely different from each other. No man, therefore, with whatsoever ecclesiastical office he is dignified, can deprive another man that is not of his church and faith either of liberty or of any part of his worldly goods upon the account of that difference between them in religion. For whatsoever is not lawful to the whole Church cannot by any ecclesiastical right become lawful to any of its members.

--But this is not all. It is not enough that ecclesiastical men abstain from violence and pillage and all manner of persecution. He that pretends to be a successor of the apostles, and takes upon him the office of teaching, is obliged also to admonish his hearers of the duties of peace and goodwill towards all men, as well towards the erroneous as the orthodox; towards those that differ from them in faith and worship as well as towards those that agree with them therein. And he ought industriously to exhort all men, whether private persons or magistrates (if any such there be in his church), to charity, meekness, and toleration, and diligently endeavor to ally and temper all that heat and unreasonable averseness of mind which either any man's fiery zeal for his own sect or the craft of others has kindled against dissenters. I will not undertake to represent how happy and how great would be the fruit, both in Church and State, if the pulpits everywhere sounded with this doctrine of peace and toleration, lest I should seem to reflect too severely upon those men whose dignity I desire not to detract from, nor would have it diminished either by others or themselves. But this I say, that thus it ought to be. And if anyone that professes himself to be a minister of the Word of God, a preacher of the gospel of peace, teaches otherwise, he either understands not or neglects the business of his calling and shall one day give account thereof unto the Prince of Peace. If Christians are to be admonished that they abstain from all manner of revenge, even after repeated provocations and multiplied injuries, how much more ought they who suffer nothing, who have had no harm done them, forbear violence and abstain from all manner of ill-usage towards those from whom they have received none! This caution and temper they ought certainly to use towards those. who mind only their own business and are solicitous for nothing but that (whatever men think of them) they may worship God in that manner which they are persuaded is acceptable to Him and in which they have the strongest hopes of eternal salvation. In private domestic affairs, in the management of estates, in the conservation of bodily health, every man may consider what suits his own convenience and follow what course he likes best. No man complains of the ill-management of his neighbor's affairs. No man is angry with another for an error committed in sowing his land or in marrying his daughter. Nobody corrects a spendthrift for consuming his substance in taverns. Let any man pull down, or build, or make whatsoever expenses he pleases, nobody murmurs, nobody controls him; he has his liberty. But if any man do not frequent the church, if he do not there conform his behavior exactly to the accustomed ceremonies, or if he brings not his children to be initiated in the sacred mysteries of this or the other congregation, this immediately causes an uproar. The neighborhood is filled with noise and clamor. Everyone is ready to be the avenger of so great a crime, and the zealots hardly have the patience to refrain from violence and rapine so long until the cause is heard and the poor man be, according to form, condemned to the loss of liberty, goods, or life. Oh, that our ecclesiastical orators of every sect would apply themselves with all the strength of arguments that they are able to the confounding of men's errors! But let them spare their persons. Let them not supply their want of reasons with the instruments of force, which belong to another jurisdiction and do ill become a Churchman's hands. Let them not call in the magistrate's authority to the aid of their eloquence or learning, lest perhaps, while they pretend only love for the truth, their intemperate zeal, breathing nothing but fire and sword, betray their ambition and show that what they desire is temporal dominion. For it will be very difficult to persuade men of sense that he who with dry eyes and satisfaction of mind can deliver his brother to the executioner to be burnt alive, does sincerely and heartily concern himself to save that brother from the flames of hell in the world to come.

--In the last place let us now consider what is the magistrate's duty in the business of toleration, which certainly is very considerable.

--We have already proved that the care of souls does not belong to the magistrate. Not a magisterial care, I mean (if I may so call it), which consists in prescribing by laws and compelling by punishments. But a charitable care, which consists in teaching, admonishing, and persuading, cannot be denied unto any man. The care, therefore, of every man's soul belongs unto himself and is to be left unto himself. But what if he neglects the care of his soul? I answer: What if he neglects the care of his health or of his estate, which things are nearly related to the government of the magistrate than the other? Will the magistrate provide by an express law that such a one shall not become poor or sick? Laws provide, as much as is possible, that the goods and health of subjects be not injured by the fraud and violence of others; they do not guard them from the negligence or ill-husbandry of the possessors themselves. No man can be forced to be rich or healthful whether he will or no. Nay, God Himself will not save men against their wills. Let us suppose, however, that some prince were desirous to force his subjects to accumulate riches, or to preserve the health and strength of their bodies. Shall it be provided by law that they must consult none but Roman physicians, and shall everyone be bound to live according to their prescriptions? What, shall no potion, no broth, be taken, but what is prepared either in the Vatican, suppose, or in a Geneva shop? Or, to make these subjects rich, shall they all be obliged by law to become merchants or musicians? Or, shall everyone turn grocer, or smith, because there are some that maintain their families plentifully and grow rich in those professions? But, it may be said, there are a thousand ways to wealth, but one only way to heaven. It is well said, indeed, especially by those that plead for compelling men into this or the other way. For if there were several ways that led thither, there would not be so much as a pretence left for compulsion. But now, if I be marching on with my utmost vigor in that way which, according to the sacred geography, leads straight to Jerusalem, why am I beaten and ill-used by others because, perhaps, I wear not buskins; because my hair is not of the right cut; because, perhaps, I have not been dipped in the right fashion; because I eat flesh upon the road, or some other food which agrees with my stomach; because I avoid certain by-ways, which seem unto me to lead into briars or precipices; because, among the several paths that are in the same road, I choose that to walk in which seems to be the straightest and cleanest; because I avoid to keep company with some travelers that are less grave and others that are more sour than they ought to be; or, in fine, because I follow a guide that either is, or is not, clothed in white, or crowned with a mitre? Certainly, if we consider right, we shall find that, for the most part, they are such frivolous things as these that (without any prejudice to religion or the salvation of souls, if not accompanied with superstition or hypocrisy) might either be observed or omitted. I say they are such-like things as these which breed implacable enmities among Christian brethren, who are all agreed in the substantial and truly fundamental part of religion.

--But let us grant unto these zealots, who condemn all things that are not of their mode, that from these circumstances are different ends. What shall we conclude from thence? There is only one of these which is the true way to eternal happiness: but in this great variety of ways that men follow, it is still doubted which is the right one. Now, both the care of the commonwealth, nor the right enacting of laws, does discover this way that leads to heaven more certainly to the magistrate than every private man's search and study discovers it unto himself. I have a weak body, sunk under a languishing disease, for which (I suppose) there is one only remedy, but that unknown. Does it therefore belong unto the magistrate to prescribe me a remedy, because there is but one, and because it is unknown? Because there is but one way for me to escape death, will it therefore be safe for me to do whatsoever the magistrate ordains? Those things that every man ought sincerely to inquire into himself, and by meditation, study, search, and his own endeavors, attain the knowledge of, cannot be looked upon as the peculiar possession of any sort of men. Princes, indeed, are born superior unto other men in power, but in nature equal. Neither the right nor the art of ruling does necessarily carry along with it the certain knowledge of other things, and least of all of true religion. For if it were so, how could it come to pass that the lords of the earth should differ as vastly as they do in religious matters? But let us grant that it is probable the way to eternal life may be better known by a prince than by his subjects, or at least that in this incertitude of things the safest and most commodious way for private persons is to follow his dictates. You will say: "What then?" If he should bid you follow merchandise for your livelihood, would you decline that course for fear it should not succeed? I answer: I would turn merchant upon the prince's command, because, in case I should have ill-success in trade, he is abundantly able to make up my loss some other way. If it be true, as he pretends, that he desires I should thrive and grow rich, he can set me up again when unsuccessful voyages have broken me. But this is not the case in the things that regard the life to come; if there I take a wrong course, if in that respect I am once undone, it is not in the magistrate's power to repair my loss, to ease my suffering, nor to restore me in any measure, much less entirely, to a good estate. What security can be given for the Kingdom of Heaven?

--Perhaps some will say that they do not suppose this infallible judgment, that all men are bound to follow in the affairs of religion, to be in the civil magistrate, but in the Church. What the Church has determined, that the civil magistrate orders to be observed; and he provides by his authority that nobody shall either act or believe in the business of religion otherwise than the Church teaches. So that the judgment of those things is in the Church; the magistrate himself yields obedience thereunto and requires the like obedience from others. I answer: Who sees not how frequently the name of the Church, which was venerable in time of the apostles, has been made use of to throw dust in the people's eyes in the following ages? But, however, in the present case it helps us not. The one only narrow way which leads to heaven is not better known to the magistrate than to private persons, and therefore I cannot safely take him for my guide, who may probably be as ignorant of the way as myself, and who certainly is less concerned for my salvation than I myself am. Among so many kings of the Jews, how many of them were there whom any Israelite, thus blindly following, had not fallen into idolatry and thereby into destruction? Yet, nevertheless, you bid me be of good courage and tell me that all is now safe and secure, because the magistrate does not now enjoin the observance of his own decrees in matters of religion, but only the decrees of the Church. Of what Church, I beseech you? of that, certainly, which likes him best. As if he that compels me by laws and penalties to enter into this or the other Church, did not interpose his own judgment in the matter. What difference is there whether he led me himself, or delivers me over to be led by others? I depend both ways upon his will, and it is he that determines both ways of my eternal state. Would an Israelite that had worshipped Baal upon the command of his king have been in any better condition because somebody had told him that the king ordered nothing in religion upon his own head, nor commanded anything to be done by his subjects in divine worship but what was approved by the counsel of priests, and declared to be of divine right by the doctors of their Church? If the religion of any Church become, therefore, true and saving, because the head of that sect, the prelates and priests, and those of that tribe, do all of them, with all their might, extol and praise it, what religion can ever be accounted erroneous, false, and destructive? I am doubtful concerning the doctrine of the Socinians, I am suspicious of the way of worship practiced by the Papists, or Lutherans; will it be ever a jot safer for me to join either unto the one or the other of those Churches, upon the magistrate's command, because he commands nothing in religion but by the authority and counsel of the doctors of that Church?

--But, to speak the truth, we must acknowledge that the Church (if a convention of clergymen, making canons, must be called by that name) is for the most part more apt to be influenced by the Court than the Court by the Church. How the Church was under the changes of both orthodox and Arian emperors is very well known. Or if those things be too remote, our modern English history affords us fresh examples in the reigns of Henry VIII, Edward VI, Mary, and Elizabeth, how easily and smoothly the clergy changed their decrees, their articles of faith, their form of worship, everything according to the inclination of those kings and queens. Yet were those kings and queens of such different minds in point of religion, and enjoined thereupon such different things, that no man in his wits (I had almost said none but an atheist) will presume to say that any sincere and upright worshipper of God could, with a safe conscience, obey their several decrees. To conclude, it is the same thing whether a king that prescribes laws to another man's religion pretend to do it by his own judgment, or by the ecclesiastical authority and advice of others. The decisions of churchmen, whose differences and disputes are sufficiently known, cannot be any sounder or safer than his; nor can all their suffrages joined together add a new strength to the civil power. Though this also must be taken notice of- that princes seldom have any regard to the suffrages of ecclesiastics that are not favorers of their own faith and way of worship.

--But, after all, the principal consideration, and which absolutely determines this controversy, is this: Although the magistrate's opinion in religion is sound, and the way that he appoints is truly Evangelical, yet, if I be not thoroughly persuaded thereof in my own mind, there will be no safety for me in following it. No way whatsoever that I shall walk in against the dictates of my conscience will ever bring me to the mansions of the blessed. I may grow rich by an art that I take not delight in; I may be cured of some disease by remedies that I have not faith in; but I *cannot* be saved by a religion that I distrust and by a worship that I abhor. It is in vain for an unbeliever to take up the outward show of another man's profession. Faith only and inward sincerity are the things that procure acceptance with God. The most likely and most approved remedy can have no effect upon the patient, if his stomach reject it as soon as taken; and you will in vain cram a medicine down a sick man's throat, which his particular constitution will be sure to turn into poison. In a word, whatsoever may be doubtful in religion, yet this at least is certain, that no religion which I believe not to be true can be either true or profitable unto me. In vain, therefore, do princes compel their subjects to come into their Church communion, under pretence of saving their souls. If they believe, they will come of their own accord, if they believe not, their coming will nothing avail them. How great soever, in fine, may be the pretence of good-will and charity, and concern for the salvation of men's souls, men cannot be forced to be saved whether they will or no. And therefore, when all is done, they must be left to their own consciences.

--Having thus at length freed men from all dominion over one another in matters of religion; let us now consider what they are to do. All men know and acknowledge that God ought to be publicly worshipped; why otherwise do they compel one another unto the public assemblies? Men, therefore, constituted in this liberty are to enter into some religious society, that they meet together, not only for mutual edification, but to own to the world that they worship God and offer unto His Divine Majesty such service as they themselves are not ashamed of any such as they think not unworthy of Him, nor unacceptable to Him; and, finally, that by the purity of doctrine, holiness of life, and decent form of worship, they may draw others unto the love of the true religion, and perform such other things in religion as cannot be done by each private man apart.

--These religious societies I call Churches; and these, I say, the magistrate ought to tolerate, for the business of these assemblies of the people is nothing but what is lawful for every man in particular to take care of- I mean the salvation of their souls; nor in this case is there any difference between the National Church and other separated congregations.

--But as in every Church there are two things especially to be considered- the outward form and rites of worship, and the doctrines and articles of things must be handled each distinctly that so the whole matter of toleration may the more clearly be understood.

--Concerning outward worship, I say, in the first place, that the magistrate has no power to enforce by law, either in his own Church, or much less in another, the use of any rites or ceremonies whatsoever in the worship of God. And this, not only because these Churches are free societies, but because whatsoever is practiced in the worship of God is only so far justifiable as it is believed by those that practice it to be acceptable unto Him. Whatsoever is not done with that assurance of faith is neither well in itself, nor can it be acceptable to God. To impose such things, therefore, upon any people, contrary to their own judgment, is in effect to command them to offend God, which, considering that the end of all religion is to please Him, and that liberty is essentially necessary to that end, appears to be absurd beyond expression.

--But perhaps it may be concluded from hence that I deny unto the magistrate all manner of power about indifferent things, which, if it be not granted, the whole subject-matter of law-making is taken away. No, I readily grant that indifferent things, and perhaps none but such, are subjected to the legislative power. But it does not therefore follow that the magistrate may ordain whatsoever he pleases concerning anything that is indifferent. The public good is the rule and measure of all law-making. If a thing be not useful to the commonwealth, though it be never so indifferent, it may not presently be established by law.

--And further, things never so indifferent in their own nature, when they are brought into the Church and worship of God, are removed out of the reach of the magistrate's jurisdiction, because in that use they have no connection at all with civil affairs. The only business of the Church is the salvation of souls, and it no way concerns the commonwealth, or any member of it, that this or the other ceremony be there made use of. Neither the use nor the omission of any ceremonies in those religious assemblies does either advantage or prejudice the life, liberty, or estate of any man. For example, let it be granted that the washing of an infant with water is in itself an indifferent thing, let it be granted also that the magistrate understand such washing to be profitable to the curing or preventing of any disease the children are subject unto, and esteem the matter weighty enough to be taken care of by a law. In that case he may order it to be done. But will anyone therefore say that a magistrate has the same right to ordain by law that all children shall be baptized by priests in the sacred font in order to the purification of their souls? The extreme difference of these two cases is visible to everyone at first sight. Or let us apply the last case to the child of a Jew, and the thing speaks itself. For what hinders but a Christian magistrate may have subjects that are Jews? Now, if we acknowledge that such an injury may not be done unto a Jew as to compel him, against his own opinion, to practice in his religion a thing that is in its nature indifferent, how can we maintain that anything of this kind may be done to a Christian?

--Again, things in their own nature indifferent cannot, by any human authority, be made any part of the worship of God- for this very reason: because they are indifferent. For, since indifferent things are not capable, by any virtue of their own, to propitiate the Deity, no human power or authority can confer on them so much dignity and excellency as to enable them to do it. In the common affairs of life that use of indifferent things which God has not forbidden is free and lawful, and therefore in those things human authority has place. But it is not so in matters of religion. Things indifferent are not otherwise lawful in the worship of God than as they are instituted by God Himself and as He, by some positive command, has ordained them to be made a part of that worship which He will vouchsafe to accept at the hands of poor sinful men. Nor, when an incensed Deity shall ask us, "Who has required these, or such-like things at your hands?" will it be enough to answer Him that the magistrate commanded them. If civil jurisdiction extends thus far, what might not lawfully be introduced into religion? What hodgepodge of ceremonies, what superstitious inventions, built upon the magistrate's authority, might not (against conscience) is imposed upon the worshippers of God? For the greatest part of these ceremonies and superstitions consists in the religious use of such things as are in their own nature indifferent; nor are they sinful upon any other account than because God is not the author of them. The sprinkling of water and the use of bread and wine are both in their own nature and in the ordinary occasions of life altogether indifferent. Will any man, therefore, say that these things could have been introduced into religion and made a part of divine worship if not by divine institution? If any human authority or civil power could have done this, why might it not also enjoin the eating of fish and drinking of ale in the holy banquet as a part of divine worship? Why not the sprinkling of the blood of beasts in churches, and expiations by water or fire, and abundance more of this kind? But these things, how indifferent soever they are in common uses, when they come to be annexed unto divine worship, without divine authority, they are as abominable to God as the sacrifice of a dog. And why is a dog so abominable? What difference is there between a dog and a goat, in respect of the divine nature, equally and infinitely distant from all affinity with matter, unless it be that God required the use of one in His worship and not of the other? We see, therefore, that indifferent things, how much soever they are under the power of the civil magistrate, yet cannot, upon that pretence, be introduced into religion and imposed upon religious assemblies, because, in the worship of God, they wholly cease to be indifferent. He that worships God does it with design to please Him and procure His favor. But that cannot be done by him who, upon the command of another, offers unto God that which he knows will be displeasing to Him, because not commanded by Himself. This is not to please God, or appease his wrath, but willingly and knowingly to provoke Him by a manifest contempt, which is a thing absolutely repugnant to the nature and end of worship.

--But it will be here asked: "If nothing belonging to divine worship be left to human discretion, how is it then that Churches themselves have the power of ordering anything about the time and place of worship and the like?" To this I answer that in religious worship we must distinguish between what is part of the worship itself and what is but a circumstance. That is a part of the worship which is believed to be appointed by God and to be well-pleasing to Him, and therefore that is necessary. Circumstances are such things which, though in general they cannot be separated from worship, yet the particular instances or modifications of them are not determined, and therefore they are indifferent. Of this sort are the time and place of worship, habit and posture of him that worships. These are circumstances, and perfectly indifferent, where God has not given any express command about them. For example: among the Jews the time and place of their worship and the habits of those that officiated in it were not mere circumstances, but a part of the worship itself, in which, if anything were defective, or different from the institution, they could not hope that it would be accepted by God. But these, to Christians under the liberty of the Gospel, are mere circumstances of worship, which the prudence of every Church may bring into such use as shall be judged most subservient to the end of order, decency, and edification. But, even under the Gospel, those who believe the first or the seventh day to be set apart by God, and consecrated still to His worship, to them that portion of time is not a simple circumstance, but a real part of Divine worship, which can neither be changed nor neglected.

--In the next place: As the magistrate has no power to impose by his laws the use of any rites and ceremonies in any Church, so neither has he any power to forbid the use of such rites and ceremonies as are already received, approved, and practiced by any Church; because, if he did so, he would destroy the Church itself: the end of whose institution is only to worship God with freedom after its own manner.

--You will say, by this rule, if some congregations should have a mind to sacrifice infants, or (as the primitive Christians were falsely accused) lustfully pollute themselves in promiscuous uncleanness, or practice any other such heinous enormities, is the magistrate obliged to tolerate them, because they are committed in a religious assembly? I answer: No. These things are not lawful in the ordinary course of life, nor in any private house; and therefore neither are they so in the worship of God, or in any religious meeting. But, indeed, if any people congregated upon account of religion should be desirous to sacrifice a calf, I deny that that ought to be prohibited by a law. Meliboeus, whose calf it is, may lawfully kill his calf at home, and burn any part of it that he thinks fit. For no injury is thereby done to anyone, no prejudice to another man's goods. And for the same reason he may kill his calf also in a religious meeting. Whether the doing so be well-pleasing to God or no, it is their part to consider that do it. The part of the magistrate is only to take care that the commonwealth receive no prejudice, and that there be no injury done to any man, either in life or estate. And thus what may be spent on a feast may be spent on a sacrifice. But if peradventure such were the state of things that the interest of the commonwealth required all slaughter of beasts should be forborne for some while, in order to the increasing of the stock of cattle that had been destroyed by some extraordinary murrain, who sees not that the magistrate, in such a case, may forbid all his subjects to kill any calves for any use whatsoever? Only it is to be observed that, in this case, the law is not made about a religious, but a political matter; nor is the sacrifice, but the slaughter of calves, thereby prohibited.

--By this we see what difference there is between the Church and the Commonwealth. Whatsoever is lawful in the Commonwealth cannot be prohibited by the magistrate in the Church. Whatsoever is permitted unto any of his subjects for their ordinary use, neither can nor ought to be forbidden by him to any sect of people for their religious uses. If any man may lawfully take bread or wine, either sitting or kneeling in his own house, the law ought not to abridge him of the same liberty in his religious worship; though in the Church the use of bread and wine be very different and be there applied to the mysteries of faith and rites of Divine worship. But those things that are prejudicial to the commonweal of a people in their ordinary use and are, therefore, forbidden by laws, those things ought not to be permitted to Churches in their sacred rites. Only the magistrate ought always to be very careful that he does not misuse his authority to the oppression of any Church, under pretence of public good.

--It may be said: "What if a Church be idolatrous, is that also to be tolerated by the magistrate?" I answer: What power can be given to the magistrate for the suppression of an idolatrous Church, which may not in time and place be made use of to the ruin of an orthodox one? For it must be remembered that the civil power is the same everywhere, and the religion of every prince is orthodox to himself. If, therefore, such a power be granted unto the civil magistrate in spirituals as that at Geneva, for example, he may extirpate, by violence and blood, the religion which is their reputed idolatrous, by the same rule another magistrate, in some neighboring country, may oppress the reformed religion and, in India, the Christian. The civil power can either change everything in religion, according to the prince's pleasure, or it can change nothing. If it be once permitted to introduce anything into religion by the means of laws and penalties, there can be no bounds put to it; but it will in the same manner be lawful to alter everything, according to that rule of truth which the magistrate has framed unto himself. No man whatsoever ought, therefore, to be deprived of his terrestrial enjoyments upon account of his religion. Not even Americans, subjected unto a Christian prince, are to be punished either in body or goods for not embracing our faith and worship. If they are persuaded that they please God in observing the rites of their own country and that they shall obtain happiness by that means, they are to be left unto God and themselves. Let us trace this matter to the bottom. Thus it is: An inconsiderable and weak number of Christians, destitute of everything, arrive in a Pagan country; these foreigners beseech the inhabitants, by the bowels of humanity, that they would succor them with the necessaries of life; those necessaries are given them, habitations are granted, and they all join together, and grow up into one body of people. The Christian religion by this means takes root in that country and spreads itself, but does not suddenly grow the strongest. While things are in this condition peace, friendship, faith, and equal justice are preserved among them. At length the magistrate becomes a Christian, and by that means their party becomes the most powerful. Then immediately all compacts are to be broken, all civil rights to be violated, that idolatry may be extirpated; and unless these innocent Pagans, strict observers of the rules of equity and the law of Nature and no ways offending against the laws of the society, I say, unless they will forsake their ancient religion and embrace a new and strange one, they are to be turned out of the lands and possessions of their forefathers and perhaps deprived of life itself. Then, at last, it appears what zeal for the Church, joined with the desire of dominion, is capable to produce, and how easily the pretence of religion, and of the care of souls, serves for a cloak to covetousness, rapine, and ambition.

--Now whosoever maintains that idolatry is to be rooted out of any place by laws, punishments, fire, and sword, may apply this story to himself. For the reason of the thing is equal, both in America and Europe. And neither Pagans there, nor any dissenting Christians here, can, with any right, be deprived of their worldly goods by the predominating faction of a court-church; nor are any civil rights to be either changed or violated upon account of religion in one place more than another.

--But idolatry, say some, is a sin and therefore not to be tolerated. If they said it were therefore to be avoided, the inference were good. But it does not follow that because it is a sin it ought therefore to be punished by the magistrate. For it does not belong unto the magistrate to make use of his sword in punishing everything, indifferently, that he takes to be a sin against God. Covetousness, uncharitableness, idleness, and many other things are sins by the consent of men, which yet no man ever said were to be punished by the magistrate. The reason is because they are not prejudicial to other men's rights, nor do they break the public peace of societies. Nay, even the sins of lying and perjury are nowhere punishable by laws; unless, in certain cases, in which the real turpitude of the thing and the offence against God are not considered, but only the injury done unto men's neighbors and to the commonwealth. And what if in another country, to a Muslim or a Pagan prince, the Christian religion seem false and offensive to God; may not the Christians for the same reason, and after the same manner, be destroyed there?

--But it may be urged further that, by the Law of Moses, idolaters were to be rooted out. True, indeed, by the Law of Moses; but that is not obligatory to us Christians. Nobody pretends that everything generally enjoined by the Law of Moses ought to be practiced by Christians; but there is nothing more frivolous than that common distinction of moral, judicial, and ceremonial law, which men ordinarily make use of. For no positive law whatsoever can oblige any people but those to whom it is given. "Hear, O Israel," sufficiently restrains the obligations of the Law of Moses only to that people. And this consideration alone is answer enough unto those that urge the authority of the Law of Moses for the inflicting of capital punishment upon idolaters. But, however, I will examine this argument a little more particularly.

--The case of idolaters, in respect of the Jewish commonwealth, falls under a double consideration. The first is of those who, being initiated in the Mosaic rites, and made citizens of that commonwealth, did afterwards apostatize from the worship of the God of Israel. These were proceeded against as traitors and rebels, guilty of no less than high treason. For the commonwealth of the Jews, different in that from all others, was an absolute theocracy; nor was there, or could there be, any difference between that commonwealth and the Church. The laws established there concerning the worship of One Invisible Deity were the civil laws of that people and a part of their political government, in which God Himself was the legislator. Now, if anyone can show me where there is a commonwealth at this time, constituted upon that foundation, I will acknowledge that the ecclesiastical laws do there unavoidably become a part of the civil, and that the subjects of that government both may and ought to be kept in strict conformity with that Church by the civil power. But there is absolutely no such thing under the Gospel as a Christian commonwealth. There are, indeed, many cities and kingdoms that have embraced the faith of Christ, but they have retained their ancient form of government, with which the law of Christ has not at all meddled. He, indeed, has taught men how, by faith and good works, they may obtain eternal life; but He instituted no commonwealth. He prescribed unto His followers no new and peculiar form of government, nor put

He the sword into any magistrate's hand, with commission to make use of it in forcing men to forsake their former religion and receive His.

--Secondly, foreigners and such as were strangers to the commonwealth of Israel were not compelled by force to observe the rites of the Mosaic law; but, on the contrary, in the very same place where it is ordered that an Israelite that was an idolater should be put to death, there it is provided that strangers should not be vexed nor oppressed. I confess that the seven nations that possessed the land which was promised to the Israelites were utterly to be cut off; but this was not singly because they were idolaters. For if that had been the reason, why were the Moabites and other nations to be spared? No: the reason is this. God being in a peculiar manner the King of the Jews, He could not suffer the adoration of any other deity (which was properly an act of high treason against Himself) in the land of Canaan, which was His kingdom. For such a manifest revolt could no ways consist with His dominion, which was perfectly political in that country. All idolatry was, therefore, to be rooted out of the bounds of His kingdom because it was an acknowledgment of another god, that is say, another king, against the laws of Empire. The inhabitants were also to be driven out, that the entire possession of the land might be given to the Israelites. And for the like reason the Emims and the Horims were driven out of their countries by the children of Esau and Lot; and their lands, upon the same grounds, given by God to the invaders.(2) But, though all idolatry was thus rooted out of the land of Canaan, yet every idolater was not brought to execution. The whole family of Rahab, the whole nation of the Gibeonites, joined with Joshua, and were allowed by treaty; and there were many captives among the Jews who were idolaters. David and Solomon subdued many countries outside the confines of the Land of Promise and carried their conquests as far as Euphrates. Among so many captives taken, so many nations reduced under their obedience, we find not one man forced into the Jewish religion and the worship of the true God and punished for idolatry, though all of them were certainly guilty of it. If anyone, indeed, becoming a proselyte, desired to be made a denizen of their commonwealth, he was obliged to submit to their laws; that is, to embrace their religion. But this he did willingly, on his own accord, not by constraint. He did not unwillingly submit, to show his obedience, but he sought and solicited for it as a privilege. And, as soon as he was admitted, he became subject to the laws of the commonwealth, by which all idolatry was forbidden within the borders of the land of Canaan. But that law (as I have said) did not reach to any of those regions, however subjected unto the Jews that were situated without those bounds.

- Exod. 22, 20, 21.

-(2) Deut. 2.

--Thus far concerning outward worship. Let us now consider articles of faith.

--The articles of religion are some of them practical and some speculative. Now, though both sorts consist in the knowledge of truth, yet these terminate simply in the understanding, those influence the will and manners. Speculative opinions, therefore, and articles of faith (as they are called) which are required only to be believed, cannot be imposed on any Church by the law of the land. For it is absurd that things should be enjoined by laws which are not in men's power to perform. And to believe this or that to be true does not depend upon our will. But of this enough has been said already. "But." will some say; "let men at least profess that they believe." A sweet religion, indeed, that obliges men to dissemble and tell lies, both to God and man, for the salvation of their souls! If the magistrate thinks to save men thus, he seems to understand little of the way of salvation. And if he does it not in order to save them, why is he so solicitous about the articles of faith as to enact them by a law?

--Further, the magistrate ought not to forbid the preaching or professing of any speculative opinions in any Church because they have no manner of relation to the civil rights of the subjects. If a Roman Catholic believe that to be really the body of Christ which another man calls bread, he does no injury thereby to his neighbor. If a Jew does not believe the New Testament to be the Word of God, he does not thereby alter anything in men's civil rights. If a heathen doubts both Testaments, he is not therefore to be punished as a pernicious citizen. The power of the magistrate and the estates of the people may be equally secure whether any man believes these things or no. I readily grant that these opinions are false and absurd. But the business of laws is not to provide for the truth of opinions, but for the safety and security of the commonwealth and of every particular man's goods and person. And so it ought to be. For the truth certainly would do well enough if she were once left to shift for herself. She seldom has received and, I fear, never will receive much assistance from the power of great men, to whom she is but rarely known and more rarely welcome. She is not taught by laws, nor has she any need of force to procure her entrance into the minds of men. Errors, indeed, prevail by the assistance of foreign and borrowed succors. But if Truth makes not her way into the understanding by her own light, she will be but the weaker for any borrowed force violence can add to her. Thus much for speculative opinions. Let us now proceed to practical ones.

--A good life, in which consist not the least part of religion and true piety, concerns also the civil government; and in it lies the safety both of men's souls and of the commonwealth. Moral actions belong, therefore, to the jurisdiction both of the outward and inward court; both of the civil and domestic governor; I mean both of the magistrate and conscience. Here, therefore, is great danger, lest one of these jurisdictions entrench upon the other, and discord arises between the keeper of the public peace and the overseers of souls. But if what has been already said concerning the limits of both these governments be rightly considered, it will easily remove all difficulty in this matter.

--Every man has an immortal soul, capable of eternal happiness or misery; whose happiness depending upon his believing and doing those things in this life which are necessary to the obtaining of God's favor, and are prescribed by God to that end. It follows from thence, first, that the observance of these things is the highest obligation that lies upon mankind and that our utmost care, application, and diligence ought to be exercised in the search and performance of them; because there is nothing in this world that is of any consideration in comparison with eternity. Secondly, that seeing one man does not violate the right of another by his erroneous opinions and undue manner of worship, nor is his perdition any prejudice to another man's affairs, therefore, the care of each man's salvation belongs only to himself. But I would not have this understood as if I meant hereby to condemn all charitable admonitions and affectionate endeavors to reduce men from errors, which are indeed the greatest duty of a Christian. Anyone may employ as many exhortations and arguments as he pleases, towards the promoting of another man's salvation. But all force and compulsion are to be forbidden. Nothing is to be done imperiously. Nobody is obliged in that matter to yield obedience unto the admonitions or injunctions of another, further than he himself is persuaded. Every man in that has the supreme and absolute authority of judging for himself. And the reason is because nobody else is concerned in it, nor can receive any prejudice from his conduct therein.

--But besides their souls, which are immortal, men have also their temporal lives here upon earth; the state whereof being frail and fleeting, and the duration uncertain, they have need of several outward conveniences to the support thereof, which are to be procured or preserved by pains and industry. For those things that are necessary to the comfortable support of our lives are not the spontaneous products of nature, nor do offer themselves fit and prepared for our use. This part, therefore, draws on another care and necessarily gives another employment. But the depravity of mankind being such that they had rather injuriously prey upon the fruits of other men's labors than take pains to provide for themselves, the necessity of preserving men in the possession of what honest industry has already acquired and also of preserving their liberty and strength, whereby they may acquire what they father want, obliges men to enter into society with one another, that by mutual assistance and joint force they may secure unto each other their properties, in the things that contribute to the comfort and happiness of this life, leaving in the meanwhile to every man the care of his own eternal happiness, the attainment whereof can neither be facilitated by another man's industry, nor can the loss of it turn to another man's prejudice, nor the hope of it be forced from him by any external violence. But, forasmuch as men thus entering into societies, grounded upon their mutual compacts of assistance for the defense of their temporal goods, may, nevertheless, be deprived of them, either by the pillage and fraud of their fellow citizens, or by the hostile violence of foreigners, the remedy of this evil consists in arms, riches, and multitude of citizens; the remedy of the other in laws; and the care of all things relating both to one and the other is committed by the society to the civil magistrate. This is the original, this is the use, and these are the bounds of the legislative (which is the supreme) power in every commonwealth. I mean that provision may be made for the security of each man's private possessions; for the peace, riches, and public commodities of the whole people; and, as much as possible, for the increase of their inward strength against foreign invasions.

--These things being thus explained, it is easy to understand to what end the legislative power ought to be directed and by what measures regulated; and that is the temporal good and outward prosperity of the society; which is the sole reason of men's entering into society, and the only thing they seek and aim at in it. And it is also evident what liberty remains to men in reference to their eternal salvation, and that is that everyone should do what he in his conscience is persuaded to be acceptable to the Almighty, on whose good pleasure and acceptance depends their eternal happiness. For obedience is due, in the first place, to God and, afterwards to the laws.

--But some may ask: "What if the magistrate should enjoin anything by his authority that appears unlawful to the conscience of a private person?" I answer that, if government is faithfully administered and the counsels of the magistrates be indeed directed to the public good, this will seldom happen. But if, perhaps, it do so fall out, I say, that such a private person is to abstain from the action that he judges unlawful, and he is to undergo the punishment which it is not unlawful for him to bear. For the private judgment of any person concerning a law enacted in political matters, for the public good, does not take away the obligation of that law, nor deserve a dispensation. But if the law, indeed, be concerning things that lie not within the verge of the magistrate's authority (as, for example, that the people, or any party among them, should be compelled to embrace a strange religion, and join in the worship and ceremonies of another Church), men are not in these cases obliged by that law, against their consciences. For the political society is instituted for no other end, but only to secure every man's possession of the things of this life. The care of each man's soul and of the things of heaven, which neither does belong to the commonwealth nor can be subjected to it, is left entirely to every man's self. Thus the safeguard of men's lives and of the things that belong unto this life is the business of the commonwealth; and the preserving of those things unto their owners is the duty of the magistrate. And therefore the magistrate cannot take away these worldly things from this man or party and give them to that; nor change propriety among fellow subjects (no not even by a law), for a cause that has no relation to the end of civil government, I mean for their religion, which whether it be true or false does no prejudice to the worldly concerns of their fellow subjects, which are the things that only belong unto the care of the commonwealth.

--But what if the magistrate believes such a law as this to be for the public good? I answer: As the private judgment of any particular person, if erroneous, does not exempt him from the obligation of law, so the private judgment (as I may call it) of the magistrate does not give him any new right of imposing laws upon his subjects, which neither was in the constitution of the government granted him, nor ever was in the power of the people to grant, much less if he make it his business to enrich and advance his followers and fellow-sectaries with the spoils of others. But what if the magistrate believes that he has a right to make such laws and that they are for the public good, and his subjects believe the contrary? Who shall be judge between them? I answer: God alone. For there is no judge upon earth between the supreme magistrate and the people. God, I say, is the only judge in this case, who will retribute unto everyone at the last day according to his deserts; that is, according to his sincerity and uprightness in endeavoring to promote piety, and the public weal, and peace of mankind. But what shall be done in the meanwhile? I answer: The principal and chief care of everyone ought to be of his own soul first, and, in the next place, of the public peace; though yet there are very few will think it is peace there, where they see all laid fallow.

--There are two sorts of contests among men, the one managed by law, the other by force; and these are of that nature that where the one ends, the other always begins. But it is not my business to inquire into the power of the magistrate in the different constitutions of nations. I only know what usually happens where controversies arise without a judge to determine them. You will say, then, the magistrate being the stronger will have his will and carry his point. Without doubt; but the question is not here concerning the doubtfulness of the event, but the rule of right.

--But to come to specifics. I say, first, no opinions contrary to human society, or to those moral rules which are necessary to the preservation of civil society, are to be tolerated by the magistrate. But of these, indeed, examples in any Church are rare. For no sect can easily arrive to such a degree of madness as that it should think fit to teach, for doctrines of religion, such things as manifestly undermine the foundations of society and are, therefore, condemned by the judgment of all mankind; because their own interest, peace, reputation, everything would be thereby endangered.

--Another more secret evil, but more dangerous to the commonwealth, is when men arrogate to themselves, and to those of their own sect, some peculiar prerogative covered over with a false show of deceitful words, but in effect opposite to the civil right of the community. For example: we cannot find any sect that teaches, expressly and openly, that men are not obliged to keep their promise; that princes may be dethroned by those that differ from them in religion; or that the dominion of all things belongs only to themselves. For these things, proposed thus nakedly and plainly, would soon draw on them the eye and hand of the magistrate and awaken all the care of the commonwealth to watchfulness against the spreading of so dangerous an evil. But, nevertheless, we find those that say the same things in other words. What else do they mean who teach that faith is not to be kept with heretics? Their meaning, forsooth, is that the privilege of breaking faith belongs unto themselves; for they declare all that are not of their communion to be heretics, or at least may declare them so whensoever they think fit. What can be the meaning of their asserting that kings excommunicated forfeit their crowns and kingdoms? It is evident that they thereby arrogate unto themselves the power of deposing kings, because they challenge the power of excommunication, as the peculiar right of their hierarchy. That dominion is founded in grace is also an assertion by which those that maintain it do plainly lay claim to the possession of all things. For they are not so wanting to themselves as not to believe, or at least as not to profess themselves to be the truly pious and faithful. These, therefore, and the like, who attribute unto the faithful, religious, and orthodox, that is, in plain terms, unto themselves, any peculiar privilege or power above other mortals, in civil concernments; or who upon pretence of religion do challenge any manner of authority over such as are not associated with them in their ecclesiastical communion, I say these have no right to be tolerated by the magistrate; as neither those that will not own and teach the duty of tolerating all men in matters of mere religion. For what do all these and the like doctrines signify, but that they may and are ready upon any occasion to seize the Government and possess themselves of the estates and fortunes of their fellow subjects; and that they only ask leave to be tolerated by the magistrate so long until they find themselves strong enough to effect it?

--Again: That religion can have no right to be tolerated by the magistrate which is constituted upon such a bottom that all those who enter into it do thereby *ipso facto* deliver themselves up to the protection and service of another prince. For by this means the magistrate would give way to the settling of a foreign jurisdiction in his own country and suffer his own people to be listed, as it were, for soldiers against his own Government. Nor does the frivolous and fallacious distinction between the Court and the Church afford any remedy to this inconvenience; especially when both the one and the other are equally subject to the absolute authority of the same person, who has not only power to persuade the members of his Church to whatsoever he lists, either as purely religious, or in order thereunto, but can also enjoin it them on pain of eternal fire. It is ridiculous for anyone to profess himself to be a Muslim only in his religion, but in everything else a faithful subject to a Christian magistrate, while at the same time he acknowledges himself bound to yield blind obedience to the Imam of Constantinople, who himself is entirely obedient to the

Ottoman Emperor and frames the feigned oracles of that religion according to his pleasure. But this Muslim living among Christians would yet more apparently renounce their government if he acknowledged the same person to be head of his Church who is the supreme magistrate in the state.

--Lastly, those are not at all to be tolerated who deny the being of a God. Promises, covenants, and oaths, which are the bonds of human society, can have no hold upon an atheist. The taking away of God, though but even in thought, dissolves all; besides also, those that by their atheism undermine and destroy all religion, can have no pretence of religion whereupon to challenge the privilege of a toleration. As for other practical opinions, though not absolutely free from all error, if they do not tend to establish domination over others, or civil impunity to the Church in which they are taught, there can be no reason why they should not be tolerated.

--It remains that I say something concerning those assemblies which, being vulgarly called and perhaps having sometimes been conventicles and nurseries of factions and seditions, are thought to afford against this doctrine of toleration. But this has not happened by anything peculiar unto the genius of such assemblies, but by the unhappy circumstances of an oppressed or ill-settled liberty. These accusations would soon cease if the law of toleration were once so settled that all Churches were obliged to lay down toleration as the foundation of their own liberty, and teach that liberty of conscience is every man's natural right, equally belonging to dissenters as to themselves; and that nobody ought to be compelled in matters of religion either by law or force. The establishment of this one thing would take away all ground of complaints and tumults upon account of conscience; and these causes of discontents and animosities being once removed, there would remain nothing in these assemblies that were not more peaceable and less apt to produce disturbance of state than in any other meetings whatsoever. But let us examine particularly the heads of these accusations.

--You will say that assemblies and meetings endanger the public peace and threaten the commonwealth. I answer: If this be so, why are there daily such numerous meetings in markets and Courts of Judicature? Why are crowds upon the Exchange and a concourse of people in cities suffered? You will reply: "Those are civil assemblies, but these we object against are ecclesiastical." I answer: It is a likely thing, indeed, that such assemblies as are altogether remote from civil affairs should be most apt to embroil them. Oh, but civil assemblies are composed of men that differ from one another in matters of religion, but these ecclesiastical meetings are of persons that are all of one opinion. As if an agreement in matters of religion were in effect a conspiracy against the commonwealth; or as if men would not be so much the more warmly unanimous in religion the less liberty they had of assembling. But it will be urged still that civil assemblies are open and free for anyone to enter into, whereas religious conventicles are more private and thereby give opportunity to clandestine machinations. I answer that this is not strictly true, for many civil assemblies are not open to everyone. And if some religious meetings be private, who are they (I beseech you) that are to be blamed for it, those that desire, or those that forbid their being public! Again, you will say that religious communion does exceedingly unite men's minds and affections to one another and is therefore the more dangerous. But if this be so, why is not the magistrate afraid of his own Church; and why does he not forbid their assemblies as things dangerous to his Government? You will say because he himself is a part and even the head of them. As if he were not also a part of the commonwealth, and the head of the whole people!

--Let us therefore deal plainly. The magistrate is afraid of other Churches, but not of his own, because he is kind and favorable to the one, but severe and cruel to the other. These he treats like children, and indulges them even to wantonness. Those he uses as slaves and, howsoever blamelessly they demean themselves, recompenses them no otherwise than by galleys, prisons, confiscations, and death. These he cherishes and defends; those he continually scourges and oppresses. Let him turn the tables. Or let those dissenters enjoy but the same privileges in civil matters as his other subjects, and he will quickly find that these religious meetings will be no longer dangerous. For if men enter into seditious conspiracies, it is not religion inspires them to it in their meetings, but their sufferings and oppressions that make them willing to ease themselves. Just and moderate governments are everywhere quiet, everywhere safe; but oppression raises ferments and makes men struggle to cast off an uneasy and tyrannical yoke. I know that seditions are very frequently raised upon pretence of religion, but it is as true that for religion subjects are frequently ill treated and live miserably. Believe me, the stirs that are made proceed not from any peculiar temper of this or that Church or religious society, but from the common disposition of all mankind, who when they groan under any heavy burthen endeavor naturally to shake off the yoke that galls their necks. Suppose this business of religion were let alone, and that there were some other distinction made between men and men upon account of their different complexions, shapes, and features, so that those who have black hair (for example) or grey eyes should not enjoy the same privileges as other citizens; that they should not be permitted either to buy or sell, or live by their callings; that parents should not have the government and education of their own children; that all should either be excluded from the benefit of the laws, or meet with partial judges; can it be doubted but these persons, thus distinguished from others by the color of their hair and eyes, and united together by one common persecution, would be as dangerous to the magistrate as any others that had associated themselves merely upon the account of religion? Some enter into company for trade and profit; others for want of business have their clubs for claret. Neighborhood joins some and religion others. But there is only one thing which gathers people into seditious commotions, and that is oppression.

--You will say "What, will you have people to meet at divine service against the magistrate's will?" I answer: Why, I pray, against his will? Is it not both lawful and necessary that they should meet? Against his will, do you say? That is what I complain of; that is the very root of all the mischief. Why are assemblies less sufferable in a church than in a theatre or market? Those that meet there are not either more vicious or more turbulent than those that meet elsewhere. The business in that is that they are ill used, and therefore they are not to be suffered. Take away the partiality that is used towards them in matters of common right; change the laws, take away the penalties unto which they are subjected, and all things will immediately become safe and peaceable; nay, those that are averse to the religion of the magistrate will think themselves so much the more bound to maintain the peace of the commonwealth as their condition is better in that place than elsewhere; and all the several separate congregations, like so many guardians of the public peace, will watch one another, that nothing may be innovated or changed in the form of the government, because they can hope for nothing better than what they already enjoy- that is, an equal condition with their fellow-subjects under a just and moderate government. Now if that Church which agrees in religion with the prince be esteemed the chief support of any civil government, and that for no other reason (as has already been shown) than because the prince is kind and the laws are favorable to it, how much greater will be the security of government where all good subjects, of whatever Church they be, without any distinction upon account of religion, enjoying the same favor of the prince and the same benefit of the laws, shall become the common support and guard of it, and where none will have any occasion to fear the severity of the laws but those that do injuries to their neighbors and offend against the civil peace?

--That we may draw towards a conclusion. The sum of all we drive at is that every man may enjoy the same rights that are granted to others. Is it permitted to worship God in the Roman manner? Let it be permitted to do it in the Geneva form also. Is it permitted to speak Latin in the market-place? Let those that have a mind to it be permitted to do it also in the Church. Is it lawful for any man in his own house to kneel, stand, sit, or use any other posture; and to clothe himself in white or black, in short or in long garments? Let it not be made unlawful to eat bread, drink wine, or wash with water in the church. In a word, whatsoever things are left free by law in the common occasions of life let them remain free unto every Church in divine worship. Let no man's life, or body, or house, or estate, suffer any manner of prejudice upon these accounts. Can you allow of the Presbyterian discipline? Why should not the Episcopal also have what they like? Ecclesiastical authority, whether it be administered by the hands of a single person or many, is everywhere the same; and neither has any jurisdiction in things civil, nor any manner of power of compulsion, nor anything at all to do with riches and revenues.

--Ecclesiastical assemblies and sermons are justified by daily experience and public allowance. These are allowed to people of someone persuasion; why not to all? If anything pass in a religious meeting seditious and contrary to the public peace, it is to be punished in the same manner and no otherwise than as if it had happened in a fair or market. These meetings ought not to be sanctuaries for factious and scandalous people. Nor ought it to be less lawful for men to meet in churches than in halls; nor are one part of the subjects to be esteemed more blamable for their meeting together than others. Everyone is to be accountable for his own actions, and no man is to be laid under a suspicion or odium for the fault of another. Those that are seditious, murderers, thieves, robbers, adulterers, slanderers, etc., of whatsoever Church, whether national or not, ought to be punished and suppressed. But those whose doctrine is peaceable and whose manners are pure and blameless ought to be upon equal terms with their fellow-subjects. Thus if solemn assemblies, observations of festivals, public worship be permitted to anyone sort of professors, all these things ought to be permitted to the Presbyterians, Independents, Anabaptists, Arminians, Quakers, and others, with the same liberty. Nay, if we may openly speak the truth, and as becomes one man to another, neither Pagan nor Muslim, nor Jew, ought to be excluded from the civil rights of the commonwealth because of his religion. The Gospel commands no such thing. The Church which "judgeth not those that are without" wants it not. And the commonwealth, which embraces indifferently all men that are honest, peaceable, and industrious, requires it not. Shall we suffer a Pagan to deal and trade with us, and shall we not suffer him to pray unto and worship God? If we allow the Jews to have private houses and dwellings among us, why should we not allow them to have synagogues? Is their doctrine more false, their worship more abominable, or is the civil peace more endangered by their meeting in public than in their private houses? But if these things may be granted to Jews and Pagans, surely the condition of any Christians ought not to be worse than theirs in a Christian commonwealth.

- I Cor. 5. 12, 13.

--You will say, perhaps: "Yes, it ought to be; because they are more inclinable to factions, tumults, and civil wars." I answer: Is this the fault of the Christian religion? If it be so, truly the Christian religion is the worst of all religions and ought neither to be embraced by any particular person, nor tolerated by any commonwealth. For if this is the genius, the nature of the Christian religion, to be turbulent and destructive to the civil peace, that Church itself which the magistrate indulges will not always be innocent. But far be it from us to say any such thing of that religion which carries the greatest opposition to covetousness, ambition, discord, contention, and all manner of inordinate desires, and is the most modest and peaceable religion that ever was. We must, therefore, seek another cause of those evils that are charged upon religion. And, if we consider right, we shall find it to consist wholly in the subject that I am treating of. It is not the diversity of opinions (which cannot be avoided), but the refusal of toleration to those that are of different opinions (which might have been granted), that has produced all the bustles and wars that have been in the Christian world upon account of religion. The heads and leaders of the Church, moved by avarice and insatiable desire of dominion, making use of the immoderate ambition of magistrates and the credulous superstition of the giddy multitude, have incensed and animated them against those that dissent from themselves, by preaching unto them, contrary to the laws of the Gospel and to the precepts of charity, that schismatics and heretics are to be outed of their possessions and destroyed. And thus have they mixed together and confounded two things that are in themselves most different, the Church and the commonwealth. Now as it is very difficult for men patiently to suffer themselves to be stripped of the goods which they have got by their honest industry, and, contrary to all the laws of equity, both human and divine, to be delivered up for a prey to other men's violence and rapine; especially when they are otherwise altogether blameless; and that the occasion for which they are thus treated does not at all belong to the jurisdiction of the magistrate, but entirely to the conscience of every particular man for the conduct of which he is accountable to God only; what else can be expected but that these men, growing weary of the evils under which they labor, should in the end think it lawful for them to resist force with force, and to defend their natural rights (which are not forfeitable upon account of religion) with arms as well as they can? That this has been hitherto the ordinary course of things is abundantly evident in history, and that it will continue to be so hereafter is but too apparent in reason. It cannot indeed, be otherwise so long as the principle of persecution for religion shall prevail, as it has done hitherto, with magistrate and people, and so long as those that ought to be the preachers of peace and concord shall continue with all their art and strength to excite men to arms and sound the trumpet of war. But that magistrates should thus suffer these incendiaries and disturbers of the public peace might justly be wondered at if it did not appear that they have been invited by them unto a participation of the spoil, and have therefore thought fit to make use of their covetousness and pride as means whereby to increase their own power. For who does not see that these good men are, indeed, more ministers of the government than ministers of the Gospel and that, by flattering the ambition and favoring the dominion of princes and men in authority, they endeavor with all their might to promote that tyranny in the commonwealth which otherwise they should not be able to establish in the Church? This is the unhappy agreement that we see between the Church and State. Whereas if each of them would contain itself within its own bounds- the one attending to the worldly welfare of the commonwealth, the other to the salvation of souls- it is impossible that any discord should ever have happened between them. Sed pudet hoec opprobria, etc. God Almighty grant, I beseech Him, that the gospel of peace may at length be preached, and that civil magistrates, growing more careful to conform their own consciences to the law of God and less solicitous about the binding of other men's consciences by human laws, may, like fathers of their country, direct all their counsels and endeavors to promote universally the civil welfare of all their children, except only of such as are arrogant, ungovernable, and injurious to their brethren; and that all ecclesiastical men, who boast themselves to be the successors of the Apostles, walking peaceably and modestly in the Apostles' steps, without intermeddling with State Affairs, may apply themselves wholly to promote the salvation of souls.

---- FAREWELL.

--PERHAPS it may not be amiss to add a few things concerning heresy and schism. A Turk is not, nor can be, either heretic or schismatic to a Christian; and if any man falls off from the Christian faith to Islam, he does not thereby become a heretic or schismatic, but an apostate and an infidel. This nobody doubts of; and by this it appears that men of different religions cannot be heretics or schismatics to one another.

--We are to inquire, therefore, what men are of the same religion. Concerning which it is manifest that those who have one and the same rule of faith and worship are of the same religion; and those who have not the same rule of faith and worship are of different religions. For since all things that belong unto that religion are contained in that rule, it follows necessarily that those who agree in one rule are of one and the same religion, and vice versa. Thus Turks and Christians are of different religions, because these take the Holy Scriptures to be the rule of their religion, and those the Koran. And for the same reason there may be different religions also even among Christians. The Papists and Lutherans, though both of them profess faith in Christ and are therefore called Christians, yet are not both of the same religion, because these acknowledge nothing but the Holy Scriptures to be the rule and foundation of their religion, those take in also traditions and the decrees of Popes and of these together make the rule of their religion; and thus the Christians of St. John (as they are called) and the Christians of Geneva are of different religions, because these also take only the Scriptures, and those I know not what traditions, for the rule of their religion.

--This being settled, it follows, first, that heresy is a separation made in ecclesiastical communion between men of the same religion for some opinions no way contained in the rule itself; and, secondly, that among those who acknowledge nothing but the Holy Scriptures to be their rule of faith, heresy is a separation made in their Christian communion for opinions not contained in the express words of Scripture. Now this separation may be made in a twofold manner:

--1. When the greater part, or by the magistrate's patronage the stronger part, of the Church separates itself from others by excluding them out of her communion because they will not profess their belief of certain opinions which are not the express words of the Scripture. For it is not the paucity of those that are separated, nor the authority of the magistrate, that can make any man guilty of heresy, but he only is a heretic who divides the Church into parts, introduces names and marks of distinction, and voluntarily makes a separation because of such opinions.

--2. When anyone separates himself from the communion of a Church because that Church does not publicly profess some certain opinions which the Holy Scriptures do not expressly teach.

--Both these are heretics because they err in fundamentals, and they err obstinately against knowledge; for when they have determined the Holy Scriptures to be the only foundation of faith, they nevertheless lay down certain propositions as fundamental which are not in the Scripture, and because others will not acknowledge these additional opinions of theirs, nor build upon them as if they were necessary and fundamental, they therefore make a separation in the Church, either by withdrawing themselves from others, or expelling the others from them. Nor does it signify anything for them to say that their confessions and symbols are agreeable to Scripture and to the analogy of faith; for if they be conceived in the express words of Scripture, there can be no question about them, because those things are acknowledged by all Christians to be of divine inspiration and therefore fundamental. But if they say that the articles which they require to be professed are consequences deduced from the Scripture, it is undoubtedly well done of them who believe and profess such things as seem unto them so agreeable to the rule of faith. But it would be very ill done to obtrude those things upon others unto whom they do not seem to be the indubitable doctrines of the Scripture; and to make a separation for such things as these, which neither are nor can be fundamental, is to become heretics; for I do not think there is any man arrived to that degree of madness as that he dare give out his consequences and interpretations of Scripture as divine inspirations and compare the articles of faith that he has framed according to his own fancy with the authority of Scripture. I know there are some propositions so evidently agreeable to Scripture that nobody can deny them to be drawn from thence, but about those, therefore, there can be no difference. This only I say- that however clearly we may think this or the other doctrine to be deduced from Scripture, we ought not therefore to impose it upon others as a necessary article of faith because we believe it to be agreeable to the rule of faith, unless we would be content also that other doctrines should be imposed upon us in the same manner, and that we should be compelled to receive and profess all the different and contradictory opinions of Lutherans, Calvinists, Remonstrants, Anabaptists, and other sects which the contrivers of symbols, systems, and confessions are accustomed to deliver to their followers as genuine and necessary deductions from the Holy Scripture. I cannot but wonder at the extravagant arrogance of those men who think that they themselves can explain things necessary to salvation more clearly than the Holy Ghost, the eternal and infinite wisdom of God.

--Thus much concerning heresy, which word in common use is applied only to the doctrinal part of religion. Let us now consider schism, which is a crime near akin to it; for both these words seem unto me to signify an ill-grounded separation in ecclesiastical communion made about things not necessary. But since use, which is the supreme law in matter of language, has determined that heresy relates to errors in faith, and schism to those in worship or discipline, we must consider them under that distinction.

--Schism, then, for the same reasons that have already been alleged, is nothing else but a separation made in the communion of the Church upon account of something in divine worship or ecclesiastical discipline that is not any necessary part of it. Now, nothing in worship or discipline can be necessary to

Christian communion but what Christ our legislator, or the Apostles by inspiration of the Holy Spirit, have commanded in express words.

--In a word, he that denies not anything that the Holy Scriptures teach in express words, nor makes a separation upon occasion of anything that is not manifestly contained in the sacred text - however he may be nicknamed by any sect of Christians and declared by some or all of them to be utterly void of true Christianity- yet in deed and in truth this man cannot be either a heretic or schismatic.

--These things might have been explained more largely and more advantageously, but it is enough to have hinted at them thus briefly to a person of your parts.

-THE END-

THE REASONABLENESS OF CHRISTIANITY

by John Locke
1695

The little satisfaction and consistency that is to be found, in most of the systems of divinity I have met with, made me betake myself to the sole reading of the Scriptures (to which they all appeal) for the understanding the Christian Religion. From that, by an attentive and unbiased search, I have received, Reader, I here deliver to you. If by this my labor you receive any light, or confirmation in the truth, join with me in thanks to the Father of lights, for his condescension to our understandings. If upon a fair and unprejudiced examination, you find I have mistaken the sense and tenor of the Gospel, I beseech you, as a true Christian, in the spirit of the Gospel, (which is that of charity,) and in the words of sobriety, set me right, in the doctrine of salvation.

It is obvious to anyone, who reads the New Testament, that the doctrine of redemption, and consequently of the gospel, is founded upon the supposition of Adam's fall. To understand, therefore, what we are restored to by Jesus Christ, we must consider what the Scriptures show we lost by Adam. This I thought worthy of a diligent and unbiased search: since I found the two extremes that men run into on this point, either on the one hand shook the foundations of all religion, or, on the other, made Christianity almost nothing: for while some men would have all Adam's posterity doomed to eternal, infinite punishment, for the transgression of Adam, whom millions had never heard of, and no one had authorized to transact for him, or be his representative; this seemed to others so little consistent with the justice or goodness of the great and infinite God, that they thought there was no redemption necessary, and consequently, that there was none; rather than admit of it upon a supposition so derogatory to the honor and attributes of that infinite Being; and so made Jesus Christ nothing but the restorer and preacher of pure natural religion; thereby doing violence to the whole tenor of the New Testament. And, indeed, both sides will be suspected to have trespassed this way, against the written word of God, by anyone, who does but take it to be a collection of writings, designed by God, for the instruction of the illiterate bulk of mankind, in the way to salvation; and therefore, generally, and in necessary points, to be understood in the plain direct meaning of the words and phrases: such as they may be supposed to have had in the mouths of the speakers, who used them according to the language of that time and country wherein they lived; without such learned, artificial, and forced senses of them, as are sought out, and put upon them, in most of the systems of divinity, according to the notions that each one has been bred up in.

To one that, thus unbiased, reads the Scriptures, what Adam fell from (is visible) was the state of perfect obedience, which is called justice in the New Testament; though the word, which in the original signifies justice, be translated righteousness: and by this fall he lost paradise, wherein was tranquility and the tree of life; i.e. he lost bliss and immortality. The penalty annexed to the breach of the law, with the sentence pronounced by God upon it, shows this. The penalty stands thus, Gen. ii. 17, "In the day that you eatest thereof, you shall surely die." How was this executed? He did eat: but, in the day he did eat, he did not actually die; but was turned out of paradise from the tree of life, and shut out for ever from it, lest he should take thereof, and live forever. This shows, that the state of paradise was a state of immortality, of life without end; which he lost that very day that he eat: his life began from thence to shorten, and fallow, and to have an end; and from thence to his actual death, was but like the time of a prisoner, between the sentence passed, and the execution, which was in view and certain. Death then entered, and showed his face, which before was shut out, and not known. So St. Paul, Rom. v. 12, "By one man sin entered into the world, and death by sin;" i.e. a state of death and mortality: and, 1 Cor. xv. 22, "In Adam all die;" i.e. by reason of his transgression, all men are mortal, and come to die.

This is so clear in these cited places, and so much the current of the New Testament, that nobody can deny, but that the doctrine of the gospel is, that death came on all men by Adam's sin; only they differ about the signification of the word death: for some will have it to be a state of guilt, wherein not only he, but all his posterity was so involved, that everyone descended of him deserved endless torment, in hell-fire. I shall say nothing more here, how far, in the apprehensions of men, this consists with the justice and goodness of God, having mentioned it above: but it seems a strange way of understanding a law, which requires the plainest and directs words that by death should be meant eternal life in misery. Could anyone be supposed, by a law, that says, "For felony you shall die;" not that he should lose his life; but be kept alive in perpetual, exquisite torments? And would anyone think himself fairly dealt with, that was so used?

To this, they would have it be also a state of necessary sinning, and provoking God in every action that men do: a yet harder sense of the word death than the other. God says, that "in the day that you eatest of the forbidden fruit, you shall die;" i.e. you and your posterity shall be, ever after, incapable of doing anything, but what shall be sinful and provoking to me and shall justly deserve my wrath and indignation. Could a worthy man be supposed to put such terms upon the obedience of his subjects? Much less can the righteous God be supposed, as a punishment of one sin, wherewith he is displeased, to put man under the necessity of sinning continually, and so multiplying the provocation. The reason of this strange interpretation, we shall perhaps find, in some mistaken places of the New Testament. I must confess, by death here, I can understand nothing but a ceasing to be, the losing of all actions of life and sense. Such a death came on Adam, and all his posterity, by his first disobedience in paradise; under which death they should have lain forever, had it not been for the redemption by Jesus Christ. If by death, threatened to Adam, were meant the corruption of human nature in his posterity, it is strange, that the New Testament should not anywhere take notice of it, and tell us, that corruption seized on all, because of Adam's transgression, as well as it tells us so of death. But, as I remember, everyone's sin is charged upon himself only.

Another part of the sentence was, "Cursed is the ground for your sake: in sorrow shall you eat of it all the days of your life; in the sweat of your face shall you eat bread, till you return unto the ground; for out of it were you taken; dust you are, and to dust shall you return," Gen. iii. 17—19. This shows, that paradise was a place of bliss, as well as immortality; without drudgery, and without sorrow. But, when man was turned out, he was exposed to the toil, anxiety, and frailties of this mortal life, which should end in the dust, out of which he was made, and to which he should return; and then have no more life or sense, than the dust had, out of which he was made.

As Adam was turned out of paradise, so all his posterity were born out of it, out of the reach of the tree of life; all, like their father Adam, in a state of mortality, void of the tranquility and bliss of paradise. Rom. v. 12, "By one man sin entered into the world, and death by sin." But here will occur the common objection, that so many stumble at: "How does it consist with the justice and goodness of God that the posterity of Adam should suffer for his sin; the innocent be punished for the guilty?" Very well, if keeping one from what he has no right to, be called a punishment; the state of immortality, in paradise, is not due to the posterity of Adam, more than to any other creature. Nay, if God afford them a temporary, mortal life, it is his gift; they owe it to his bounty; they could not claim it as their right, nor does he injure them when he takes it from them. Had he taken from mankind anything that was their right, or did he put men in a state of misery, worse than not being, without any fault or demerit of their own; this, indeed, would be hard to reconcile with the notion we have of justice; and much more with the goodness, and other attributes of the supreme Being, which he has declared of himself; and reason, as well as revelation, must acknowledge to be in him; unless we will confound good and evil, God and Satan. That such a state of extreme, irremediable torment is worse than no being at all; if everyone's own sense did not determine against the vain philosophy, and foolish metaphysics of some men; yet our Savior's peremptory decision, Matt. xxvi. 24, has put it past doubt, that one may be in such an estate, that it had been better for him not to have been born. But that such a temporary life, as we now have, with all its frailties and ordinary miseries, is better than no being, is evident, by the high value we put upon it ourselves. And therefore, though all die in Adam, yet none are truly punished, but for their own deeds. Rom. ii. 6, "God will render to everyone," How? "According to his deeds. To those that obey unrighteousness, indignation and wrath, tribulation and anguish, upon every soul of man that does evil," ver. 9. 2 Cor. v. 10, "We must appear before the judgment seat of Christ that everyone may receive the things done in his body, according to that he has done, whether it be good or bad." And Christ himself, who knew for what he should condemn men at the last day, assures us, in the two places, where he describes his proceeding at the great judgment, that the sentence of condemnation passes only upon the workers of iniquity, such as neglected to fulfill the law in acts of charity, Matt. vii. 23, Luke xiii. 27, Matt. xxv. 41, 42, etc. "And again, John v. 29, our Savior tells the Jews, that all shall come forth of their graves, they that have done good to the resurrection of life; and they that have done evil, unto the resurrection of damnation." But here is no condemnation of anyone, for what his fore-father Adam had done; which it is not likely should have been omitted, if that should have been a cause why anyone was adjudged to the fire, with the devil and his angels. And he tells his disciples, that when he comes again with his angels, in the glory of his Father, that then he will render to everyone according to his works, Matt. xvi. 27.

Adam being thus turned out of paradise, and all his posterity born out of it, the consequence of it was, that all men should die, and remain under death for ever, and so be utterly lost.

From this estate of death, Jesus Christ restores all mankind to life; 1 Cor. xv. 22, "As in Adam all die, so in Christ shall all be made alive." How this shall be, the same apostle tells us in the foregoing ver. 21. "By man death came, by man also came the resurrection from the dead." Whereby it appears, that the life, which Jesus Christ restores to all men, is that life, which they receive again at the resurrection. Then they recover from death, which otherwise all mankind should have continued under, lost forever; as appears by St. Paul's arguing, 1 Cor. xv. concerning the resurrection.

And thus men are, by the second Adam, restored to life again; that so by Adam's sin they may none of them lose anything, which by their own righteousness they might have a title to: for righteousness, or an exact obedience to the law, seems, by the Scripture, to have a claim of right to eternal life, Rom. iv. 4. "To him that works," i.e. does the works of the law, "is the reward not reckoned of grace, but of debt." And Rev. xxii. 14, "Blessed are they who do his commandments, that they may have right to the tree of life, which is in the paradise of God." If any of the posterity of Adam were just, they shall not lose the reward of it, eternal life and bliss, by being his mortal issue: Christ will bring them all to life again; and then they shall be put everyone upon his own trial, and receive judgment, as he is found to be righteous, or not. And the righteous, as our Savior says, Matt. xxv. 46, shall go into eternal life. Nor shall anyone miss it, who has done, what our Savior directed the lawyer, who asked, Luke x. 25, What he should do to inherit eternal life? "Do this," i.e. what is required by the law, "and you shall live."

On the other side, it seems the unalterable purpose of the divine justice, that no unrighteous person, no one that is guilty of any breach of the law, should be in paradise: but that the wages of sin should be to every man, as it was to Adam, an exclusion of him out of that happy state of immortality, and bring death upon him. And this is so conformable to the eternal and established law of right and wrong, that it is spoken of too, as if it could not be otherwise. St. James says, chap. i. 15, "Sin, when it is finished, bringeth forth death," as it were, by a natural and necessary production. "Sin entered into the world, and death by sin," says St. Paul, Rom. v. 12: and vi. 23, "The wages of sin is death." Death is the purchase of any, of every sin. Gal. iii. 10, "Cursed is everyone, who continues not in all things which are written in the book of the law to do them." And of this St. James gives a reason, chap. ii. 10, 11, "Whosoever shall keep the whole law, and yet offend in one point, he is guilty of all: for he that said, Do not commit adultery, said also, Do not kill:" i.e. he that offends in anyone point, sins against the authority which established the law.

Here then we have the standing and fixed measures of life and death. Immortality and bliss, belong to the righteous; those who have lived in an exact conformity to the law of God, are out of the reach of death; but an exclusion from paradise and loss of immortality is the portion of sinners; of all those who have any way broke that law, and failed of a complete obedience to it, by the guilt of anyone transgression. And thus mankind by the law is put upon the issues of life or death, as they are righteous or unrighteous, just, or unjust; i.e. exact performers or transgressors of the law.

But yet, "all having sinned," Rom. iii. 23, "and come short of the glory of God," i.e. the Kingdom of God in heaven, (which is often called his glory,) "both Jews and Gentiles;" ver. 22, so that, "by the deeds of the law," no one could be justified, ver. 20, it follows, that no one could then have eternal life and bliss.

Perhaps, it will be demanded, "Why did God give so hard a law to mankind, that to the apostle's time no one of Adam's issue had kept it? As appears by Rom. iii. and Gal. iii. 21, 22."

Answer. It was such a law as the purity of God's nature required, and must be the law of such a creature as man; unless God would have made him a rational creature, and not required him to have lived by the law of reason; but would have countenanced in him irregularity and disobedience to that light which he had, and that rule which was suitable to his nature; which would have been to have authorized disorder, confusion, and wickedness in his creatures: for that this law was the law of reason, or as it is called, of nature; we shall see by and by: and if rational creatures will not live up to the rule of their reason, who shall excuse them? If you will admit them to forsake reason in one point, why not in another? Where will you stop? To disobey God in any part of his commands, (and it is he that commands what reason does,) is direct rebellion; which, if dispensed with in any point, government and order are at an end; and there can be no bounds set to the lawless exorbitances of unconfined man. The law therefore was, as St. Paul tells us, Rom. vii. 12, "holy, just, and good," and such as it ought, and could not otherwise be.

This then being the case, that whoever is guilty of any sin should certainly die, and cease to be; the benefit of life, restored by Christ at the resurrection, would have been no great advantage, (for as much as, here again, death must have seized upon all mankind, because all have sinned; for the wages of sin is everywhere death, as well after as before the resurrection,) if God had not found out a way to justify some, i.e. so many as obeyed another law, which God gave; which in the New Testament is called "the law of faith," Rom. iii. 27, and is opposed to "the law of works." And therefore the punishment of those who would not follow him, was to lose their souls, i.e. their lives, Mark viii. 35—38, as is plain, considering the occasion it was spoke on.

The better to understand the law of faith, it will be convenient, in the first place, to consider the law of works. The law of works then, in short, is that law which requires perfect obedience, without any remission or abatement; so that, by that law, a man cannot be just, or justified, without an exact performance of every tittle. Such a perfect obedience, in the New Testament, is termed δικαιοσύνη, which we translate righteousness.

The language of this law is, "Do this and live, transgress and die." Lev. xviii. 5, "You shall keep my statutes and my judgments, which if a man do, he shall live in them." Ezek. xx. 11, "I gave them my statutes, and showed them my judgments, which if a man do, he shall even live in them. Moses, says St. Paul, Rom. x. 5, describes the righteousness, which is of the law, that the man, which does these things, shall live in them." Gal. iii. 12, "The law is not of faith; but that man, that does them, shall live in them." On the other side, transgress and die; no dispensation, no atonement. Ver-10, "Cursed is everyone that continues not in all things which are written in the book of the law to do them."

Where this law of works was to be found, the New Testament tells us, that is in the law delivered by Moses, John i. 17, "The law was given by Moses, but grace and truth came by Jesus Christ." Chap. vii. 19, "Did not Moses give you the law?" says our Savior, "and yet none of you keep the law." And this is the law, which he speaks of, where he asks the lawyer, Luke x. 26, "What is written in the law? How read you? ver. 28, This do, and you shall live." This is that which St. Paul so often styles the law, without any other distinction, Rom. ii. 13, "Not the hearts of the law are just before God, but the doers of the law are justified." it is needless to quote any more places; his epistles are full of it, especially this of the Romans.

"But the law given by Moses, being not given to all mankind, how are all men sinners; since, without a law, there is no transgression?" To this the apostle, ver. 14, answers, "For when the Gentiles, which have not the law, do (i.e. find it reasonable to do) by nature the things contained in the law; these, having not the law, are a law unto themselves; which show the work of the law written in their hearts; their consciences also bearing witness, and among themselves their thoughts accusing or excusing one another." By which, and other places in the following chapter, it is plain, that under the law of works, is comprehended also the law of nature, knowable by reason, as well as the law given by Moses. For, says St. Paul, Rom. iii. 9, 23, "We have proved both Jews and Gentiles, that they are all under sin: for all have sinned, and come short of the glory of God:" which they could not do without a law.

Nay, whatever God requires anywhere to be done, without making any allowance for faith, that is a part of the law of works: so that forbidding Adam to eat of the tree of knowledge was part of the law of works. Only we must take notice here, that some of God's positive commands, being for peculiar ends, and suited to particular circumstances of times, places, and persons; have a limited and only temporary obligation by virtue of God's positive injunction; such as was that part of Moses' law, which concerned the outward worship or political constitution of the Jews; and is called the ceremonial and judicial law, in contradistinction to the moral part of it; which being conformable to the eternal law of right, is of eternal obligation; and therefore remains in force still, under the gospel; nor is abrogated by the law of faith, as St. Paul found some ready to infer, Rom. iii. 31, "Do we then make void the law, through faith? God forbid; yes we establish the law."

Nor can it be otherwise: for, were there no law of works, there could be no law of faith. For there could be no need of faith, which should be counted to men for righteousness; if there were no law, to be the rule and measure of righteousness, which men failed in their obedience to. Where there is no law, there is no sin; all are righteous equally, with or without faith.

The rule, therefore, of right, is the same that ever it was; the obligation to observe it is also the same: the difference between the law of works, and the law of faith, is only this: that the law of works makes no allowance for failing on any occasion. Those that obey are righteous; those that in any part disobey, are unrighteous, and must not expect life, the reward of righteousness. But, by the law of faith, faith is allowed to supply the defect of full obedience: and so the believers are admitted to life and immortality, as if they were righteous. Only here we must take notice, that when St. Paul says, that the gospel establishes the law, he means the moral part of the law of Moses; for that he could not mean the ceremonial, or political part of it, is evident, by what I quoted out of him just now, where he says, That the Gentiles do, by nature, the things contained in the law, their consciences bearing witness. For the Gentiles neither did, nor thought of, the judicial or ceremonial institutions of Moses; 'twas only the moral part their consciences were concerned in. As for the rest, St. Paul tells the Galatians, chap. iv. they are not under that part of the law, which ver. 3, he calls elements of the world; and ver. 9, weak and beggarly elements. And our Savior himself, in this gospel sermon on the mount, tells them, Matt. v. 17, That, whatever they might think, he was not come to dissolve the law, but to make it more full and strict: for that which is meant by πληρῶσαι is evident from the following part of that chapter, where he gives the precepts in a stricter sense, than they were received in before. But they are all precepts of the moral law, which he re-enforces. What should become of the ritual law, he tells the woman of Samaria, in these words, John iv. 21, 23, "The hour comes, when you shall, neither in this mountain, nor yet at Jerusalem, worship the Father. But the true worshippers shall worship the Father in spirit and in truth; for the Father seeks such to worship him."

Thus then, as to the law, in short: the civil and ritual part of the law, delivered by Moses, obliges not Christians, though, to the Jews, it were a part of the law of works; it being a part of the law of nature, that man ought to obey every positive law of God, whenever he shall please to make any such addition to the law of his nature. But the moral part of Moses' law, or the moral law, (which is everywhere the same, the eternal rule of right,) obliges Christians, and all men, everywhere, and is to all men the standing law of works. But Christian believers have the privilege to be under the law of faith too; which is that law, whereby God justifies a man for believing, though by his works he be not just or righteous, i.e. though he come short of perfect obedience to the law of works. God alone does or can justify, or make just, those who by their works are not so: which he does, by counting their faith for righteousness, i.e. for a complete performance of the law. Rom. iv. 3, "Abraham believed God, and it was counted to him for righteousness." Ver. 5, "To him that believeth on him that justifies the ungodly, his faith is counted for righteousness." Ver. 6, "Even as David also describes the blessedness of the man unto whom God imputes righteousness without works;" i.e. without a full measure of works, which is exact obedience. Ver. 7,

Saying, "Blessed are they whose iniquities are forgiven, and whose sins are covered." Ver. 8, "Blessed is the man, to whom the Lord will not impute sin."

This faith, for which God justified Abraham, what was it? It was the believing God, when he engaged his promise in the covenant he made with him. This will be plain to anyone, who considers these places together, Gen. xv. 6, "He believed in the Lord, or believed the Lord." For that the Hebrew phrase, "believing in," signifies no more but believing, is plain from St. Paul's citation of this place, Rom. iv. 3, where he repeats it thus: "Abraham believed God," which he thus explains, ver. 18—22, "Who against hope believed in hope, that he might become the father of many nations: according to that which was spoken, so shall your seed be. And, being not weak in faith, he considered not his own body now dead, when he was about an hundred years old, nor yet the deadness of Sarah's womb. He staggered not at the promise of God, through unbelief; but was strong in faith giving glory to God. And being fully persuaded, that what he had promised he was also able to perform. And therefore it was imputed to him for righteousness." By which it is clear, that the faith which God counted to Abraham for righteousness, was nothing but a firm belief of what God declared to him; and a steadfast relying on him, for the accomplishment of what he had promised.

"Now this," says St. Paul, ver. 23, 24, "was not writ for his [Abraham's] sake alone, but for us also;" teaching us, that as Abraham was justified for his faith, so also ours shall be accounted to us for righteousness, if we believe God, as Abraham believed him. Whereby it is plain meant the firmness of our faith, without staggering, and not the believing the same propositions that Abraham believed; that is that though he and Sarah were old, and past the time and hopes of children, yet he should have a son by her, and by him become the father of a great people, which should possess the land of Canaan. This was what Abraham believed, and was counted to him for righteousness. But nobody, I think, will say, that anyone's believing this now, shall be imputed to him for righteousness. The law of faith then, in short, is for everyone to believe what God requires him to believe, as a condition of the covenant he makes with him: and not to doubt of the performance of his promises. This the apostle intimates in the close here, ver. 24, "But for us also, to whom it shall be imputed, if we believe on him that raised up Jesus our Lord from the dead." We must, therefore, examine and see what God requires us to believe now, under the revelation of the gospel; for the belief of one invisible, eternal, omnipotent God, maker of heaven and earth, etc. was required before, as well as now.

What we are now required to believe to obtain eternal life, is plainly set down in the gospel. St. John tells us, John iii. 36, "He that believeth on the Son has eternal life; and he that believeth not the Son, shall not see life." What this believing on him is, we are also told in the next chapter: "The woman said unto him, I know that the Messiah comes: when he is come, he will tell us all things. Jesus said unto her, I that speak unto you, am he. The woman then went into the city, and said to the men, come see a man that has told me all things that ever I did: is not this the Messiah? and many of the Samaritans believed on him for the saying of the woman, who testified, he told me all that ever I did. So when the Samaritans were come unto him, many more believed because of his words, and said to the woman, We believe not any longer, because of your saying; for we have heard ourselves, and we know that this man is truly the Savior of the world, the Messiah." John iv. 25, 26, 29, 39, 40, 41, 42.

By which place it is plain, that believing on the Son is the believing that Jesus was the Messiah; giving credit to the miracles he did, and the profession he made of himself. For those who are said to believe on him, for the saying of the woman, ver. 39, tell the woman that they now believed not any longer, because of her saying: but that having heard him themselves, they knew, i.e. believed, past doubt, that he was the Messiah.

This was the great proposition that was then controverted, concerning Jesus of Nazareth, "Whether he was the Messiah or no?" And the assent to that was that which distinguished believers from unbelievers. When many of his disciples had forsaken him, upon his declaring that he was the bread of life, which came down from heaven, "He said to his apostles, Will you also go away?" Then Simon Peter answered him, "Lord, to whom shall we go? You have the words of eternal life. And we believe, and are sure, that you are the Messiah, the Son of the living God," John vi. 69. This was the faith which distinguished them from apostates and unbelievers, and was sufficient to continue them in the rank of apostles: and it was upon the same proposition, "That Jesus was the Messiah, the Son of the living God," owned by St. Peter, that our Savior said, he would build his church, Matt. xvi. 16—18.

To convince men of this, he did his miracles; and their assent to, or not assenting to this, made them to be, or not to be, of his church; believers, or not believers: "The Jews came round about him, and said unto him, How long do you make us doubt? If you be the Messiah, tell us plainly. Jesus answered them, I told you, and you believed not: the works that I do in my Father's name, they bear witness of me. But you believe not, because you are not of my sheep," John x. 24—26. Similarly, St. John tells us, that "many deceivers are entered into the world, who confesses not that Jesus, the Messiah, is come in the flesh. This is a deceiver and an antichrist; whosoever abides not in the doctrine of the Messiah, has not God. He that abides in the doctrine of the Messiah," i.e. that Jesus is he, "has both the Father and the Son," 2 John 7, 9. That this is the meaning of the place, is plain from what he says in his foregoing epistle, "Whosoever believeth that Jesus is the Messiah, is born of God," 1 John v. 1. And therefore, drawing to a close of his gospel, and showing the end for which he writ it, he has these words: "Many other signs truly did Jesus in the presence of his disciples, which are not written in this book: but these are written that you may believe that Jesus is the Messiah, the Son of God; and that believing, you might have life through his name," John xx. 30, 31. Whereby it is plain, that the gospel was writ to induce men into a belief of this proposition, "That Jesus of Nazareth was the Messiah;" which if they believed, they should have life.

Accordingly the great question among the Jews was, whether he was the Messiah or no? and the great point insisted on and promulgated in the gospel, was, that he was the Messiah. The first glad tidings of his birth, brought to the shepherds by an angel, was in these words: "Fear not: for, behold, I bring you good tidings of great joy, which shall be to all people: for to you is born this day, in the city of David, a Savior, who is the Messiah, the Lord," Luke ii. 11. Our Savior discoursing with Martha about the means of attaining eternal life, said to her, John xi. 27, "Whosoever believeth in me shall never die. Believe you this? She said unto him, Yes, Lord, I believe that you are the Messiah, the Son of God, which should come into the world." This answer of hers showed what it is to believe in Jesus Christ, so as to have eternal life; that is to believe that he is the Messiah, the son of God, whose coming was foretold by the prophets. And thus Andrew and Philip express it: Andrew says to his brother Simon, "we have found the Messiah, which is, being interpreted, the Christ. Philip said to Nathanael, we have found him, of whom Moses in the law and the prophets did write, Jesus of Nazareth, the son of Joseph," John i. 41, 45. According to what the evangelist says in this place, I have, for the clearer understanding of the Scripture, all along put Messiah for Christ: Christ being but the Greek name for the Hebrew Messiah, and both signifying the Anointed.

And that he was the Messiah, was the great truth he took pains to convince his disciples and apostles of; appearing to them after his resurrection: as may be seen, Luke xxiv. which we shall more particularly consider in another place. There we read what gospel our Savior preached to his disciples and apostles; and that as soon as he was raised from the dead, twice, the very day of his resurrection.

And, if we may gather what was to be believed by all nations from what was preached unto them, we may certainly know what they were commanded, Matt. ult. to teach all nations, by what they actually did teach all nations. We may observe, that the preaching of the apostles everywhere in the Acts, tended to this one point, to prove that Jesus was the Messiah. Indeed, now, after his death, his resurrection was also commonly required to be believed, as a necessary article, and sometimes solely insisted on: it being a mark and undoubted evidence of his being the Messiah, and necessary now to be believed by those who would receive him as the Messiah. For since the Messiah was to be a Savior and a king, and to give life and a kingdom to those who received him, as we shall see by and by; there could have been no pretence to have given him out for the Messiah, and to require men to believe him to be so, who thought him under the power of death, and corruption of the grave. And therefore those who believed him to be the Messiah must believe that he was raised from the dead: and those who believed him to be raised from the dead could not doubt of his being the Messiah. But of this more in another place.

Let us see therefore, how the apostles preached Christ, and what they proposed to their hearers to believe. St. Peter at Jerusalem, Acts ii. by his first sermon, converted three thousand souls. What was his word, which, as we are told, ver. 41, "they gladly received, and thereupon were baptized?" That may be seen from ver. 22 to 36. In short, this; which is the conclusion, drawn from all that he had said, and which he presses on them, as the thing they were to believe, that is "Therefore let all the house of Israel know assuredly, that God has made that same Jesus, whom you have crucified, Lord and Messiah," ver. 36.

To the same purpose was his discourse to the Jews, in the temple, Acts iii. the design whereof you have, ver. 18. "But those things that God before had showed, by the mouth of all his prophets, that the Messiah should suffer, he has so fulfilled."

In the next chapter, Acts iv. Peter and John being examined, about the miracle on the lame man, profess it to have been done in the name of Jesus of Nazareth, who was the Messiah, in whom alone there was salvation, ver. 10—12. The same thing they confirm to them again, Acts v. 29—32. "And daily in the temple, and in every house, they ceased not to teach and preach Jesus the Messiah," ver. 42.

What was Stephen's speech to the council, Acts vii. but a reprehension to them that they were the betrayers and murderers of the Just One? Which is the title, by which he plainly designs the Messiah whose coming was foreshown by the prophets, ver. 51, 52. And that the Messiah was to be without sin, (which is the import of the word Just,) was the opinion of the Jews appears from John ix. ver. 22, compared with 24.

Act viii. Philip carries the gospel to Samaria: "Then Philip went down to Samaria, and preached to them." What was it he preached? You have an account of it in this one word, "the Messiah," ver. 5. This being that alone which was required of them, to believe that Jesus was the Messiah; which when they believed they were baptized. "And when they believed Philip's preaching the gospel of the Kingdom of God, and the name of Jesus the Messiah, they were baptized, both men and women," ver. 12.

Philip being sent from thence by a special call of the Spirit, to make an eminent convert; out of Isaiah preaches to him Jesus, ver. 35. And what it was he preached concerning Jesus, we may know by the profession of faith the eunuch made, upon which he was admitted to baptism, ver. 37. "I believe that Jesus Christ is the Son of God:" which is as much as to say, I believe that he, whom you call Jesus Christ, is really and truly the Messiah that was promised. For, that believing him to be the Son of God, and to be the Messiah, was the same thing, may appear, by comparing John i. 45, with ver. 49, where Nathanael owns Jesus to be the Messiah, in these terms: "You are the Son of God; you are the king of Israel." So the Jews, Luke xxii. 70, asking Christ, whether he were the Son of God, plainly demanded of him, whether he were the Messiah? Which is evident, by comparing that with the three preceding verses. They ask him, ver. 67, Whether he were the Messiah. He answers, "If I tell you, you will not believe:" but withal tells them, that from thenceforth he should be in possession of the kingdom of the Messiah, expressed in these words, ver. 69. "Hereafter shall the Son of Man sit on the right hand of the power of God:" which made them all cry out, "Are you then the Son of God?" i.e. Do you then own yourself to be the Messiah? To which he replies, "You say that I am." That the Son of God was the known title of the Messiah at that time, among the Jews, we may see also from what the Jews say to Pilate, John xix. 7. "We have a law, and by our law he ought to die, because he made himself the Son of God;" i.e. by making himself the Messiah, the prophet which was to come, but falsely; and therefore he deserves to die by the law, Deut. xviii. 20. That this was the common signification of the Son of God, is father evident, from what the chief priests, mocking him, said, when he was on the cross, Matt. xxvii. 42. "He saved others, himself he cannot save: if he be the king of Israel, let him now come down from the cross, and we will believe him. He trusted in God, let him deliver him now, if he will have him; for he said, I am the Son of God;" i.e. He said, he was the Messiah: but it is plainly false; for, if he were, God would deliver him: for the Messiah is to be king of Israel, the Savior of others; but this man cannot save himself. The chief priests mention here the two titles, then in use, whereby the Jews commonly designed the Messiah, that is "Son of God, and king of Israel." That of Son of God was so familiar a compellation of the Messiah, who was then so much expected and talked of, that the Romans, it seems, who lived among them, had learned it, as appears from ver. 54. "Now when the centurion and they that were with him, watching Jesus, saw the earthquake, and those things that were done, they feared greatly, saying, truly this was the Son of God;" this was that extraordinary person that was looked for.

Acts ix. St. Paul, exercising the commission to preach the gospel, which he had received in a miraculous way, ver. 20. "Straightway preached Christ in the synagogues, that he is the Son of God;" i.e. that Jesus was the Messiah: for Christ, in this place, is evidently a proper name. And that this was it, which Paul preached, appears from ver. 22. "Saul increased the more in strength, and confounded the Jews, who dwelt in Damascus, proving that this is the very Christ," i.e. the Messiah.

Peter, when he came to Cornelius at Cæsarea, who, by a vision, was ordered to send for him, as St. Peter on the other side was by a vision commanded to go to him; what does he teach him? His whole discourse, Acts x. tends to show what, he says, God commanded the apostles, "To preach unto the people, and to testify, that it is he [Jesus] which was ordained of God to be the judge of the quick and the dead. And that it was to him, that all the prophets give witness, that, through his name, whosoever believeth in him, shall have remission of sins," ver. 42, 43. "This is the word, which God sent to the children of Israel; that word, which was published throughout all Judea, and began from Galilee, after the baptism which John preached," ver. 36, 37. And these are the words, which had been promised to Cornelius, Acts xi. 14, "Whereby he and all his house should be saved:" which words amount only to thus much: that Jesus was the Messiah, the Savior that was promised. Upon their receiving of this, (for this was all was taught them,) the Holy Ghost fell on them, and they were baptized. it is observable here, that the Holy Ghost fell on them, before they were baptized, which, in other places, converts received not till after baptism. The reason whereof seems to be this, that God, by bestowing on them the Holy Ghost, did thus declare from Heaven, that the Gentiles, upon believing Jesus to be the Messiah, ought to be admitted into the church by baptism, as well as the Jews. Whoever reads St. Peter's defense, Acts xi. when he was accused by those of the circumcision, that he had not kept that distance, which he ought, with the uncircumcised, will be of this opinion; and see by what he says, ver. 15, 16, 17, that this was the ground, and an irresistible authority to him for doing so strange a thing, as it appeared to the Jews, (who alone yet were members of the Christian church,) to admit Gentiles into their communion, upon their believing. And therefore St. Peter, in the foregoing chapter, Acts x. before he would baptize them, proposes this question, "to those of the circumcision, which came with him, and were astonished, because that on the Gentiles also was poured out the gift of the Holy Ghost: can anyone forbid water, that these should not be baptized, who have received the Holy Ghost as well as we?" ver. 47. And when some of the sect of the Pharisees, who believed, thought it needful that the converted Gentiles should be circumcised and keep the law of Moses, Acts xv. "Peter rose up and said unto them, men and brethren, you know that a good while ago God made choice among us, that the Gentiles," that is Cornelius, and those here converted with him, "by my mouth should hear the gospel and believe. And God, who knows the hearts, bare them witness, giving them the Holy Ghost, even as he did unto us, and put no difference between us and them, purifying their hearts by faith," v. 7—9. So that both Jews and Gentiles, who believed Jesus to be the Messiah, received thereupon the seal of baptism; whereby they were owned to be his, and distinguished from unbelievers. From what is above said, we may observe that this preaching Jesus to be the Messiah is called the Word, and the Word of God: and believing it, receiving the Word of God. Vid. Acts x. 36, 37. and xi. 1, 19, 20. and the word of the gospel, Acts xv. 7. And so likewise in the history of the gospel, what Mark, chap. iv. 14, 15, calls simply the word, St. Luke calls the word of God, Luke viii. 11. And St. Matthew, chap. xiii. 19, the word of the kingdom; which were, it seems, in the gospel-writers synonymous terms, and are so to be understood by us.

But to go on: Acts xiii. Paul preaches in the synagogue at Antioch, where he makes it his business to convince the Jews, that "God, according to his promise, had of the seed of David raised to Israel a Savior Jesus." v. 24. That he was He of whom the prophets writ, v. 25—29, i.e. the Messiah: and that, as a demonstration of his being so, God had raised him from the dead, v. 30. From whence he argues thus, v. 32, 33. We evangelize to you, or bring you this gospel, "how that the promise which was made to our fathers, God has fulfilled the same unto us, in that he has raised Jesus again;" as it is also written in the second Psalm, "You are my Son, this day I have begotten you." And having gone on to prove him to be the Messiah, by his resurrection from the dead, he makes this conclusion, v. 38, 39. "Be it known unto you, therefore, men and brethren, that through this man is preached unto you forgiveness of sins; and by him all who believe are justified from all things, from which they could not be justified by the law of Moses." This is in this chapter called "the Word of God," over and over again: compare v. 42, with 44, 46, 48, 49, and chap. xii. v. 24.

Acts xvii. 2—4. At Thessalonica, "Paul, as his manner was, went into the synagogue, and three Sabbath days reasoned with the Jews out of the Scriptures; opening and alleging, that the Messiah must needs have suffered, and risen again from the dead: and that this Jesus, whom I preach unto you, is the Messiah. And some of them believed, and consorted with Paul and Silas: but the Jews which believed not set the city in an uproar." Can there be anything plainer, than that the assenting to this proposition, that Jesus was the Messiah, was that which distinguished the believers from the unbelievers? For this was that alone, which, three Sabbaths, Paul endeavored to convince them of, as the text tells us in direct words.

From thence he went to Berea, and preached the same thing: and the Bereans are commended, v. 11, for searching the Scriptures, whether those things, i.e. which he had said, v. 2, 3, concerning Jesus' being the Messiah, were true or no.

The same doctrine we find him preaching at Corinth, Acts xviii. 4—6. "And he reasoned in the synagogue every Sabbath, and persuaded the Jews and the Greeks. And when Silas and Timothy were come from Macedonia, Paul was pressed in spirit, and testified to the Jews, that Jesus was the Messiah. And when they opposed themselves, and blasphemed, he shook his raiment, and said unto them, Your blood be upon your own heads, I am clean; from henceforth I will go unto the Greeks."

Upon the like occasion he tells the Jews at Antioch, Acts xiii. 46, "It was necessary that the word of God should first have been spoken to you; but seeing you put it off from you, we turn to the Gentiles." it is plain here, St. Paul's charging their blood on their own heads, is for opposing this single truth, that Jesus was the Messiah; that salvation or perdition depends upon believing or rejecting this one proposition. I mean, this is all that is required to be believed by those who acknowledge but one eternal and invisible God, the maker of heaven and earth, as the Jews did. For that there is something more required to salvation, besides believing, we shall see hereafter. In the mean time, it is fit here on this occasion to take notice, that though the apostles in their preaching to the Jews, and the devout, (as we translate the word σεόμενοι, who were proselytes of the gate, and the worshippers of one eternal and invisible God,) said nothing of the believing in this one true God, the maker of heaven and earth; because it was needless to press this to those who believed and professed it already (for to such, it is plain, were most of their discourses hitherto.) Yet when they had to do with idolatrous heathens, who were not yet come to the knowledge of the one only true God; they began with that, as necessary to be believed; it being the foundation on which the other was built, and without which it could signify nothing.

Thus Paul speaking to the idolatrous Lystrians, who would have sacrificed to him and Barnabas, says, Acts xiv. 15, "We preach unto you, that you should turn from these vanities unto the living God, who made heaven and earth, and the sea, and all things that are therein: who in times past suffered all nations to walk in their own ways. Nevertheless he left not himself without witness, in that he did good, and gave us rain from heaven, and fruitful seasons, filling our hearts with food and gladness."

Thus also he proceeded with the idolatrous Athenians, Acts xvii. telling them, upon occasion of the altar, dedicated to the unknown God, "whom you ignorantly worship, him declare I unto you. God who made the world, and all things therein, seeing that he is Lord of heaven and earth, dwells not in temples made with hands.—Forasmuch then as we are the offspring of God, we ought not to think that the Godhead is like unto gold, or silver, or stone, graven by are, or man's device. And the time of this ignorance God winked at; but now commands all men everywhere to repent; because he has appointed a day in which he will judge the world in righteousness, by that man whom he has ordained: whereof he has given assurance unto all men, in that he has raised him from the dead." So that we see, where anything more was necessary to be proposed to be believed, as there was to the heathen idolaters, there the apostles were careful not to omit it.

Acts xviii. 4, "Paul at Corinth reasoned in the synagogue every Sabbath-day, and testified to the Jews, that Jesus was the Messiah." Ver. 11, "And he continued there a year and six months, teaching the word of God among them;" i.e. The good news, that Jesus was the Messiah; as we have already shown is meant by "the Word of God."

Apollos, another preacher of the gospel, when he was instructed in the way of God more perfectly, what did he teach but this same doctrine? As we may see in this account of him, Acts xviii. 27. That, "when he was come into Achaia, he helped the brethren much, who had believed through grace. For he mightily convinced the Jews, and that publicly, showing by the Scriptures that Jesus was the Messiah."

St. Paul, in the account he gives of himself before Festus and Agrippa, professes this alone to be the doctrine he taught after his conversion: for, says he, Acts xxvi. 22, "Having obtained help of God, I continue unto this day, witnessing both to small and great, saying none other things than those which the prophets and Moses did say should come: that the Messiah should suffer, and that he should be the first that should rise from the dead, and should show light unto the people, and to the Gentiles." Which was no more than to prove that Jesus was the Messiah. This is that, which, as we have above observed, is called the Word of God; Acts xi. 1. compared with the foregoing chapter, from v. 34. to the end. And xiii. 42. compared with 44, 46, 48, 49, and xvii. 13. compared with v. 11, 13. It is also called, "the Word of the Gospel," Acts xv. 7. And this is that Word of God, and that Gospel, which, wherever their discourses are set down, we find the apostles preached; and was that faith, which made both Jews and Gentiles believers and members of the church of Christ; purifying their hearts, Acts xv. 9, and carrying with it remission of sins, Acts x. 43. So that all that was to be believed for justification, was no more but this single proposition, that "Jesus of Nazareth was the Christ, or the Messiah." All, I say, that was to be believed for justification: for that it was not all that was required to be done for justification, we shall see hereafter.

Though we have seen above from what our Savior has pronounced himself, John iii. 36, "that he that believeth on the Son has everlasting life; and he that believeth not the Son, shall not see life, but the wrath of God abides on him;" and are taught from John iv. 39, compared with v. 42, that believing on him, is believing that he is the Messiah, the Savior of the world; and the confession made by St. Peter, Matt. xvi. 16, that he is "the Messiah, the Son of the living God," being the rock, on which our Savior has promised to build his church; though this I say, and what else we have already taken notice of, be enough to convince us what it is we are in the gospel required to believe to eternal life, without adding what we have observed from the preaching of the apostles; yet it may not be amiss, for the father clearing this matter, to observe what the evangelists deliver concerning the same thing, though in different words; which, therefore, perhaps, are not so generally taken notice of to this purpose.

We have above observed, from the words of Andrew and Philip compared, that "the Messiah, and him of whom Moses in the law and the prophets did write," signify the same thing. We shall now consider that place, John i. a little father. Ver. 41, "Andrew says to Simon, we have found the Messiah." Philip, on the same occasion, v. 45, says to Nathanael, "we have found him of whom Moses in the law and the prophets did write, Jesus of Nazareth, the son of Joseph." Nathanael, who disbelieved this, when, upon Christ's speaking to him, he was convinced of it, declares his assent to it in these words: "Rabbi, you are the Son of God; you are the king of Israel." From which it is evident, that to believe him to be "Him of whom Moses and the prophets did write," or to be "the Son of God," or to be "the king of Israel," was in effect the same as to believe him to be the Messiah: and an ascent to that, was what our Savior received for believing. For, upon Nathanael's making a confession in these words, "You are the Son of God, you are the king of Israel, Jesus answered and said to him, Because I said to you I saw you under the fig-tree, do you believe? You shall see greater things than these," ver. 51. I desire anyone to read the latter part of the first of John, from ver. 25, with attention, and tell me, whether it be not plain, that this phrase, The Son of God, is an expression used for the Messiah. To which let him add Martha's declaration of her faith, John xi. 27, in these words: "I believe that you are the Messiah, the Son of God, who should come into the world;" and that passage of St. John xx. 31, "That you might believe that Jesus is the Messiah, the Son of God; and that, believing, you might have life through his name:" and then tell me whether he can doubt that Messiah, the Son of God, were synonymous terms, at that time, among the Jews.

The prophecy of Daniel, chap. ix. when he is called "Messiah the Prince;" and the mention of his government and kingdom, and the deliverance by him, in Isaiah, Daniel, and other prophecies, understood of the Messiah; were so well known to the Jews, and had so raised their hopes of him about this time, which, by their account, was to be the time of his coming, to restore the kingdom of Israel; that Herod no sooner heard of the magi's inquiry after "Him that was born king of the Jews," Matt. ii. but he forthwith "demanded of the chief priests and scribes, where the Messiah should be born," ver. 4. Not doubting but, if there were any king born to the Jews, it was the Messiah: whose coming was now the general expectation, as appears, Luke iii. 15, "The people being in expectation, and all men musing in their hearts, of John, whether he were the Messiah or not." And when the priests and Levites sent to ask him who he was; he, understanding their meaning, answers, John i. 20, "That he was not the Messiah;" but he bears witness, that Jesus "is the Son of God," i.e. the Messiah, ver. 34.

This looking for the Messiah, at this time, we see also in Simeon; who is said to be "waiting for the consolation of Israel," Luke ii. 21. And having the child Jesus in his arms, he says he had "seen the salvation of the Lord," ver. 30. And, "Anna coming at the same instant into the temple, she gave thanks also unto the Lord, and spoke of him to all them that looked for redemption in Israel," ver. 38. And of Joseph of Arimathea, it is said, Mark xv. 43, That "he also expected the Kingdom of God:" by all which was meant the coming of the Messiah; and Luke xix. 11, it is said, "They thought that the Kingdom of God should immediately appear."

This being premised, let us see what it was that John the Baptist preached, when he first entered upon his ministry. That St. Matthew tells us, chap. iii. 1, 2, "In those days came John the Baptist preaching in the wilderness of Judea, saying, repent; for the kingdom of heaven is at hand." This was a declaration of the coming of the Messiah: the kingdom of heaven, and the Kingdom of God, being the same, as is clear out of several places of the evangelists; and both signifying the kingdom of the Messiah. The profession which John the Baptist made, when sent to the Jews, John i. 19, was, that "he was not the Messiah;" but that Jesus was. This will appear to anyone, who will compare ver. 26—34, with John iii. 27, 30. The Jews being very inquisitive to know, whether John were the Messiah; he positively denies it; but tells them, he was only his forerunner; and that there stood one among them, who would follow him, whose shoe laces he was not worthy to untie. The next day, seeing Jesus, he says, he was the man; and that his own baptizing in water was only that Jesus might be manifested to the world; and that he knew him not, till he saw the Holy Ghost descend upon him: he that sent him to baptize, having told him, that he on whom he should see the Spirit descend, and rest upon, he it was that should baptize with the Holy Ghost; and that therefore he witnessed, that "this was the Son of God," ver. 34, i.e. the Messiah; and, chap. iii. 26, etc. they come to John the Baptist, and tell him, that Jesus baptized, and that all men went to him. John answers, He has his authority from heaven; you know I never said, I was the Messiah, but that I was sent before him. He must increase, but I must decrease; for God has sent him, and he speaks the words of God; and God has given all things into the hands of his Son, "And he that believes on the Son, has eternal life;" the same doctrine, and nothing else but what was preached by the apostles afterwards: as we have seen all through the Acts. v. g. that Jesus was the Messiah. And thus it was that John bears witness of our Savior, as Jesus himself says, John v. 33.

This also was the declaration given of him at his baptism, by a voice from heaven: "This is my beloved Son in whom I am well pleased." Matt. iii. 17. Which was a declaration of him to be the Messiah, the Son of God being (as we have showed) understood to signify the Messiah. To which we may add the first mention of him after his conception, in the words of the angel to Joseph, Matt. i. 21. "You shall call his name Jesus," or Savior; "for he shall save his people from their sins." It was a received doctrine in the Jewish nation, that at the coming of the Messiah, all their sins should be forgiven them. These words, therefore, of the angel, we may look upon as a declaration, that Jesus was the Messiah; whereof these words, "his people," are a father mark: which suppose him to have a people, and consequently to be a king.

After his baptism, Jesus himself enters upon his ministry. But, before we examine what it was he proposed to be believed, we must observe, that there is a threefold declaration of the Messiah.

1. By miracles. The spirit of prophecy had now for many ages forsaken the Jews; and, though their commonwealth were not quite dissolved, but that they lived under their own laws, yet they were under a foreign dominion, subject to the Romans. In this state their account of the time being up, they were in expectation of the Messiah, and of deliverance by him in a kingdom he was to set up, according to their ancient prophecies of him: which gave them hopes of an extraordinary man yet to come from God, who, with an extraordinary and divine power, and miracles, should evidence his mission, and work their deliverance. And, of any such extraordinary person, who should have the power of doing miracles, they had no other expectation, but only of their Messiah. One great prophet and worker of miracles, and only one more, they expected; who was to be the Messiah. And therefore we see the people justified their believing in him, i.e. their believing him to be the Messiah, because of the miracles he did; John vii. 41. "And many of the people believed in him, and said, When the Messiah comes, will he do more miracles, than this man has done?" And when the Jews, at the feast of dedication, John x. 24, 25, coming about him, said unto him, "How long do you make us doubt? If you be the Messiah, tell us plainly; Jesus answered them, I told you, and you believed not; the works that I do in my Father's name bear witness of me." And, John v. 36, he says, "I have a greater witness than that of John; for the works, which the Father has given me to do, the same works that I do, bear witness of me, that the Father has sent me." Where, by the way, we may observe, that his being "sent by the Father," is but another way of expressing the Messiah; which is evident from this place here, John v. compared with that of John x. last quoted. For there he says, that his works bear witness of him: And what was that witness? that is That he was "the Messiah." Here again he says, that his works bear witness of him: And what is that witness? that is "That the Father sent him." By which we are taught, that to be sent by the Father, and to be the Messiah, was the same thing, in his way of declaring himself. And accordingly we find, John iv. 53, and xi. 45, and elsewhere, many hearkened and assented to his testimony, and believed on him, seeing the things that he did.

2. Another way of declaring the coming of the Messiah was by phrases and parable that did signify or intimate his coming; though not in direct words pointing out the person. The most usual of these were, "The Kingdom of God, and of heaven;" because it was that which was often spoken of the Messiah, in the Old Testament, in very plain words: and a kingdom was that which the Jews most looked after and wished for. In that known place, Isa. ix. "The government shall be upon his shoulders; he shall be called the Prince of peace: of the increase of his government and peace there shall be no end; upon the throne of David, and upon his kingdom, to order it, and to establish it with judgment, and with justice, from henceforth even forever." Micah v. 2, "But you, Bethlehem Ephrata, though you be little among the thousands of Judah, yet out of you shall he come forth unto me, that is to be the Ruler in Israel." And Daniel, besides that he calls him "Messiah the Prince," chap. ix. 25, in the account of his vision "of the Son of man," chap. vii. 13, 14, says, "There was given him dominion, glory, and a kingdom, that all people, nations, and languages should serve him: his dominion is an everlasting dominion, which shall not pass away; and his kingdom that which shall not be destroyed." So that the Kingdom of God, and the kingdom of heaven, were common phrases among the Jews, to signify the times of the Messiah. Luke xiv. 15, "One of the Jews that sat at meat with him, said unto him, Blessed is he that shall eat bread in the Kingdom of God." Chap. xvii. 20, The Pharisees demanded, "when the Kingdom of God should come?" And St. John Baptist "came, saying, Repent; for the kingdom of heaven is at hand;" a phrase he would not have used in preaching, had it not been understood.

There are other expressions that signified the Messiah, and his coming, which we shall take notice of, as they come in our way.

3. By plain and direct words, declaring the doctrine of the Messiah, speaking out that Jesus was he; as we see the apostles did, when they went about preaching the gospel, after our Savior's resurrection. This

was the open clear way, and that which one would think the Messiah himself, when he came, should have taken; especially, if it were of that moment, that upon men's believing him to be the Messiah depended the forgiveness of their sins. And yet we see, that our Savior did not: but on the contrary, for the most part, made no other discovery of himself, at least in Judea, and at the beginning of his ministry, but in the two former ways, which were more obscure; not declaring himself to be the Messiah, any otherwise than as it might be gathered from the miracles he did, and the conformity of his life and actions with the prophecies of the Old Testament concerning him: and from some general discourses of the kingdom of the Messiah being come, under the name of the "Kingdom of God, and of heaven." Nay, so far was he from publicly owning himself to be the Messiah, that he forbids the doing of it: Mark viii. 27—30. "He asked his disciples, Who do men say that I am? And they answered, John the Baptist; but some say Elias; and others, one of the prophets." (So that it is evident, that even those, who believed him an extraordinary person, knew not yet who he was, or that he gave himself out for the Messiah; though this was in the third year of his ministry, and not a year before his death.) "And he said unto them, But who say you that I am? And Peter answered and said unto him, You are the Messiah. And he charged them that they should tell no man of him." Luke iv. 41. "And devils came out of many, crying, You are the Messiah, the Son of God: and he, rebuking them, suffered them not to speak, that they knew him to be the Messiah." Mark iii. 11, 12. "Unclean spirits, when they saw him, fell down before him, and cried, saying, You are the Son of God: and he strictly charged them that they should not make him known." Here again we may observe, from the comparing of the two texts, that "You are the Son of God," or, "You are the Messiah," were indifferently used for the same thing. But to return to the matter in hand.

This concealment of himself will seem strange, in one who came to bring light into the world, and was to suffer death for the testimony of the truth. This reserve will be thought to look, as if he had a mind to conceal himself, and not to be known to the world for the Messiah, nor to be believed on as such. But we shall be of another mind, and conclude this proceeding of his according to divine wisdom, and suited to a fuller manifestation and evidence of his being the Messiah; when we consider that he was to fill out the time foretold of his ministry; and after a life illustrious in miracles and good works, attended with humility, meekness, patience, and sufferings, and every way conformable to the prophecies of him; should be led as a sheep to the slaughter, and with all quiet and submission be brought to the cross, though there were no guilt, nor fault found in him. This could not have been, if, as soon as he appeared in public, and began to preach, he had presently professed himself to have been the Messiah; the king that owned that kingdom, he published to be at hand. For the Sanhedrin would then have laid hold on it, to have got him into their power, and thereby have taken away his life; at least they would have disturbed his ministry, and hindered the work he was about. That this made him cautious, and avoid, as much as he could, the occasions of provoking them and falling into their hands, is plain from John vii. 1. "After these things Jesus walked in Galilee;" out of the way of the chief priests and rulers; "for he would not walk in Jewry, because the Jews sought to kill him." Thus, making good what he foretold them at Jerusalem, when, at the first Passover after his beginning to preach the gospel, upon his curing the man at the pool of Bethesda, they sought to kill him, John v. 16, "You have not," says he, ver. 38, "his word abiding among you; for whom he has sent, him you believe not." This was spoken more particularly to the Jews of Jerusalem, who were the forward men, zealous to take away his life: and it imports, that, because of their unbelief and opposition to him, the word of God, i.e. the preaching of the kingdom of the Messiah, which is often called "the word of God," did not stay among them, he could not stay among them, preach and explain to them the kingdom of the Messiah.

That the word of God, here, signifies "the word of God," that should make Jesus known to them to be the Messiah, is evident from the context: and this meaning of this place is made good by the event. For, after this, we hear no more of Jesus at Jerusalem, until the Pentecost came; though it is not to be doubted, but that he was there the next Passover, and other feasts between; but privately. And now at Jerusalem, at the feast of Pentecost, near fifteen months after, he says little of anything, and not a word of the kingdom of heaven being come, or at hand; nor did he any miracle there. And returning to Jerusalem at the feast of tabernacles, it is plain, that from this time 'till then, which was a year and a half, he had not taught them at Jerusalem.

For, 1. it is said, John vii. 2, 15, that, he teaching in the temple at the feast of tabernacles, "the Jews marveled, saying, How knows this man letters, having never learned?" A sign they had not been used to his preaching: for, if they had, they would not now have marveled.

2. Ver. 19, He says thus to them: "Did not Moses give you the law, and yet none of you keep the law? Why do you go about to kill me? One work," or miracle, "I did here among you, and you all marvel. Moses therefore gave unto you circumcision, and you on the Sabbath-day circumcise a man: if a man on the Sabbath-day receive circumcision, that the law of Moses should not be broken, are you angry with me, because I have made a man every way whole on the Sabbath-day?" Which is a direct defense of what he did at Jerusalem, a year and a half before the work he here speaks of. We find he had not preached to them there, from that time to this; but had made good what he had told them, ver. 38, "You have not the word of God remaining among you, because whom he has sent you believe not." Whereby, I think, he signifies his not staying, and being frequent among them at Jerusalem, preaching the gospel of the kingdom; because their great unbelief, opposition, and malice to him, would not permit it.

This was manifestly so in fact: for the first miracle he did at Jerusalem, which was at the second Passover after his baptism, brought him in danger of his life. Hereupon we find he forbore preaching again there, 'till the feast of tabernacles, immediately preceding his last Passover: so that 'till the half a year before his passion, he did but one miracle, and preached but once publicly at Jerusalem. These trials he made there; but found their unbelief such, that if he had staid and persisted to preach the good tidings of the kingdom, and to show himself by miracles among them, he could not have had time and freedom to do those works which his Father had given him to finish, as he says, ver. 36, of this fifth of St. John.

When, upon the curing of the withered hand on the Sabbath-day, "The Pharisees took counsel with the Herodians, how they might destroy him, Jesus withdrew himself, with his disciples, to the sea: and a great multitude from Galilee followed him, and from Judea, and from Jerusalem, and from Idumea, and from beyond Jordan, and they about Tyre and Sidon, a great multitude; when they had heard what great things he did, came unto him, and he healed them all, and charged them, that they should not make him known: that it might be fulfilled which was spoken by the prophet Isaiah, saying, Behold, my servant, whom I have chosen; my beloved, in whom my soul is well pleased: I will put my spirit upon him, and he shall show judgment to the Gentiles. He shall not strive, nor cry; neither shall any man hear his voice in the streets." Matt. xii, Mark iii.

And, John xi. 47, upon the news of our Savior's raising Lazarus from the dead, "The chief priests and Pharisees convened the Sanhedrin, and said, What do we? For this man does many miracles." Ver. 53, "Then from that day forth they took counsel together for to put him to death." Ver. 54, "Jesus therefore walked no more openly among the Jews." His miracles had now so much declared him to be the Messiah, that the Jews could no longer bear him, nor he trust himself among them; "But went thence unto a country near to the wilderness, into a city called Ephraim; and there continued with his disciples." This was but a little before his last Passover, as appears by the following words, ver. 55. "And the Jews Passover was nigh at hand," and he could not, now his miracles had made him so well known, have been secure, the little time that remained, 'till his hour was fully come, if he had not, with his wonted and necessary caution, withdrawn; "And walked no more openly among the Jews," 'till his time (at the next Passover) was fully come; and then again he appeared among them openly.

Nor would the Romans have suffered him, if he had gone about preaching, that he was the king whom the Jews expected. Such an accusation would have been forwardly brought against him by the Jews, if they could have heard it out of his own mouth; and that had been his public doctrine to his followers, which was openly preached by the apostles after his death, when he appeared no more. And of this they were accused, Acts xvii. 5—9. "But the Jews, which believed not, moved with envy, took unto them certain lewd fellows of the baser sort, and gathered a company, and set all the city in an uproar, and assaulted the house of Jason, and sought to bring them out to the people. And when they found them [Paul and Silas] not, they drew Jason, and certain brethren, unto the rulers of the city, crying, These that have turned the world upside down, are come hither also; whom Jason has received: and these all do contrary to the decrees of Cæsar, saying, That there is another king, one Jesus. And they troubled the people, and the rulers of the city, when they heard these things: and when they had taken security of Jason and the other, they let them go."

Though the magistrates of the world had no great regard to the talk of a king who had suffered death, and appeared no longer anywhere; yet, if our Savior had openly declared this of himself in his life time, with a train of disciples and followers everywhere owning and crying him up for their king; the Roman governors of Judea could not have forborne to have taken notice of it, and have made use of their force against him. This the Jews were not mistaken in; and therefore made use of it as the strongest accusation, and likeliest to prevail with Pilate against him, for the taking away his life; it being treason, and an unpardonable offence, which could not escape death from a Roman deputy, without the forfeiture of his own life. Thus then they accuse him to Pilate, Luke xxiii. 2. "We found this fellow perverting the nation, forbidding to give tribute to Cæsar, saying, that he himself is a king;" or rather "the Messiah, the King."

Our Savior, indeed, now that his time was come, (and he in custody, and forsaken of all the world, and so out of all danger of raising any sedition or disturbance,) owns himself to Pilate to be a king; after first having told Pilate, John xviii. 36, "That his kingdom was not of this world;" and, for a kingdom in another world, Pilate knew that his master at Rome concerned not himself. But had there been any the least appearance of truth in the allegations of the Jews, that he had perverted the nation, forbidding to pay tribute to Cæsar, or drawing the people after him, as their king; Pilate would not so readily have pronounced him innocent. But we see what he said to his accusers, Luke xxiii. 13, 14. "Pilate, when he had called together the chief priests and the rulers of the people, said unto them, You have brought this man unto me as one that perverted the people; and behold, I, having examined him before you, have found no fault in this man, touching those things whereof you accuse him: no, nor yet Herod, for I sent you to him; and, lo, nothing worthy of death is done by him." And therefore, finding a man of that mean condition, and innocent life, (no mover of seditions, or disturber of the public peace) without a friend or a follower, he would have dismissed him, as a king of no consequence; as an innocent man, falsely and maliciously accused by the Jews.

How necessary this caution was in our Savior, to say or do nothing that might justly offend, or render him suspected to the Roman governor: and how glad the Jews would have been to have had any such thing against him, we may see, Luke xx. 20. The chief priests and the scribes "watched him, and sent forth spies, who should feign themselves just men, that might take hold of his words, that so they might deliver him unto the power and authority of the governor." And the very thing wherein they hoped to entrap him in this place was paying tribute to Cæsar; which they afterwards falsely accused him of. And what would they have done, if he had before them professed himself to have been the Messiah, their King and deliverer?

And here we may observe the wonderful providence of God, who had so ordered the state of the Jews, at the time when his son was to come into the world, that though neither their civil constitution nor religious worship were dissolved, yet the power of life and death was taken from them; whereby he had an opportunity to publish "the kingdom of the Messiah;" that is, his own royalty, under the name of "the Kingdom of God, and of heaven;" which the Jews well enough understood, and would certainly have put him to death for, had the power been in their own hands. But this being no matter of accusation to the Romans, hindered him not from speaking of the "kingdom of heaven," as he did, sometimes in reference to his appearing in the world, and being believed on by particular persons; sometimes in reference to the power should be given him by the Father at his resurrection; and sometimes in reference to his coming to judge the world at the last day, in the full glory and completion of his kingdom. These were ways of declaring himself, which the Jews could lay no hold on, to bring him in danger with Pontius Pilate, and get him seized and put to death.

Another reason there was, that hindered him as much as the former, from professing himself, in express words, to be the Messiah; and that was, that the whole nation of the Jews, expecting at this time their Messiah, and deliverance, by him, from the subjection they were in to a foreign yoke, the body of the people would certainly, upon his declaring himself to be the Messiah, their king, have rose up in rebellion, and set him at the head of them. And indeed, the miracles that he did, so much disposed them to think him to be the Messiah, that, though shrouded under the obscurity of a mean condition, and a very private simple life; though he passed for a Galilean (his birth at Bethlehem being then concealed), and assumed not to himself any power or authority, or so much as the name of the Messiah; yet he could hardly avoid being set up by a tumult, and proclaimed their king. So John tells us, chap. vi. 14, 15, "Then those men, when they had seen the miracles that Jesus did, said, this is of a truth that prophet that should come into the world. When therefore Jesus perceived that they would come to take him by force to make him king, he departed again into a mountain, himself alone." This was upon his feeding of five thousand with five barley loaves and two fishes. So hard was it for him, doing those miracles which were necessary to testify his mission and which often drew great multitudes after him, Matt. iv. 25, to keep the heady and heavy multitude from such disorder, as would have involved him in it; and have disturbed the course, and cut short the time of his ministry; and drawn on him the reputation and death of a turbulent, seditious criminal; contrary to the design of his coming, which was, to be offered up a lamb blameless, and void of offence; his innocence appearing to all the world, even to him that delivered him up to be crucified. This it would have been impossible to have avoided, if, in his preaching everywhere, he had openly assumed to himself the title of their Messiah; which was all was wanting to set the people in a flame; who drawn by his miracles, and the hopes of finding a Deliverer in so extraordinary a man, followed him in great numbers. We read everywhere of multitudes, and in Luke xii. 1, of myriads that were gathered about him. This conflux of people, thus disposed, would not have failed, upon his declaring himself to be the Messiah, to have made a commotion, and with force set him up for their King. It is plain, therefore, from these two reasons, why (though he came to preach the gospel, and convert the world to a belief of his being the Messiah; and though he says so much of his kingdom, under the title of the Kingdom of God, and the kingdom of heaven) he yet makes it not his business to persuade them, that he himself is the Messiah, nor does, in his public preaching, declare himself to be him. He inculcates to the people, on all occasions, that the Kingdom of God is come: he shows the way of admittance into this kingdom, that is repentance and baptism; and teaches the laws of it, that is good life, according to the strictest rules of virtue and morality. But who the King was of this kingdom, he leaves to his miracles to point out, to those who would consider what he did, and make the right use of it now; or to witness to those who should hearken to the apostles hereafter when they preached it in plain words, and called upon them to believe it, after his resurrection, when there should be no longer room to fear, that it should cause any disturbance in civil societies, and the governments of the world. But he could not declare himself to be the Messiah, without manifest danger of tumult and sedition: and the miracles he did declare it so much, that he was fain often to hide himself, and withdraw from the concourse of the people. The leper that he cured, Mark i, though forbid to say anything, yet "blazed it so abroad, that Jesus could no more openly enter into the city, but was without in desert places," living in retirement, as appears from Luke v. 16, and there "they came to him from every quareer." And thus he did more than once.

This being established, let us take a view of the spread of the gospel by our Savior himself, and see what it was he taught the world, and required men to believe.

The first beginning of his ministry, whereby he showed himself, seems to be at Cana in Galilee, soon after his baptism; where he turned water into wine: of which St. John, chap. ii. 11, says thus: "This beginning of miracles Jesus made, and manifested his glory, and his disciples believed in him." His disciples here believed in him, but we hear not of any other preaching to them, but by this miracle, whereby he "manifested his glory," i.e. of being the Messiah, the Prince. So Nathanael, without any other preaching, but only our Savior's discovering to him, that he knew him after an extraordinary manner, presently acknowledges him to be the Messiah; crying, "Rabbi, you are the Son of God; you are the King of Israel."

From hence, staying a few days at Capernaum, he goes to Jerusalem, to the Passover, and there he drives the traders out of the temple, John ii. 12—15, saying, "Make not my Father's house a house of merchandise." Where we see he uses a phrase, which, by interpretation, signifies that he was the "Son of God," though at that time unregarded. Ver. 16, Hereupon the Jews demand, "What sign do you show us, since you doest these things?" Jesus answered, "Destroy you this temple, and in three days I will raise it again." This is an instance of what way Jesus took to declare himself: for it is plain, by their reply, the Jews understood him not, nor his disciples neither; for it is said, ver. 22, "When, therefore, he was risen from the dead, his disciples remembered, that he said this to them: and they believed the Scripture, and the saying of Jesus to them."

This, therefore, we may look on in the beginning, as a pattern of Christ's preaching, and showing himself to the Jews, which he generally followed afterwards; that is such a manifestation of himself, as everyone at present could not understand; but yet carried such an evidence with it, to those who were well disposed now, or would reflect on it when the whole course of his ministry was over, as was sufficient clearly to convince them that he was the Messiah.

The reason of this method used by our Savior, the Scripture gives us here, at this his first appearing in public, after his entrance upon his ministry, to be a rule and light to us in the whole course of it: for the next verse taking notice, that many believed on him, "because of his miracles," (which was all the preaching they had,) it is said, ver. 24, "But Jesus did not commit himself unto them, because he knew all men;" i.e. he declared not himself so openly to be the Messiah, their King, as to put himself into the power of the Jews, by laying himself open to their malice; who, he knew, would be so ready to lay hold on it to accuse him; for, as the next verse 25, shows, he knew well enough what was in them. We may here further observe, that "believing in his name" signifies believing him to be the Messiah. Ver. 22, tells us, that "many at the Passover believed in his name, when they saw the miracles that he did." What other faith could these miracles produce in them who saw them, but that this was he of whom the Scripture spoke, who was to be their Deliverer?

While he was now at Jerusalem, Nicodemus, a ruler of the Jews, comes to him, John iii. 1—21, to whom he preaches eternal life by faith in the Messiah, ver. 15 and 17, but in general terms, without naming himself to be that Messiah, though his whole discourse tends to it. This is all we hear of our Savior the first year of his ministry, but only his baptism, fasting, and temptation in the beginning of it, and spending the rest of it after the Passover, in Judea with his disciples, baptizing there. But "when he knew that the Pharisees reported, that he made and baptized more disciples than John, he left Judea," and got out of their way again into Galilee, John iv. 1, 3.

In his way back, by the well of Sichar, he discourses with the Samaritan woman; and after having opened to her the true and spiritual worship which was at hand, which the woman presently understands of the times of the Messiah, who was then looked for; thus she answers, ver. 25, "I know that the Messiah comes: when he is come, he will tell us all things." Whereupon our Savior, though we hear no such thing from him in Jerusalem or Judea, or to Nicodemus; yet here, *to this Samaritan woman*, he in plain and direct words owns and declares, that he himself, who talked with her, was the Messiah, ver. 26.

This would seem very strange, that he should be more free and open to a Samaritan, than he was to the Jews, were not the reason plain, from what we have observed above. He was now out of Judea, among a people with whom the Jews had no commerce; ver. 9, who were not disposed, out of envy, as the Jews were, to seek his life, or to accuse him to the Roman governor, or to make an insurrection, to set a Jew up for their King. What the consequence was of his discourse with this Samaritan woman, we have an account, ver. 28, 39—42. "She left her water-pot, and went her way into the city, and said to the men, Come, see a man who told me all things that ever I did: Is not this the Messiah? And many of the Samaritans of that city believed on him for the saying of the woman, which testified, He told me all that ever I did. So when the Samaritans were come unto him, they besought him that he would stay with them: and he abode there two days. And many more believed because of his own word; and said unto the woman, Now we believe not because of your saying: for we have heard him ourselves; and we know," (i.e. are fully persuaded) "that this is indeed the Messiah, the Savior of the world." By comparing ver. 39, with 41 and 42, it is plain, that "believing on him" signifies no more than believing him to be the Messiah.

From Sichar Jesus goes to Nazareth, the place he was bred up in; and there reading in the synagogue a prophecy concerning the Messiah, out of the lxi. of Isaiah, he tells them, Luke iv. 21, "This day is this Scripture fulfilled in your ears."

But being in danger of his life at Nazareth, he leaves it for Capernaum: and then, as St. Matthew informs us, chap. iv. 17, "He began to preach and say, Repent; for the kingdom of heaven is at hand." Or, as St. Mark has it, chap. i. 14, 15, "Preaching the gospel of the Kingdom of God, and saying, The time is fulfilled, and the Kingdom of God is at hand; repent you, and believe the gospel;" i.e. believe this good news. This removing to Capernaum, and seating himself there in the borders of Zebulon and Naphtali, was, as St. Matthew observes, chap. iv. 13—16, that a prophecy of Isaiah might be fulfilled. Thus the actions and circumstances of his life answered the prophecies, and declared him to be the Messiah. And by what St. Mark says in this place, it is manifest, that the gospel which he preached and required them to believe, was no other but the good tidings of the coming of the Messiah, and of his kingdom, the time being now fulfilled.

In his way to Capernaum, being come to Cana, a nobleman of Capernaum came to him, ver. 47, "And besought him that he would come down and heal his son; for he was at the point of death." Ver. 48, "Then said Jesus unto him, Except you see signs and wonders, you will not believe." Then he returning homewards, and finding that his son began to "mend at the same hour which Jesus said unto him, Your son lives; he himself believed, and his whole house," ver. 53.

Here this nobleman is by the apostles pronounced to be a believer. And what does he believe? Even that which Jesus complains, ver. 48, "they would not believe, except they saw signs and wonders; which could be nothing but what those of Samaria in the same chapter believed, that is that he was the Messiah. For we nowhere in the gospels hear of anything else, that had been proposed to be believed by them.

Having done miracles, and cured all their sick at Capernaum, he says, "Let us go to the adjoining towns, that I may preach there also; for this I came forth," Mark i. 38. Or, as St. Luke has it, chap. iv. 43, he tells the multitude, who would have kept him, that he might not go from them, "I must evangelize," or tell the good tidings of "the Kingdom of God to other cities also; for therefore am I sent." And St. Matthew, chap. iv. 23, tells us how he executed this commission he was sent on: "And Jesus went about all Galilee, teaching in their synagogues, and preaching the gospel of the kingdom, and curing all diseases." This then was what he was sent to preach everywhere, that is the gospel of the kingdom of the Messiah; and by the miracles and good he did he let them know who the Messiah was.

Hence he goes up to Jerusalem, to the second Passover, since the beginning of his ministry. And here, discoursing to the Jews, who sought to kill him upon occasion of the man whom he had cured carrying his bed on the Sabbath-day, and for making God his Father, he tells them that he wrought these things by the power of God, and that he shall do greater things; for that the dead shall, at his summons, be raised; and that he, by a power committed to him from his Father, shall judge them; and that he is sent by his Father, and that whoever shall hear his word, and believe in him that sent him, has eternal life. This though a clear description of the Messiah, yet we may observe, that here, to the angry Jews, who sought to kill him, he says not a word of his kingdom, nor so much as names the Messiah; but yet that he is the Son of God, and sent from God, he refers them to the testimony of John the Baptist; to the testimony of his own miracles, and of God himself in the voice from heaven, and of the Scriptures, and of Moses. He leaves them to learn from these the truth they were to believe, that is that he was the Messiah sent from God. This you may read more at large, John v. 1—47.

The next place where we find him preaching was on the mount, Matt. v. and Luke vi. This is by far the longest sermon we have of his, anywhere; and, in all likelihood, to the greatest auditory: for it appears to have been to the people gathered to him from Galilee, and Judea, and Jerusalem, and from beyond Jordan, and that came out of Idumea, and from Tyre and Sidon, mentioned Mark iii. 7, 8. and Luke vi. 17. But in this whole sermon of his, we do not find one word of believing, and therefore no mention of the Messiah, or any intimation to the people who himself was. The reason whereof we may gather from Matt. xii. 16, where "Christ forbids them to make him known;" which supposes them to know already who he was. For that this 12th chapter of St. Matthew ought to precede the sermon in the mount, is plain, by comparing it with Mark ii. beginning at ver. 13, to Mark iii. 8, and comparing those chapters of St. Mark with Luke vi. And I desire my reader, once for all, here to take notice that I have all along observed the order of time in our Savior's preaching, and have not, as I think, passed by any of his discourses. In this sermon, our Savior only teaches them what were the laws of his kingdom, and what they must do who were admitted into it, of which I shall have occasion to speak more at large in another place, being at present only inquiring what our Savior proposed as matter of faith to be believed.

After this, John the Baptist sends to him this message, Luke vii. 19, asking, "Are you he that should come, or do we expect another?" That is, in short, Are you the Messiah? And if you are, why do you let me, your forerunner, languish in prison? Must I expect deliverance from any other? To which Jesus returns this answer, ver. 22, 23, "Tell John what you have seen and heard; the blind see, the lame walk, the lepers are cleansed, the deaf hear, the dead are raised, to the poor the gospel is preached; and blessed is he who is not offended in me." What it is to be "offended, or scandalized in him," we may see by comparing Matt. xiii. 28, and Mark iv. 17, with Luke viii. 13. For what the two first call "scandalized," the last call "standing off from, or forsaking," i.e. not receiving him as the Messiah (vid. Mark vi. 1—6.) or revolting from him. Here Jesus refers John, as he did the Jews before, to the testimony of his miracles, to know who he was; and this was generally his preaching, whereby he declared himself to be the Messiah, who was the only prophet to come, whom the Jews had any expectation of; nor did they look for any other person to be sent to them with the power of miracles, but only the Messiah. His miracles, we see by his answer to John the Baptist, he thought a sufficient declaration among them, that he was the Messiah. And therefore, upon his curing the possessed of the devil, the dumb, and blind, Matt. xii. the people, who saw the miracles, said, ver. 23, "Is not this the son of David?" As much as to say, Is not this the Messiah? Whereat the Pharisees being offended, said, "He cast out devils by Beelzebub." Jesus, showing the falsehood and vanity of their blasphemy, justifies the conclusion the people made from this miracle, saying, ver. 28, that his casting out devils by the Spirit of God, was evidence that the kingdom of the Messiah was come.

One thing more there was in the miracles done by his disciples, which showed him to be the Messiah: that they were done in his name. "In the name of Jesus of "Nazareth, rise up and walk," says St. Peter to the lame man, whom he cured in the temple, Acts iii. 6. And how far the power of that name reached, they themselves seem to wonder, Luke x. 17. "And the seventy returned again with joy, saying, Lord, even the devils are subject to us in your name."

From this message from John the Baptist, he takes occasion to tell the people that John was the forerunner of the Messiah; that from the time of John the Baptist the kingdom of the Messiah began; to which time all the prophets and the law pointed, Luke vii. and Matt. xi.

Luke viii. 1, "Afterwards he went through every city and village, preaching and showing the good tidings of the Kingdom of God." Here we see as everywhere, what his preaching was, and consequently what was to be believed.

Soon after, he preaches from a boat to the people on the shore. His sermon at large we may read, Matt. xiii. Mark iv. and Luke viii. But this is very observable, that this second sermon of his, here, is quite different from his former in the mount: for that was all so plain and intelligible, that nothing could be more so; whereas this is all so involved in parables, that even the apostles themselves did not understand it. If we inquire into the reason of this, we shall possibly have some light, from the different subjects of these two sermons. There he preached to the people only morality; clearing the precepts of the law from the false glosses which were received in those days, and setting forth the duties of a good life in their full obligation and extent, beyond what the judiciary laws of the Israelites did, or the civil laws of any country could prescribe, or take notice of. But here, in this sermon by the seaside, he speaks of nothing but the kingdom of the Messiah, which he does all in parables. One reason whereof St. Matthew gives us, chap. xiii. 35, "That it might be fulfilled which was spoken by the prophets," saying, "I will open my mouth in parables; I will utter things that have been kept secret from the foundations of the world." Another reason our Savior himself gives of it, ver. 11, 12, Because to you is given to know the mysteries of the kingdom of heaven, but to them it is not given. For whosoever has, to him shall be given, and he shall have more abundantly; but whosoever has not," i.e. improves not the talents that he has, "from him shall be taken away even that he has."

One thing it may not be amiss to observe, that our Savior here, in the explanation of the first of these parables to his apostles, calls the preaching of the kingdom of the Messiah, simply, "The word," and Luke viii. 21, "The word of God:" from whence St. Luke, in the Acts, often mentions it under the name of the "word," and "the word of God," as we have elsewhere observed. To which I shall here add that of Acts viii. 4, "Therefore they that were scattered abroad, went everywhere preaching the word;" which word, as we have found by examining what they preached all through their history, was nothing but this, that "Jesus was the Messiah:" I mean, this was all the doctrine they proposed to be believed: for what they taught, as well as our Savior, contained a great deal more; but that concerned practice, and not belief. And therefore our Savior says, in the place before quoted, Luke viii. 21, "they are my mother and my brethren, who hear the word of God, and do it:" obeying the law of the Messiah their king being no less required, than their believing that Jesus was the Messiah, the king and deliverer that was promised them.

Matt. ix. 13, we have an account again of this preaching; what it was, and how: "And Jesus went about all the cities and villages, teaching in their synagogues, and preaching the gospel of the kingdom, and healing every sickness and every disease among the people." He acquainted them, that the kingdom of the Messiah was come, and left it to his miracles to instruct and convince them, that he was the Messiah.

Matt. x. when he sent his apostles abroad, their commission to preach we have, ver. 7, 8, in these words: "As you go, preach saying, The kingdom of heaven is at hand: heal the sick," etc. All that they had to preach was, that the kingdom of the Messiah was come.

Whosoever should not receive them, the messengers of these good tidings, nor hearken to their message, incurred a heavier doom than Sodom and Gomorrah, at the Day of Judgment, ver. 14, 15. But ver. 32, "Whosoever shall confess me before men; I will confess him before my Father who is in heaven." What this confessing of Christ is, we may see by comparing John xii. 42. with ix. 22. "Nevertheless, among the chief rulers also many believed on him; but because of the Pharisees they did not confess him, lest they should be put out of the synagogue. And chap. ix. 22, "These words spoke his parents, because they feared the Jews; for the Jews had agreed already, that if any man did confess that he was the Messiah, he should be put out of the synagogue." By which places it is evident, that to confess him was to confess that he was the Messiah. From which, give me leave to observe also, (what I have cleared from other places, but cannot be too often remarked, because of the different sense has been put upon that phrase) that is "that believing on, or in him," (for εἰς αὐτὸν is rendered either way by the English translation,) signifies believing that he was the Messiah. For many of the rulers (the text says) "believed on him:" but they durst not confess what they believed, "for fear they should be put out of the synagogue." Now the offence, for which it was agreed that anyone should be put out of the synagogue, was, if he "did confess, that Jesus was the Messiah." Hence we may have a clear understanding of that passage of St. Paul to the Romans, where he tells them positively, what is the faith he preaches, Rom. x. 8, 9, "That is the word of faith which we preach, that if you shall confess with your mouth the Lord Jesus, and believe in your heart, that God has raised him from the dead, you shall be saved;" and that also of 1 John iv. 14, 15, "We have seen, and do testify, that the Father sent the Son to be the Savior of the world: whosoever shall confess, that Jesus is the Son of God, God dwells in him, and he in God." Where confessing Jesus to be the Son of God, is the same with confessing him to be the Messiah; those two expressions being understood among the Jews to signify the same thing, as we have shown already.

How calling him the Son of God, came to signify that he was the Messiah, would not be hard to show. But it is enough, that it appears plainly, that it was so used, and had that import among the Jews at that time: which if anyone desires to have further evidenced to him, he may add Matt. xxvi. 63. John vi. 69. and xi. 27. and xx. 31. to those places before occasionally taken notice of.

As was the apostle's commission, such was their performance; as we read, Luke xi. 6, "They departed and went through the towns, preaching the gospel, and healing everywhere." Jesus bid them preach,

"Saying, The kingdom of heaven is at hand." And St. Luke tells us, they went through the towns preaching the gospel; a word which in Saxon answers well the Greek εὐαγγέλιον, and signifies, as that does, "good news." So that what the inspired writers call the gospel, is nothing but the good tidings, that the Messiah and his kingdom was come; and so it is to be understood in the New Testament, and so the angel calls it, "good tidings of great joy," Luke ii. 10, bringing the first news of our Savior's birth. And this seems to be all that his disciples were at that time sent to preach.

So, Luke ix. 59, 60, to him that would have excused his present attendance, because of burying his father; "Jesus said unto him, let the dead bury their dead, but go you and preach the Kingdom of God." When I say, this was all they were to preach, I must be understood that this was the faith they preached; but with it they joined obedience to the Messiah, whom they received for their king. So likewise, when he sent out the seventy, Luke x. their commission was in these words, ver. 9, "Heal the sick, and say unto them, the Kingdom of God is come nigh unto you."

After the return of his apostles to him, he sits down with them on a mountain; and a great multitude being gathered about them, St. Luke tells us, chap. ix. 11, "The people followed him, and he received them, and spoke unto them of the Kingdom of God, and healed them that had need of healing." This was his preaching to this assembly, which consisted of five thousand men, besides women and children: all which great multitude he fed with five loaves and two fishes, Matt. xiv. 21. And what this miracle wrought upon them, St. John tells us, chap. vi. 14, 15, "Then these men, when they had seen the miracle that Jesus did, said, This is of a truth that prophet that should come into the world," i.e. the Messiah. For the Messiah was the only person that they expected from God, and this the time they looked for him. And hence John the Baptist, Matt. xi. 3, styles him, "He that should come;" as in other places, "come from God," or "sent from God," are phrases used for the Messiah.

Here we see our Savior keep to his usual method of preaching: he speaks to them of the Kingdom of God, and does miracles; by which they might understand him to be the Messiah, whose kingdom he spoke of. And here we have the reason also, why he so much concealed himself, and forbore to own his being the Messiah. For what the consequence was, of the multitude's but thinking him so, when they were got together, St. John tells us in the very next words: "When Jesus then perceived, that they would come and take him by force to make him a king, he departed again into a mountain himself alone." If they were so ready to set him up for their king, only because they gathered from his miracles that he was the Messiah, while he himself said nothing of it: what would not the people have done, and what would not the scribes and Pharisees have had an opportunity to accuse him of, if he had openly professed himself to have been the Messiah, that king they looked for? But this we have taken notice of already.

From hence going to Capernaum, whither he was followed by a great part of the people, whom he had the day before so miraculously fed; he, upon the occasion of their following him for the loaves, bids them seek for the meat that endures to eternal life: and thereupon, John vi. 22—69, declares to them his being sent from the Father; and that those who believed in him should be raised to eternal life: but all this very much involved in a mixture of allegorical terms of eating, and of bread; bread of life, which came down from heaven, etc. Which is all comprehended and expounded in these short and plain words, ver. 47 and 54, "Verily, verily, I say unto you, he that believeth on me has everlasting life, and I will raise him up at the last day." The sum of all which discourse is, that he was the Messiah sent from God; and that those who believed him to be so, should be raised from the dead at the last day, to eternal life. These whom he spoke to here were of those who, the day before, would by force have made him king; and therefore it is no wonder he should speak to them of himself, and his kingdom and subjects, in obscure and mystical terms; and such as should offend those who looked for nothing but the grandeur of a temporal kingdom in this world, and the protection and prosperity they had promised themselves under it. The hopes of such a kingdom, now that they had found a man that did miracles, and therefore concluded to be the Deliverer they expected; had the day before almost drawn them into an open insurrection, and involved our Savior in it. This he thought fit to put a stop to; they still following him, it is like, with the same design. And therefore, though he here speaks to them of his kingdom, it was in a way that so plainly confused their expectation, and shocked them, that when they found themselves disappointed of those vain hopes, and that he talked of their eating his flesh, and drinking his blood, that they might have life; the Jews said, ver. 52, "How can this man give us his flesh to eat? And many, even of his disciples said, it was a hard saying: Who can hear it?" And so were scandalized in him, and forsook him, ver. 60, 66. But what the true meaning of this discourse of our Savior was, the confession of St. Peter, who understood it better, and answered for the rest of the apostles, shows: when Jesus answered him, ver. 67, "Will you also go away?" Then Simon Peter answered him, "Lord, to whom shall we go? You have the words of eternal life:" i.e. you teach us the way to attain eternal life; and accordingly, "we believe, and are sure, that you are the Messiah, the Son of the living God." This was the eating his flesh and drinking his blood, whereby those who did so had eternal life.

Sometime after this, he inquires of his disciples, Mark viii. 27, who the people took him for? They telling him, "for John the Baptist," or one of the old prophets risen from the dead; he asked, what they themselves thought. And here again, Peter answers in these words, Mark viii. 29, "You are the Messiah," Luke ix. 20, "The Messiah of God." And Matt. xvi. 16, "You are the Messiah, the Son of the living God:" Which expressions, we may hence gather, amount to the same thing. Whereupon our Savior tells Peter, Matt. xvi. 17, 18, That this was such a truth "as flesh and blood could not reveal to him, but only his Father who was in heaven;" and that this was the foundation, on which he was "to build his church:" by all the parts of which passage it is more than probable, that he had never yet told his apostles in direct words, that he was the Messiah; but that they had gathered it from his life and miracles. For which we may imagine to ourselves this probable reason; because that, if he had familiarly, and in direct terms, talked to his apostles in private, that he was the Messiah the Prince, of whose kingdom he preached so much in public everywhere; Judas, whom he knew false and treacherous, would have been readily made use of, to testify against him, in a matter that would have been really criminal to the Roman governor. This, perhaps, may help to clear to us that seemingly abrupt reply of our Savior to his apostles, John vi. 70, when they confessed him to be the Messiah: I will, for the better explaining of it, set down the passage at large. Peter having said, "We believe and are sure that you are the Messiah, the Son of the living God; Jesus answered them, have not I chosen you twelve, and one of you is διάολος?" This is a reply, seeming at first sight, nothing to the purpose; when yet it is sure all our Savior's discourses were wise and pertinent. It seems therefore to me to carry this sense, to be understood afterwards by the eleven (as that of destroying the temple, and raising it again in three days was) when they should reflect on it, after his being betrayed by Judas: you have confessed, and believe the truth concerning me; I am the Messiah your king: but do not wonder at it, that I have never openly declared it to you; for among you twelve, whom I have chosen to be with me, there is one who is an informer, or false accuser, (for so the Greek word signifies, and may, possibly, here be so translated, rather than devil) who, if I had owned myself in plain words to have been the "Messiah, the king of Israel," would have betrayed me, and informed against me.

That he was yet cautious of owning himself to his apostles, positively, to be the Messiah, appears father from the manner wherein he tells Peter, ver. 18, that he will build his church upon that confession of his, that he was the Messiah: I say unto you, "You are Cephas," or a rock, "and upon this rock I will build my church, and the gates of hell shall not prevail against it." Words too doubtful to be laid hold on against him, as a testimony that he professed himself to be the Messiah; especially if we join with them the following words, ver. 19, "And I will give you the keys of the kingdom of heaven, and what you shall bind on earth, shall be bound in heaven; and what you shall loose on earth, shall be loosed in heaven." Which being said personally to Peter, render the foregoing words of our Savior (wherein he declares the fundamental article of his church to be the believing him to be the Messiah) the more obscure and doubtful, and less liable to be made use of against him; but yet such as might afterwards be understood. And for the same reason, he yet, here again, forbids the apostles to say that he was the Messiah, ver. 20.

From this time (say the evangelists) "Jesus began to show to his disciples," i.e. his apostles, (who are often called disciples,) "that he must go to Jerusalem, and suffer many things from the elders, chief priests, and scribes; and be killed, and be raised again the third day," Matt. xvi. 21. These, though all marks of the

Messiah, yet how little understood by the apostles, or suited to their expectation of the Messiah, appears from Peter's rebuking him for it in the following words, Matt. xvi. 22. Peter had twice before owned him to be the Messiah, and yet he cannot here bear that he should suffer, and be put to death, and be raised again. Whereby we may perceive, how little yet Jesus had explained to the apostles what personally concerned himself. They had been a good while witnesses of his life and miracles: and thereby being grown into a belief that he was the Messiah, were, in some degree, prepared to receive the specifics that were to fill up that character, and answer the prophecies concerning him. This, from henceforth, he began to open to them (though in a way which the Jews could not form an accusation out of;) the time of the accomplishment of all, in his sufferings, death, and resurrection, now drawing on. For this was in the last year of his life: he being to meet the Jews at Jerusalem but once more at the Passover, and then they should have their will upon him: and, therefore, he might now begin to be a little more open concerning himself: though yet so, as to keep himself out of the reach of any accusation, that might appear just or weighty to the Roman deputy.

After his reprimand to Peter, telling him, "That he savored not the things of God, but of man," Mark viii. 34, he calls the people to him, and prepares those, who would be his disciples, for suffering, telling them, ver. 38, "Whosoever shall be ashamed of me and my words in this adulterous and sinful generation, of him also shall the Son of man be ashamed, when he comes in the glory of his Father, with the holy angels:" and then subjoins, Matt. xvi. 27, 28, two great and solemn acts, wherein he would show himself to be the Messiah, the king: "For the Son of man shall come in the glory of his Father, with his angels; and then he shall render to every man according to his works." This is evidently meant of the glorious appearance of his kingdom, when he shall come to judge the world at the last day; described more at large, Matt. xxv. "When the Son of man shall come in his glory, and all the holy angels with him, then shall he sit upon the throne of his glory. Then shall the King say to them on his right hand," etc.

But what follows in the place above quoted, Matt. xvi. 28, "Verily, verily, there be some standing here, who shall not taste of death, till they see the Son of man coming in his kingdom;" importing that dominion, which some there should see him exercise over the nation of the Jews; was so covered, by being annexed to the preaching, ver. 27, (where he spoke of the manifestation and glory of his kingdom, at the day of judgment,) that though his plain meaning here in ver. 28, be, that the appearance and visible exercise of his kingly power in his kingdom was so near, that some there should live to see it; yet if the foregoing words had not cast a shadow over these latter, but they had been left plainly to be understood, as they plainly signified; that he should be a King, and that it was so near, that some there should see him in his kingdom; this might have been laid hold on, and made the matter of a plausible and seemingly just accusation against him, by the Jews before Pilate. This seems to be the reason of our Savior's inverting here the order of the two solemn manifestations to the world, of his rule and power; thereby perplexing at present his meaning, and securing himself, as was necessary, from the malice of the Jews, which always lay at catch to entrap him, and accuse him to the Roman governor; and would, no doubt, have been ready to have alleged these words, "Some here shall not taste of death, till they see the Son of man coming in his kingdom," against him, as criminal, had not their meaning been, by the former verse, perplexed, and the sense at that time rendered unintelligible, and not applicable by any of his auditors to a sense that might have been prejudicial to him before Pontius Pilate. For how well the chief of the Jews were disposed towards him, St. Luke tells us, chap. xi. 54, "Laying wait for him, and seeking to catch something out of his mouth, that they might accuse him;" which may be a reason to satisfy us of the seemingly doubtful and obscure way of speaking, used by our Savior in other places; his circumstances being such, that without such a prudent carriage and reserve, he could not have gone through the work which he came to do; nor have performed all the parts of it, in a way correspondent to the descriptions given of the Messiah; and which would be afterwards fully understood to belong to him, when he had left the world.

After this, Matt. xvii. 10, etc. he, without saying it in direct words, begins, as it were, to own himself to his apostles to be the Messiah, by assuring them, that as the scribes, according to the prophecy of Malachi, chap. iv. 5, rightly said, that Elias was to usher in the Messiah; so indeed Elias was already come, though the Jews knew him not, and treated him ill; whereby "they understood that he spoke to them of John the Baptist," ver. 13. And a little after he somewhat more plainly intimates, that he is the Messiah, Mark ix. 41, in these words: "Whosoever shall give you a cup of water to drink in my name, because you belong to the Messiah." This, as I remember, is the first place where our Savior ever mentioned the name of Messiah; and the first time that he went so far towards the owning, to any of the Jewish nation, himself to be him.

In his way to Jerusalem, bidding one follow him, Luke ix. 59, who would first bury his father, ver. 60, "Jesus said unto him, Let the dead bury their dead; but go you and preach the Kingdom of God." And Luke x. 1, sending out the seventy disciples, he says to them, ver. 9, "Heal the sick, and say, The Kingdom of God is come nigh unto you." He had nothing else for these, or for his apostles, or anyone, it seems, to preach, but the good news of the coming of the kingdom of the Messiah. And if any city would not receive them, he bids them, ver. 10, "Go into the streets of the same, and say, Even the very dust of your city, which cleaves on us, do we wipe off against you; notwithstanding, be you sure of this, that the Kingdom of God is come nigh unto you." This they were to take notice of, as that which they should dearly answer for, that is that they had not with faith received the good tidings of the kingdom of the Messiah.

After this, his brethren say unto him, John vii. 2, 3, 4, (the feast of tabernacles being near,) "Depart hence, and go into Judea, that your disciples also may see the works that you doest: for there is no man that does anything in secret, and he himself seeks to be known openly. If you do these things, show yourself to the world." Here his brethren, which, the next verse tells us, "did not believe in him," seem to upbraid him with the inconsistency of his carriage; as if he designed to be received for the Messiah, and yet was afraid to show himself: to whom he justified his conduct (mentioned ver. 1.) in the following verses, by telling them, "That the world" (meaning the Jews especially) "hated him, because he testified of it, that the works thereof are evil; and that his time had not yet fully come," wherein to quit his reserve, and abandon himself freely to their malice and fury. Therefore, though he "went up unto the feast," it was "not openly, but, as it were, in secret," ver. 10. And here, coming into the temple about the middle of the feast, he justifies his being sent from God; and that he had not done anything against the law, in curing the man at the pool of Bethesda, John v. 1—16, on the Sabbath-day; which, though done above a year and a half before, they made use of as a pretence to destroy him. But what was the true reason of seeking his life, appears from what we have in this vii chapter, ver. 25—34, "Then said some of them at Jerusalem, Is not this he whom they seek to kill? But lo, he speaketh boldly, and they say nothing unto him. Do the rulers know indeed, that this is the very Messiah? Howbeit, we know this man whence he is; but when the Messiah comes, no man knows whence he is. Then cried Jesus in the temple, as he taught, You both know me and you know whence I am: and I am not come of myself, but he that sent me is true, whom you know not. But I know him; for I am from him, and he has sent me. Then they sought [an occasion] to take him, but no man laid hands on him, because his hour was not yet come. And many of the people believed on him, and said, When the Messiah comes, will he do more miracles than these, which this man has done? The Pharisees heard that the people murmured such things concerning him; and the Pharisees and chief priests sent officers to take him. Then said Jesus unto them, Yet a little while am I with you, and then I go to him that sent me: you shall seek me, and not find me; and where I am, there you cannot come. Then said the Jews among themselves, Where will he go, that we shall not find him?" Here we find that the great fault in our Savior, and the great provocation to the Jews, was his being taken for the Messiah; and doing such things as made the people "believe in him;" i.e. believe that he was the Messiah. Here also our Savior declares, in words very easy to be understood, at least after his resurrection, that he was the Messiah: for, if he were "sent from God," and did his miracles by the Spirit of God, there could be no doubt but he was the Messiah. But yet this declaration was in a way that the Pharisees and priests could not lay hold on, to make an accusation of, to the disturbance of his ministry, or the seizure of his person, how much soever they desired it: for his time was not yet come. The officers they had sent to apprehend him, charmed with his discourse, returned without laying hands on him, ver. 45, 46. And when the chief priests asked them, "Why they brought him not?" They answered, "Never man spoke like this man." Whereupon the Pharisees reply, "Are you also deceived? Have any of the rulers, or of the Pharisees, believed on him? But this people, who know not the law, are cursed." This shows what was meant "by believing on him," that is believing that he was the Messiah. For, say they, have any of the rulers, who are skilled in the law, or of the devout and learned Pharisees, acknowledged him to be the Messiah? For as for those who in the division among the people concerning him, say, "That he is the Messiah," they are ignorant and vile wretches, know nothing of the Scripture, and being accursed, are given up by God, to be deceived by this impostor, and to take him for the Messiah. Therefore, notwithstanding their desire to lay hold on him, he goes on; and ver. 37, 38, "In the last and great day of the feast, Jesus stood and cried, saying, If any man thirst, let him come unto me and drink: he that believeth on me, as the Scripture has said, out of his belly shall flow rivers of living water." And thus he here again declares himself to be the Messiah; but in the prophetic style, as we may see by the next verse of this chapter, and those places in the Old Testament, that these words of our Savior refer to.

In the next chapter, John viii. all that he says concerning himself, and what they were to believe, tends to this, that is that he was sent from God his Father; and that, if they did not believe that he was the Messiah, they should die in their sins: but this, in a way, as St. John observes, ver. 27, that they did not well understand. But our Savior himself tells them, ver. 28, "When you have lift up the Son of man, then you shall know that I am he."

Going from them, he cures the man born blind, whom meeting with again, after the Jews had questioned him, and cast him out, John ix. 35—38, "Jesus said to him, Do you believe on the Son of God? He answered, Who is he, Lord, that I might believe on him? And Jesus said unto him, You have both seen him, and it is he that talks with you. And he said, Lord, I believe." Here we see this man is pronounced a believer, when all that was proposed to him to believe, was that Jesus was "the Son of God," which was, as we have already shown, to believe that he was the Messiah.

In the next chapter, John x. 1—21, he declares the laying down of his life both for Jews and Gentiles; but in a parable which they understood not, ver. 6—20.

As he was going to the feast of the dedication, the Pharisees ask him, Luke xvii. 20, "When the Kingdom of God," i.e. of the Messiah, "should come?" He answers, That it should not come with pomp and observation, and great concourse; but that it was already begun among them. If he had stopped here, the sense had been so plain, that they could hardly have mistaken him; or have doubted, but that he meant, that the Messiah was already come, and among them; and so might have been prone to infer, that Jesus took upon him to be him. But here, as in the place before taken notice of, subjoining to this future revelation of himself, both in his coming to execute vengeance on the Jews, and in his coming to judgment, mixed together, he so involved his sense, that it was not easy to understand him. And therefore the Jews came to him again in the temple, John x. 23, and said, "How long do you make us doubt? If you be the Christ tell us plainly. Jesus answered, I told you, and you believed not: the works that I do in my Father's name, they bear witness of me. But you believed not, because you are not of my sheep, as I told you." The believing here, which he accuses them of not doing, is plainly their not believing him to be the Messiah, as the foregoing words evince; and in the same sense it is evidently meant in the following verses of this chapter.

From hence Jesus going to Bethabara, and thence returning into Bethany; upon Lazarus's death, John xi. 25—27, Jesus said to Martha, "I am the resurrection and the life; he that believeth in me, though he were dead, yet shall he live; and whosoever lives and believeth in me shall not die for ever." So I understand ἀποθάνῃ εἰς τὸν αἰῶνα, answerable to ζήσεται εἰς τὸν αἰῶνα, of the Septuagint, Gen. iii. 22, or John vi. 51, which we read right, in our English translation, "live forever." But whether this saying of our Savior here, can with truth be translated, "He that lives and believeth in me shall never die," will be apt to be questioned. But to go on, "Believe you this? She said unto him, Yes, Lord, I believe that you are the Messiah, the Son of God, which should come into the world." This she gives as a full answer to our Savior's demands; this being that faith, which, whoever had, wanted no more to make them believers.

We may observe father, in this same story of the raising of Lazarus, what faith it was our Savior expected, by what he says, ver. 41, 42, "Father, I thank you, that you have heard me; and I know that you hear me always. But because of the people who stand by, I said it, that they may believe that you have sent me." And what the consequence of it was, we may see, ver. 45, "Then many of the Jews who came to Mary, and had seen the things which Jesus did, believed on him;" which belief was, that he was "sent from the Father;" which, in other words, was, that he was the Messiah. That this is the meaning, in the evangelists, of the phrase, of "believing on him," we have a demonstration in the following words, ver. 47, 48, "Then gathered the chief priests and Pharisees a council, and said, What do we? For this man does many miracles; and if we let him alone, all men will believe on him." Those who here say, all men would believe on him, were the chief priests and Pharisees, his enemies, who sought his life, and therefore could have no other sense nor thought of this faith in him, which they spoke of; but only the believing him to be the Messiah: and that that was their meaning, the adjoining words show: "If we let him alone, all the world will believe on him;" i.e. believe him to be the Messiah. "And the Romans will come and take away both our place and nation." Which reasoning of theirs was thus grounded: If we stand still, and let the people "believe on him," i.e. receive him for the Messiah: they will thereby take him and set him up for their king, and expect deliverance by him; which will draw the Roman arms upon us, to the destruction of us and our country. The Romans could not be thought to be at all concerned in any other belief whatsoever, that the people might have on him. It is therefore plain, that "believing on him," was, by the writers of the gospel, understood to mean the "believing him to be the Messiah." The Sanhedrin therefore, ver. 53, 54, from that day forth consulted to put him to death. "Jesus therefore walked not yet" (for so the word ἔτι signifies, and so I think it ought here to be translated) "boldly," or open-faced, "among the Jews," i.e. of Jerusalem." Ἔτι cannot here be translated "no more," because, within a very short time after, he appeared openly at the Passover and by his miracles and speech declared himself more freely than ever he had done; and all the week before his passion, taught daily in the temple, Matt. xx. 17. Mark. x. 32. Luke xviii. 31, etc. The meaning of this place seems therefore to be this: that his time being not yet come, he durst not yet show himself openly and confidently before the scribes and Pharisees, and those of the Sanhedrin at Jerusalem, who were full of malice against him, and had resolved his death: "But went thence into a country near the wilderness, into a city called Ephraim, and there continued with his disciples," to keep himself out of the way until the Passover, "which was nigh at hand," ver. 55. In his return thither, he takes the twelve aside, and tells them before-hand what should happen to him at Jerusalem, whither they were now going; and that all things that are written by the prophets, concerning the Son of man, should be accomplished; that he should be betrayed to the chief priests and scribes: and that they should condemn him to death and deliver him to the Gentiles; that he should be mocked, and spit on, and scourged and put to death; and the third day he should rise again. But St. Luke tells us, chap. xviii. 34, That the apostles "understood none of these things, and this saying was hid from them; neither knew they the things which were spoken." They believed him to be the Son of God, the Messiah sent from the Father; but their notion of the Messiah was the same with the rest of the Jews, that he should be a temporal prince and deliverer: accordingly we see, Mark x. 35, that, even in this their last journey with him to Jerusalem, two of them, James and John, coming to him, and falling at his feet, said, "Grant unto us that we may sit one on your right hand, and the other on your left hand, in your glory:" or, as St. Matthew has it, chap. xx. 21, "in your kingdom." That which distinguished them from the unbelieving Jews, was, that they believed Jesus to be the very Messiah, and so received him as their King and Lord.

And now, the hour being come that the Son of man should be glorified, he, without his usual reserve, makes his public entry into Jerusalem, riding on a young ass! "As it is written, Fear not, daughter of Zion; behold, your King comes, sitting on an ass's colt." But "these things," says St. John, chap. xii. 16, "his disciples understood not, at the first; but when Jesus was glorified, then remembered they that these things were written of him, and that they had done these things unto him." Though the apostles believed him to be the Messiah, yet there were many occurrences of his life, which they understood not (at the time when they happened) to be foretold of the Messiah; which, after his ascension, they found exactly to quadrate. Thus according to what was foretold of him, he rode into the city, "all the people crying, Hosanna, blessed is the King of Israel, that comes in the name of the Lord." This was so open a declaration of his being the

Messiah, that, Luke xix. 39, "Some of the Pharisees from among the multitude said unto him, Master, rebuke your disciples." But he was so far now from stopping them, or disowning this acknowledgment of his being the Messiah, that he said unto them, "I tell you, that if these should hold their peace, the stones would immediately cry out." And again upon the like occasion of their crying, "Hosanna to the Son of David," in the temple, Matt. xxi. 15, 16, "When the chief priests and scribes were sore displeased, and said unto him, Hear you what they say? Jesus said unto them, Yes; have you never read, Out of the mouths of babes and sucklings you have perfected praise?" And now, ver. 14, 15, "He cures the blind and the lame openly in the temple. And when the chief priests and scribes saw the wonderful things that he did, and the children crying in the temple, Hosanna, they were enraged." One would not think that after the multitude of miracles that our Savior had now been doing for above three years together, the curing the lame and blind should so much move them. But we must remember that though his ministry had abounded with miracles, yet the most of them had been done about Galilee, and in parts remote from Jerusalem. There is but one left on record, hitherto done in that city; and that had so ill a reception, that they sought his life for it: as we may read John v. 16. And therefore we hear not of his being at the next Passover, because he was there only privately, as an ordinary Jew: the reason whereof we may read, John vii. 1, "After these things Jesus walked in Galilee; for he would not walk in Jewry, because the Jews sought to kill him."

Hence we may guess the reason why St. John omitted the mention of his being at Jerusalem, at the third Passover, after his baptism; probably because he did nothing memorable there. Indeed when he was at the feast of tabernacles, immediately preceding this his last Passover, he cured the man born blind: but it appears not to have been done in Jerusalem itself, but on the way, as he retired to the mount of Olives; for there seems to have been nobody by when he did it, but his apostles. Compare ver. 2. with ver. 8, 10, of John ix. This, at least, is remarkable, that neither the cure of this blind man, nor that of the other infirm man, at the Passover, above a twelve-month before, at Jerusalem, was done in the sight of the scribes, Pharisees, chief priests, or rulers. Nor was it without reason, that in the former part of his ministry, he was cautious of showing himself to them to be the Messiah. But now, that he was come to the last scene of his life, and that the Passover was come, the appointed time, wherein he was to complete the work he came for, in his death and resurrection, he does many things in Jerusalem itself before the face of the scribes, Pharisees, and whole body of the Jewish nation, to manifest himself to be the Messiah. And, as St. Luke says, chap. xix. 47, 48, "he taught daily in the temple: but the chief priests, and the scribes, and the chief of the people, sought to destroy him; and could not find what they might do; for all the people were very attentive to hear him." What he taught we are left to guess, by what we have found him constantly preaching elsewhere: but St. Luke tells us, chap. xx. 1, "He taught in the temple, and evangelized;" or, as we translate it, "preached the gospel;" which, as we have showed, was the making known to them the good news of the kingdom of the Messiah. And this we shall find he did, in what now remains of his history.

In the first discourse of his, which we find upon record, after this, John xii. 20, etc. he foretells his crucifixion, and the belief of all sorts, both Jews and Gentiles, on him after that. Whereupon the people say to him, ver. 34, "We have heard out of the law, that the Messiah abides for ever: and how say you, that the Son of man must be lifted up? Who is this Son of man?" In his answer, he plainly designs himself under the name of Light; which was what he had declared himself to them to be, the last time that they had seen him in Jerusalem. For then at the feast of tabernacles, but six months before, he tells them in the very place where he now is, that is in the temple, "I am the Light of the world; whosoever follows me shall not walk in darkness, but shall have the light of life;" as we may read, John viii. 12. And ix. 5, he says, "As long as I am in the world, I am the Light of the world." But neither here, nor anywhere else, does he, even in these four or five last days of his life, (though he knew his hour was come, and was prepared to his death, ver. 27, and scrupled not to manifest himself to the rulers of the Jews to be the Messiah, by doing miracles before them in the temple,) ever once in direct words own himself to the Jews to be the Messiah; though by miracles and other ways he did everywhere make it known unto them, so that it might be understood. This could not be without some reason; and the preservation of his life, which he came now to Jerusalem on purpose to lay down, could not be it. What other could it then be, but the same which had made him use caution in the former part of his ministry; so to conduct himself, that he might do the work which he came for, and in all parts answer the character given of the Messiah, in the law and the prophets? He had fulfilled the time of his ministry; and now taught and did miracles openly in the temple, before the rulers and the people, not fearing to be seized. But he would not be seized for anything that might make him a criminal to the government: and therefore he avoided giving those, who, in the division that was about him, inclined towards him, occasion of tumult for his sake: or to the Jews, his enemies, matter of just accusation, against him, out of his own mouth, by professing himself to be the Messiah, the King of Israel, in direct words. It was enough that by words and deeds he declared it so to them, that they could not but understand him; which it is plain they did, Luke xx. 16, 19. Matt. xxi. 45. But yet neither his actions, which were only doing of good; nor words, which were mystical and parabolic (as we may see, Matt. xxi. and xxii, and the parallel places of Matthew and Luke;) nor any of his ways of making himself known to be the Messiah; could be brought in testimony, or urged against him, as opposite or dangerous to the government. This preserved him from being condemned as a criminal; and procured him a testimony from the Roman governor, his judge, that he was an innocent man, sacrificed to the envy of the Jewish nation. So that he avoided saying that he was the Messiah, that to those who would call to mind his life and death, after his resurrection, he might the more clearly appear to be so. It is father to be remarked, that though he often appeals to the testimony of his miracles, who he is, yet he never tells the Jews, that he was born at Bethlehem, to remove the prejudice that lay against him, while he passed for a Galilean, and which was urged as a proof that he was not the Messiah, John vii. 41, 42. The healing of the sick, and doing good miraculously, could be no crime in him, nor accusation against him. But the naming of Bethlehem for his birth-place might have wrought as much upon the mind of Pilate, as it did on Herod's; and have raised a suspicion in Pilate, as prejudicial to our Savior's innocence as Herod was to the children born there. His pretending to be born at Bethlehem, as it was liable to be explained by the Jews could not have failed to have met with a sinister interpretation in the Roman governor, and have rendered Jesus suspected of some criminal design against the government. And hence we see, that when Pilate asked him, John xix. 9, "Whence are you? Jesus gave him no answer."

Whether our Savior had not an eye to this straightness, this narrow room that was left to his conduct, between the new converts and the captious Jews, when he says, Luke xii. 50, "I have a baptism to be baptized with, and πῶς συνέχομαι, how am I distressed until it be accomplished!" I leave to be considered. "I am come to send fire on the earth," says our Savior, "and what if it be already kindled?" i.e. There begin already to be divisions about me, John vii. 12, 43, and ix. 16, and x. 19. And I have not the freedom, the latitude, to declare myself openly to be the Messiah; though I am he, that must not be spoken on, until after my death. My way to my throne is closely hedged in on every side, and much straitened; within which I must keep, until it bring me to my cross in its due time and manner; so that it do not cut short the time, nor cross the end of my ministry.

And therefore, to keep up this inoffensive character, and not to let it come within the reach of accident or calumny, he withdrew, with his apostles, out of the town, every evening; and kept himself retired out of the way, Luke xxi. 37. "And in the day-time he was teaching in the temple, and every night he went out and abode in the mount, that is called the Mount of Olives," that he might avoid all concourse to him in the night, and give no occasion of disturbance, or suspicion of himself, in that great conflux of the whole nation of the Jews, now assembled in Jerusalem at the Passover.

But to return to his preaching in the temple: he bids them, John xii. 36, "To believe in the Light, while they have it." And he tells them, ver. 46, "I am the Light come into the world, that everyone who believes in me, should not remain in darkness;" which believing in him, was the believing him to be the Messiah, as I have elsewhere showed.

The next day, Matt. xxi. he rebukes them for not having believed John the Baptist, who had testified that he was the Messiah. And then, in a parable, declares himself to be the "Son of God," whom they should destroy; and that for it God would take away the kingdom of the Messiah from them, and give it to the Gentiles. That they understood him thus, is plain from Luke xxi. 16, "And when they heard it, they said, God forbid." And ver. 19, "For they knew that he had spoken this parable against them."

Much to the same purpose was his next parable, concerning "the kingdom of heaven," Matt. xxi. 1—10. That the Jews not accepting of the kingdom of the Messiah, to whom it was first offered, other should be brought in.

The scribes and Pharisees and chief priests, not able to bear the declaration he made of himself to be the Messiah (by his discourses and miracles before them, ἔμπροσθεν αὐτῶν, John xii. 37, which he had never done before) impatient of his preaching and miracles, and being unable otherwise to stop the increase of his followers, (for, "said the Pharisees among themselves, Perceive you how you prevail nothing? Behold, the world is gone after him,") John xii. 19. So that "the chief priests, and the scribes, and the chief of the people sought to destroy him," the first day of his entrance into Jerusalem, Luke xix. 47. The next day again, they were intent upon the same thing, Mark xi. 17, 18, "And he taught in the temple; and the scribes and the chief priests heard it, and sought how they might destroy him; for they feared him, because all the people were astonished at his doctrine."

The next day but one, upon his telling them the kingdom of the Messiah should be taken from them, "The chief priests and scribes sought to lay hands on him the same hour, and they feared the people," Luke xx. 19. If they had so great a desire to lay hold on him, why did they not? They were the chief priests and the rulers, the men of power. The reason St. Luke plainly tells us in the next verse: "And they watched him, and sent forth spies, who should feign themselves just men, that they might take hold of his words, that so they might deliver him unto the power and authority of the governor." They wanted matter of accusation against him, to the power they were under; that they watched for, and that they would have been glad of, if they could have "entangled him in his talk;" as St. Matthew expresses it, chap. xxii. 15. If they could have laid hold on any word, that had dropped from him, that they might have rendered him guilty, or suspected to the Roman governor; that would have served their turn, to have laid hold upon him, with hopes to destroy him. For their power not answering their malice, they could not put him to death by their own authority, without the permission and assistance of the governor; as they confess, John xviii. 31, "It is not lawful for us to put any man to death." This made them so earnest for a declaration in direct words, from his own mouth, that he was the Messiah. It was not that they would more have believed in him, for such a declaration of himself, than they did for his miracles, or other ways of making himself known, which it appears they understood well enough. But they wanted plain direct words, such as might support an accusation, and be of weight before a heathen judge. This was the reason why they pressed him to speak out, John x. 24, "Then came the Jews round about him, and said unto him, How long do you hold us in suspense? If you be the Messiah, tell us plainly, παῤῥησίᾳ;" i.e. in direct words: for that St. John uses it in that sense we may see, chap. xi. 11—14, "Jesus said to them, Lazarus sleeps. His disciples said, If he sleeps, he shall do well. Howbeit, Jesus spoke of his death; but they thought he had spoken of taking rest in sleep. Then said Jesus to them plainly, παῤῥησίᾳ, Lazarus is dead." Here we see what is meant by παῤῥησίᾳ, plain, direct words, such as express the same thing without a figure; and so they would have had Jesus pronounce himself to be the Messiah. And the same thing they press again, Matt. xxvi. 63, the high priest adjuring him by the living God, to tell them whether he were the Messiah the Son of God; as we shall have occasion to take notice by-and-by.

This we may observe in the whole management of their design against his life. It turned upon this, that they wanted and wished for a declaration from him in direct words, that he was the Messiah; something from his own mouth that might offend the Roman power, and render him criminal to Pilate. In the 21st verse of this xx of Luke, "They asked him, saying, Master, we know that you say and teach rightly; neither accepts you the person of any, but teach the way of God truly. Is it lawful for us to give tribute to Cæsar, or no?" By this captious question they hoped to catch him, which way soever he answered. For if he had said they ought to pay tribute to Cæsar, it would be plain he allowed their subjection to the Romans; and so in effect disowned himself to be their King and Deliverer; whereby he would have contradicted what his carriage and doctrine seemed to aim at, the opinion that was spread among the people, that he was the Messiah. This would have quashed the hopes, and destroyed the faith of those that believed on him; and have turned the ears and hearts of the people from him. If on the other side he answered, No, it is not lawful to pay tribute to Cæsar, they had out of his own mouth wherewithal to condemn him before Pontius Pilate. But St. Luke tells us, ver. 23, "He perceived their craftiness, and said unto them, Why tempt you me?" i.e. Why do you lay snares for me? "You hypocrites, show me the tribute money;" so it is, Matt. xxii. 19, "Whose image and inscription has it? They said Cæsar's." He said unto them, "Render therefore to Cæsar the things that are Cæsar's, and to God the things that are God's." By the wisdom and caution of which unexpected answer, he defeated their whole design: "and they could not take hold of his words before the people; and they marveled at his answer, and held their peace." Luke xx. 26. "And leaving him, they departed." Matt. xxii. 22.

He having, by this reply (and what he answered to the Sadducees, concerning the resurrection, and to the lawyer about the first commandment, Mark xii.) answered so little to their satisfaction or advantage, they durst ask him no more questions, any of them. And now, their mouths being stopped, he himself begins to question them about the Messiah; asking the Pharisees, Matt. xxii. 41, "What think you of the Messiah? Who's son is he? They say unto him, the Son of David." Wherein though they answered right, yet he shows them in the following words, that, however they pretended to be studiers and teachers of the law, yet they understood not clearly the Scriptures concerning the Messiah; and thereupon he sharply rebukes their hypocrisy, vanity, pride, malice, covetousness, and ignorance; and particularly tells them, ver. 13, "You shut up the kingdom of heaven against men: for you neither go in yourselves, nor suffer you them that are entering, to go in." Whereby he plainly declares to them, that the Messiah was come, and his kingdom begun; but that they refused to believe in him themselves, and did all they could to hinder others from believing in him; as is manifest throughout the New Testament; the history whereof sufficiently explains what is meant here by "the kingdom of heaven," which the scribes and Pharisees would neither go into themselves, nor suffer others to enter into. And they could not choose but understand him, though he named not himself in the case.

Provoked anew by his rebukes, they get presently to council, Matt. xxvi. 3, 4. "Then assembled together the chief priests, and the scribes and the elders of the people, unto the palace of the high priest, who was called Caiaphas, and consulted that they might take Jesus by subtlety, and kill him. But they said, Not on the feast-day, lest there should be an uproar among the people. For they feared the people," says Luke, chap. xxii. 2.

Having in the night got Jesus into their hands, by the treachery of Judas, they presently led him away bound to Annas, the father-in-law of Caiaphas. Annas, probably, having examined him, and getting nothing out of him for his purpose, sends him away to Caiaphas, John xviii. 24, where the chief priests, the scribes, and the elders were assembled, Matt. xxvi. 57. John xviii. 13, 19. "The high priest then asked Jesus of his disciples, and of his doctrine. Jesus answered him, I spoke openly to the world: I ever taught in the synagogue, and in the temple, whither the Jews always resort, and in secret have I said nothing." A proof that he had not in private, to his disciples, declared himself in express words to be the Messiah, the Prince. But he goes on: "Why do you ask me?" Ask Judas, who has been always with me. "Ask them who heard me, what I have said unto them; behold, they know what I said." Our Savior, we see here, warily declines, for the reasons above-mentioned, all discourse of his doctrine. The Sanhedrin, Matt. xxvi. 59, "sought false witness against him:" but when "they found none that were sufficient," or came up to the point they desired, which was to have something against him to take away his life (for so I think the words ἴσαι and ἴση mean, Mark xiv. 56, 59.) they try again what they can get out of him himself, concerning his being the Messiah; which, if he owned in express words, they thought they should have enough against him at the tribunal of the Roman governor, to make him "læsæ majestatis reum," and to take away his life. They therefore say to him, Luke xxii. 67, "If you be the Messiah, tell us." Nay, as St. Matthew has it, the high priest adjures him by the living God, to tell him whether he was the Messiah. To which our Savior replies, "If I tell you, you will not believe; and if I also ask you, you will not answer me, nor let me go." If I tell you, and prove to you, by the testimony given me from heaven, and by the works that I have done among you, you will not believe in me, that I am the Messiah. Or if I should ask where the Messiah is to be born, and what state he should come in; how he should appear, and other things that you think in me are not reconcilable with the Messiah; you will not answer me, nor let me go, as one that has no pretence to be the Messiah, and you are not afraid should be received for such. But yet I tell you, "Hereafter shall the Son of man sit on the right hand of the power of God," ver. 70. "Then say they all, Are you then the Son of God? And he said unto them, You say that I am." By which discourse with them, related at large here by St. Luke, it is plain, that the answer of our Savior, set down by St. Matthew, chap. xxvi. 64, in these words, "You have said;" and by St. Mark, chap. xiv. 62, in these, "I am;" is in answer only to this question, "Are you then the Son of God?" and not to that other, "Are you the Messiah?" which preceded, and he had answered to before; though Matthew and Mark, contracting the story, set them down together, as if making but one question, omitting all the intervening discourse; whereas it is plain out of St. Luke, that they were two distinct questions, to which Jesus gave two distinct answers. In the first whereof he, according to his usual caution, declined saying in plain express words, that he was the Messiah; though in the latter he owned himself to be "the Son of God." Which though they, being Jews, understood to signify the Messiah, yet he knew could be no legal or weighty accusation against him before a heathen; and so it proved. For upon his answering to their question, "Are you then the Son of God? You say that I am;" they cry out, Luke xxii. 71, "What need we any further witness? For we ourselves have heard out of his own mouth." And so thinking they had enough against him, they hurry him away to Pilate.

Pilate asking them, John xviii. 29—32, "What accusation bring you against this man? They answered and said, If he were not a criminal we would not have delivered him up unto you." Then said Pilate unto them, "Take him, and judge him according to your law." But this would not serve their turn, who aimed at his life, and would be satisfied with nothing else. "The Jews therefore said unto him, It is not lawful for us to put any man to death." And this was also, "That the saying of Jesus might be fulfilled, which he spoke, signifying what death he should die." Pursuing therefore their design of making him appear, to Pontius Pilate, guilty of treason against Cæsar, Luke xxiii. 2, "They began to accuse him, saying, We found this fellow perverting the nation, and forbidding to give tribute to Cæsar; saying, that he himself is the Messiah, the King;" all which were inferences of theirs, from his saying, he was "the Son of God:" which Pontius Pilate finding (for it is consonant that he examined them to the precise words he had said), their accusation had no weight with him. However, the name of king being suggested against Jesus, he thought himself concerned to search it to the bottom, John xviii. 33—37. "Then Pilate entered again into the judgment hall, and called Jesus, and said unto him, Are you the king of the Jews? Jesus answered him, Do you say this of yourself, or did others tell it to you of me? Pilate answered, Am I a Jew? Your own nation and the chief priests have delivered you unto me: what have you done? Jesus answered, My kingdom is not of this world: if my kingdom were of this world, then would my servants fight, that I should not be delivered to the Jews; but now my kingdom is not from hence. Pilate therefore said unto him, Are you a king then? Jesus answered, You say that I am a king. For this end was I born, and for this cause I came into the world, that I should bear witness to the truth: everyone that is of the truth hearth my voice."

In this dialogue between our Savior and Pilate, we may observe, 1. That being asked, Whether he were "The king of the Jews?" he answered so, that though he deny it not, yet he avoids giving the least offense, that he had any design upon the government. For, though he allows himself to be a king, yet, to obviate any suspicion, he tells Pilate, "his kingdom is not of this world;" and evidences it by this, that if he had pretended to any title to that country, his followers, which were not a few, and were forward enough to believe him their king, would have fought for him, if he had had a mind to set himself up by force, or his kingdom were so to be erected. "But my kingdom," says he, "is not from hence," is not of this fashion, or of this place.

2. Pilate being, by his words and circumstances, satisfied that he laid no claim to his province, or meant any disturbance of the government; was yet a little surprised to hear a man in that poor garb, without retinue, or so much as a servant, or a friend, own himself to be a king; and therefore asks him, with some kind of wonder, "Are you a king then?"

3. That our Savior declares, that his great business into the world was, to testify and make good this great truth, that he was a king; i.e. in other words, that he was the Messiah.

4. That whoever were followers of truth, and got into the way of truth and happiness, received this doctrine concerning him, that is That he was the Messiah, their King.

Pilate being thus satisfied that he neither meant, nor could there arise, any harm from his pretence, whatever it was, to be a king; tells the Jews, ver. 31, "I find no fault in this man." But the Jews were the fiercer, Luke xxiii. 5. saying, "He stirred up the people to sedition, by his preaching through all Jewry, beginning from Galilee to this place." And then Pilate, learning that he was of Galilee, Herod's jurisdiction, sent him to Herod; to whom also "the chief priests and scribes," ver. 10, "vehemently accused him." Herod, finding all their accusations either false or frivolous, thought our Savior a bare object of contempt; and so turning him only into ridicule, sent him back to Pilate: who, calling unto him the chief priests, and the rulers, and the people, ver. 14, "Said unto them, You have brought this man unto me, as one that perverted the people; and behold, I having examined him before you, have found no fault in this man, touching these things whereof you accuse him; no, nor yet Herod; for I sent you to him: and lo, nothing worthy of death is done by him." And therefore he would have released him: "For he knew the chief priests had delivered him through envy," Mark xv. 10. And when they demanded Barabbas to be released, but as for Jesus, cried, "Crucify him;" Luke xxiii. 22; "Pilate said unto them the third time, Why? What evil has he done? I have found no cause of death in him; I will, therefore, chastise him, and let him go.

We may observe, in all this whole prosecution of the Jews, that they would rather have got it out of Jesus' own mouth, in express words, that he was the Messiah: which not being able to do, with all their heart and endeavor; all the rest that they could allege against him not amounting to a proof before Pilate, that he claimed to be king of the Jews; or that he had caused, or done anything towards a mutiny or insurrection among the people (for upon these two, as we see, their whole charge turned); Pilate again and again pronounced him innocent: for so he did a fourth, and a fifth time; bringing him out to them, after he had whipped him, John xix. 4, 6. And after all, "when Pilate saw that he could prevail nothing, but that rather a tumult was made, he took water, and washed his hands before the multitude, saying, I am innocent of the blood of this just man: see you to it:" Matt. xxvii. 24. Which gives us a clear reason of the cautious and wary conduct of our Savior, in not declaring himself, in the whole course of his ministry, so much as to his disciples, much less to the multitude, or to the rulers of the Jews, in express words, to be the Messiah the King; and why he kept himself always in prophetical or parabolic terms (he and his disciples preaching only the Kingdom of God, i.e. of the Messiah, to be come), and left to his miracles to declare who he was; though this was the truth, which he came into the world, as he says himself, John xviii. 37, to testify and which his disciples were to believe.

When Pilate, satisfied of his innocence, would have released him; and the Jews persisted to cry out, "Crucify him, crucify him," John xix. 6, "Pilate says to them, Take him yourselves, and crucify him: for I do not find any fault in him." The Jews then, since they could not make him a state criminal, by alleging his saying, that he was "the Son of God," say, by their law it was a capital crime, ver. 7. "The Jews answered to Pilate, We have a law, and by our law he ought to die; because he made himself the Son of God," i.e. because, by saying "he is the Son of God," he has made himself the Messiah, the prophet, which was to come. For we find no other law but that against false prophets, Deut. xviii. 20, whereby "making himself the Son of God," deserved death. After this, Pilate was the more desirous to release him, ver. 12, 13. "But the Jews cried out, saying, If you let this man go, you are not Cæsar's friend; whosoever maketh himself a king, speaketh against Cæsar." Here we see the stress of their charge against Jesus; whereby they hoped to take away his life, that is that he "made himself king." We see also upon what they grounded this accusation, that is because he had owned himself to be "the Son of God." For he had in their hearing, never made or professed himself to be a king. We see here, likewise, the reason why they were so desirous to draw from his own mouth a confession in express words, that he was the Messiah; that is that they might have what might be a clear proof that he did so. And, last of all, we see reason why, though in expressions which they understood, he owned himself to them to be the Messiah; yet he avoided declaring it to them in such words as might look criminal at Pilate's tribunal. He owned himself to be the Messiah plainly, to the understanding of the Jews; but in ways that could not, to the understanding of Pilate, make it appear that he had laid claim to the kingdom of Judea; or went about to make himself king of that country. But whether his saying that he was "the Son of God," was criminal by their law, that Pilate troubled not himself about.

He that considers what Tacitus, Suetonius, Seneca de benef. l. 3. c. 26. say of Tiberius and his reign, will find how necessary it was for our Savior, if he would not die as a criminal and a traitor, to take great heed to his words and actions; that he did or said not anything that might be offensive, or give the least indignation to the Roman government. It behooved an innocent man, who was taken notice of, for something extraordinary in him, to be very wary under a jealous and cruel prince, who encouraged information, and filled his reign with executions for treason; under whom, words spoken innocently, or in jest, if they could be misconstrued, were made treason, and prosecuted with a rigor, that made it always the same thing to be accused and condemned. And therefore we see, that when the Jews told Pilate, John xix. 12, that he should not be a friend to Cæsar, if he let Jesus go (for that whoever made himself king, was a rebel against Cæsar:) he asks them no more whether they would take Barabbas, and spare Jesus, but (though against his conscience) gives him up to death, to secure his own head.

One thing more there is, that gives us light into this wise and necessarily cautious management of himself, which manifestly agrees with it and makes a part of it: and that is, the choice of his apostles: exactly suited to the design and foresight of the necessity of keeping the declaration of the kingdom of the Messiah, which was now expected, within certain general terms, during his ministry. It was not fit to open himself too plainly or forwardly to the heady Jews, that he himself was the Messiah; that was to be left to the observation of those who would attend to the purity of his life, the testimony of his miracles, and the conformity of all with the predictions concerning him: by these marks, those he lived among were to find it out, without an express promulgation that he was the Messiah until after his death. His kingdom was to be opened to them by degrees, as well to prepare them to receive it, as to enable him to be long enough among them, to perform what was the work of the Messiah to be done; and fulfill all those several parts of what was foretold of him in the Old Testament, and we see applied to him in the New.

The Jews had no other thoughts of their Messiah, but of a mighty temporal prince, that should raise their nation into a higher degree of power, dominion, and prosperity than ever it had enjoyed. They were filled with the expectation of a glorious earthly kingdom. It was not, therefore, for a poor man, the son of a carpenter, and (as they thought) born in Galilee, to pretend to it. None of the Jews, no, not his disciples, could have borne this, if he had expressly avowed this at first, and began his preaching and the opening of his kingdom this way, especially if he had added to it, that in a year or two, he should die an ignominious death upon the cross. They are therefore prepared for the truth by degrees. First, John the Baptist tells them, "The Kingdom of God" (a name by which the Jews called the kingdom of the Messiah) "is at hand." Then our Savior comes, and he tells them "of the Kingdom of God;" sometimes that it is at hand, and upon some occasions, that it is come; but says, in his public preaching, little or nothing of himself. Then come the apostles and evangelists after his death, and they, in express words, teach what his birth, life, and doctrine had done before, and had prepared the well-disposed to receive, that is that "Jesus is the Messiah."

To this design and method of publishing the gospel, was the choice of the apostles exactly adjusted; a company of poor, ignorant, illiterate men; who, as Christ himself tells us, Matt. xi. 25, and Luke x. 21, were not of the "wise and prudent" men of the world: they were, in that respect, but mere children. These, convinced by the miracles they saw him daily do, and the blameless life he led, might be disposed to believe him to be the Messiah: and though they, with others, expected a temporal kingdom on earth, might yet rest satisfied in the truth of their master (who had honored them with being near his person) that it would come, without being too inquisitive after the time, manner, or seat of his kingdom, as men of letters, more studied in their rabbis, or men of business, more versed in the world, would have been forward to have been. Men, great or wise in knowledge, or ways of the world, would hardly have been kept from prying more narrowly into his design and conduct; or from questioning him about the ways and measures he would take, for ascending the throne; and what means were to be used towards it, and when they should in earnest set about it. Abler men, of higher births or thoughts, would hardly have been hindered from whispering, at least to their friends and relations, that their master was the Messiah; and that, though he concealed himself to a fit opportunity, and until things were ripe for it, yet they should, ere long, see him break out of his obscurity, cast off the cloud, and declare himself, as he was, King of Israel. But the ignorance and lowness of these good, poor men, made them of another temper. They went along, in an implicit trust on him, punctually keeping to his commands, and not exceeding his commission. When he sent them to preach the gospel, he bid them preach "the Kingdom of God" to be at hand; and that they did, without being more particular than he had ordered, or mixing their own prudence with his commands, to promote the kingdom of the Messiah. They preached it, without giving, or so much as intimating that their master was he: which men of another condition, and a higher education, would scarce have forborne to have done. When he asked them, who they thought him to be; and Peter answered, "The Messiah, the Son of God," Matt. xvi. 16, he plainly shows by the following words, that he himself had not told them so; and at the same time, ver. 20. forbids them to tell this opinion of him to anybody. How obedient they were to him in this, we may not only conclude from the silence of the evangelists concerning any such thing, published by them anywhere before his death; but from the exact obedience three of them paid to a like command of his. He takes Peter, James, and John, into a mountain; and there Moses and Elias coming to him, he is transfigured before them, Matt. xvii. 9. He charges them, saying, "See that you tell no man what you have seen, until the Son of man shall be risen from the dead." And St. Luke tells us, what punctual observers they were of his orders in this case, chap. ix. 36, "They kept silent and told no man in those days, any of those things which they had seen."

Whether twelve other men, of quicker parts, and of a station or breeding, which might have given them any opinion of themselves, or their own abilities, would have been so easily kept from meddling, beyond just what was prescribed them, in a matter they had so much interest in; and have said nothing of what they might, in human prudence, have thought would have contributed to their master's reputation, and made way for his advancement to his kingdom; I leave to be considered. And it may suggest matter of meditation, whether St. Paul was not for this reason, by his learning, parts, and warmer temper, better fitted for an apostle after, than during our Savior's ministry: and therefore, though a chosen vessel, was not by the divine wisdom called, until after Christ's resurrection.

I offer this only as a subject of magnifying the admirable plan of the divine wisdom, in the whole work of our redemption, as far as we are able to trace it, by the footsteps which God has made visible to human reason. For though it be as easy to omnipotent power to do all things by an immediate over-ruling will, and so to make any instruments work, even contrary to their nature, in subservience to his ends; yet his wisdom is not usually at the expense of miracles, (if I may so say,) but only in cases that require them, for the evidencing of some revelation or mission to be from him. He does constantly (unless where the confirmation of some truth requires it otherwise) bring about his purposes by means operating according to their natures. If it were not so, the course and evidence of things would be confounded, miracles would lose their name and force; and there could be no distinction between natural and supernatural.

There had been no room left to see and admire the wisdom, as well as innocence of our Savior, if he had rashly everywhere exposed himself to the fury of the Jews, and had always been preserved by a miraculous suspension of their malice, or a miraculous rescuing him out of their hands. It was enough for him once to escape from the men of Nazareth, who were going to throw him down a precipice, for him never to preach to them again. Our Savior had multitudes that followed him for the loaves; who barely seeing the miracles that he did, would have made him king. If to the miracles he did, he had openly added, in express words, that he was the Messiah, and the king they expected to deliver them, he would have had more followers, and warmer in the cause, and readier to set him up at the head of a tumult. These indeed God, by a miraculous influence, might have hindered from any such attempt: but then posterity could not have believed, that the nation of the Jews did, at that time, expect the Messiah, their king and deliverer; or that Jesus, who declared himself to be that king and deliverer, showed any miracles among them, to convince them of it; or did anything worthy to make him be credited or received. If he had gone about preaching to the multitude, which he drew after him, that he was the "Messiah, the king of Israel," and this had been evidenced to Pilate; God could indeed, by a supernatural influence upon his mind, have made Pilate pronounce him innocent, and not condemn him as a criminal, who had openly for three years together, preached sedition to the people, and endeavored to persuade them, that he was "the Messiah, their king," of the royal blood of David, come to deliver them. But then I ask, Whether posterity would not either have suspected the story, or that some arts had been used to gain that testimony from Pilate? Because he could not (for nothing) have been so favorable to Jesus, as to be willing to release so turbulent and seditious a man; to declare him innocent, and to cast the blame and guilt of his death, as unjust, upon the envy of the Jews.

But now, the malice of the chief priests, scribes and Pharisees; the headiness of the mob, animated with hopes, and raised with miracles; Judas's treachery, and Pilate's care of his government, and of the peace of his province, all working naturally as they should; Jesus, by the admirable wariness of his carriage, and an extraordinary wisdom, visible in his whole conduct; weathers all these difficulties, does the work he comes for, uninterruptedly goes about preaching his full appointed time, sufficiently manifests himself to be the Messiah, in all the specifics the Scriptures had foretold of him; and when his hour is come, suffers death: but is acknowledged, both by Judas that betrayed, and Pilate that condemned him, to die innocent. For, to use his own words, Luke xxiv. 46, "Thus it is written, and thus it behooved the Messiah to suffer." And of his whole conduct we have a reason and clear resolution in those words to St. Peter, Matt. xxvi. 53, "Do you think that I cannot now pray to my Father, and he shall presently give me more than twelve legions of angels? But how then shall the Scripture be fulfilled, that thus it must be?"

Having this clue to guide us, let us now observe, how our Savior's preaching and conduct comported with it in the last scene of his life. How cautious he had been in the former part of his ministry, we have already observed. We never find him to use the name of the Messiah but once, until he now came to Jerusalem, this last Passover. Before this, his preaching and miracles were less at Jerusalem) where he used to make but very short stays) than anywhere else. But now he comes six days before the feast, and is every day in the temple teaching; and there publicly heals the blind and the lame, in the presence of the scribes, Pharisees, and chief priests. The time of his ministry drawing to an end, and his hour coming, he cared not how much the chief priests, elders, rulers, and the Sanhedrin, were provoked against him by his doctrine and miracles: he was as open and bold in his preaching, and doing the works of the Messiah now at Jerusalem, and in the sight of the rulers, and of all the people; as he had been before cautious and reserved there, and careful to be little taken notice of in that place, and not to come in their way more than needs. All that he now took care of was, not what they should think of him, or design against him, (for he knew they would seize him,) but to say or do nothing that might be a just matter of accusation against him, or render him criminal to the governor. But, as for the grandees of the Jewish nation, he spares them not, but sharply now reprehends their miscarriages publicly in the temple; where he calls them more than once, "hypocrites;" as is to be seen, Matt. xxiii. And concludes all with no softer a compellation than "serpents," and "a generation of vipers."

After this severe reproof of the scribes and Pharisees, being retired with his disciples into the "Mount of Olives" over against the temple, and there foretelling the destruction of it; his disciples ask him, Matt. xxiv. 3, etc. "When it should be, and what should be the sign of his coming?" He says, to them, "Take heed that no man deceive you: for many shall come in my name," (i.e. taking on them the name and dignity of the Messiah, which is only mine,) saying, "I am the Messiah, and shall deceive many." But be not you by them misled, nor by persecution driven away from this fundamental truth, that I am the Messiah: "for many shall be scandalized," and apostatize; "but he that endures to the end, the same shall be saved: and this gospel of the kingdom shall be preached in all the world:" i.e. the good news of me, the Messiah, and my kingdom, shall be spread through the world. This was the great and only point of belief they were warned to stick to; and this is inculcated again, ver. 23—26, and Mark xiii. 21—23, with this emphatical application to them, in both these evangelists, "Behold, I have told you beforehand; remember, you are forewarned."

This was in answer to the apostles inquiry, concerning his "coming, and the end of the world," ver. 3. For so we translate τῆς συντελείας τ αἰῶνος. We must understand the disciples here to put their question, according to the notion and way of speaking of the Jews. For they had two worlds, as we translate it, ὁ νῦν αἰὼν, καὶ ὁ μέλλων αἰὼν; "the present world," and the "world to come." The Kingdom of God, as they called it, or the time of the Messiah, they called ὁ μέλλων αἰὼν, "the world to come," which they believed was to put an end to "this world;" and that then the just should be raised from the dead, to enjoy in that "new world" a happy eternity, with those of the Jewish nation, who should be then living.

These two things, that is the visible and powerful appearance of his kingdom, and the end of the world, being confounded in the apostles question, our Savior does not separate them, nor distinctly reply to them apart; but, leaving the inquirers in the common opinion, answers at once concerning his coming to take vengeance on the Jewish nation, and put an end to their church worship and commonwealth; which was their ὁ νῦν αἰὼν, "present world," which they counted should last until the Messiah came; and so it did, and then had an end put to it. And to this he joins his last coming to judgment, in the glory of his Father, to put a final end to this world, and all the dispensation belonging to the posterity of Adam upon earth. This joining them together, made his answer obscure, and hard to be understood by them then; nor was it safe for him to speak plainer of his kingdom, and the destruction of Jerusalem; unless he had a mind to be accused for having designs against the government. For Judas was among them: and whether no other but his apostles were comprehended under the name of "his disciples," who were with him at this time, one cannot determine. Our Savior, therefore, speaks of his kingdom in no other style, but that which he had all along hitherto used, that is "the Kingdom of God," Luke xxi. 31, "When you see these things come to pass, know you that the Kingdom of God is nigh at hand." And continuing on his discourse with them, he has the same expression, Matt. xxv. 1, "Then the kingdom of heaven shall be like unto ten virgins." At the end of the following parable of the talents, he adds, ver. 31, "When the Son of man shall come in his glory, and all the holy angels with him, then shall he sit upon the throne of his glory. And before him shall be gathered all the nations. And he shall set the sheep on his right hand, and the goats on his left. Then shall the King say," etc. Here he describes to his disciples the appearance of his kingdom, wherein he will show himself a king in glory upon his throne; but this in such a way, and so remote, and so unintelligible to an heathen magistrate; that, if it had been alleged against him, it would have seemed rather the dream of a crazy brain, than the contrivance of an ambitious or dangerous man, designing against the government: the way of expressing what he meant, being in the prophetic style, which is seldom so plain as to be understood, till accomplished. It is plain, that his disciples themselves comprehended not what kingdom he here spoke of, from their question to him after his resurrection, "Will you at this time restore again the kingdom unto Israel?"

Having finished these discourses, he prepares for the Passover, and eats it with his disciples; and at supper tells them, that one of them should betray him; and adds, John xiii. 19, "I tell it you now, before it comes, that when it is come to pass, you may know that I am." He does not say out, "the Messiah;" Judas should not have that to say against him, if he would; though that be the sense in which he uses this expression, ἐγὼ εἰμι, "I am," more than once. And that this is the meaning of it is clear from Mark xii. 6, Luke xxi. 8. In both which evangelists the words are, "For many shall come in my name, saying, ἐγὼ εἰμι, I am;" the meaning whereof we shall find explained in the parallel place of St. Matthew, chap. xxiv. 5, "For many shall come in my name, saying, ἐγὼ εἰμι ὁ Χριςὸς, I am the Messiah." Here, in this place of John xiii. Jesus foretells what should happen to him, that is that he should be betrayed by Judas; adding this prediction to the many other specifics of his death and suffering, which he had at other times foretold to them. And here he tells them the reason of these his predictions, that is that afterwards they might be a confirmation to their faith. And what was it that he would have them believe, and be confirmed in the belief of? Nothing but this, ὅτι ἐγὼ εἰμι ὁ Χριςὸς, "that he was the Messiah." The same reason he gives,

John xiv. 28, You have heard how I said unto you, I go away, and come again unto you: and now I have told you, before it comes to pass, that when it comes to pass, you might believe."

When Judas had left them, and was gone out, he talks a little freer to them of his glory and his kingdom, than ever he had previously. For now he speaks plainly of himself, and of his kingdom, John xiii. 31, "Therefore when he [Judas] was gone out, Jesus said, Now is the Son of man glorified, and God is also glorified in him. And, if God be glorified in him, God shall also glorify him in himself, and shall straightway glorify him." And Luke xxii. 29, "And I will appoint unto you a kingdom, as my Father has appointed unto me; that you may eat and drink with me at my table, in my kingdom." Though he has everywhere, all along through his ministry, preached the "gospel of the kingdom," and nothing else but that and repentance, and the duties of a good life: yet it has been always "the Kingdom of God," and "the kingdom of heaven:" and I do not remember, that "anywhere, until now, he uses any such expression, as my kingdom." But here now he speaks in the first person, "I will appoint you a kingdom," and, "in my kingdom:" and this we see is only to the eleven, now Judas was gone from them.

With these eleven, whom he was just now leaving, he has a long discourse, to comfort them for the loss of him; and to prepare them for the persecution of the world, and to exhort them to keep his commandments, and to love one another. And here one may expect all the articles of faith should be laid down plainly, if anything else were required of them to believe, but what he had taught them, and they believed already, that is "That he was the Messiah." John xiv. 1, "You believe in God, believe also in me." Ver. 29, "I have told you before it come to pass, that when it is come to pass, you may believe." It is believing on him without anything else. John xvi. 31, "Jesus answered them, Do you now believe?" This was in answer to their profession, ver. 30, "Now are we sure that you know all things, and need not that any man should ask you: by this we believe that you came forth from God."

John xvii. 20, "Neither pray I for these alone, but for them also which shall believe on me through their word." All that is spoke of believing, in this his last sermon to them, is only "believing on him," or believing that "he came from God;" which was no other than believing him to be the Messiah.

Indeed, John xiv. 9, our Savior tells Philip, "He that has seen me, has seen the Father." And adds, ver. 10, "Believe you not that I am in the Father, and the Father in me? The words that I speak unto you, I speak not of myself: but the Father that dwells in me, he does the works." Which being in answer to Philip's words, ver. 9, "Show us the Father," seem to import thus much: "No man has seen God at any time," he is known only by his works. And that he is my Father, and I the Son of God, i.e. the Messiah, you may know by the works I have done; which it is impossible I could do of myself, but by the union I have with God my Father. For that by being "in God," and "God in him," he signifies such an union with God, that God operates in and by him, appears not only by the words above cited out of ver. 10 (which can scarce otherwise be made coherent sense), but also from the same phrase, used again by our Savior presently after, ver. 20, "At that day," that is after his resurrection, when they should see him again, "you shall know that I am in the Father, and you in me, and I in you;" i.e. by the works that I shall enable you to do, through a power I have received from the Father: which whosoever sees me do, must acknowledge the Father to be in me; and whosoever sees you do, must acknowledge me to be in you. And therefore he says, ver. 12, "Verily, verily, I say unto you, he that believeth on me, the works that I do shall he do also, because I go unto my Father." Though I go away, yet I shall be in you, who believe in me; and you shall be enabled to do miracles also, for the carrying on of my kingdom, as I have done; that it may be manifested to others, that you are sent by me, as I have evidenced to you, that I am sent by the Father. And hence it is that he says, in the immediately preceding ver. 11, "Believe me that I am in the Father, and the Father in me; if not, believe me for the sake of the works themselves." Let the works that I have done convince you, that I am sent by the Father; that he is with me, and that I do nothing but by his will; and by virtue of the union I have with him; and that consequently I am the Messiah, who am anointed, sanctified, and separated by the Father, to the work for which he sent me.

To confirm them in this faith, and to enable them to do such works as he had done, he promises them the Holy Ghost, John xiv. 25, 26. "These things I have said unto you, being yet present with you."

But when I am gone, "The Holy Ghost, the Paraclet," (which may signify Monitor, as well as Comforter, or Advocate,) "which the Father shall send you in my name, he shall show you all things, and bring to your remembrance all things which I have said." So that considering all that I have said, and laying it together, and comparing it with what you shall see come to pass; you may be more abundantly assured, that I am the Messiah; and fully comprehend, that I have done and suffered all things foretold of the Messiah, and that were to be accomplished and fulfilled by him, according to the Scriptures. But be not filled with grief, that I leave you, John xvi. 7, "It is expedient for you, that I go away; for if I go not away, the Paraclet will not come unto you." One reason why, if he went not away, the Holy Ghost could not come, we may gather from what has been observed, concerning the prudent and wary carriage of our Savior all through his ministry, that he might not incur death with the least suspicion of a criminal. And therefore, though his disciples believed him to be the Messiah, yet they neither understood it so well, nor were so well confirmed in the belief of it, as after that, he being crucified and risen again, they had received the Holy Ghost; and with the gifts of the Holy Spirit, a fuller and clearer evidence and knowledge that he was the Messiah. They then were enlightened to see how his kingdom was such as the Scriptures foretold; though not such as they, till then, had expected. And now this knowledge and assurance, received from the Holy Ghost, was of use to them after his resurrection; when they could now boldly go about, and openly preach, as they did, that Jesus was the Messiah; confirming that doctrine by the miracles which the Holy Ghost empowered them to do. But until he was dead and gone, they could not do this. Their going about openly preaching, as they did after his resurrection, that Jesus was the Messiah, and doing miracles everywhere, to make it good, would not have consisted with that character of humility, peace and innocence, which the Messiah was to sustain, if they had done it before his crucifixion. For this would have drawn upon him the condemnation of a criminal, either as a stirrer of sedition against the public peace, or as a pretender to the kingdom of Israel. Hence we see, that they, who before his death preached only the "gospel of the kingdom;" that "the Kingdom of God was at hand;" as soon as they had received the Holy Ghost, after his resurrection, changed their style, and everywhere in express words declare, that Jesus is the Messiah, that King which was to come. This, the following words here in St. John xvi. 8—14, confirm; where he goes on to tell them, "And when he is come, he will convince the world of sin; because they believed not on me." Your preaching then, accompanied with miracles, by the assistance of the Holy Ghost, shall be a conviction to the world, that the Jews sinned in not believing me to be the Messiah. "Of righteousness," or justice; "because I go to my Father, and you see me no more." By the same preaching and miracles you shall confirm the doctrine of my ascension; and thereby convince the world, that I was that just one, who is, therefore, ascended to the Father into heaven, where no unjust person shall enter. "Of judgment; because the prince of this world is judged." And by the same assistance of the Holy Ghost you shall convince the world that the devil is judged or condemned by your casting of him out, and destroying his kingdom, and his worship, wherever you preach. Our Savior adds, "I have yet many things to say unto you, but you cannot bear them now." They were yet so full of a temporal kingdom, that they could not bear the discovery of what kind of kingdom his was, nor what a king he was to be: and therefore he leaves them to the coming of the Holy Ghost, for a father and fuller discovery of himself, and the kingdom of the Messiah; for fear they should be scandalized in him, and give up the hopes they now had in him, and forsake him. This he tells them, ver. 1, of this xvi chapter: "These things I have said unto you, that you may not be scandalized." The last thing he had told them, before his saying this to them, we find in the last verses of the preceding chapter: "When the Paraclet is come, the Spirit of truth, he shall witness concerning me." He shall show you who I am, and witness it to the world; and then, "You also shall bear witness, because you have been with me from the beginning." He shall call to your mind what I have said and done, that you may understand it, and know, and bear witness concerning me. And again here, John xvi. after he had told them they could not bear what he had more to say, he adds, ver. 13, "Howbeit, when the Spirit of truth is come, he will guide you into all truth; and he will show you things to come: he shall glorify me." By the Spirit, when he comes, you shall be fully instructed concerning me; and though you cannot yet, from what I have said to you, clearly comprehend my kingdom and glory, yet he shall make it known to you wherein it consists: and though I am now in a mean state, and ready to be given up to contempt, torment, and death, so that you know not what to think of it; yet the Spirit, when he comes, "shall glorify me," and fully satisfy you of my power and kingdom; and that I sit on the right hand of God, to order all things for the good and increase of it, till I come again at the last day, in the fullness of glory.

Accordingly, the apostles had a full and clear sight and persuasion of this, after they had received the Holy Ghost; and they preached it everywhere boldly and openly, without the least remainder of doubt or uncertainty. But that, even so late as this, they understood not his death and resurrection, is evident from ver. 17, 18, "Then said some of his disciples among themselves, What is it that he said unto us; A little while, and you shall not see me; and again, a little while, and you shall see me; and because I go to the Father? They said therefore, What is this that he said, A little while? We know not what he said." Upon which he goes on to discourse to them of his death and resurrection, and of the power they should have of doing miracles. But all this he declares to them in a mystical and involved way of speaking: as he tells them himself, ver. 25, "These things have I spoken to you in proverbs;" i.e. in general, obscure, enigmatic, or figurative terms (all which, as well as allusive apologues, the Jews called proverbs or parables). Hitherto my declaring of myself to you has been obscure, and with reserve: and I have not spoken of myself to you in plain and direct words, because you "could not bear it." A Messiah, and not a King, you could not understand: and a King living in poverty and persecution, and dying the death of a slave and criminal upon a cross; you could not put together. And I had told you in plain words, that I was the Messiah, and given you a direct commission to preach to others, that I professedly owned myself to be the Messiah, you and they would have been ready to have made a commotion, to have set me upon the throne of my father David, and to fight for me; and that your Messiah, your King, in whom are your hopes of a kingdom, should not be delivered up into the hands of his enemies, to be put to death; and of this Peter will instantly give you a proof. But "the time comes, when I shall no more speak unto you in parables; but I shall show unto you plainly of the Father." My death and resurrection, and the coming of the Holy Ghost, will speedily enlighten you, and then I shall make you know the will and design of my Father; what a kingdom I am to have, and by what means, and to what end, ver. 27. And this the Father himself will show unto you: "For he loves you, because you have loved me, and have believed that I came out from the Father." Because you have believed that I am "the Son of God, the Messiah;" that he has anointed and sent me; though it has not yet been fully discovered to you, what kind of kingdom it shall be, nor by what means brought about. And then our Savior, without being asked, explaining to them what he had said, and making them understand better what before they stuck at, and complained secretly among themselves that they understood not; they thereupon declare, ver. 30, "Now are we sure that you know all things, and need not that any man should ask you." It is plain, you know men's thoughts and doubts before they ask. "By this we believe that you came forth from God. Jesus answered, Do you now believe?" Notwithstanding that you now believe, that I came from God, and am the Messiah, sent by him: "Behold, the hour comes, yes, is now come, that you shall be scattered;" and as it is Matt. xxvi. 31, and "shall all be scandalized in me." What it is to be scandalized in him, we may see by what followed hereupon, if that which he says to St. Peter, Mark xiv. did not sufficiently explain it.

This I have been the more particular in; that it may be seen, that in this last discourse to his disciples (where he opened himself more than he had hitherto done; and where, if anything more was required to make them believers than what they already believed, we might have expected they should have heard of it) there were no new articles proposed to them, but what they believed before, that is that he was the Messiah, the Son of God, sent from the Father; though of his manner of proceeding, and his sudden leaving of the world, and some few specifics, he made them understand something more than they did before. But as to the main design of the gospel, that is that he had a kingdom, that he should be put to death, and rise again, and ascend into heaven to his Father, and come again in glory to judge the world; this he had told them: and so had acquainted them with the great counsel of God, in sending him the Messiah, and omitted nothing that was necessary to be known or believed in it. And so he tells them himself, John xv. 15, "Henceforth I call you not servants: for the servant knows not what his Lord does: but I have called you friends; for all things that I have heard of my Father, I have made known unto you;" though perhaps you do not so fully comprehend them, as you will shortly, when I am risen and ascended.

To conclude all, in his prayer, which shuts up this discourse, he tells the Father, what he had made known to his apostles; the result whereof we have John xvii. 8, "I have given unto them the words which you gave me, and they have received them, and they have believed that you didst send me." Which is, in effect, that he was the Messiah promised and sent by God. And then he prays for them, and adds, ver. 20, 21, "Neither pray I for these alone, but for them also who shall believe on me through their word." What that word was, through which others should believe in him, we have seen in the preaching of the apostles, all through the history of the Acts, that is this one great point, that Jesus was the Messiah. The apostles, he says, ver. 25, "know that you have sent me;" i.e. are assured that I am the Messiah. And in ver. 21 and 23, he prays, "That the world may believe" (which, ver. 23, is called knowing) "that you has sent me." So that what Christ would have believed by his disciples, we may see by this his last prayer for them, when he was leaving the world, as by what he preached while he was in it.

And, as a testimony of this, one of his last actions, even when he was upon the cross, was to confirm his doctrine, by giving salvation to one of the thieves that was crucified with him, upon his declaration that he believed him to be the Messiah: for so much the words of his request imported, when he said, "Remember me, Lord, when you comest into your kingdom," Luke xxiii. 42. To which Jesus replied, ver. 43, "Verily, I say unto you, To-day shall you be with me in paradise." An expression very remarkable: for as Adam, by sin, lost paradise, i.e. a state of happy immortality; here the believing thief, through his faith in Jesus the Messiah, is promised to be put in paradise, and so re-instated in an happy immortality.

Thus our Savior ended his life. And what he did after his resurrection, St. Luke tells us, Acts i. 3, That he showed himself to the apostles, "forty days, speaking things concerning the Kingdom of God." This was what our Savior preached in the whole course of his ministry, before his passion: and no other mysteries of faith does he now discover to them after his resurrection. All he says, is concerning the Kingdom of God; and what it was he said concerning that, we shall see presently out of the other evangelists; having first only taken notice, that when now they asked him, ver. 6, "Lord, wilt you at this time restore again the kingdom of Israel? He said unto them, ver. 7, it is not for you to know the times and the seasons, which the Father has put in his own power: but you shall receive power, after that the Holy Ghost is come upon you; and you shall be witnesses unto me, unto the utmost parts of the earth." Their great business was to be witnesses to Jesus, of his life, death, resurrection, and ascension; which, put together, were undeniable proofs of his being the Messiah. This was what they were to preach, and what he said to them, concerning the Kingdom of God; as will appear by what is recorded of it in the other evangelists.

When on the day of his resurrection he appeared to the two going to Emmaus, Luke xxiv. they declare, ver. 21, what his disciples faith in him was: "But we trusted that it had been he that should have redeemed Israel:" i.e. we believed that he was the Messiah, come to deliver the nation of the Jews. Upon this, Jesus tells them they ought to believe him to be the Messiah, notwithstanding what had happened: nay, they ought, by his sufferings and death, to be confirmed in that faith, that he was the Messiah. And ver. 26, 27, "Beginning at Moses and all the prophets, he expounded unto them, in all the Scriptures, the things concerning himself," how, "that the Messiah ought to have suffered these things, and to have entered into his glory." Now he applies the prophecies of the Messiah to himself, which we read not, that he did ever do before his passion. And afterwards appearing to the eleven, Luke xxiv. 36, he said unto them, ver. 44—47, "These are the words, which I spoke unto you, while I was yet with you, that all things must be fulfilled which are written in the law of Moses, and in the prophets, and in the psalms concerning me. Then he opened their understanding, that they might understand the Scripture, and said unto them: Thus it is written, and thus it behooved the Messiah to suffer, and to rise from the dead the third day; and that repentance and remission of sins should be preached in his name among all nations, beginning at Jerusalem." Here we see what it was he had preached to them, though not in so plain open words before his crucifixion; and what it is he now makes them understand; and what it was that was to be preached to all nations, that is That he was the Messiah that had suffered, and rose from the dead the third day, and fulfilled all things that were written in the Old Testament concerning the Messiah; and that those who believed this, and repented, should receive remission of their sins, through this faith in him. Or, as St. Mark has it, chap. xvi. 15, "Go into all the world, and preach the gospel to every creature; he that believeth, and is baptized, shall be saved; but he that believeth not, shall be damned," ver. 16. What the "gospel," or "good news," was, we have showed already, that is The happy tidings of the Messiah being come. Ver. 20, And "they went forth and preached everywhere, the Lord working with them, and confirming the word with signs following." What the "word" was which they preached, and the Lord confirmed with miracles, we have seen already, out of the history of their Acts. I have already given an account of their preaching everywhere, as it is recorded in the Acts, except some few places, where the kingdom of "the Messiah" is mentioned under the name of "the Kingdom of God;" which I forbore to set down, until I had made it plain out of the evangelists, that that was no other but the kingdom of the Messiah.

It may be seasonable therefore, now, to add to those sermons we have formerly seen of St. Paul, (wherein he preached no other article of faith, but that Jesus was "the Messiah," the King, who being risen from the dead, now reigns, and shall more publicly manifest his kingdom, in judging the world at the last day,) what father is left upon record of his preaching. Acts xix. 8, at Ephesus, "Paul went into the synagogues, and spoke boldly for the space of three months; disputing and persuading, concerning the Kingdom of God." And, Acts xx. 25, at Miletus he thus takes leave of the elders of Ephesus: "And now, behold, I know that you all, among whom I have gone preaching the Kingdom of God, shall see my face no more." What this preaching the Kingdom of God was, he tells you, ver. 20, 21, "I have kept nothing back from you, which was profitable unto you; but have showed you, and have taught you publicly, and from house to house; testifying both to the Jews, and to the Greeks, repentance towards God, and faith towards our Lord Jesus Christ." And so again, Acts xxviii. 23, 24, "When they [the Jews at Rome] had appointed him [Paul] a day, there came many to him into his lodging; to whom he expounded and testified the Kingdom of God; persuading them concerning Jesus, both out of the law of Moses, and out of the prophets, from morning to evening. And some believed the things which were spoken, and some believed not." And the history of the Acts is concluded with this account of St. Paul's preaching: "And Paul dwelt two whole years in his own hired house, and received all that came in unto him, preaching the Kingdom of God, and teaching those things which concern the Lord Jesus the Messiah." We may therefore here apply the same conclusion to the history of our Savior, writ by the evangelists, and to the history of the apostles, writ in the Acts, which St. John does to his own gospel, chap. xx. 30, 31, "Many other signs did Jesus before his disciples;" and in many other places the apostles preached the same doctrine, "which are not written" in these books; "but these are written that you may believe that Jesus is the Messiah, the Son of God; and that believing you may have life in his name."

What St. John thought necessary and sufficient to be believed, for the attaining eternal life, he here tells us. And this not in the first dawning of the gospel; when, perhaps, some will be apt to think less was required to be believed, than after the doctrine of faith, and mystery of salvation, was more fully explained, in the epistles writ by the apostles, for it is to be remembered, that St. John says this, not as soon as Christ was ascended; for these words, with the rest of St. John's gospel, were not written until many years after not only the other gospels, and St. Luke's history of the Acts, but in all appearance, after all the epistles written by the other apostles. So that more than years after our Savior's passion (for so long after, both Epiphanius and St. Jerome assure us this gospel was written) St. John knew nothing else required to be believed, for the attaining of life, but that "Jesus is the Messiah, the Son of God."

To this, it is likely, it will be objected by some, that to believe only that Jesus of Nazareth is the Messiah, is but an historical, and not a justifying, or saving faith.

To which I answer that I allow to the makers of systems and their followers to invent and use what distinctions they please, and to call things by what names they think fit. But I cannot allow to them, or to any man, an authority to make a religion for me, or to alter that which God has revealed. And if they please to call the believing that which our Savior and his apostles preached, and proposed alone to be believed, a historical faith; they have their liberty. But they must have a care, how they deny it to be a justifying or saving faith, when our Savior and his apostles have declared it so to be; and taught no other which men should receive, and whereby they should be made believers unto eternal life: unless they can so far make bold with our Savior, for the sake of their beloved systems, as to say, that he forgot what he came into the world for; and that he and his apostles did not instruct people right in the way and mysteries of salvation. For that this is the sole doctrine pressed and required to be believed in the whole tenor of our Savior's and his apostles preaching, we have showed through the whole history of the evangelists and the Acts. And I challenge them to show that there was any other doctrine, upon their assent to which, or disbelief of it, men were pronounced believers or unbelievers; and accordingly received into the church of Christ, as members of his body; as far as mere believing could make them so: or else kept out of it. This was the only gospel-article of faith which was preached to them. And if nothing else was preached everywhere, the apostle's argument will hold against any other articles of faith to be believed under the gospel, Rom. x. 14, "How shall they believe that whereof they have not heard?" For to preach any other doctrines necessary to be believed, we do not find that anybody was sent.

Perhaps it will further be urged, that this is not a "saving faith;" because such a faith as this the devils may have, and it was plain they had; for they believed and declared "Jesus to be the Messiah." And St. James, ch. ii. 19, tells us, "The devils believe and tremble;" and yet they shall not be saved. To which I answer:

1. That they could not be saved by any faith, to whom it was not proposed as a means of salvation, nor ever promised to be counted for righteousness. This was an act of grace shown only to mankind. God dealt so favorably with the posterity of Adam, that if they would believe Jesus to be the Messiah, the promised King and Savior, and perform what other conditions were required of them by the covenant of grace; God would justify them, because of this belief. He would account this faith to them for righteousness, and look on it as making up the defects of their obedience; which being thus supplied, by what was taken instead of it, they were looked on as just or righteous; and so inherited eternal life. But this favor shown to mankind, was never offered to the fallen angels. They had no such proposals made to them: and therefore, whatever of this kind was proposed to men, it availed not devils, whatever they performed of it. This covenant of grace was never offered to them.

2. I answer; that though the devils believed, yet they could not be saved by the covenant of grace; because they performed not the other condition required in it, altogether as necessary to be performed as this of believing: and that is repentance. Repentance is as absolute a condition of the covenant of grace as faith; and as necessary to be performed as that. John the Baptist, who was to prepare the way for the Messiah, "Preached the baptism of repentance for the remission of sins," Mark i. 4.

As John began his preaching with "Repent; for the kingdom of heaven is at hand," Mat. iii. 2; so did our Savior begin his, Matt. iv. 17, "From that time began Jesus to preach, and to say, Repent; for the kingdom of heaven is at hand." Or, as St. Mark has it in that parallel place, Mark i. 14, 15, "Now, after that John was put in prison, Jesus came into Galilee, preaching the gospel of the Kingdom of God, and saying, The time is fulfilled, and the Kingdom of God is at hand: repent you, and believe the gospel." This was not only the beginning of his preaching, but the sum of all that he did preach; that is That men should repent, and believe the good tidings which he brought them; that "the time was fulfilled" for the coming of the Messiah. And this was what his apostles preached, when he sent them out, Mark vi. 12, "And they, going out, preached that men should repent." Believing Jesus to be the Messiah, and repenting, were so necessary and fundamental parts of the covenant of grace, that one of them alone is often put for both. For here St. Mark mentions nothing but their preaching repentance: as St. Luke, in the parallel place, chap. ix. 6, mentions nothing but their evangelizing, or preaching the good news of the kingdom of the Messiah: and St. Paul often, in his epistles, puts faith for the whole duty of a Christian. But yet the tenor of the gospel is what Christ declares, Luke xii. 3, 5, "Unless you repent, you shall all likewise perish." And in the parable of the rich man in hell, delivered by our Savior, Luke xvi. repentance alone is the means proposed, of avoiding that place of torment, ver. 30, 31. And what the tenor of the doctrine which should be preached to the world should be, he tells his apostles, after his resurrection, Luke xxiv. 27, that is "That repentance and remission of sins" should be preached "in his name," who was the Messiah. And accordingly, believing Jesus to be the Messiah, and repenting, was what the apostles preached. So Peter began, Acts ii. 38, "Repent, and be baptized." These two things were required for the remission of sins, that is entering themselves in the Kingdom of God; and owning and professing themselves the subjects of Jesus, whom they believed to be the Messiah, and received for their Lord and King; for that was to be "baptized in his name:" baptism being an initiating ceremony, known to the Jews, whereby those, who leaving heathenism, and professing a submission to the law of Moses, were received into the commonwealth of Israel. And so it was made use of by our Savior, to be that solemn visible act, whereby those who believed him to be the Messiah, received him as their king, and professed obedience to him, were admitted as subjects into his kingdom: which, in the gospel, is called "the Kingdom of God;" and in the Acts and epistles, often by another name, that is the "Church."

The same St. Peter preaches again to the Jews, Acts iii. 19, "Repent, and be converted, that your sins may be blotted out."

What this repentance was which the new covenant required, as one of the conditions to be performed by all those who should receive the benefits of that covenant; is plain in the Scripture, to be not only a sorrow for sins past, but (what is a natural consequence of such sorrow, if it be real) a turning from them into a new and contrary life. And so they are joined together, Acts iii. 19, "Repent and turn about;" or, as we render it, "be converted." And Acts xxvi. 20, "Repent and turn to God."

And sometimes "turning about" is put alone to signify repentance, Matt. xiii. 15, Luke xxii. 32, which in other words is well expressed by "newness of life." For it being certain that he, who is really sorry for his sins, and abhors them, will turn from them, and forsake them; either of these acts, which have so natural a connection one with the other, may be, and is often put for both together. Repentance is a hearty sorrow for our past misdeeds, and a sincere resolution and endeavor, to the utmost of our power, to conform all our actions to the law of God. So that repentance does not consist in one single act of sorrow, (though that being the first and leading act gives denomination to the whole,) but in "doing works meet for repentance;" in a sincere obedience to the law of Christ, the remainder of our lives. This was called for by John the Baptist, the preacher of repentance, Matt. iii. 8, "Bring forth fruits meet for repentance." And by St. Paul here, Acts xxvi. 20, "Repent and turn to God, and do works meet for repentance." There are works to follow belonging to repentance, as well as sorrow for what is past.

These two, faith and repentance, i.e. believing Jesus to be the Messiah, and a good life, are the indispensable conditions of the new covenant, to be performed by all those who would obtain eternal life. The reasonableness, or rather necessity of which, that we may the better comprehend, we must a little look back to what was said in the beginning.

Adam being the Son of God, and so St. Luke calls him, chap. iii. 38, had this part also of the likeness and image of his father, that is that he was immortal. But Adam, transgressing the command given him by his heavenly Father, incurred the penalty; forfeited that state of immortality, and became mortal. After this, Adam begot children: but they were "in his own likeness, after his own image;" mortal, like their father.

God nevertheless, out of his infinite mercy, willing to bestow eternal life on mortal men, sends Jesus Christ into the world; who being conceived in the womb of a virgin (that had not known man) by the immediate power of God, was properly the Son of God; according to what the angel declared unto his mother, Luke i. 30—35, "The Holy Ghost shall come upon you, and the power of the Highest shall over-shadow you: therefore also that holy thing, which shall be born of you, shall be called the Son of God." So that being the Son of God, he was like the Father, immortal; as he tells us, John v. 26, "As the Father has life in himself, so has he given to the Son to have life in himself."

And that immortality is a part of that image, wherein those (who were the immediate sons of God, so as to have no other father) were made like their father, appears probable, not only from the places in Genesis concerning Adam, above taken notice of, but seems to me also to be intimated in some expressions, concerning Jesus the Son of God, in the New Testament. Col. i. 15, he is called "the image of the invisible God." Invisible seems put in, to obviate any gross imagination, that he (as images used to do) represented God in any corporeal or visible resemblance. And there is father subjoined, to lead us into the meaning of it, "The first-born of every creature;" which is father explained, ver. 18, where he is termed "The first-born from the dead;" thereby making out, and showing himself to be the image of the invisible; that death has no power over him; but being the Son of God, and not having forfeited that sonship by any transgression; was the heir of eternal life, as Adam should have been, had he continued in his filial duty. In the same sense the apostle seems to use the word image in other places, that is Rom. viii. 29, "Whom he did foreknow, he also did predestinate to be conformed to the image of his Son, that he might be the first-born among many brethren." This image, to which they were conformed, seems to be immortality and eternal life: for it is remarkable, that in both these places, St. Paul speaks of the resurrection; and that Christ was "The first-born among many brethren;" he being by birth the Son of God, and the others only by adoption, as we see in this same chapter ver. 15—17, "You have received the Spirit of adoption, whereby we cry, Abba, Father; the Spirit itself bearing witness with our spirit, that we are the children of God. And if children, then heirs, and joint-heirs with Christ; if so be that we suffer with him, that we may also be glorified together." And hence we see, that our Savior vouchsafes to call those, who at the day of judgment are, through him, entering into eternal life, his brethren; Matt. xxv. 40, "Inasmuch as you have done it unto one of the least of these my brethren." May we not in this find a reason, why God so frequently in the New Testament, and so seldom, if at all, in the Old, is mentioned under the single title of the father? And therefore our Savior says, Matt. xi. "No man knows the Father, save the Son, and he to whomsoever the Son will reveal him." God has now a son again in the world, the first-born of many brethren, who all now, by the Spirit of adoption, can say, Abba, Father. And we, by adoption, being for his sake made his brethren, and the sons of God, come to share in that inheritance, which was his natural right; he being by birth the Son of God: which inheritance is eternal life. And again, ver. 23, "We groan within ourselves, waiting for the adoption, to wit, the redemption of our body;" whereby is plainly meant, the change of these frail mortal bodies, into the spiritual immortal bodies at the resurrection; "When this mortal shall have put on immortality," 1 Cor. xv. 54; which in that chapter, ver. 42—44, he father expresses thus; "So also is the resurrection of the dead. It is sown in corruption, it is raised in incorruption; it is sown in dishonor, it is raised in glory; it is sown in weakness, it is raised in power; it is sown a natural body, it is raised a spiritual body," etc. To which he subjoins, ver. 49, "As we have born the image of the earthly," (i.e. as we have been mortal, like earthly Adam, our father, from whom we are descended, when he was turned out of paradise,) "we shall also bear the image of the heavenly;" into whose sonship and inheritance being adopted, we shall, at the resurrection, receive that adoption we expect, "even the redemption of our bodies;" and after his image, which is the image of the Father, become immortal. Hear what he says himself, Luke xx. 35, 36, "They who shall be accounted worthy to obtain that world, and the resurrection from the dead, neither marry, nor are given in marriage. Neither can they die anymore; for they are equal to the angels, and are the sons of god, being the sons of the resurrection." And he that shall read St. Paul's arguing, Acts xiii. 32, 33, will find that the great evidence that Jesus was the "Son of God," was his resurrection. Then the image of his Father appeared in him, when he visibly entered into the state of immortality. For thus the apostle reasons, "We preach to you, how that the promise which was made to our fathers, God has fulfilled the same unto us, in that he has raised up Jesus again; as it is also written in the second psalm, You are my Son, this day have I begotten you."

This may serve a little to explain the immortality of the sons of God, who are in this like their Father, made after his image and likeness. But that our Savior was so, he himself father declares, John x. 18, where speaking of his life, he says, "No one takes it from me, but I lay it down of myself; I have power to lay it down, and I have power to take it up again." Which he could not have had, if he had been a mortal man, the son of a man, of the seed of Adam; or else had by any transgression forfeited his life. "For the wages of sin is death;" and he that has incurred death for his own transgression, cannot lay down his life for another, as our Savior professes he did. For he was the just one, Acts vii. 52, and xxii. 14, "Who knew no sin;" 2

Cor. v. 21, "Who did no sin, neither was guile found in his mouth." And thus, "As by man came death, so by man came the resurrection of the dead. For as in Adam all die, so in Christ shall all be made alive."

For this laying down his life for others, our Savior tells us, John x. 17, "Therefore does my Father love me, because I lay down my life, that I might take it again." And his obedience and suffering was rewarded with a kingdom: which he tells us, Luke xxii. "His Father had appointed unto him:" and which, it is evident out of the epistle to the Hebrews, chap. xii. 2, he had a regard to in his sufferings: "Who for the joy that was set before him, endured the cross, despising the shame, and is set down at the right hand of the throne of God." Which kingdom, given him upon this account of his obedience, suffering, and death, he himself takes notice of in these words, John xvii. 1—4, "Jesus lifted up his eyes to heaven, and said, Father, the hour is come: glorify your Son, that your Son also may glorify you: as you have given him power over all flesh, that he should give eternal life to as many as you have given him. And this is life eternal, that they may know you the only true God, and Jesus, the Messiah, whom you have sent. I have glorified you on earth: I have finished the work which you gave me to do." And St. Paul, in his epistle to the Philippians, chap. ii. 8—11, "He humbled himself, and became obedient unto death, even the death of the cross. Wherefore God also has highly exalted him, and given him a name that is above every name; that at the name of Jesus every knee should bow, of things in heaven, and things in earth, and things under the earth; and that every tongue should confess, that Jesus Christ is Lord."

Thus God, we see, designed his Son Jesus Christ a kingdom, an everlasting kingdom in heaven. But though, "as in Adam all die, so in Christ shall all be made alive;" and all men shall return to life again at the last day; yet all men having sinned, and thereby "come short of the glory of God," as St. Paul assures us, Rom. iii. 23, i.e. not attaining to the heavenly kingdom of the Messiah, which is often called the glory of God; (as may be seen, Rom. v. 2, and xv. 7; and ii. 7; Matt. xvi. 27; Mark vii. 38. For no one who is unrighteous, i.e. comes short of perfect righteousness, shall be admitted into the eternal life of that kingdom; as is declared, 1 Cor. vi. 9, "The unrighteous shall not inherit the Kingdom of God;") and death, the wages of sin, being the portion of all those who had transgressed the righteous law of God; the son of God would in vain have come into the world to lay the foundations of a kingdom, and gather together a select people out of the world, if, (they being found guilty at their appearance before the judgment-seat of the righteous Judge of all men at the last day,) instead of entrance into eternal life in the kingdom he had prepared for them, they should receive death, the just reward of sin which everyone of them was guilty of; this second death would have left him no subjects; and instead of those ten thousand times ten thousand, and thousands of thousands, there would not have been one left him to sing praises unto his name, saying, "Blessing, and honor, and glory, and power, be unto him that sits on the throne, and unto the lamb forever and ever." God therefore, out of his mercy to mankind, and for the erecting of the kingdom of his Son, and furnishing it with subjects out of every kindred, and tongue, and people, and nation; proposed to the children of men, that as many of them as would believe Jesus his Son (whom he sent into the world) to be the Messiah, the promised Deliverer; and would receive him for their King and Ruler; should have all their past sins, disobedience, and rebellion forgiven them: and if for the future they lived in a sincere obedience to his law, to the utmost of their power; the sins of human frailty for the time to come, as well as all those of their past lives; should, for his Son's sake, because they gave themselves up to him, to be his subjects, be forgiven them: and so their faith, which made them be baptized into his name, (i.e. enroll themselves in the kingdom of Jesus the Messiah, and profess themselves his subjects, and consequently live by the laws of his kingdom,) should be accounted to them for righteousness; i.e. should supply the defects of a scanty obedience in the sight of God; who, counting faith to them for righteousness, or complete obedience, did thus justify, or make them just, and thereby capable of eternal life.

Now, that this is the faith for which God of his free grace justifies sinful man, (for "it is God alone that justifies," Rom. viii. 33, Rom. iii. 26,) we have already showed, by observing through all the history of our Savior and the apostles, recorded in the evangelists, and in the Acts, what he and his apostles preached, and proposed to be believed. We shall show now, that besides believing him to be the Messiah, their King, it was father required, that those who would have the privilege, advantage, and deliverance of his kingdom, should enter themselves into it; and by baptism being made denizens, and solemnly incorporated into that kingdom, live as became subjects obedient to the laws of it. For if they believed him to be the Messiah, their King, but would not obey his laws, and would not have him to reign over them; they were but the greater rebels; and God would not justify them for a faith that did but increase their guilt, and oppose diametrically the kingdom and design of the Messiah; "Who gave himself for us, that he might redeem us from all iniquity, and purify unto himself a peculiar people zealous of good works," Titus ii. 14. And therefore St. Paul tells the Galatians, That that which avails is faith; but "faith working by love." And that faith without works, i.e. the works of sincere obedience to the law and will of Christ, is not sufficient for our justification, St. James shows at large, chap. ii.

Neither, indeed, could it be otherwise; for life, eternal life, being the reward of justice or righteousness only, appointed by the righteous God (who is of purer eyes than to behold iniquity) to those who only had no taint or infection of sin upon them, it is impossible that he should justify those who had no regard to justice at all whatever they believed. This would have been to encourage iniquity, contrary to the purity of his nature; and to have condemned that eternal law of right, which is holy, just, and good; of which no one precept or rule is abrogated or repealed; nor indeed can be, while God is a holy, just, and righteous God, and man a rational creature. The duties of that law, arising from the constitution of his very nature, are of eternal obligation; nor can it be taken away or dispensed with, without changing the nature of things, overturning the measures of right and wrong, and thereby introducing and authorizing irregularity, confusion, and disorder in the world. Christ's coming into the world was not for such an end as that; but, on the contrary, to reform the corrupt state of degenerate man; and out of those who would mend their lives, and bring forth fruit meet for repentance, erect a new kingdom.

This is the law of that kingdom, as well as of all mankind; and that law, by which all men shall be judged at the last day. Only those who have believed Jesus to be the Messiah, and have taken him to be their King, with a sincere endeavor after righteousness, in obeying his law; shall have their past sins not imputed to them; and shall have that faith taken instead of obedience, where frailty and weakness made them transgress, and sin prevailed after conversion; in those who hunger and thirst after righteousness, (or perfect obedience,) and do not allow themselves in acts of disobedience and rebellion, against the laws of that kingdom they are entered into.

He did not expect, it is true, a perfect obedience, void of slips and falls: he knew our make, and the weakness of our constitution too well, and was sent with a supply for that defect. Besides, perfect obedience was the righteousness of the law of works; and then the reward would be of debt, and not of grace; and to such there was no need of faith to be imputed to them for righteousness. They stood upon their own legs, were just already, and needed no allowance to be made them for believing Jesus to be the Messiah, taking him for their king, and becoming his subjects. But that Christ does require obedience, sincere obedience, is evident from the law he himself delivers (unless he can be supposed to give and inculcate laws, only to have them disobeyed) and from the sentence he will pass when he comes to judge.

The faith required was, to believe Jesus to be the Messiah, the Anointed: who had been promised by God to the world. Among the Jews (to whom the promises and prophecies of the Messiah were more immediately delivered) anointing was used to three sorts of persons, at their inauguration; whereby they were set apart to three great offices, that is of priests, prophets, and kings. Though these three offices be in holy writ attributed to our Savior, yet I do not remember that he anywhere assumes to himself the title of a priest, or mentions anything relating to his priesthood; nor does he speak of his being a prophet but very sparingly, and only once or twice, as it were by the by: but the gospel, or the good news of the kingdom of the Messiah, is what he preaches everywhere, and makes it his great business to publish to the world. This he did not only as most agreeable to the expectation of the Jews, who looked for the Messiah, chiefly as coming in power to be their king and deliverer: but as it best answered the chief end of his coming, which was to be a king, and, as such, to be received by those who would be his subjects in the kingdom which he came to erect. And though he took not directly on himself the title of king, until he was in custody, and in the hands of Pilate; yet it is plain, "King" and "King of Israel," were the familiar and received titles of the

Messiah. See John i. 50, Luke xix. 38, compared with Matt. xxi. 9; and Mark xi. 9, John xii. 13, Matt. xxi. 5, Luke xxiii. 2, compared with Matt. xxvii. 11; and John xviii. 33—37, Mark xv. 12, compared with Matt. xxvii. 22, 42.

What those were to do, who believed him to be the Messiah, and received him for their king, that they might be admitted to be partakers with him of his kingdom in glory, we shall best know by the laws he gives them, and requires them to obey; and by the sentence which he himself will give, when sitting on his throne they shall all appear at his tribunal, to receive everyone his doom from the mouth of this righteous judge of all men.

What he proposed to his followers to be believed, we have already seen, by examining his and his apostles preaching, step by step, all through the history of the four evangelists, and the Acts of the Apostles. The same method will best and plainest show us, whether he required of those who believed him to be the Messiah, anything besides that faith, and what it was. For, he being a king, we shall see by his commands what he expects from his subjects: for, if he did not expect obedience to them, his commands would be but mere mockery; and if there were no punishment for the transgressors of them, his laws would not be the laws of a king, and that authority to command, and power to chastise the disobedient, but empty talk, without force, and without influence.

We shall therefore from his injunctions (if any such there is) see what he has made necessary to be performed, by all those who shall be received into eternal life, in his kingdom prepared in the heavens. And in this we cannot be deceived. What we have from his own mouth, especially if repeated over and over again, in different places and expressions, will be past doubt and controversy. I shall pass by all that is said by St. John Baptist, or any other before our Savior's entry upon his ministry, and public promulgation of the laws of his kingdom.

He began his preaching with a command to repent, as St. Matthew tells us, iv. 17. "From that time Jesus began to preach, saying, Repent; for the kingdom of heaven is at hand." And Luke v. 32, he tells the scribes and Pharisees, "I come not to call the righteous;" (those who were truly so, needed no help, they had a right to the tree of life), "but sinners, to repentance."

In his sermon, as it is called, in the mount, Luke vi. and Matt. v. etc. he commands they should be exemplary in good works: "Let your light so shine among men, that they may see your good works, and glorify your Father which is in heaven," Matt. v. 15. And that they might know what he came for, and what he expected of them, he tells them, ver. 17—20, "Think not that I am come to dissolve," or loosen, "the law, or the prophets: I am not come to dissolve," or loosen, "but to make it full," or complete; by giving it you in its true and strict sense. Here we see he confirms, and at once re-enforces all the moral precepts in the Old Testament. "For verily I say to you, Till heaven and earth pass, one jot or one tittle, shall in no wise pass from the law, till all be done. Whosoever therefore shall break one of these least commandments, and shall teach men so, he shall be called the least (i, e. as it is interpreted, shall not be at all) in the kingdom of heaven." Ver. 21, "I say unto you, That except your righteousness," i.e. your performance of the eternal law of right, "shall exceed the righteousness of the scribes and Pharisees, you shall in no case enter into the kingdom of heaven." And then he goes on to make good what he said, ver. 17, that is "That he was come to complete the law," that is by giving its full and clear sense, free from the corrupt and loosening glosses of the scribes and Pharisees, ver. 22—26. He tells them, That not only murder, but causeless anger, and so much as words of contempt, were forbidden. He commands them to be reconciled and kind towards their adversaries; and that upon pain of condemnation. In the following part of his sermon, which is to be read Luke vi. and more at large, Matt. v. vi. vii. he not only forbids actual uncleanness, but all irregular desires, upon pain of hell-fire; causeless divorces; swearing in conversation, as well as forswearing in judgment; revenge; retaliation; ostentation of charity, of devotion, and of fasting; repetitions in prayer, covetousness, worldly care, censoriousness: and on the other side commands loving our enemies, doing good to those that hate us, blessing those that curse us, praying for those that despitefully use us; patience and meekness under injuries, forgiveness, liberality, compassion: and closes all his particular injunctions, with this general golden rule, Matt. vii. 12, "All things whatsoever you would that men should do to you, do you even so to them, for this is the law and the prophets." And to show how much he is in earnest, and expects obedience to these laws, he tells them, Luke vi. 35, That if they obey, "great shall be their reward;" they "shall be called the sons of the Highest." And to all this, in the conclusion, he adds the solemn sanction; "Why call you me, Lord, Lord, and do not the things that I say?" It is in vain for you to take me for the Messiah your King, unless you obey me. "Not everyone who calls me, Lord, Lord, shall enter into the kingdom of heaven," or be the Sons of God; "but he that does the will of my father which is in heaven." To such disobedient subjects, though they have prophesied and done miracles in my name, I shall say at the day of judgment, "Depart from me, you workers of iniquity; I know you not."

When, Matt. xii. he was told, that his mother and brethren sought to speak with him, ver. 49, "Stretching out his hands to his disciples, he said, Behold my mother and my brethren; for whosoever shall do the will of my Father, who is in heaven, he is my brother, and sister, and mother." They could not be children of the adoption, and fellow heirs with him of eternal life, who did not do the will of his heavenly Father.

Matt. xv. and Mark vi. the Pharisees finding fault, that his disciples ate with unclean hands, he makes this declaration to his apostles: "Do you not perceive, that whatsoever from without enters into a man cannot defile him, because it enters not into his heart, but his belly? That which comes out of the man, that defiles the man; for from within, out of the heart of men, proceed evil thoughts, adulteries, fornications, murders, thefts, false witnesses, covetousness, wickedness, deceit, lasciviousness, an evil eye, blasphemy, pride, foolishness. All these ill things come from within, and defile a man."

He commands self-denial, and the exposing ourselves to suffering and danger, rather than to deny or disown him: and this upon pain of losing our souls; which are of more worth than the entire world. This we may read, Matt. xvi. 24—27, and the parallel places, Mark viii. and Luke ix.

The apostles disputing among them, who should be greatest in the kingdom of the Messiah, Matt. xviii. 1, he thus determines the controversy, Mark ix. 35, "If anyone will be first, let him be last of all, and servant of all:" and setting a child before them adds, Matt. xviii. 3, "Verily I say unto you, Unless you turn, and become as children, you shall not enter into the kingdom of heaven."

Matt. xviii. 15, "If your brother shall trespass against you, go and tell him his fault between you and him alone: if he shall hear you, you have gained your brother. But if he will not hear you, then take with you one or two more, that in the mouth of two or three witnesses every word may be established. And if he shall neglect to hear them, tell it to the church: but if he neglects to hear the church, let him be unto you, as a heathen and publican." Ver. 21, "Peter said, Lord, how often shall my brother sin against me and I forgive him? Seven times? Jesus said unto him, I say not unto you, seven times; but seventy times seven." And then ends the parable of the servant, who being himself forgiven, was rigorous to his fellow-servant, with these words, ver. 34, "and his Lord was angry, and delivered him to the tormentors, till he should pay all that was due to him. So likewise shall my heavenly Father do also unto you, if you from your hearts forgive not everyone his brother their trespasses."

Luke x. 25, to the lawyer, asking him, "What shall I do to inherit eternal life? He said, What is written in the law? How do you read this?" He answered, "You shall love the Lord your God with all your heart, and with all your soul, and with all your strength, and with all your mind; and your neighbor as yourself." Jesus said, "This do, and you shall live." And when the lawyer, upon our Savior's parable of the good Samaritan, was forced to confess, that he that showed mercy was his neighbor; Jesus dismissed him with this charge, ver. 37, "Go, and do you likewise."

Luke xi. 41, "Give alms, of such things as you have; behold all things are clean unto you."

Luke xii. 15, "Take heed, and beware of covetousness." Ver. 22, "Be not solicitous what you shall eat, or what you shall drink, nor what you shall put on;" be not fearful, or apprehensive of want; "for it is your Father's pleasure to give you a kingdom. Sell that you have, and give alms: and provide yourselves bags that wax not old, a treasure in the heavens that fails not: for where your treasure is, there will your heart be also. Let your loins be girded, and your lights burning; and you yourselves like unto men that wait for the Lord when he will return. Blessed are those servants, whom the Lord, when he comes, shall find watching. Blessed is that servant, whom the Lord having made ruler of his household, to give them their portion of meat in due season, the Lord, when he comes, shall find so doing. Of a truth I say unto you, that he will make him ruler over all that he has. But if that servant say in his heart, my Lord delays his coming; and shall begin to beat the men servants, and maidens, and to eat and drink, and to be drunken; the Lord of that servant will come in a day when he looks not for him, and at an hour when he is not aware; and will cut him in sunder, and will appoint him his portion with unbelievers. And that servant who knew his lord's will, and prepared not himself, neither did according to his will, shall be beaten with many stripes. But he that knew not and did commit things worthy of stripes, shall be beaten with few stripes. For unto whomsoever much is given, of him shall much be required: and to whom men have committed much, of him they will ask the more."

Luke xiv. 11, "Whosoever exalteth himself shall be abased: and he that humbles himself shall be exalted."

Ver. 12, "When you make a dinner, or supper, call not your friends, or your brethren, neither your kinsmen, nor your neighbors; lest they also bid you again, and a recompense be made you. But when you make a feast, call the poor, and maimed, the lame and the blind; and you shall be blessed, for they cannot recompense you; for you shall be recompensed at the resurrection of the just."

Ver. 33, "So likewise, whosoever he is of you, that is not ready to forego all that he has, he cannot be my disciple."

Luke xiv. 9, "I say unto you, make to yourselves friends of the mammon of unrighteousness: that when you fail, they may receive you into everlasting habitations. If you have not been faithful in the unrighteous mammon, who will commit to your trust the true riches? And if you have not been faithful in that which is another man's, who shall give you that which is your own?"

Luke xvii. 3, "If your brother trespass against you, rebuke him; and if he repent forgive him. And if he trespasses against you seven times in a day, and seven times in a day turn again unto you, saying, I repent, you shall forgive him."

Luke xviii. 1, "He spoke a parable to them to this end, that men ought always to pray, and not to faint."

Ver. 18, "One comes to him and asks him, saying, Master, what shall I do to inherit eternal life? Jesus said unto him, If you will enter into life, keep the commandments. He says, Which? Jesus said, You know the commandments. You shall not kill; you shall not commit adultery; you shall not steal; you shall not bear false witness; defraud not; honor your father and your mother; and you shall love your neighbor as yourself. He said, all these have I observed from my youth. Jesus hearing this, loved him, and said unto him, Yet you lack one thing: sell all that you have, and give it to the poor, and you shall have treasure in heaven; and come, follow me." To understand this right, we must take notice, that this young man asks our Savior, what he must do to be admitted effectually into the kingdom of the Messiah. The Jews believed, that when the Messiah came, those of their nation that received him, should not die; but that they, with those who, being dead, should then be raised again by him, should enjoy eternal life with him. Our Savior, in answer to this demand, tells the young man, that to obtain the eternal life of the kingdom of the Messiah, he must keep the commandments. And then enumerating several of the precepts of the law, the young man says, he had observed these from his childhood. For which the text tells us, Jesus loved him. But our Savior, to try whether in earnest he believed him to be the Messiah, and resolved to take him to be his king, and to obey him as such, bids him give all that he has to the poor, and come, and follow him; and he should have treasure in heaven. This I look on to be the meaning of the place; this, of selling all he had, and giving it to the poor, not being a standing law of his kingdom; but a probationary command to this young man; to try whether he truly believed him to be the Messiah, and was ready to obey his commands, and relinquish all to follow him, when he, his prince, required it.

And therefore we see, Luke xix. 14, where our Savior takes notice of the Jews not receiving him as the Messiah, he expresses it thus: "We will not have this man to reign over us." It is not enough to believe him to be the Messiah, unless we also obey his laws, and take him to be our king to reign over us.

Matt. xxii. 11—13, he that had not on the wedding-garment, though he accepted of the invitation, and came to the wedding, was cast into utter darkness. By the wedding-garment, it is evident good works are meant here; that wedding-garment of fine linen, clean, and white, which we are told, Rev. xix, 8, is the δικαιώματα, "righteous acts of the saints;" or, as St. Paul calls it, Ephes. iv. 1, "The walking worthy of the vocation wherewith we are called." This appears from the parable itself: "The kingdom of heaven," says our Savior, ver. 2, "is like unto a king, who made a marriage for his son." And here he distinguishes those who were invited, into three sorts: 1. Those who were invited, and came not; i.e. those who had the gospel, the good news of the Kingdom of God proposed to them, but believed not. 2. Those who came, but had not on a wedding-garment; i.e. believed Jesus to be the Messiah, but were not new clad (as I may so say) with a true repentance, and amendment of life: nor adorned with those virtues, which the apostle, Col. iii. requires to be put on. 3. Those who were invited, did come, and had on the wedding-garment; i.e. heard the gospel, believed Jesus to be the Messiah, and sincerely obeyed his laws. These three sorts are plainly designed here; whereof the last only were the blessed, who were to enjoy the kingdom prepared for them.

Matt. xxiii. "Do not be called Rabbi; for one is your master, even the Messiah, and you are all brethren. And call no man your father upon the earth: for one is your Father which is in heaven. Neither be called masters: for one is your master, even the Messiah. But he that is greatest among you, shall be your servant. And whosoever shall exalt himself, shall be abased; and he that shall humble himself, shall be exalted."

Luke xxi. 34, "Take heed to yourselves, lest your hearts be at any time overcharged with surfeiting and drunkenness, and cares of this life."

Luke xxii. 25, "He said unto them, the kings of the Gentiles exercise lordship over them; and they that exercise authority upon them, are called benefactors. But you shall not be so. But he that is greatest among you, let him be as the younger; and he that is chief, as he that does serve."

John xiii. 34, "A new commandment I give unto you, That you love one another: as I have loved you, that you also love one another. By this shall all men know that you are my disciples, if you love one another." This command, of loving one another, is repeated again, chap. xv. 12, and 17.

John xiv. 15, "If you love me, keep my commandments." Ver. 21, "He that has my commandments, and keepeth them, he it is that loves me: and he that loves me, shall be loved of my Father, and I will love him, and manifest myself to him." Ver. 23, "If a man loves me he will keep my words." Ver. 24, "He that does not love me, does not keep my sayings."

John xv. 8, "In this is my Father glorified, that you bear much fruit; so shall you be my disciples." Ver. 14, "You are my friends, if you do whatsoever I command you."

Thus we see our Savior not only confirmed the moral law; and clearing it from the corrupt commentaries of the scribes and Pharisees, showed the strictness as well as obligation of its injunctions; but moreover, upon occasion, requires the obedience of his disciples to several of the commands he afresh lays upon them; with the enforcement of unspeakable rewards and punishments in another world, according to their obedience or disobedience. There is not, I think, any of the duties of morality, which he has not, somewhere or other, by himself and his apostles, inculcated over and over again to his followers in express terms. And is it for nothing that he is so instant with them to bring forth fruit? Does he, their King, command, and is it an indifferent thing? Or will their happiness or misery not at all depend upon it, whether they obey or no? They were required to believe him to be the Messiah; which faith is of grace promised to be reckoned to them, for the completing of their righteousness, wherein it was defective: but righteousness, or obedience to the law of God, was their great business, which, if they could have attained by their own performances, there would have been no need of this gracious allowance, in reward of their faith: but eternal life, after the resurrection, had been their due by a former covenant, even that of works; the rule whereof was never abolished, though the rigor was abated. The duties enjoined in it were duties still. Their obligations had never ceased; nor was a willful neglect of them ever dispensed with. But their past transgressions were pardoned, to those who received Jesus, the promised Messiah, for their king; and their future slips covered, if renouncing their former iniquities, they entered into his kingdom, and continued his subjects with a steady resolution and endeavor to obey his laws. This righteousness therefore, a complete obedience, and freedom from sin, are still sincerely to be endeavored after. And it is no-where promised, that those who persist in a willful disobedience to his laws, shall be received into the eternal bliss of his kingdom, how much soever they believe in him.

A sincere obedience, how can anyone doubt to be, or scruple to call, a condition of the new covenant, as well as faith; whoever reads our Savior's sermon on the mount, to omit all the rest? Can anything be more express than these words of our Lord? Matt. vi. 14, "If you forgive men their trespasses, your heavenly Father will also forgive you: but if you forgive not men their trespasses, neither will your Father forgive your trespasses." And John xiii. 17, "If you know these things, happy are you if you do them." This is so indispensable a condition of the new covenant, that believing without it, will not do, nor be accepted; if our Savior knew the terms on which he would admit men into life. "Why do you call me, Lord, Lord," says he, Luke vi. 46, "and do not the things which I say?" It is not enough to believe him to be the Messiah, the Lord, without obeying him. For that these he speaks to here, were believers, is evident from the parallel place, Matt. vii. 21—23, where it is thus recorded: "Not everyone who says, Lord, Lord, shall enter into the kingdom of heaven; but he that does the will of my father, which is in heaven." No rebels, or refractory disobedient, shall be admitted there, though they have so far believed in Jesus, as to be able to do miracles in his name: as is plain out of the following words: "Many will say to me in that day, Have we not prophesied in your name, and in your name have cast out devils, and in your name have done many wonderful works? And then will I profess unto them, I never knew you; depart from me, you workers of iniquity."

This part of the new covenant, the apostles also, in their preaching the gospel of the Messiah, ordinarily joined with the doctrine of faith.

St. Peter, in his first sermon, Acts ii. when they were pricked in heart, and asked, "What shall we do?" says, ver. 38, "Repent, and be baptized, every one of you in the name of Jesus Christ, for the remission of sins." The same he says to them again in his next speech, Acts iv. 26, "Unto you first, God having raised up his Son Jesus, sent him to bless you." How was this done? "in turning away everyone from your iniquities."

The same doctrine they preach to the high priest and rulers, Acts v. 30, "The God of our fathers raised up Jesus, whom you slew, and hanged on a tree. He has God exalted with his right hand, to be a Prince and a Savior, for to give repentance to Israel, and forgiveness of sins; and we are witnesses of these things, and so is also the Holy Ghost, whom God has given to them that obey him."

Acts xvii. 30, St. Paul tells the Athenians, That now under the gospel, "God commands all men everywhere to repent."

Acts xx. 21, St. Paul, in his last conference with the elders of Ephesus, professes to have taught them the whole doctrine necessary to salvation: "I have," says he, "kept back nothing that was profitable unto you; but have showed you, and have taught you publicly, and from house to house; testifying both to the Jews and to the Greeks:" and then gives an account what his preaching had been, that is "Repentance towards God, and faith towards our Lord Jesus the Messiah." This was the sum and substance of the gospel which St. Paul preached, and was all that he knew necessary to salvation; that is "Repentance, and believing Jesus to be the Messiah:" and so takes his last farewell of them, whom he shall never see again, ver. 32, in these words, "And now, brethren, I commend you to God, and to the word of his grace, which is able to build you up, and to give you an inheritance among all them that are sanctified." There is an inheritance conveyed by the word and covenant of grace; but it is only to those who are sanctified.

Acts xxiv. 24, "When Felix sent for Paul," that he and his wife Drusilla might hear him, "concerning the faith in Christ;" Paul reasoned of righteousness, or justice; and temperance; the duties we owe to others, and to ourselves; and of the judgment to come; until he made Felix to tremble. Whereby it appears, that "temperance and justice" were fundamental parts of the religion that Paul professed, and were contained in the faith which he preached. And if we find the duties of the moral law not pressed by him everywhere, we must remember, that most of his sermons left upon record, were preached in their synagogues to the Jews, who acknowledged their obedience due to all the precepts of the law; and would have taken it amiss to have been suspected not to have been more zealous for the law than he. And therefore it was with reason that his discourses were directed chiefly to what they yet wanted, and were averse to, the knowledge and embracing of Jesus, their promised Messiah. But what his preaching generally was, if we will believe him himself, we may see, Acts xxvi. where giving an account to king Agrippa, of his life and doctrine, he tells him, ver. 20, "I showed unto them of Damascus, and at Jerusalem, and throughout all the coasts of Judea, and then to the Gentiles, that they should repent and turn to God, and do works meet for repentance."

Thus we see, by the preaching of our Savior and his apostles, that he required of those who believed him to be the Messiah, and received him for their Lord and Deliverer, that they should live by his laws: and that (though in consideration of their becoming his subjects, by faith in him, whereby they believed and took him to be the Messiah, their former sins should be forgiven, yet) he would own none to be his, nor receive them as true denizens of the new Jerusalem, into the inheritance of eternal life; but leave them to the condemnation of the unrighteous; who renounced not their former miscarriages, and lived in a sincere obedience to his commands. What he expects from his followers, he has sufficiently declared as a legislator: and that they may not be deceived, by mistaking the doctrine of faith, grace, free-grace, and the pardon and forgiveness of sins, and salvation by him, (which was the great end of his coming,) he more than once declares to them, for what omissions and miscarriages he shall judge and condemn to death, even those who have owned him, and done miracles in his name: when he comes at last to render to everyone according to what he had done in the flesh, sitting upon his great and glorious tribunal, at the end of the world.

The first place where we find our Savior to have mentioned the day of judgment, is John v. 28, 29, in these words: "the hour is coming, in which all that are in their grave shall hear his [i.e. the Son of God's] voice, and shall come forth; they that have done good, unto the resurrection of life; and they that have done evil, unto the resurrection of damnation." That which puts the distinction, if we will believe our Savior, is the having done good or evil. And he gives a reason of the necessity of his judging or condemning those "who have done evil," in the following words, ver. 30, "I can of myself do nothing. As I hear I judge; and my judgment is just; because I seek not my own will, but the will of my Father who has sent me." He could not judge of himself; he had but a delegated power of judging from the Father, whose will he obeyed in it; and who was of purer eyes than to admit any unjust person into the kingdom of heaven.

Matt. vii. 22, 23, speaking again of that day, he tells what his sentence will be, "Depart from me, you workers of iniquity." Faith in the penitent and sincerely obedient, supplies the defect of their performances; and so by grace they are made just. But we may observe, none are sentenced or punished for unbelief, but only for their misdeeds. "They are workers of iniquity" on whom the sentence is pronounced.

Matt. xiii. 41, "At the end of the world, the Son of man shall send forth his angels; and they shall gather out of his kingdom all scandals, and them which do iniquity; and cast them into a furnace of fire; there shall be wailing and gnashing of teeth." And again, ver. 49, "The angels shall sever the wicked from among the just; and shall cast them into the furnace of fire."

Matt. xvi. 24, "For the Son of man shall come in the glory of his Father, with his angels: and then he shall reward every man according to his works."

Luke xiii. 26, "Then shall you begin to say, We have eaten and drank in your presence, and you have taught in our streets. But he shall say, I tell you, I know you not; depart from me, you workers of iniquity."

Matt. xxv. 31—46, "When the Son of man shall come in his glory; and before him shall be gathered all nations; he shall set the sheep on his right hand, and the goats on his left. Then shall the king say to them on his right hand, Come, you blessed of my Father, inherit the kingdom prepared for you from the foundation of the world; for I was an hungered, and you gave me meat; I was thirsty, and you gave me drink; I was a stranger, and you took me in; naked, and you clothed me; I was sick, and you visited me; I was in prison, and you came unto me. Then shall the righteous answer him, saying, Lord, when saw we you hungering, and fed you? etc. And the King shall answer and say unto them, Verily, I say unto you, Inasmuch as you have done it unto one of the least of these my brethren, you have done it unto me. Then shall he say unto them on the left hand, Depart from me, you cursed, into everlasting fire, prepared for the devil and his angels: for I was an hungered, and you gave me no meat; I was thirsty, and you gave me no drink; I was a stranger, and you took me not in; naked, and you clothed me not; sick, and in prison, and you visited me not. Insomuch that you did it not to one of these, you did it not to me. And these shall go into everlasting punishment; but the righteous into life eternal."

These, I think, are all the places where our Savior mentions the last judgment, or describes his way of proceeding in that great day; wherein, as we have observed, it is remarkable, that everywhere the sentence follows doing or not doing, without any mention of believing or not believing. Not that any, to whom the gospel has been preached, shall be saved, without believing Jesus to be the Messiah: for all being sinners, and transgressors of the law, and so unjust; are all liable to condemnation; unless they believe, and so through grace are justified by God, for this faith, which shall be accounted to them for righteousness. But the rest wanting this cover, this allowance for their transgressions, must answer for all their actions; and being found transgressors of the law, shall, by the letter and sanction of that law, be condemned for not having paid a full obedience to that law; and not for want of faith. That is not the guilt on which the punishment is laid; though it is the want of faith, which lays open their guilt uncovered; and exposes them to the sentence of the law, against all that are unrighteous.

The common objection here, is, if all sinners shall be condemned, but such as have a gracious allowance made them; and so are justified by God, for believing Jesus to be the Messiah, and so taking him for their King, whom they are resolved to obey to the utmost of their power; "What shall become of all mankind, who lived before our Savior's time, who never heard of his name, and consequently could not believe in him?" To this the answer is so obvious and natural, that one would wonder how any reasonable man should think it worth the urging. No-body was, or can be required to believe, what was never proposed to him to believe. Before the fullness of time, which God from the counsel of his own wisdom had appointed to send his Son in, he had, at several times, and in different manners, promised to the people of Israel, an extraordinary person to come; who, raised from among themselves, should be their Ruler and Deliverer. The time, and other circumstances of his birth, life, and person, he had in sundry prophecies so particularly described, and so plainly foretold, that he was well known, and expected by the Jews, under the name of the Messiah, or Anointed, given him in some of these prophecies. All then that was required, before his appearing in the world, was to believe what God had revealed, and to rely with a full assurance on God, for the performance of his promise; and to believe, that in due time he would send them the Messiah, this anointed King, this promised Savior and Deliverer, according to his word. This faith in the promises of God, this relying and acquiescing in his word and faithfulness, the Almighty takes well at our hands, as a great mark of homage, paid by us poor frail creatures, to his goodness and truth, as well as to his power and wisdom: and accepts it as an acknowledgment of his peculiar providence, and benignity to us. And therefore our Savior tells us, John xii. 44, "He that believes on me, believes not on me, but on him that sent me." The works of nature show his wisdom and power; but it is his peculiar care of mankind most eminently discovered in his promises to them, that shows his bounty and goodness; and consequently engages their hearts in love and affection to him. This oblation of a heart, fixed with dependence on, and affection to him, is the most acceptable tribute we can pay him, the foundation of true devotion, and life of all religion. What a value he puts on this depending on his word, and resting satisfied in his promises, we have an example in Abraham; whose faith "was counted to him for righteousness," as we have before remarked out of Rom. iv. And his relying firmly on the promise of God, without any doubt of its performance, gave him the name of the father of the faithful; and gained him so much favor with the Almighty, that he was called the "friend of God;" the highest and most glorious title that can be bestowed on a creature. The thing promised was no more but a son by his wife Sarah; and a numerous posterity by him, which should possess the land of Canaan. These were but temporal blessings, and (except the birth of a son) very remote, such as he should never live to see, nor in his own person have the benefit of. But because he questioned not the performance of it; but rested fully satisfied in the goodness, truth, and faithfulness of God, who had promised, it was counted to him for righteousness. Let us see how St. Paul expresses it, Rom. iv. 18—22, "Who, against hope, believed in hope, that he might become the father of many nations; according to that which was spoken, So shall thy seed be. And being not weak in faith, he considered not his own body now dead, when he was above an hundred years old, neither yet the deadness of Sarah's womb. He staggered not at the promise of God through unbelief, but was strong in faith: giving glory to God, and being fully persuaded, that what he had promised he was able to perform. And therefore it was imputed to him for righteousness." St. Paul having here emphatically described the strength and firmness of Abraham's faith, informs us, that he thereby "gave glory to God;" and therefore it was accounted to him for righteousness." This is the way that God deals with poor frail mortals. He is graciously pleased to take it well of them, and give it the place of righteousness, and a kind of merit in his sight; if they believe his promises, and have a steadfast relying on his veracity and goodness. St. Paul, Heb. xi. 6, tells us, "Without faith it is impossible to please God:" but at the same time tells us what faith that is. "For," says he, "he that comes to God, must believe that he is; and that he is a rewarder of them that diligently seek him." He must be persuaded of God's mercy and goodwill to those who seek to obey him; and rest assured of his rewarding those who rely on him, for whatever, either by the light of nature, or particular promises, he has revealed to them of his tender mercies, and taught them to expect from his bounty. This description of faith (that we might not mistake what he means by that faith, without which we cannot please God, and which recommended the saints of old) St. Paul places in the middle of the list of those who were eminent for their faith; and whom he sets as patterns to the converted Hebrews, under persecution, to encourage them to persist in their confidence of deliverance by the coming of Jesus Christ, and in their belief of the promises they now had under the gospel. By those examples he exhorts them not to "draw back" from the hope that was set before them, nor apostatize from the profession of the Christian religion. This is plain from ver. 35—38, of the precedent chapter: "Cast not away therefore your confidence, which has great recompense of reward. For you have great need of persisting or perseverance;" (for so the Greek word signifies here, which our translation renders "patience." Vide Luke viii. 15.) "that after you have done the will of God, you might receive the promise. For yet a little while, and he that shall come will come, and will not tarry. Now the just shall live by faith. But if any man draws back, my soul shall have no pleasure in him."

The examples of faith, which St. Paul enumerates and proposes in the following words, chap. xi. plainly show, that the faith whereby those believers of old pleased God, was nothing but a steadfast reliance on the goodness and faithfulness of God, for those good things, which either the light of nature, or particular promises, had given them grounds to hope for. Of what avail this faith was with God, we may see, ver. 4, "By faith Abel offered unto God a more excellent sacrifice than Cain; by which he obtained witness that he was righteous." Ver. 5, "By faith Enoch was translated, that he should not see death: for before his translation he had this testimony, that he pleased God." Ver. 7, "Noah being warned of God of things not seen as yet;" being wary, "by faith prepared an ark, to the saving of his house; by which he condemned the world, and became heir of the righteousness which is by faith." And what it was that God so graciously accepted and rewarded, we are told, ver. 11, "Through faith also Sarah herself received strength to conceive seed, and was delivered of a child, when she was past age." How she came to obtain this grace from God, the apostle tells us, "Because she judged him faithful who had promised." Those therefore, who pleased God, and were accepted by him before the coming of Christ, did it only by believing the promises, and relying on the goodness of God, as far as he had revealed it to them. For the apostle, in the following words, tells us, ver. 13, "These all died in faith, not having received (the accomplishment of) the promises; but having seen them afar off: and were persuaded of them, and embraced them." This was all that was required of them; to be persuaded of, and embrace the promises which they had. They could be "persuaded of" no more than was proposed to them; "embrace" no more than was revealed; according to the promises they had received, and the dispensations they were under. And if the faith of things "seen afar off;" if their trusting in God for the promises he then gave them; if a belief of the Messiah to come; were sufficient to render those who lived in the ages before Christ acceptable to God, and righteous before him: I desire those who tell us, that God will not (nay, some go so far as to say, cannot) accept any, who do not believe every article of their particular creeds and systems, to consider, why God, out of his infinite mercy, cannot as well justify men now, for believing Jesus of Nazareth to be the promised Messiah, the King and Deliverer; as those heretofore, who believed only that God would, according to his promise, in due time, send the Messiah, to be a King and Deliverer.

There is another difficulty often to be met with, which seems to have something of more weight in it: and that is, that "though the faith of those before Christ (believing that God would send the Messiah, to be a Prince and a Savior to his people, as he had promised), and the faith of those since his time (believing Jesus to be that Messiah, promised and sent by God), shall be accounted to them for righteousness; yet what shall become of all the rest of mankind, who, having never heard of the promise or news of a Savior; not a word of a Messiah to be sent, or that was come; have had no thought or belief concerning him?"

To this I answer; that God will require of every man, "according to what a man has, and not according to what he has not." He will not expect the improvement of ten talents, where he gave but one; nor require anyone should believe a promise of which he has never heard. The apostle's reasoning, Rom. x. 14, is very just: "How shall they believe in him, of whom they have not heard?" But though there be many who being strangers to the commonwealth of Israel, were also strangers to the oracles of God, committed to that people; many, to whom the promise of the Messiah never came, and so were never in a capacity to believe or reject that revelation; yet God had, by the light of reason, revealed to all mankind, who would make use of that light, that he was good and merciful. The same spark of the divine nature and knowledge in man, which making him a man, showed him the law he was under, as a man; showed him also the way of atoning the merciful, kind, compassionate Author and Father of him and his being, when he had transgressed that law. He that made use of this candle of the Lord, so far as to find what was his duty, could not miss to find also the way to reconciliation and forgiveness, when he had failed of his duty: though, if he used not his reason this way, if he put out or neglected this light, he might, perhaps, see neither.

The law is the eternal, immutable standard of right. And a part of that law is, that a man should forgive, not only his children, but his enemies, upon their repentance, asking pardon, and amendment. And therefore he could not doubt that the author of this law, and God of patience and consolation, who is rich in mercy, would forgive his frail offspring, if they acknowledged their faults, disapproved the iniquity of their transgressions, begged his pardon, and resolved in earnest, for the future, to conform their actions to this rule, which they owned to be just and right. This way of reconciliation, this hope of atonement, the light of nature revealed to them: and the revelation of the gospel, having said nothing to the contrary, leaves them to stand and fall to their own Father and Master, whose goodness and mercy is over all his works.

I know some are forward to urge that place of the Acts, chap. iv. as contrary to this. The words, ver. 10 and 12, stand thus: "Be it known unto you all, and to all the people of Israel, that by the name of Jesus Christ of Nazareth, whom you crucified, whom God raised from the dead, even by him, does this man" [i.e. the lame man restored by Peter] "stand here before you whole. This is the stone which is set at naught by you builders, which is become the head of the corner. Neither is there salvation in any other: for there is none other name under heaven given among men, in which we must be saved." Which, in short, is, that Jesus is the only true Messiah, neither is there any other person, but he, given to be a mediator between God and man; in whose name we may ask, and hope for salvation.

It will here possibly be asked, "*Quorsum perditio hæc?*" What need was there of a Savior? What advantage have we by Jesus Christ?

It is enough to justify the fitness of anything to be done, by resolving it into the "wisdom of God," who had done it; though our short views, and narrow understandings, may utterly incapacitate us to see that wisdom, and to judge rightly of it. We know little of this visible, and nothing at all of the state of that intellectual world, wherein infinite numbers and degrees of spirits are out of the reach of our ken, or guess; and therefore know not what transactions there were between God and our Savior, in reference to his kingdom. We know not what need there was to set up a head and a chieftain, in opposition to "the prince of this world, the prince of the power of the air," etc. whereof there are more than obscure intimations in Scripture. And we shall take too much upon us, if we shall call God's wisdom or providence to account, and pertly condemn for needless all that our weak, and perhaps biased, understanding cannot account for.

Though this general answer be reply enough to the aforementioned demand, and such as a rational man, or fair searcher after truth, will acquiesce in; yet in this particular case, the wisdom and goodness of God has shown itself so visibly to common apprehensions, that it has furnished us abundantly wherewithal to satisfy the curious and inquisitive; who will not take a blessing, unless they be instructed what need they had of it, and why it was bestowed upon them. The great and many advantages we receive by the coming of Jesus the Messiah, will show, that it was not without need that he was sent into the world.

The evidence of our Savior's mission from heaven is so great, in the multitude of miracles he did before all sorts of people, that what he delivered cannot but be received as the oracles of God, and unquestionable verity. For the miracles he did were so ordered by the divine providence and wisdom, that they never were, nor could be denied by any of the enemies, or opposers of Christianity.

Though the works of nature, in every part of them, sufficiently evidence a deity; yet the world made so little use of their reason, that they saw him not, where, even by the impressions of himself, he was easy to be found. Sense and lust blinded their minds in some, and a careless inadvertency in others, and fearful apprehensions in most, (who either believed there were, or could not but suspect there might be, superior unknown beings,) gave them up into the hands of their priests, to fill their heads with false notions of the Deity, and their worship with foolish rites, as they pleased: and what dread or craft once began, devotion soon made sacred, and religion immutable. In this state of darkness and ignorance of the true God, vice and superstition held the world. Nor could any help be had, or hoped for, from reason; which could not be heard, and was judged to have nothing to do in the case; the priests, everywhere, to secure their empire, having excluded reason from having anything to do in religion. And in the crowd of wrong notions, and invented rites, the world had almost lost the sight of the one only true God. The rational and thinking part of mankind, it is true, when they sought after him, they found the one supreme, invisible God; but if they acknowledged and worshipped him, it was only in their own minds. They kept this truth locked up in their own breasts as a secret, nor ever durst venture it among the people; much less among the priests, those wary guardians, of their own creeds and profitable inventions. Hence we see, that reason, speaking ever so clearly to the wise and virtuous, had never authority enough to prevail on the multitude; and to persuade the societies of men, that there was but one God, that alone was to be owned and worshipped. The belief and worship of one God, was the national religion of the Israelites alone: and if we will consider it, it was introduced and supported among the people by revelation. They were in Goshen, and had light, while the rest of the world was in almost Egyptian darkness, "without God in the world." There was no part of mankind, who had quicker parts, or improved them more; that had a greater light of reason, or followed it father in all sorts of speculations, than the Athenians; and yet we find but one Socrates among them, that opposed and laughed at their polytheism, and wrong opinions of the Deity; and we see how they rewarded him for it. Whatsoever Plato, and the soberest of the philosophers, thought of the nature and being of the one God, they were fain, in their outward professions and worship, to go with the herd, and keep to their religion established by law: which what it was, and how it had disposed the minds of these knowing and quick-sighted Grecians, St. Paul tells us, Acts xvii. 22—29, "You men of Athens," says he, "I perceive, that in all things you are very religious. For as I passed by, and beheld your devotions, I found an altar with this inscription, to the unknown god. Whom therefore you ignorantly worship, him I declare unto you. God that made the world, and all things therein, seeing that he is Lord of heaven and earth, dwells not in temples made with hands: neither is worshipped with men's hands, as though he needed anything, seeing that he giveth unto all life, and breath, and all things; and has made of one blood all the nations of men, for to dwell on the face of the earth; and has determined the times before appointed, and the bounds of their habitations; that they should seek the Lord, if haply they might feel him out and find him, though he be not far from everyone of us." Here he tells the Athenians, that they, and the rest of the world (given up to superstition) whatever light there was in the works of creation and providence, to lead them to the true God; yet few of them found him. He was everywhere near them; yet they were but like people groping and feeling for something in the dark, and did not see him with a full and clear day-light; "but thought the Godhead like to gold and silver, and stone, graven by are and man's device."

In this state of darkness and error, in reference to the "true God," our Savior found the world. But the clear revelation he brought with him, dissipated this darkness; made the "one invisible true God" known to the world: and that with such evidence and energy, that polytheism and idolatry have no-where been able to withstand it: but wherever the preaching of the truth he delivered, and the light of the gospel has come, those mists have been dispelled. And, in effect, we see, that since our Savior's time, the "belief of one God" has prevailed and spread itself over the face of the earth. For even to the light that the Messiah brought into the world with him, we must ascribe the owning and profession of one God, which the Muslim religion has derived and borrowed from it. So that in this sense it is certainly and manifestly true of our Savior, what St. John says of him, 1 John iii. 8, "For this purpose the Son of God was manifested, that he might destroy the works of the devil." This light the world needed, and this light is received from him: that there is but "one God," and he "eternal, invisible;" not like to any visible objects, nor to be represented by them.

If it be asked, whether the revelation to the patriarchs by Moses did not teach this, and why that was not enough? The answer is obvious; that however clearly the knowledge of one invisible God, maker of heaven and earth, was revealed to them; yet that revelation was shut up in a little corner of the world; among a people, by that very law, which they received with it, excluded from a commerce and communication with the rest of mankind. The Gentile world, in our Savior's time, and several ages before, could have no attestation of the miracles on which the Hebrews built their faith, but from the Jews themselves, a people not known to the greatest part of mankind; contemned and thought vilely of, by those nations that did know them; and therefore very unfit and unable to propagate the doctrine of one God in the world, and diffuse it through the nations of the earth, by the strength and force of that ancient revelation, upon which they had received it. But our Savior, when he came, threw down this wall of partition; and did not confine his miracles or message to the land of Canaan, or the worshippers at Jerusalem. But he himself preached at Samaria, and did miracles in the borders of Tyre and Sidon, and before multitudes of people gathered from all quarters. And after his resurrection, sent his apostles among the nations, accompanied with miracles; which were done in all parts so frequently, and before so many witnesses of all sorts, in broad day-light, that, as I have before observed, the enemies of Christianity have never dared to deny them; no, not Julian himself: who neither wanted skill nor power to inquire into the truth: nor would have failed to have proclaimed and exposed it, if he could have detected any falsehood in the history of the gospel; or found the least ground to question the matter of fact published of Christ and his apostles. The number and evidence of the miracles done by our Savior and his followers, by the power and force of truth, bore down this mighty and accomplished emperor, and all his parts, in his own dominions. He durst not deny so plain a matter of fact, which being granted, the truth of our Savior's doctrine and mission unavoidably follows; notwithstanding whatsoever artful suggestions his wit could invent, or malice should offer to the contrary.

Next to the knowledge of one God; maker of all things; "a clear knowledge of their duty was wanting to mankind." This part of knowledge, though cultivated with some care by some of the heathen philosophers, yet got little footing among the people. All men, indeed, under pain of displeasing the gods, were to frequent the temples: everyone went to their sacrifices and services: but the priests made it not their business to teach them virtue. If they were diligent in their observations and ceremonies; punctual in their feasts and solemnities, and the tricks of religion; the holy tribe assured them the gods were pleased, and they looked no father. Few went to the schools of the philosophers to be instructed in their duties, and to know what was good and evil in their actions. The priests sold the better pennyworths, and therefore had all the custom. Lustrations and processions were much easier than a clean conscience, and a steady course of virtue; and an expiatory sacrifice that atoned for the want of it, was much more convenient than a strict and holy life. No wonder then, that religion was everywhere distinguished from, and preferred to virtue; and that it was dangerous heresy and profaneness to think the contrary. So much virtue as was necessary to hold societies together, and to contribute to the quiet of governments, the civil laws of commonwealths taught, and forced upon men that lived under magistrates. But these laws being for the most part made by such, who had no other aims but their own power, reached no farther than those things that would serve to tie men together in subjection; or at most were directly to conduce to the prosperity and temporal happiness of any people. But natural religion, in its full extent, was no-where, that I know, taken care of, by the force of natural reason. It should seem, by the little that has hitherto been done in it, that it is too hard a task for unassisted reason to establish morality in all its parts, upon its true foundation, with a clear and convincing light. And it is at least a surer and shorter way, to the apprehensions of the vulgar, and mass of mankind, that one manifestly sent from God, and coming with visible authority from him, should, as a king and law-maker, tell them their duties; and require their obedience; then leave it to the long and sometimes intricate deductions of reason, to be made out to them. Such trains of reasoning the greatest part of mankind have neither leisure to weigh; nor, for want of education and use, skill to judge of. We see how unsuccessful in this the attempts of philosophers were before our Savior's time. How short their several systems came of the perfection of a true and complete morality, is very visible. And if, since that, the Christian philosophers have much out-done them: yet we may observe, that the first knowledge of the truths they have added, is owing to revelation: though as soon as they are heard and considered, they are found to be agreeable to reason; and such as can by no means be contradicted. Everyone may observe a great many truths, which he receives at first from others, and readily assents to, as consonant to reason, which he would have found it hard, and perhaps beyond his strength, to have discovered himself. Native and original truth is not so easily wrought out of the mine, as we, who have it delivered already dug and fashioned into our hands, are apt to imagine. And how often at fifty or sixty year old are thinking men told what they wonder how they could miss thinking of? Which yet their own contemplations did not, and possibly never would have helped them to. Experience shows, that the knowledge of morality, by mere natural light, (how agreeable soever it be to it,) makes but a slow progress, and little advance in the world. And the reason of it is not hard to be found in men's necessities, passions, vices, and mistaken interests; which turn their thoughts another way: and the designing leaders, as well as following herd, find it not to their purpose to employ much of their meditations this way. Or whatever else was the cause, it is plain, in fact, that human reason unassisted failed men in its great and proper business of morality. It never from unquestionable principles, by clear deductions, made out an entire body of the "law of nature." And he that shall collect all the moral rules of the philosophers, and compare them with those contained in the New Testament, will find them to come short of the morality delivered by our Savior, and taught by his apostles; a college made up, for the most part, of ignorant, but inspired fishermen.

Though yet, if anyone should think, that out of the sayings of the wise heathens before our Savior's time, there might be a collection made of all those rules of morality, which are to be found in the Christian religion; yet this would not at all hinder, but that the world, nevertheless, stood as much in need of our Savior, and the morality delivered by him. Let it be granted (though not true) that all the moral precepts of the gospel were known by somebody or other, among mankind before. But where, or how, or of what use, is not considered. Suppose they may be picked up here and there; some from Solon and Bias in Greece, others from Tully in Italy: and to complete the work, let Confucius, as far as China, be consulted; and Anacharsis, the Scythian, contribute his share. What will all this do, to give the world a complete morality that may be to mankind the unquestionable rule of life and manners? I will not here urge the impossibility of collecting from men, so far distant from one another, in time and place, and languages. I will suppose there was a Stobeus in those times, who had gathered the moral sayings from all the sages of the world. What would this amount to, towards being a steady rule; a certain transcript of a law that we are under? Did the sayings of Aristippus, or Confucius, give it an authority? Was Zeno a law-giver to mankind? If not, what he or any other philosopher delivered, was but a saying of his. Mankind might hearken to it, or reject it, as they pleased; or as it suited their interest, passions, principles or humors. They were under no obligation; the opinion of this or that philosopher was of no authority. And if it were, you must take all he said under the same character. All his dictates must go for law, certain and true; or none of them. And then, if you will take any of the moral sayings of Epicurus (many whereof Seneca quotes with esteem and approbation) for precepts of the law of nature, you must take all the rest of his doctrine for such too; or else his authority ceases: and so no more is to be received from him, or any of the sages of old, for parts of the law of nature, as carrying with it an obligation to be obeyed, but what they prove to be so. But such a body of ethics, proved to be the law of nature, from principles of reason, and teaching all the duties of life; I think nobody will say the world had before our Savior's time. It is not enough, that there were up and down scattered sayings of wise men, conformable to right reason. The law of nature, is the law of convenience too: and it is no wonder that those men of parts, and studious of virtue, (who had occasion to think on any particular part of it,) should, by meditation, light on the right even from the observable convenience and beauty of it; without making out its obligation from the true principles of the law of nature, and foundations of morality. But these incoherent proverbs of philosophers, and wise men, however excellent in themselves, and well intended by them; could never make a morality, whereof the world could be convinced; could never rise to the force of a law, that mankind could with certainty depend on. Whatsoever should thus be universally useful, as a standard to which men should conform their manners, must have its authority, either from reason or revelation. It is not every writer of morality, or compiler of it from others, that can thereby be erected into a law-giver to mankind; and a dictator of rules, which are therefore valid, because they are to be found in his books; under the authority of this or that philosopher. He, that anyone will pretend to set up in this kind, and have his rules pass for authentic directions, must show, that either he builds his doctrine upon principles of reason, self-evident in themselves; and that he deduces all the parts of it from thence, by clear and evident demonstration: or must show his commission from heaven, that he comes with authority from God, to deliver his will and commands to the world. In the former way, no-body that I know, before our Savior's time, ever did, or went about to give us a morality. It is true, there is a law of nature: but who is there that ever did, or undertook to give it us all entire, as a law; no more, nor no less, than what was contained in, and had the obligation of that law? Who ever made out all the parts of it, put them together, and showed the world their obligation? Where was there any such code, that mankind might have recourse to, as their unerring rule, before our Savior's time? If there was not, it is plain there was need of one to give us such a morality; such a law, which might be the sure guide of those who had a desire to go right; and, if they had a mind, need not mistake their duty, but might be certain when they had performed, when failed in it. Such a law of morality Jesus Christ has given us in the New Testament; but by the latter of these ways, by revelation. We have from him a full and sufficient rule for our direction, and conformable to that of reason. But the truth and obligation of its precepts have their force, and are put past doubt to us, by the evidence of his mission. He was sent by God: his miracles show it; and the authority of God in his precepts cannot be questioned. Here morality has a sure standard, that revelation vouches, and reason cannot gainsay, nor question; but both together witness to come from God the great law-maker. And such an one as this, out of the New Testament, I think the world never had, nor can anyone say, is anywhere else to be found. Let me ask anyone, who is forward to think that the doctrine of morality was full and clear in the world, at our Savior's birth; whither would he have directed Brutus and Cassius, (both men of parts and virtue, the one whereof believed, and the other disbelieved a future being,) to be satisfied in the rules and obligations of all the parts of their duties; if they should have asked him, Where they might find the law they were to live by, and by which they should be charged, or acquitted, as guilty, or innocent? If to the sayings of the wise, and the declarations of philosophers, he sends them into a wild wood of uncertainty, to an endless maze, from which they should never get out: if to the religions of the world, yet worse: and if to their own reason, he refers them to that which had some light and certainty; but yet had hitherto failed all mankind in a perfect rule; and we see, resolved not the doubts that had arisen among the studious and thinking philosophers; nor had yet been able to convince the civilized parts of the world, that they had not given, nor could, without a crime, take away the lives of their children, by exposing them.

If anyone shall think to excuse human nature, by laying blame on men's negligence, that they did not carry morality to an higher pitch; and make it out entire in every part, with that clearness of demonstration which some think it capable of; he helps not the matter. Be the cause what it will, our Savior found mankind under a corruption of manners and principles, which ages after ages had prevailed, and must be confessed, was not in a way or tendency to be mended. The rules of morality were in different countries and sects different. And natural reason no-where had cured, nor was like to cure the defects and errors in them. Those just measures of right and wrong, which necessity had anywhere introduced, the civil laws prescribed, or philosophy recommended, stood on their true foundations. They were looked on as bonds of society, and conveniences of common life, and laudable practices. But where was it that their obligation was thoroughly known and allowed, and they received as precepts of a law; of the highest law, the law of nature? That could not be, without a clear knowledge and acknowledgment of the law-maker, and the great rewards and punishments, for those that would, or would not obey him. But the religion of the heathens, as was before observed, little concerned itself in their morals. The priests, that delivered the oracles of heaven, and pretended to speak from the gods, spoke little of virtue and a good life. And, on the other side, the philosophers, who spoke from reason, made not much mention of the Deity in their ethics. They depended on reason and her oracles, which contain nothing but truth: but yet some parts of that truth lie too deep for our natural powers easily to reach, and make plain and visible to mankind; without some light from above to direct them. When truths are once known to us, though by tradition, we are apt to be favorable to our own parts; and ascribe to our own understandings the discovery of what, in reality, we borrowed from others: or, at least, finding we can prove, what at first we learn from others, we are forward to conclude it an obvious truth, which, if we had sought, we could not have missed. Nothing seems hard to our understandings that is once known: and because what we see, we see with our own eyes; we are apt to overlook, or forget the help we had from others who showed it us, and first made us see it; as if we were not at all beholden to them, for those truths they opened the way to, and led us into. For knowledge being only of truths that are perceived to be so, we are favorable enough to our own faculties, to conclude, that they of their own strength would have attained those discoveries, without any foreign assistance; and that we know those truths, by the strength and native light of our own minds, as they did from whom we received them by theirs, only they had the luck to be before us. Thus the whole stock of human knowledge is claimed by everyone, as his private possession, as soon as he (profiting by others discoveries) has got it into his own mind: and so it is; but not properly by his own single industry, nor of his own acquisition. He studies, it is true, and takes pains to make a progress in what others have delivered: but their pains were of another sort, who first brought those truths to light, which he afterwards derives from them. He that travels the roads now, applauds his own strength and legs that have carried him so far in such a scantling of time; and ascribes all to his own vigor; little considering how much he owes to their pains, who cleared the woods, drained the bogs, built the bridges, and made the ways passable; without which he might have toiled much with little progress. A great many things which we have been bred up in the belief of, from our cradles, (and are notions grown familiar, and, as it were, natural to us, under the gospel,) we take for unquestionable obvious truths, and easily demonstrable; without considering how long we might have been in doubt or ignorance of them, had revelation been silent. And many are beholden to revelation, who do not acknowledge it. It is not diminishing to revelation, that reason gives its suffrage too, to the truths revelation has discovered. But it is our mistake to think, that because reason confirms them to us, we had the first certain knowledge of them from thence; and in that clear evidence we now possess them. The contrary is manifest, in the defective morality of the Gentiles, before our Savior's time; and the want of reformation in the principles and measures of it, as well as practice. Philosophy seemed to have spent its strength, and done its utmost: or if it should have gone farther, as we see it did not, and from undeniable principles given us ethics in a science like mathematics, in every part demonstrable; this yet would not have been so effectual to man in this imperfect state, nor proper for the cure. The greatest part of mankind want leisure or capacity for demonstration; nor can carry a train of proofs, which in that way they must always depend upon for conviction, and cannot be required to assent to, until they see the demonstration. Wherever they stick, the teachers are always put upon proof, and must clear the doubt by a thread of coherent deductions from the first principle, how long, or how intricate soever they be. And you may as soon hope to have all the day-laborers and tradesmen, the spinsters and dairy-maids, perfect mathematicians, as to have them perfect in ethics this way. Hearing plain commands, is the sure and only course to bring them to obedience and practice. The greatest part cannot know, and therefore they must believe. And I ask, whether one coming from heaven in the power of God, in full and clear evidence and demonstration of miracles, giving plain and direct rules of morality and obedience; be not likelier to enlighten the bulk of mankind, and set them right in their duties, and bring them to do them, than by reasoning with them from general notions and principles of human reason? And were all the duties of human life clearly demonstrated, yet I conclude, when well considered, that method of teaching men their duties would be thought proper only for a few, who had much leisure, improved understandings, and were used to abstract reasonings. But the instruction of the people was best still to be left to the precepts and principles of the gospel. The healing of the sick, the restoring sight to the blind by a word, the raising and being raised from the dead, are matters of fact, which they can without difficulty conceive, and that he who does such things, must do them by the assistance of a divine power. These things lie level to the most ordinary apprehension: he that can distinguish between sick and well, lame and sound, dead and alive, is capable of this doctrine. To one who is once persuaded that Jesus Christ was sent by God to be a King, and a Savior of those who do believe in him; all his commands become principles; *there needs no other proof for the truth of what he says, but that he said it.* And then there needs no more, but to read the inspired books, to be instructed: all the duties of morality lie there clear, and plain, and easy to be understood. And here I appeal, whether this is not the surest, the safest, and most effectual way of teaching: especially if we add this father consideration that as it suits the lowest capacities of reasonable creatures, so it reaches and satisfies, nay, enlightens the highest. The most elevated understandings cannot but submit to the authority of this doctrine as divine; which coming from the mouths of a company of illiterate men, has not only the attestation of miracles, but reason to confirm it: since they delivered no precepts but such, as though reason of itself had not clearly made out, yet it could not but assent to, when thus discovered, and think itself indebted for the discovery. The credit and authority our Savior and his apostles had over the minds of men, by the miracles they did, tempted them not to mix (as we find in that of all the sects and philosophers, and other religions) any conceits, any wrong rules, anything tending to their own by-interest, or that of a party, in their morality. No hint of prepossession, or fancy; no footsteps of pride, or vanity; no touch of ostentation, or ambition: appears to have a hand in it. It is all pure, all sincere; nothing too much, nothing wanting; but such a complete rule of life, as the wisest men must acknowledge, tends entirely to the good of mankind, and that all would be happy, if all would practice it.

3. The outward forms of worshipping the Deity, wanted a reformation. Stately buildings, costly ornaments, peculiar and uncouth habits, and a numerous huddle of pompous, fantastical, cumbersome ceremonies, everywhere attended divine worship. This, as it had the peculiar name, so it was thought the principal part, if not the whole of religion. Nor could this, possibly, be amended, while the Jewish ritual stood; and there was so much of it mixed with the worship of the true God. To this also our Savior, with the knowledge of the infinite, invisible, supreme Spirit, brought a remedy, in a plain, spiritual, and suitable worship. Jesus says to the woman of Samaria, "The hour comes, when you shall neither in this mountain, nor yet at Jerusalem, worship the Father. But the true worshippers shall worship the Father, both in Spirit and in truth; for the Father seeks such to worship him." To be worshipped in spirit and truth, with application of mind, and sincerity of heart, was what God henceforth only required. Magnificent temples, and confinement to certain places, were now no longer necessary for his worship, which by a pure heart

might be performed anywhere. The splendor and distinction of habits, and pomp of ceremonies, and all outside performances, might now be spared. God, who was a spirit, and made known to be so, required none of those, but the spirit only; and that in public assemblies, (where some actions must lie open to the view of the world), all that could appear and be seen, should be done decently, and in order, and to edification. Decency, order and edification, were to regulate all their public acts of worship, and beyond what these required, the outward appearance (which was of little value in the eyes of God) was not to go. Having shut indecency and confusion out of their assemblies, they need not be solicitous about useless ceremonies. Praises and prayer, humbly offered up to the Deity, were the worship he now demanded; and in this everyone was to look after his own heart, and to know that it was that alone which God had regard to, and accepted.

4. Another great advantage received by our Savior, is the great encouragement he brought through a virtuous and pious life; great enough to surmount the difficulties and obstacles that lie in the way to it, and reward the pains and hardships of those who stuck firm to their duties, and suffered for the testimony of a good conscience. The portion of the righteous has been in all ages taken notice of, to be pretty scanty in this world. Virtue and prosperity do not often accompany one another; and therefore virtue seldom had many followers. And it is no wonder she prevailed not much in a state, where the inconveniencies that attended her were visible, and at hand; and the rewards doubtful, and at a distance. Mankind, who are and must be allowed to pursue their happiness, nay, cannot be hindered; could not but think themselves excused from a strict observation of rules, which appeared so little to consist of their chief end, happiness; while they kept them from the enjoyments of this life; and they had little evidence and security of another. It is true they might have argued the other way, and concluded, That because the good were most of them ill-treated here, there was another place where they should meet with better usage; but it is plain they did not: their thoughts of another life were at best obscure, and their expectations uncertain. Of manes, and ghosts, and the shades of departed men, there was some talk; but little certain, and less minded. They had the names of Styx and Acheron, of Elysian fields and seats of the blessed: but they had them generally from their poets, mixed with their fables. And so they looked more like the inventions of wit, and ornaments of poetry, than the serious persuasions of the grave and the sober. They came to them bundled up among their tales, and for tales they took them. And that which rendered them more suspected, and less useful to virtue, was, that the philosophers seldom set their rules on men's minds and practices, by consideration of another life. The chief of their arguments were from the excellency of virtue; and the highest they generally went, was the exalting of human nature, whose perfection lay in virtue. And if the priest at any time talked of the ghosts below, and a life after this; it was only to keep men to their superstitious and idolatrous rites; whereby the use of this doctrine was lost to the credulous multitude, and its belief to the quicker-sighted; who suspected it presently of priestcraft. Before our Savior's time the doctrine of a future state, though it was not wholly hid, yet it was not clearly known in the world. It was an imperfect view of reason, or, perhaps, the decayed remains of an ancient tradition, which seemed rather to float on men's fancies, than sink deep into their hearts. It was something they knew not what, between being and not being. Something in man they imagined might escape the grave; but a perfect complete life, of an eternal duration, after this, was what entered little into their thoughts and less into their persuasions. And they were so far from being clear herein, that we see no nation of the world publicly professed it, and built upon it: no religion taught it; and it was no-where made an article of faith, and principle of religion, until Jesus Christ came; of whom it is truly said, that he, at his appearing, "brought life and immortality to light." And that not only in the clear revelation of it, and in instances shown of men raised from the dead; but he has given us an unquestionable assurance and pledge of it in his own resurrection and ascension into heaven. How has this one truth changed the nature of things in the world, and given the advantage to piety over all that could tempt or deter men from it! The philosophers, indeed, showed the beauty of virtue; they set her off so, as drew men's eyes and approbation to her; but leaving her unendowed, very few were willing to espouse her. The generality could not refuse her their esteem and commendation; but still turned their backs on her, and forsook her, as a match not for their turn. But now there being put into the

scales on her side, "an exceeding and immortal weight of glory;" interest is come about to her, and virtue now is visibly the most enriching purchase, and by much the best bargain. That she is the perfection and excellency of our nature; that she is herself a reward, and will recommend our names to future ages, is not all that can now be said of her. It is not strange that the learned heathens satisfied not many with such airy commendations. It has another relish and efficacy to persuade men, that if they live well here, they shall be happy hereafter. Open their eyes upon the endless, unspeakable joys of another life, and their hearts will find something solid and powerful to move them. The view of heaven and hell will cast a slight upon the short pleasures and pains of this present state, and give attractions and encouragements to virtue which reason and interest, and the care of ourselves, cannot but allow and prefer. Upon this foundation, and upon this only, morality stands firm, and may defy all competition. This makes it more than a name; a substantial good, worth all our aims and endeavors; and thus the gospel of Jesus Christ has delivered it to us.

5. To these I must add one advantage more by Jesus Christ, and that is the promise of assistance. If we do what we can, he will give us his Spirit to help us to do what, and how we should. It will be idle for us, who know not how our own spirits move and act us, to ask in what manner the Spirit of God shall work upon us. The wisdom that accompanies that Spirit knows better than we, how we are made, and how to work upon us. If a wise man knows how to prevail on his child, to bring him to what he desires; can we suspect that the spirit and wisdom of God should fail in it; though we perceive or comprehend not the ways of his operation? Christ has promised it, who is faithful and just; and we cannot doubt of the performance. It is not requisite on this occasion, for the enhancing of this benefit, to enlarge on the frailty of our minds, and weakness of our constitutions; how liable to mistakes, how apt to go astray, and how easily to be turned out of the paths of virtue. If anyone needs go beyond himself, and the testimony of his own conscience in this point; if he feels not his own errors and passions always tempting, and often prevailing, against the strict rules of his duty; he need but look abroad into any stage of the world, to be convinced. To a man under the difficulties of his nature, beset with temptations, and hedged in with prevailing custom; it is no small encouragement to set himself seriously on the courses of virtue, and practice of true religion; that he is from a sure hand, and an Almighty arm, promised assistance to support and carry him through.

There remains yet something to be said to those, who will be ready to object, "If the belief of Jesus of Nazareth to be the Messiah, together with those concomitant articles of his resurrection, rule, and coming again to judge the world, be all the faith required, as necessary to justification, to what purpose were the epistles written; I say, if the belief of those many doctrines contained in them be not also necessary to salvation; and what is there delivered a Christian may believe or disbelieve, and yet, nevertheless, be a member of Christ's church, and one of the faithful?"

To this I answer, that the epistles are written upon several occasions: and he that will read them as he ought, must observe what it is in them, which is principally aimed at; find what is the argument in hand, and how managed; if he will understand them right, and profit by them. The observing of this will best help us to the true meaning and mind of the writer; for that is the truth which is to be received and believed; and not scattered sentences in Scripture-language, accommodated to our notions and prejudices. We must look into the drift of the discourse, observe the coherence and connection of the parts, and see how it is consistent with itself and other parts of Scripture; if we will conceive it right. We must not cull out, as best suits our system, here and there a period or verse; as if they were all distinct and independent aphorisms; and make these the fundamental articles of the Christian faith, and necessary to salvation; unless God has made them so. There are many truths in the Bible, which a good Christian may be wholly ignorant of, and so not believe: which, perhaps, some lay great stress on, and call fundamental articles, because they are the distinguishing points of their communion. The epistles, most of them, carry on a thread of argument, which, in the style they are writ, cannot everywhere be observed without great attention, and to consider the texts as they stand, and bear a part in that, is to view them in their due light, and the way to get the true sense of them. They were writ to those who were in the faith, and true

Christians already: and so could not be designed to teach them the fundamental articles and points necessary to salvation. The epistle to the Romans was writ to all "that were at Rome, beloved of God, called to be saints, whose faith was spoken of through the world," chap. i. 7, 8. To whom St. Paul's first epistle to the Corinthians was, he shows, chap. i. 2, 4, etc. "Unto the church of God which is at Corinth, to them that are sanctified in Christ Jesus, called to be saints; with all them that in every place call upon the name of Jesus Christ our Lord, both theirs and ours. I thank my God always on your behalf, for the grace of God which is given you by Jesus Christ; that in everything you are enriched by him, in all utterance, and in all knowledge: even as the testimony of Christ was confirmed in you. So that you come behind in no gift; waiting for the coming of our Lord Jesus Christ." And so likewise the second was, "To the church of God at Corinth, with all the saints in Achaia," chap. i. 1. His next is to the churches of Galatia. That to the Ephesians was, "To the saints that were at Ephesus, and to the faithful in Christ Jesus." So likewise, "To the saints and faithful brethren in Christ at Colosse, who had faith in Christ Jesus, and love to the saints. To the church of the Thessalonians. To Timothy his son in the faith. To Titus his own son after the common faith. To Philemon his dearly beloved, and fellow-laborer." And the author to the Hebrews calls those he writes to "Holy brethren, partakers of the heavenly calling," chap. iii. 1. From whence it is evident, that all those whom St. Paul writ to, were brethren, saints, faithful in the church, and so Christians already; and therefore, wanted not the fundamental articles of the Christian religion; without a belief of which they could not be saved; nor can it be supposed, that the sending of such fundamentals was the reason of the apostle's writing to any of them. To such also St. Peter writes, as is plain from the first chapter of each of his epistles. Nor is it hard to observe the like in St. James's and St. John's epistles. And St. Jude directs his thus: "To them that are sanctified by God the Father, and preserved in Jesus Christ, and called." The epistles, therefore, being all written to those who were already believers and Christians, the occasion and end of writing them could not be to instruct them in that which was necessary to make them Christians. This, it is plain, they knew and believed already; or else they could not have been Christians and believers. And they were writ upon particular occasions; and without those occasions, had not been writ; and so cannot be thought necessary to salvation: though they resolving doubts, and reforming mistakes, are of great advantage to our knowledge and practice. I do not deny, but the great doctrines of the Christian faith are dropt here and there, and scattered up and down in most of them. But it is not in the epistles we are to learn what are the fundamental articles of faith, where they are promiscuously and without distinction mixed with other truths, in discourses that were (though for edification, indeed, yet) only occasional. We shall find and discern those great and necessary points best, in the preaching of our Savior and the apostles, to those who were yet strangers, and ignorant of the faith; to bring them in, and convert them to it. And what that was, we have seen already, out of the history of the evangelists, and the acts; where they are plainly laid down, so that nobody can mistake them. The epistles to particular churches, besides the main argument of each of them, (which was some present concernment of that particular church, to which they severally were addressed,) do in many places explain the fundamentals of the Christian religion, and that wisely; by proper accommodations to the apprehensions of those they were writ to; the better to make them imbibe the Christian doctrine, and the more easily to comprehend the method, reasons, and grounds of the great work of salvation. Thus we see, in the epistle to the Romans, adoption (a custom well known among those of Rome) is much made use of, to explain to them the grace and favor of God, in giving them eternal life; to help them to conceive how they became the children of God, and to assure them of a share in the kingdom of heaven, as heirs to an inheritance. Whereas the setting out, and confirming the Christian faith to the Hebrews, in the epistle to them, is by illusions and arguments, from the ceremonies, sacrifices, and economy of the Jews, and references to the records of the Old Testament. And as for the general epistles, they, we may see, regard the state and exigencies, and some peculiarities of those times. These holy writers, inspired from above, writ nothing but truth; and in most places, very weighty truths to us now; for the expounding, clearing, and confirming of the Christian doctrine, and establishing those in it who had embraced it. But yet every sentence of theirs must not be taken up, and looked on as a fundamental article, necessary to salvation; without an explicit belief whereof, nobody could be a member of Christ's church here, nor be admitted into his eternal kingdom hereafter. If all, or most of the truths declared in the epistles, were to be received and believed as fundamental articles, what then became of those Christians who were fallen asleep (as St. Paul witnesses in his first to the Corinthians, many were) before these things in the epistles were revealed to them? Most of the epistles not being written till above twenty years after our Savior's ascension, and some after thirty.

But father, therefore, to those who will be ready to say, "May those truths delivered in the epistles, which are not contained in the preaching of our Savior and his apostles, and are therefore, by this account, not necessary to salvation; be believed or disbelieved, without any danger? May a Christian safely question or doubt of them?"

To this I answer, That the law of faith, being a covenant of free grace, God alone can appoint what shall be necessarily believed by everyone whom he will justify. What is the faith which he will accept and account for righteousness, depends wholly on his good pleasure. For it is of grace, and not of right, that this faith is accepted. And therefore he alone can set the measures of it: and what he has so appointed and declared is alone necessary. No-body can add to these fundamental articles of faith; nor make any other necessary, but what God himself has made, and declared to be so. And what these are which God requires of those who will enter into, and receive the benefits of the new covenant, has already been shown. An explicit belief of these is absolutely required of all those to whom the gospel of Jesus Christ is preached, and salvation through his name proposed.

The other parts of divine revelation are objects of faith, and are so to be received. They are truths, whereof no one can be rejected; none that is once known to be such, may, or ought to be disbelieved. For to acknowledge any proposition to be of divine revelation and authority; and yet to deny, or disbelieve it; is to offend against this fundamental article and ground of faith, that God is true. But yet a great many of the truths revealed in the gospel, everyone does, and must confess, a man may be ignorant of; nay, disbelieve, without danger to his salvation: as is evident in those, who, allowing the authority, differ in the interpretation and meaning of several texts of Scripture, not thought fundamental: in all which, it is plain, the contending parties on one side or the other, are ignorant of, nay, disbelieve the truths delivered in holy writ; unless contrarieties and contradictions can be contained in the same words; and divine revelation can mean contrary to itself.

Though all divine revelation requires the obedience of faith, yet every truth of inspired Scriptures is not one of those that by the law of faith is required to be explicitly believed to justification. What those are, we have seen by what our Savior and his apostles proposed to, and required in those whom they converted to the faith. Those are fundamentals, which it is not enough not to disbelieve: everyone is required actually to assent to them. But any other proposition contained in the Scripture, which God has not thus made a necessary part of the law of faith, (without an actual assent to which, he will not allow anyone to be a believer,) a man may be ignorant of, without hazarding his salvation by a defect in his faith. He believes all that God has made necessary for him to believe, and assent to; and as for the rest of divine truths, there is nothing more required of him, but that he receive all the parts of divine revelation, with a docility and disposition prepared to embrace and assent to all truths coming from God; and submit his mind to whatsoever shall appear to him to bear that character. Where he, upon fair endeavors, understands it not, how can he avoid being ignorant? And where he cannot put several texts, and make them consist together, what remedy? He must either interpret one by the other, or suspend his opinion. He that thinks that more is, or can be required of poor frail man in matters of faith, will do well to consider what absurdities he will run into. God, out of the infiniteness of his mercy, has dealt with man, as a compassionate and tender Father. He gave him reason, and with it a law: that could not be otherwise than what reason should dictate: unless we should think, that a reasonable creature should have an unreasonable law. But, considering the frailty of man, apt to run into corruption and misery, he promised a Deliverer, whom in his good time he sent; and then declared to all mankind, that whoever would believe him to be the Savior promised, and take him now raised from the dead, and constituted the Lord and Judge of all men, to be their King and Ruler, should be saved. This is a plain intelligible proposition: and the all-merciful God seems herein to have consulted the poor of this world, and the bulk of mankind. These are articles that the laboring and illiterate man may comprehend. This is a religion suited to vulgar capacities; and the state of mankind in this world, destined to labor and travel. The writers and wranglers in religion fill it with niceties, and dress it up with notions, which they make necessary and fundamental parts of it; as if there were no way into the church, but through the academy or college. The greatest part of mankind has not leisure for learning and logic, and superfine distinctions of the schools. Where the hand is used to the plough and the spade, the head is seldom elevated to transcendent notions, or exercised in mysterious reasoning. It is well if men of that rank (to say nothing of women) can comprehend plain propositions, and a short reasoning about things familiar to their minds, and nearly allied to their daily experience. Go beyond this, and you amaze the greatest part of mankind; and may as well talk Arabic to a poor day-laborer, as the notions and language that the books and disputes of religion are filled with; and as soon you will be understood. The dissenting congregation are supposed by their teachers to be more accurately instructed in matters of faith, and better to understand the Christian religion, than the vulgar conformists, who are charged with great ignorance; how truly, I will not here determine. But I ask them to tell me seriously, "Do half their people have leisure to study? No, whether one in ten, of those who come to their meetings in the country, if they had time to study them, do or can understand the controversies at this time so warmly managed among them, about 'justification,' the subject of this present treatise?" I have talked with some of their teachers, who confess themselves not to understand the difference in debate between them. And yet the points they stand on, are reckoned of so great weight; so material, so fundamental in religion, that they divide communion, and separate upon them. Had God intended that none but the learned scribe, the disputer, or wise of this world, should be Christians, or be saved, thus religion should have been prepared for them, filled with speculations and niceties, obscure terms, and abstract notions. But men of that expectation, men furnished with such acquisitions, the apostle tells us, 1 Cor. i. are rather shut out from the simplicity of the gospel; to make way for those poor, ignorant, illiterate, who heard and believed promises of a Deliverer, and believed Jesus to be him; who could conceive a man dead and made alive again; and believe that he should, at the end of the world, come again and pass sentence on all men, according to their deeds. That the poor had the gospel preached to them; Christ makes a mark, as well as business of his mission, Matt. xi. 5. And if the poor had the gospel preached to them, it was, without doubt, such a gospel as the poor could understand; plain and intelligible; and so it was, as we have seen, in the preaching of Christ and his apostles.

Lex Rex - The Law, The King
ISBN: 1-4505-9240-6

A Biblical primer on the purpose, place, and power of civil government. Samuel Rutherford's Lex Rex for the modern reader.

by Thomas Adamo

The ideas in Lex Rex predate modern concepts of nationalism and politics. They are older than the United States Constitution, as well as the American Revolution – where many modern ideas of liberty originated. Lex Rex is even older than the Enlightenment that receives so much credit for concepts such as popular sovereignty, limited government, separation of powers, and individual liberty. Nevertheless, Samuel Rutherford's Lex Rex – written at a time that viewed kings as vessels of divine power – raised a Scriptural standard arguing for the dignity of the people and the accountability of earthly governments. Although some would seek to pigeonhole the book as merely a tract on civil resistance, Lex Rex contains a comprehensive examination of a Christian view of civil government. In doing so, Lex Rex actually formulates a blueprint for freedom applicable for any time and place. Rutherford hoped to demonstrate the need for government based on law instead of the arbitrary decisions of fallible humanity. Throughout this process, the Bible is the final authority and basis for law. This Scriptural base was a primary reason for both the great support and opposition that met Lex Rex.

# # #

Calvinism and the Declaration of Independence
ISBN: 1-4536-9012-3

by Thomas Adamo

The American War of Independence was one of the first political upheavals in history based primarily on ideology. Subsequent history has demonstrated the importance of philosophical justification for the instigation of any radical political action of comparable ambition to the Revolution of 1776.   However, in recent years the true nature of the ideas that helped fortify the American revolutionaries has come into question, with much of this controversy centering on the true origin of the concepts contained in the Declaration of Independence. Calvinism and the Declaration of Independence seeks to investigate whether the political traditions of the United States were entirely products of the Enlightenment or of the wider Calvinistic-Reformed-Puritan traditions of England and her American colonies.   While the Reformed tradition of the Anglo-American culture may not take exclusive credit for the ideological traditions that influenced the Revolution in the colonies, its influence was great.

# # #

Conspiracy Rhetoric
ISBN: 1-4505-7431-9

by Thomas Adamo

Conspiracy Rhetoric seeks to evaluate the growing appeal of conspiracy theories within mainstream American Society. The examination of this phenomenon as a contemporary social narrative proceeds through a content analysis of its public literature in order to determine what common links connect the various expressions of this cultural genre, and how its existence reflects on the larger culture.

# # #

Lewis Carroll's "Alice's Adventures in Wonderland"
ISBN: 1-4515-2383-1

Family Edition

"Alice was beginning to get very tired of sitting by her sister on the bank, and of having nothing to do: once or twice, she had peeped into the book her sister was reading, but it had no pictures or conversations in it, 'and what is the use of a book,' thought Alice 'without pictures or conversation?'" And so begins, one of the most fantastic adventures of all time... This original text of Alice's Adventures in Wonderland is interspersed with pieces of modern art, creating a fun reading event for the entire family.

# # #

re:Organizing America: We are what we think — both individually, and as a society. Unfortunately, many of the solutions offered to today's problems are mere panaceas that are not the result of serious deliberation. Through a variety of resources, *re:Organizing America* seeks to engage people in serious thought about the foundations of freedom and American culture. On this basis, it will become evident that an ordered liberty is the true solution to the majority of our contemporary challenges and allow for a dialogue offering real solutions for today's problems. Our editions are lightly edited, but unabridged, in order to make these ideas accessible to the widest possible audience.

The United States of America: State Papers
ISBN: 1-4538-1856-1
The Declaration of Independence, the Articles of Confederation, the Constitution, the Federalist Papers, and Washington's Farewell Address
by re:Organizing America

These essential documents, formulated over the course of twenty years, the Declaration of Independence, the Articles of Confederation, the Constitution, the Federalist Papers, and President Washington's Farewell Address, encapsulate a period of crucial significance to the United States and the world. They are the embodied results of centuries of thought, debate, and experimentation – finally espoused in a practical fashion. The foundations for the experiment of liberty and law that is the United States of America, they are the fundamental guide for securing the blessings of liberty.

# # #

John Locke's Two Essays Concerning Civil Government
ISBN: 1-4538-1859-6
by re:Organizing America

Written in 1689, Locke's Two Treatises of Government disputes the logic of the "divine right of kings," and proceeds to develop a theory of society base on the ideas of natural rights and the social contract. Locke acknowledged the necessity of the state, but saw it primarily as a tool to promote the protection of people and property, as well as the restraint of violence. Based on the consent of the governed, Locke's conception of government highlights the importance of accountability between government and citizen.

# # #

Revolutions: Three Perspectives
ISBN: 1-4538-1860-X
Rousseau's The Social Contract, Paine's Common Sense, and Burke's Reflections on the Revolution in France
by re:Organizing America

Freedom can lead to liberty, or it can descend into chaos. Rousseau's The Social Contract, Paine's Common Sense, and Burke's Reflections on the Revolution in France encompass the ideas, progress, and results of reform and revolutionary change. Rousseau reasoned that people are born free and act as a collective sovereign – owing both freedom and duty under the auspices of the general will, embodied in government. Paine wrote Common Sense in the seminal year of 1775. Using a reasoned and accessible style, he brought forth numerous arguments to demonstrate the logic of launching an American Revolution. Burke's Reflections, while specifically aimed at the French Revolution, demonstrate the superiority of practical solutions over abstract concepts. Each of these works prominently displays the importance of changes leading to freedom. These works demarcate a firm delineation between constructive and destructive change and how it affects human freedom.

# # #

Adam Smith's The Wealth of Nations
ISBN: 1-4538-1862-6
by re:Organizing America

The Wealth of Nations was the world's introduction to capitalism and economics in the modern sense. Smith developed the ideas of free trade and enlightened self interest as in ultimately bringing prosperity and forming a more just society. Freedom, labor, and responsibility form a foundation for the development and accumulation of wealth.

# # #

de Vattel's *The Law of Nations*

ISBN: 1-4538-1865-0

by re:Organizing America

The Law of Nations focuses on the rights and obligations of what we now term international relations. Outlining ideas that nations should develop reciprocal respect, this work was influential during the founding era of the United States.

# # #

Montesquieu's *The Spirit of the Laws*

ISBN: 1-4538-1867-7

by re:Organizing America

The result of over twenty years of research The Spirit of the Laws encompasses a vast array of topics and issues. This groundbreaking work provides a comprehensive examination of some of the most important topics relating to liberty. These include constitutionalism, the separation of powers, the primacy of civil liberty and the rule of law, and the power of the local community in establishing political institutions.

# # #

Autobiographies: *Benjamin Franklin & Frederick Douglass*

ISBN: 1-4538-1869-3

by re:Organizing America

Born over a century apart, one into poverty and the other into slavery, Benjamin Franklin and Frederick Douglass embody the American ideals of success through hard work, vision, and freedom. At the end of their lives, both men were renowned statesmen, admired all over the world. Each is a vivid example of the endless possibilities available to free people.

# # #

Alexis De Tocqueville's *Democracy in America*

ISBN: 1-4538-1870-7

by re:Organizing America

Summarizing the American experience up to the 1830's Democracy in America explores why the republican government of the United States was succeeding when similar undertakings had failed elsewhere. Based on first hand observations, and balancing the positive and negative attributes of American culture, Alexis de Tocqueville provides a seminal analysis of the economic, political, cultural, and religious components that led to the resounding success of the young United States of America.

# # #

www.ingramcontent.com/pod-product-compliance
Lightning Source LLC
Chambersburg PA
CBHW081346280526
45788CB00009B/2786